Cultural Memory
in
the
Present

Hent de Vries, Editor

FIGURES OF POSSIBILITY

Aesthetic Experience, Mysticism, and the Play of the Senses

Niklaus Largier

STANFORD UNIVERSITY PRESS

STANFORD, CALIFORNIA

Stanford University Press
Stanford, California

Printed in the United States of America on acid-free, archival-quality paper

Library of Congress Cataloging-in-Publication Data

Names: Largier, Niklaus, 1957– author.
Title: Figures of possibility : aesthetic experience, mysticism, and the play of the senses / Niklaus Largier.
Other titles: Cultural memory in the present.
Description: Stanford, California : Stanford University Press, 2022. | Series: Cultural memory in the present | Includes bibliographical references and index.
Identifiers: LCCN 2021029064 (print) | LCCN 2021029065 (ebook) | ISBN 9781503630437 (cloth) | ISBN 9781503631045 (paperback) | ISBN 9781503631052 (ebook)
Subjects: LCSH: Mysticism—Psychology. | Mysticism—History. | Experience (Religion) | Psychology, Religious.
Classification: LCC BV5083 .L37 2022 (print) | LCC BV5083 (ebook) | DDC 248.2/2—dc23
LC record available at https://lccn.loc.gov/2021029064
LC ebook record available at https://lccn.loc.gov/2021029065

Cover design: Rob Ehle
Cover background: Shutterstock

Contents

Introduction 1

1. Disruptions 23
2. Figuration 50
3. Reweaving Perception 62
4. Imitation 91
5. Framings 141
6. Monadic Transcriptions 184
7. Modernist Moments 218
8. Holy Fools 237

Acknowledgments 249

Notes 253

Bibliography 275

Index 295

Introduction

This book originated with the observation that, against common characterizations, modern literary and philosophical engagements with earlier mystical traditions rarely foreground moments of belief, esoteric knowledge, or an extraordinary experience of the divine. Instead, the fascination driving these engagements—from the decadent writer Joris-Karl Huysmans to the composer John Cage and the artist Dan Flavin, from Ralph Waldo Emerson to Georg Lukács and Robert Musil, from Wassily Kandinsky to Georges Bataille, Simone Weil, Paul Celan, Clarice Lispector, and Gilles Deleuze—responds to the style and the ways in which mystics made use of figures and practices of figuration. They did so, surprisingly, both in drawing attention to figures as rhetorical devices that form and transform our perception and in accentuating that the figural itself reflects the ungraspable character of the worlds of which we are a part. The mystical texts fascinate because they emphasize the fundamentally figural shapes of these worlds and their resistance to gestures of understanding. And they fascinate with the practices of figuration that they use to modulate our senses and the ways we inhabit these worlds. In doing so, the mystics draw attention away from the affiliation of figuration with metaphorical meaning and allegory. Instead, the mystics insist on the disruptive force of figures and their effects and on the invention of styles that speak the unspeakable. In their use of the example of the apostle Paul's words, "It is no longer I who live, but Christ lives in me," the stakes are made clear. According to the interpretation of this exemplary point of reference in the Christian mystical tradition and its emphasis on figure and form, the proposition is not to be taken as metaphor, as the fulfillment of a norm, or as a subjective commitment to imitation. Instead, it is understood in the sense that, through a radical dispossession, the divine cosmopoetic "matrix" (Jacob Böhme) in its concrete and dramatic incarnation has literally turned into the form of Paul's life.

I look at this not in terms of "belief" or of "religion" but of a radically negative, iconoclastic anthropology and theology, which foregrounds the convergence of figure, sensation, and imagination. Building on Paul's emphasis on dispossession and the "foolishness" of love, this has been recast, more recently, in Clarice Lispector's *Passion according to G. H.*, where the loss of self to the "spasmic moments of the world" speaks through the mirroring eyes of a dying cockroach. I argue that in such concrete, deeply material, and often expansive dramatizations of the role of the figural and its relation to the production of meaning, these mystical moments resonate with what modernity calls aesthetic experience and experimentation. They do so in privileging the figural against the hermeneutic, the representational, and the figurative that Gilles Deleuze, to take another example, reaching back to Paul Cézanne, has portrayed in his book on Francis Bacon.

To be sure, all the so-called mystical texts also produce rich archives of meaning, of scriptural hermeneutics, and of allegorical reading. They insist at each stage, however, on the fact that grace, freedom, beauty, and ecstatic absorption are not experienced through the mediation of a self in the sphere of normative orders of knowledge or allegory. As the texts show, rather than argue, these moments come about in a dramatic exposure to and a participation in the formative figures that underlie, precede, bracket, and complicate all production of meaning. Paradoxically, in this view, the figural is not opposed to the literal. Instead, it is the (hyper-)literal in its expressivity and multiplicity, perceived in the form of what I call a figural realism or a radical figuralism that moves at the limits of discourse. Thus, the mystics also challenge established modes of distinguishing the real and the imaginary, the literal and the symbolic, the material and the spiritual, the self and the other. In fact, in their notion and use of figuration the mystics—and I count Clarice Lispector drawing attention to the abject beauty of the eyes of the cockroach among them—foreground the concretely particular in its changing, often dissonant forms and effects, insisting on the force it carries and on its resistance to modes of abstraction and understanding. The seventeenth-century cobbler Jacob Böhme, to whom I return in Chapter 6, explicitly draws attention to this. Building on the medieval traditions I discuss in Chapters 3 to 5—and inspiring Georg Wilhelm Friedrich Hegel, William Blake, and Friedrich Schelling with his writings—Böhme asks his readers to return to the figural, to the world of concrete forms in their emergence and in their effects as they move through us and as they resist capture in finite modes of being, understanding, and knowing. Instead, the emergence of figures and the metamorphoses of forms that unfold through and beyond us are, in his eyes, the place of a participation in the material and spiritual "imagination" that our worlds in their concrete expression happen to be. Partaking sensually, affectively, and intellectually, not representing or understanding in terms of meaning, knowledge, or subjective experience, is at the core of his thinking and of a practice of renunciation that makes the distinction of materialism and idealism obsolete.

What figuration draws attention to is the fact that everything, each sensation, each affect, and each thought, can be seen as not a thing or a moment of representation but a concrete instance of participation, an expression in which we partake underneath the determined modes of meaning, understanding, or being, thus abandoning those very determinations and rejoining, in the words of Alfred North Whitehead, "the passing flux of immediate things."[1] The mystics, radical formalists in this regard, reach down into the dark abyss of figural expression, attending to it, drawing on it, mobilizing it in its dissonances and consonances, abandoning themselves to it, and playing with it against the attachments that make up our worlds. Looking at it from a different angle, they can be seen as foregrounding both the exposure to and the absorption into forms and effects that run up against the hermeneutic and metaphysical grasp of all knowledge—without being able to leave it behind entirely. In rearticulating this grasp in ever-richer variations of sublime allegorization and wild conceptualization, in engaging its sedimentations critically only to abandon them in the return to forms and figures, they dramatize perception and the production of meaning and create different spaces of living.

It is this emphasis on the figural that I take as the starting point in this book, insisting on the dramatic tension it establishes in relation to understanding and abstraction, hermeneutics and metaphysics—and foregrounding the realms of sensual, affective, and intellectual play this dramatization creates. The chapters that follow explore this provocative notion of the figural in mystical texts and in the literary and philosophical engagements with them. They examine the ways in which figures—sounds and words, images and things as they are used and perceived in what we often call spiritual exercises—have been taken as the rhetorical devices that support the range of possibilities and the styles of partaking, as well as sensual, aesthetic, and ethical transformations. Along these lines, practices of figuration relentlessly reinvent and reconfigure the realms of sensation, affect, imagination, and thought. In reconstructing the genealogy of these practices, I argue—against the assumption that mysticism necessarily implies a notion of "immediate experience," "pure presence," or "subjective feeling"—that "figure" and "figuration" must be seen as key terms. They allow us to think through and with the rhetoric of the mystics, their resonances in modern thought and literature, and their significance for a specific understanding of possibility in medieval and modernist contexts—and, most recently, in critical race theory and poetry with the work of Nathaniel Mackey, Fred Moten, and J. Kameron Carter.

This notion of figure, I argue throughout the book, allows us to conceive of possibility in a different way. It is to be seen as a form of virtuality that permeates the "real" in the very experience of figural effects and in the practices of figuration that undo seemingly stable, gendered, racialized, and other normative orders. Thus, figural practices challenge and suspend perspectives that focus on the possible in ontological or epistemological terms, locating it in determined forms of being or knowing.

The Austrian modernist writer Robert Musil—to whom I return in Chapter 7—draws attention to this notion of figure and figuration when he adopts rhetorical elements from a medieval mystical tradition in his novel *The Man without Qualities.* In a famous passage he introduces the protagonist as a "man without qualities," an expression he borrows from the medieval philosopher and mystic Meister Eckhart. Shortly thereafter, he talks of the protagonist, still without a name, as a person with a "sense of possibility." Strikingly, Musil deploys a notion of possibility that does not derive from an understanding of possibilities as potentialities (an apple seed that will turn into a tree), as virtual realities (that supplement and transform the real), or as forms of utopian or messianic reconciliation. Instead, he sees possibilities—in conversation with mystical texts and with the scientific interest in perception around 1900—as emerging from a "sense" that is open to the slight, even slightest, modifications of sedimented orders of perception. In his writings, both literary and essayistic, Musil points to the fact that such modifications emerge in interactions with figures that have effects on the malleable shape of ourselves and our worlds. According to him, this malleable shape of humans—he speaks of "human formlessness" and of the plasticity of man[2]—comes into view in encounters with what will be called "figures" in this book. To put it bluntly, according to Musil, in our encounters with the world we do not just see and feel things in either an immediate or a mediated way; instead, the things and environments come to us as figures and textures of figures, as shapes that assert themselves in acting on us, and as artifacts that materially embody our history—something that the German word *Wirklichkeit*, derived from *wirken*, "to be effective," reflects in its opposition to the ontological and epistemological frame that the term "reality" suggests. In acting as figures, these textures and shapes at first neither mean nor mediate anything that could be determined. Instead, Musil's "man without qualities" is the one who, in his or her lack of determining qualities, has a "sense" for the figural encounters—and for the sphere of possibilities they make emerge before they turn into sedimented orders of signification and meaning.

According to Musil, human shapes and their changes can be seen—and studied in literature, particularly in the essay and the novel—as a result of figural effects and practices of figuration that give a specific life, a specific historical form to the soul as it partakes in the world. What Musil draws attention to—also in his engagement with contemporary science, psychology, and philosophy—is the observation that a film, a house we see, a handshake, the atmospheric conditions we enter, always function not just as a neutral environment but as a figural setting, a form that acts on us, that we can explore in its effects, and that we can play with in ways of attending to it. Most important, his observations suggest that the figural effects, styles of encounter, and affordances modulate and animate our senses, our affects, and, more generally, our perception in ways that precede our understanding and our conceptual grasp of a world.

Figures and figural arrangements—a row of houses, a car accident, a view along a street, a first touch of two hands—do not just communicate some feeling or meaning that can be known. They do not just create an atmosphere that can be felt and understood. Instead, figures produce effects and differential intensities that precede and resist all mimetic assimilation in sensation, affect, imagination, and thought. Figure refers to what strikes us and makes us part of it. Mimetic assimilation, however, refers to the series of similes, analogies, and concepts that respond to this moment of striking. Think of the sound of a bird. It strikes us as we are sitting there, disrupting our world and making us part of something else. Only then it takes shape as a "song" in sensual, affective, and cognitive forms, each of them at first nothing else than a mode of resemblance that, in fitting a pattern or Gestalt, structures our recognition: a melodic sound, a pleasant feeling, a name for a bird and for the feeling that arises. These are what I call mimetic assimilations in the deployment of a world of meaning. Thus, to take an example from Musil's novel, the handshake in a scene where Ulrich, the "man without qualities," meets his cousin Diotima for the first time triggers a broad range of sensations, feelings, and thoughts. Indeed, the handshake quickly translates into the imaginary world of comparisons and similes that allow him and the narrator to picture and understand movements and constellations of sensations, affects, and thoughts that follow. Taken in itself, however, the figure and its effect, the moments of differential intensity, precede and underlie the production of similes, evoking the realization that the assimilation in sensation, affect, and meaning can never exhaust it. This is what makes the handshake not only a meaningful thing or an event but also a figure that, in acting on Ulrich, puts the entire world and its history in a state of both absorption and suspension: absorption in the figural effects that simultaneously express and disrupt a world, suspension in the possibilities of assimilation that come to nest in the historically shaped textures of it. Similarly, Marcel Proust writes of the effects of a "good book." It is, he insists, "something special, something unforeseeable, and is made up not of the sum of all previous masterpieces but of something which the most thorough assimilation . . . would not enable" us "to discover."[3]

Beyond the series of assimilations, that is, the chains of similitude and comparison they unlock, figures produce moments of disruption, which, in their force, are nothing else than the very act, the sheer fact of participation in their effects. Figures do not evoke only chains of similes and analogies; forms of assimilation and understanding; or the exploration of possible feelings, sensations, and thought. Underneath all this, the figural effects take possession and give shape to what we are before we know or guess what they might mean, breaking with the real and turning the seemingly determined historical moment into an open space of possibility. In disrupting the textures of meaning, their movements break with the known and the knowable orders of the world and open the perspective that—in Musil's simple words, which are also the words of the "fools" who speak up against the normative orders—it might all be otherwise or "just as well."[4]

Musil's "sense of possibility" is the sense that lets itself be moved by this very disruption. It is the sense that sits on the threshold of the disruption by a figural effect and that unlocks a pull into a world of similes, comparisons, and analogies, which then provide us with meaning. At the same time, it is the sense that, in the recognition that neither the similes nor the conceptual abstractions ever fully grasp the figure, pulls us back into the figural realm and opens a path into a world of endless experimentation. This threshold is the space from which possibilities, according to Musil, emerge.

Similes, analogies, and concepts tend to eclipse the figures and their effects. The former give shape to the worlds we inhabit, worlds woven tightly from and within them. However, this process never fully succeeds, since the very weave of similes and concepts is always being undone by the figural effects. Thus, in his first exploration of what "a man" with the "sense of possibility" is, Musil leaves us with nothing else than a series of comparisons that leads to the conclusion that such "possibilists are said to inhabit a more delicate medium, a hazy medium of mist, fantasy, daydreams, and the subjunctive mood." A person with this sense, he writes, "wants the forest, as it were, and the others the trees, and forest is hard to define, while trees represent so many cords of wood of definable quality."[5]

This and similar passages in Musil's novel—and in his thoughts about the form of the essay—inspire the way in which I use the term "figure" here, following his interest in perception and its modifications, and in the tension between the figural effects and mimetic assimilation. Many of the scenes and chapters in *The Man without Qualities* form experimental arrangements that study the effects of figures and figural constellations and the movements of affect, sensation, imagination, and thought they produce. While the very notion of figure is indeed abstract, the term refers in each instance to something that is concrete. In all his writings Musil draws attention to the concreteness of figural moments, their shaping force, their assimilative and disrupting effects on the life of the soul. It is the concrete thing, the concrete and inconspicuous event, the figural constellation that affects and moves and that only then turns into a series of similes, an object of meaning, an allegory, and a thought. Thus, inspired by my reading of Musil, I use the notion of figure as a name for things and moments in their concreteness as they emerge in their formative ways. I use it not in view of a "hidden meaning" but as referring to the forceful moments that give shape to perception and that enter into a tension with the worlds of signification. Figure refers, to say it simply, to the forms in movement that resist all discourse and that shape us as they shape everything else.

The figural stands on a threshold. It constitutes the ground of all assimilation in sensation, affect, and imagination and the basis of all conceptual abstraction; however, it is not a sphere of first or noumenal experience or a sphere of excessive presence but nothing else than a moment of disruption in which we participate in striking effects. On this threshold figures always affirm a world and disrupt it. They make possibilities emerge in the textures of the real when they draw our attention to the concrete moments and to the fact that in their formative function these moments break with the determined order of meaning and make us part of another world. In this, they open a tension between figure and simile, between partaking and assimilation, that will be at the core of this book.

No doubt, figures always produce series of moments of sensual and affective assimilation and mimetic repetition—all the resonances and affective traces that fill our imagination and become part of an expansive phenomenology of ourselves. The handshake I just mentioned, at the center of one of the key encounters in Musil's *The Man without Qualities*, produces a new world full of sensual, affective, and cognitive possibilities.

However, none of these possibilities are immediately known or meaningful; even if a "meaning" of the handshake will be determined at some point in the future, this does not subsist in its meaningless force in the moment when it is introduced. The very assimilation produced by the handshake, the sphere of sensual and affective attunement, the resonances, and the surplus of possible meanings it evokes break open the known texture of the world. This break brings to our attention that—beyond the modes of assimilation—the very effect of the figure, the participation it draws us into, is never exhausted. It always makes us partake in a world we do not understand, in a world that strikes, resists, and reverberates.

Erich Auerbach's essay "*Figura*," written during his exile in Istanbul, forms a surprising corollary to this notion of figuration. As I argue in Chapter 2, Auerbach develops his thoughts in correspondence with his earlier work and his reading of Dante, particularly his interest in the moments of what he perceives as the "strikingly concrete" in Dante's poetry.[6] In Auerbach's return to the use of *figura* in classical rhetoric, in Lucretius, and in the theology of the church fathers he foregrounds the "plastic" aspect of figures. He emphasizes, like Musil, the fact that figures shape perception before we enter the realm of meaning, spiritualizing interpretation, and allegorical reading. Before we ask questions about meaning and signification, figures strike us and shape our perception. They do so, according to Auerbach's reading of the early Christian theologian Tertullian, in the form of an "energetic realism," drawing us, once again, into the threshold underneath the assimilation that occurs in analogical imagination and affect and before all acts of abstraction. As Auerbach argues in his reading of classical authors, rhetorical treatises, and early Christian theology, *figura* always establishes a tension within our "tendencies" to let the realm of meaning take over, to allegorize, or to conceptualize. Against these tendencies, the figural marks a point of resistance where we are "struck," where constellations between such moments of being "struck" emerge, and where experience opens toward the strikingly concrete and its asymmetry before it is captured in meaning and thought. It is an asymmetry that does not "mean" or refer to anything or disclose some hidden immediacy or presence. "Asymmetry," when I use the term here, names the fact that the figural, seen as what has a striking effect on us, can never be fully absorbed into assimilation. In drawing attention to the concrete, it claims a fullness that can be acknowledged only in gestures of disassimilation, dispossession, and disaffiliation. The figural is the particular and concrete that strike us and that cannot be known—not because of a limit on the parts of the faculties of perception and thought, though, but because of the excessive force that asserts itself in the figure itself.

Thus, in both Musil's and Auerbach's understanding of figure, its disrupting and shaping effect produces a moment of suspense that we call possibility, the indeterminacy that is there in its asymmetrical fullness, the indeterminacy of the concrete that has not yet been grasped in forms of meanings or concepts. It is this observation that brings Auerbach's notion of figure and its emphasis on the concrete in conversation not only with Musil's experimental modernism but also with a long tradition of medieval and early modern mystical thought. While I focus on some aspects of the history of Christian mysticism in this book, similar observations could probably be made—and have been made—about other mystical traditions that address the challenges of the imposition of meaning. They appear in all forms of radical iconoclasm, negative theology, and the choice of silence. Faced with the ungraspable and unnamable divine, the medieval Christian mystical traditions, which form the object of Chapters 3 and 4 of this book, explicitly raise the question of the function of practices of figuration in light of the unsayable, of the undoing of language, and of images. In many instances, the mystical texts thematize figures and figuration not in terms of their allegorical meaning and conceptual function, not in their role of representing the divine symbolically, but in their effective force, which underlies—in the contemplative practices that we call mystical—exercises of shaping sensation, affects, and cognition. They ascribe this force of the figural not only to the symbolic orders that mediate between the creature and the divine but also to each moment in the hierarchical design of such orders. Comparable in this gesture to the role of figure in Auerbach and Musil, manuals, theories, and narratives of mystical practice use figures and figuration, often words and images they employ in prayer and contemplation, as devices that subvert discursive and cognitive orders—Musil's "sense of reality"[7]—break with them from within in concrete and striking experience, and produce experimental settings for the possibilities of an endless reweaving of perception. In short, through the undoing of sedimented old ways of seeing and the production of new figural arrangements, the world is thus made to appear and to be seen otherwise.

In focusing on the rich archive of medieval contemplative practices that I lay out in Chapters 3 and 4, I ask the reader to follow into this rather unfamiliar territory of texts that have so often exercised a fascinating force on modern readers, provoking returns to these traditions of contemplative practice from Romanticism to recent forms of new materialist thought and critical race theory. What I foreground in my presentation of the texts, however, is not something that can be cast in terms of "religious experience" or a different *Weltbild*, be it Romantic, idealist, or materialist. Instead, it is the investment of this medieval archive of texts in the very practices of figuration and in addressing questions of how to conceive of possibilities to reweave the perception of the world and the ways of inhabiting it. Thus, I do not identify mystical traditions in terms of supposed claims for an immediate experience of the world, of beauty, or of the divine but of their character as exercises of figuration that problematize all orders of perception and naming. In doing so, I foreground the reduction to the figural—in traditional terms, ascetic theology—over and against the amplification of experience in models of strategic layering of perception, affect, and thought—the symbolic theology, which I will hopefully treat in another volume on wonder and praise.

As I argue throughout this book, our attempt to conceptualize contemplative practices and their reliance on figuration in terms of an opposition between transcendence and immanence, or the infinite and finitude, is both unavoidable and wrong. What I will show is that the moments of drawing attention to figures and a specific use of and experimentation with language and media make such conceptual distinctions collapse. While the reading and contemplation of the Holy Scriptures, and the practices of prayer that build on these readings, seem to establish separate orders of this world and another world, of the human and the divine, they actually return to variations on the theme of the fullness of the worlds in which humans partake. In the notion of partaking the distinction between here and there, earth and heaven, collapses not in an imagined unity or a notion of immanence but in the irreducibly concrete creaturely multiplicity that the figures evoke.

In this collapse—in the eyes of medieval mystics the convergence of the particular and the divine—figural concreteness often turns into what modernity since the eighteenth century calls aesthetic experience. While this might, once again, look like the introduction of a perspective of transcendence in a "quasi-religious" form of aesthetic pleasure from the point of view of post-Enlightenment discursive orders, it is in fact the opposite. I thus speak, instead of transcendence, of a moment of irreducible marginality and asymmetry that the figures produce. The notion of immanence cannot do justice to this moment either. What the focus on figuration asks for, once we acknowledge the threshold position of the figural, is not a "belief" in the existence of another realm, the transcendence of the divine, the disinterested pleasure of beauty in a judgment, or of either an experiential or conceptual truth. Nor can the asymmetry of the figural—its disruptive force that underlies and resists all mimetic assimilation and conceptual grasp—be translated into ideals of humanity, compassion, tolerance, solidarity, identification, healing, otherness, difference, and understanding, that is, of a projected and imposed erasure of the concrete in a well-meaning spirit of sameness. Instead, the asymmetry, the recognition, or maybe better, the acknowledgment of the failure of meaning and concept in the disruptive encounter with the figural effects of worlds and words has no other place and time than the practice where the figure finds the space to resist and where it thus challenges the order of nature and culture alike. In the concreteness of the figure, the finite is thus realized while it makes all forms of assimilation collapse, giving way to the infinite.

It is in this acknowledgment of the asymmetry of the figural, too, that we grasp an ethical moment. To be sure, there is nothing normative in figural disruption, in terms of either an ethical "good," aesthetic "beauty," or ideal "humanity." Instead, the very practice of the acknowledgment of the figure is the place of the asymmetry, the articulation of the suppressed concrete that cannot be deployed in abstracted positions. It lets the space at the margins of our worlds open toward suspended possibilities in gestures of affirmation: the magnanimity of the reader in the perception of the strikingly concrete in Auerbach's idea of a specific will to interpretation; the contemplative mode of looking at a hill, cows, and trees in Musil's novel; the stone and the wood of the pulpit that, seen as figures, make all sermons superfluous according to Meister Eckhart; or the intervention of the slave songs at the beginning of his essays in W. E. B. Du Bois's *The Souls of Black Folk.* All these instances articulate the utter asymmetry of the figural, the marginal and disrupting position of the absorption into the concrete, and the ethical shape of submission that perception takes in the acknowledgment of the figure and the participation in its effects, devoid of all generalizations. I thus speak of acknowledgment rather than recognition. While the latter emphasizes a cognitive aspect, the former affirms an existential and temporal act, a renunciation and reformation of the will that undermine the stability of knowing subjects. In theological terms, marking the asymmetry of figural effects as supernatural gifts, we might speak of a transition from an order of nature to an order of grace here; in philosophical terms, marking the limits of knowledge, of the excess of the given in its concreteness. In both instances, we encounter the constitutive threshold again: Figure stands for the concretely real, always marginal moment that underlies and simultaneously resists mimetic assimilation and conceptual abstraction, that is, the tools of imposition and power. With some of the mystics we might thus affirm that, while it can be everything, this marginal moment is nothing—and thus, thinking with Musil, the mystics will always be "immoralists" in the eyes of normative positions.

Following a line of thought that has been deployed in Christian theologies and in the mysticism of late antiquity and the Middle Ages in terms of *theosis, theopoiesis,* and divinization, I am referring to notions of participation or partaking to characterize the specific mode of the acknowledgment of the figural. At its core lies a transition from mimetic assimilation in sensation, affect, imagination, and conceptual thought to modes of participation that always have a practical shape. The figural, thought of in this way, is the creaturely world as it resists both mimetic assimilation and conceptual grasp, calling thus for a different and always new form of acknowledgment beyond the trajectories of sameness and otherness. It is the world without content and determination that disrupts speech from within and makes us part of it.

This notion of figure and figuration as partaking, the multiple tensions and suspensions figuration produces, and the possibilities it opens are the matter of this book. It operates on three levels that often cannot be separated. "Figure" is a term that applies to the experience of perception in its movement from the striking and disruptive moment through forms of assimilation in sensation and affect, "before" it enters the sphere of meaning and conceptualization. "Figure" is a term that enables us to think of a continuity between perception, the material world in its extension, and the media that modify the shapes and movements of perception. In this sense, as shown in the texts of the mystics, figures support practices of expansion, intermingling, dramatization, and absorption in a wide range of delicate and excessive forms of pleasure and terror, reminiscence and anticipation. "Figure" is, finally, also a term that allows us to conceive of practices of experimentation with the shapes of perception, the modes of participation, and of exposure to the world that—maybe in the mode of a speculative surrealism and supernaturalism—produce possibilities in a state of suspense, undermine the spheres of meaning and concept, and displace what Musil calls the "sense of reality."

These possibilities are neither within the real nor utterly opposed to it. They also do not form a sphere of a unique or different experience. Instead, they are everywhere. The notion of figuration allows us—in what we might call a *reductio ad figuram*—to see possibilities as critical modifications of sedimented forms of knowledge, habits, and meaning, in other words, of the ontological and epistemological orders that shape and colonize worlds and peoples. These modifications, not channeled primarily through the deployment of discursive formats, are deviations and convulsions that nest within the worlds and the words whenever we return from the spheres of assimilation, meaning, and concept to the resistance and asymmetry of figures. In Chapters 3 and 4 I try to show the richness of medieval engagements with this use of figures, following the variations through the production of mystical tropes, first in their exercises of reweaving perception, then in their forms of exemplary imitation. Moving through this archive of texts allows us to see how these tropes, in returning to the most provocative one, the ungraspable divine, address the challenges of figuration and establish a range of paradigmatic forms of sensual, affective, and conceptual assimilation—however, undermining these paradigms time and again in their return to the threshold function of the figural. Most provocatively, they present us with multiple ways of designing practices and reinventing the circulation of sensation, affect, and thought that only the close reading of this rich archive can offer.

As I show based on these readings, this never means that we must end with a stable opposition between the figural and the worlds of assimilation, meaning, and concept. "Nesting," in my use of the term, refers to the fact that figuration inhabits and undergirds all sensation, imagination, and production of meaning and that what the practices of figuration ask for is the acknowledgment not of its opposition to it but, again, of the very asymmetry that is at stake here. This happens also in the movements of turning moments of meaning and conceptualization against themselves, making them into figures where we first think of them as signs. This, I argue here, has been at the core of a practice of contemplation and prayer in mystical traditions often characterized as the marginal, embodied, experiential, and somewhat subversive side of the history of medieval Christianity and dogmatic belief. As noted earlier, this is also one aspect that has made mysticism an object of fascination and engagement throughout the nineteenth and twentieth centuries. In drawing attention to the figural and the fact that it can never be fully assimilated, however, my focus is on more than a set of practices that emphasize experience instead of dogma, belief, and conceptual grasp. As I argue, the notion of the figural forces us to think along a perspective of the concrete and creaturely that, in its irreducible asymmetry, like the divine and indeed mirroring it, can never be owned or understood. Thus, I use figure here not only as a concept but also as a heuristic tool, often just an image, that allows delineation of a sphere where the "soul"—to use this seemingly archaic term that comprehends all aspects of the life of all things—is intimately woven into the textures of the world and entirely part of it, denaturalizing it and opening it to the "otherwise." It is this notion of figure—and the detours through Musil and Auerbach—that has helped me understand some of the fundamental stakes of the mystical theologies I have been working on. And it is the observation that figure cannot be conceived of without the multiple paradigms of assimilation that has made me understand that we always must return to this archive of texts and their history to grasp the very tensions that are at stake.

This book comprises eight parts. I start with an introductory meditation on the notion of figure in Chapter 1, focusing on a few characteristic moments where the disruptive force of figures and the outline of a radical figuralism come into view. In Chapter 2 I turn to a discussion of Erich Auerbach's attention to the concrete, his work on *figura*, and his engagement with the understanding of history as a continuous modification of our minds that he finds in the thought of Giambattista Vico. This is the background for the exploration of the role of practices of figuration in forms of reweaving perception and the imitation of examples at stake in medieval theories and practices of prayer, contemplation, and aesthetic experience in Chapters 3 and 4. Chapters 5, 6, and 7 focus on questions of how such practices have been framed and controlled between the fifteenth and eighteenth centuries; how they have been recast in early modern times; and how they reemerged in some forms of modernist thought and literature. In Chapter 8, the book concludes with the return to a figure that crosses the centuries, the holy fool, in my eyes the very *figura* of figuration as an agent of intervention. Not surprisingly, it is this image of the "fool" that returns also in Musil's text when he speaks of the "man without qualities."

In drawing attention to the practices of figuration, medieval Christian texts on prayer and the experience of the divine play a key role in this book. As I argue, these texts are, above all, invested in practices of shaping and reshaping sensation, emotions, and thought. At the center of this we encounter not an expression of belief, or a cognitive act of distinction between the human and the divine, or even a theory of analogy, but an investment in practices that transform and transfigure the ways of perception and of inhabiting the world. Thus, building on essays I have published in earlier versions, Chapters 3 and 4 focus on traditions of spiritual exercises that are meant to produce this transformation. Many of these practices foreground a tension between figuration, forms of assimilation, and hermeneutics, arguing for a critical focus that privileges the plastic side of perception against the imposition of meaning. At the same time, they establish and explore the tensions between the figure and the forms of assimilation that precede all hermeneutics and the empire of meaning. In all instances, we are asked to move from the meaning of a text, usually a text from the Scriptures, to an exemplary moment of mimetic assimilation—scenes from the lives of saints, for example—and to the figural threshold that can be grasped fully neither in understanding nor in the exemplary imitation itself.

In producing this movement and in rearticulating a radical negative theology, figures mark a point of suspension and dispossession where the world takes shape "otherwise." Particular moments play a role in this production of suspension and inform the contemplative practices that are at the center of my study. My main interest in identifying these moments along a line that leads from late antiquity to modern times lies neither with the characterization of specific authors nor of a conceptual framework or a definition of "mystical thought" or a universal "mystical experience" but with specific techniques, movements, and procedures that are foregrounded in the contemplative practices around the relations between figure and mimesis; the focus on reinventing sensation; the gestures of prayer; aspects of dramatization and exemplarity; visualization and imagination; the topics of the abject and disfiguration; enumeration and meditation; surrender, experiment, rapture, and delay. In focusing on these aspects of contemplative practice and their theological implications, I identify not a shared and thus idealized mystical experience or a form of belief but specific axes around which medieval contemplative practices and exercises are organized. As I show, in each instance and along each of these axes, the tension between the figural and the forms of assimilation is being evoked and complicated in a phenomenology of rhetorical effects.

In each instance the asymmetry of the figure is also being evoked in these practices that long for an experience of the world in light of the divine, beauty, and love. Articulated in moments of unity or utter ecstatic absorption, none of these forms of experience can ever be grasped or known. They give a name, however, to the asymmetrical character of the figural, the challenge of a differential intensity that disrupts the world, that suspends ontology, and that emerges in the concrete, thus negating all abstraction and all powers of subjection. In theological terms, once again, we are asked to think here of the gift of grace and of transfiguration or metamorphosis; in philosophical terms, of the excess of the concrete; in rhetorical terms, of the absorption into the figure on the thresholds of assimilation. The medieval texts that I present in Chapters 3 and 4 are, in each instance, variations on the exercises that engage these aspects of the practice of figuration.

In Chapters 5, 6, and 7—not following a strict chronological path—I identify moments and instances where these practices of participation, assimilation, and transfiguration have been discussed and reframed: first from the late Middle Ages to the Baroque, then in some of the modern voices that engage the positions that are at stake here. As I show, the discussions around the adoption of mystical tropes repeatedly answer to specific historical conditions, and they articulate new forms of conceiving of the figural challenge. Thus, among others, Jacob Böhme's cosmopoetics, Alexander Gottlieb Baumgarten's and Johann Gottfried Herder's notion of aesthetic experience, Joris-Karl Huysmans's space of decadent pleasure, Robert Musil's sense of possibility, Musil's and Georg Lukács's thoughts about the form of the essay, and Béla Balázs's notion of a new visibility of the world in silent film come into view. What also come into view are the multiple ways of framing and controlling the extravagance of figural thought and the enthusiasm it engenders, and, finally, in Chapter 8, the very foolishness that characterizes the radical abandonment to the power of figures and the ethics of asymmetry it entails—including the foolishness of this very book. It establishes, as will become clearer, a strong opposition between figurality and hermeneutic engagement only to acknowledge that hermeneutics, the arts of reading and interpretation that connect flesh, history, and spirit, are always at stake here and that the figural emerges where hermeneutic engagements realize their own finite limit position, abandoning themselves to practices of assimilation at first, to the absorbing asymmetry of the figural worlds of possibilities at last.

While I concede that specific historical shifts could be considered here, I reflect on these only in oblique ways. Thus, I refer not to historical lines of continuity or reception. Instead, after laying out what I see as a basic notion of figure and a history of medieval types of engagement with the figural in Chapters 1 to 4, in Chapter 5 I focus on a series of moments of framing the figural practices and the tensions they articulate in transitions from medieval to modern times. I argue that in the late Middle Ages and in the early modern era we move from a complex phenomenology of rhetorical effects, meant to contain practices of figuration in medieval contexts of spiritual exercises, to a framework of hermeneutic authorization and a control of "free spirits"; to a semiotics of the demonic and divine and a neutralization of inspired speech in Luther's critique of figural practices; and an entirely naturalized clarification of rational principles of discernment in Kant's elaborations of the conditions of the possibility of knowledge and his critique of "enthusiasm."

However, in Chapter 6 I draw attention to three moments of a countercurrent to these frames of control, the "monadological transcription" of the figural in the seventeenth and eighteenth centuries that resists some aspects of this very framing. I argue that in Böhme's emphasis on the cosmopoetic imagination, in his theory of the signature of things, as well as in Baumgarten's and Herder's notion of aesthetic experience, particularly in the emphasis on the "ground of the soul" and on "touch," we encounter a new monadological understanding of the figural. It takes the figure as monad, building on the idea that the entire world is folded into each moment of concrete encounter and that perception unfolds in specific forms of partaking that rearticulate the tensions between figure, assimilation, and understanding. I present the early modern notion of the emblem as the characteristic form of expression of this very tension in the sixteenth and seventeenth centuries. And I argue that in the constellation of an abstract notion, the figural image, and the expository language of assimilation—that is, the emblem in its exemplary shape—the figural, the assimilative, and the conceptual are held in a state of suspension. The form of the emblem—opposed to all subordination to metaphysical and to naturalizing conditions of possibility of knowledge—has kept its fascinating allure, returning at moments that we call Romantic, decadent, or expressionist in their diverse shapes.

Chapter 7 follows this line of inquiry further, focusing on four instances where modernism and its precursors rearticulate these tensions—my eclectic selection of these moments largely ignores the Romantic movements, which, in their attempts to think figuration anew in correlation with both an individual and a cosmopoetic imagination, would merit a separate book that moves from what I am tempted to call the reduction to the figural to the dreams of a sublime and delirious symbolic amplification. With Huysmans we turn in Chapter 7 to the so-called decadent pleasure "against nature"; with Georges Bataille to mysticism at the "limits of the possible"; with Musil and Lukács to the form of the essay, its return to mystical tropes, and its figural investment in the play of possibility on the thresholds of figure, simile, and concept; with Balázs, finally, to the figural gestures of silent film and the new visibility of the world.

In these modern instances, I am tempted to speak of transformations of the emblematic tension. What the Baroque emblem foregrounds as an irreducible constellation of concept, figure, and assimilation is now more straightforwardly and explicitly conceived of in terms of experiments: the experiment with rhetorical devices and moments of intensity in Huysmans; the limit function of the erotic excess and the mystical in Bataille; the art of the essay in Lukács and Musil; and the new practice of seeing in Bálazs. In each instance, a set of gestures enacts the experimental character of addressing the correlations of figures, thoughts, and the play of sensation and affect. In each instance, the notion of possibility is correlated with a set of expressive gestures anchored in what has been called spiritual exercises since late antiquity, creating thus, in these moments of radical modernity, a deep resonance between modernist concerns and medieval practices of prayer and contemplation.

These gestures, as I acknowledge in Chapter 8 in dialogue with more recent critical interventions by Michel Foucault and Judith Butler, are indeed gestures of a foolish exercise that transfigures the real into a place of the possible beyond its subordination to the imposition of discourse and naturalizing perspectives. It is a foolish expression of dispossession that delves into the space of possibility beyond and within the world as we know it—and that, in the best of all cases, attempts to give back to the concrete all its divine powers.

As I mentioned earlier, parts of Chapters 3, 4, 5, and 7 have been published previously in different versions. However, while preserving the richness and detail of the medieval and early modern textual archive most modern readers might not be familiar with, I have structured the presentation and analysis of these materials here along new lines. The picture of contemplative techniques that emerges is not set up in terms of particular forms of experience, theories, authors, or historical paradigm shifts but practices that are organized around mystical tropes and, more important, the specific stakes that are foregrounded in particular moments and texts. Thus, the chapters trace different aspects of the engagement with figure and figuration, foregrounding a shared interest in exploring a basic tension: the disrupting force of the figure in its concreteness, the divine contemplative depth and terror, the experimental play with it, and the forms of assimilation that the texts explore. In this tension a "sense of possibility" emerges as a sense of the concrete that creates a conversation between medieval and modernist attempts to reweave the forms of perception and of partaking beyond all naturalist temptations.

1

Disruptions

Mesmerized

Conceiving of ourselves as critical viewers at first, we often turn into partakers. What seems to be observation and abstraction becomes absorption, immersion, experience in time. Reading turns into feelings of sweetness, bitterness, disgust; looking into taste, appetite, and arousal; hearing into affective pleasure and melancholic longing; touch into an abyss of desire and joy. In short, and stating this maybe too bluntly, assimilation in all its forms is being disrupted and turns into partaking, analogical *mimesis* into figural *methexis.*

Why not begin with a simple, at first glance maybe embarrassingly trivial scene that challenges both critical distance and phenomenological exploration. A multipurpose room with an old hardwood floor, once used as a gym, in what is probably an ex-GDR school building in Berlin, Pankow. A group of dancers rehearsing, working toward a future performance. A choreography, *Chora. The Earth Is a Foreign Planet. Every Day It Shows a Different Face,* produced by Moritz Majce and Sandra Man. Silence reigns, except for the faint hum of a freeway in the distance and the irregular taps and scrapes produced by the dancers' steps. From time to time hints of a minimal soundscape float in the air, mostly rhythmical echoes that do not distract from the bodies that move. This is all there is. Figures that move, figures in no explicit and traceable form of interaction, figures in space and time. Movements that make space and time emerge, involving the spectator, attracting the gaze, holding it, redirecting it, absorbing the eyes and the ears. Affects and thoughts enter into the new space and time that unfold here, thoughts that are tempted to fill what is a pleasurable and excitable void. What strikes, however, is nothing else than a landscape of figural effects and of movements, both antitheatrical and antiperformative, resisting the powers of assimilation. It is a landscape where sensation and imagination converge, a landscape of beauty in its dispersion. Of cruelty also, of figuration and disfiguration, and of violence that pulls viewers out of themselves and into the movement of figures.

The thought arrives, surprisingly, of David Hume's skepticism and his happiness in scenes of eating and conversation—and of his melancholy that came about when he engaged in philosophical matters. As we look at the movements of the dancers unfold, no concepts emerge; neither does any kind of aesthetic empathy. There is no distance here, no way of foregrounding an event, no significance of the performative, no phenomenological line of interpretation or anything similar. Instead, thought itself turns into the movement of perception and affect; and, starting in the critically descriptive mode they are used to inhabit, spectators find themselves as skeptics absorbed in a dream of sensation, affect, and thought. While a phenomenological exploration tends to quickly set in, speaking of feelings, meanings, and intentionality, nothing of that kind happens at first. All reading of moods or of events, all search for the axiomatic lines we might want to find, for the key algorithm that governs the movements, all this is in vain in face of the radical figuralism that makes the distinction of materialist and idealist views collapse.

Indeed, when we look at the dancers, sensing the movements and following the figures, we react with procedures of assimilation that break with the figural and start to explore the rich imagination the scenes stimulate. Thinking of Henry Corbin's "imaginal" worlds, angels are coming to mind. It is an image that we, quickly moving into a critical mood and giving in to the hermeneutic temptation in a subtle interpretive framework, might want to call a cliché or a topos. Nevertheless, it is not far-fetched. Angels, each of them singular and not bound by the hierarchies of discursive thought, engaging each other in a form of language unknown to us. Angels, as in the drawing of Paul Klee that Walter Benjamin loved, looking back toward the ruins of history and alluding to a language that restores what is lost. Angels, as in Rainer Maria Rilke's vision—and as close to the suspicion of kitsch as we can get here—terrifying in their beauty and always close, too close to us in their intimate movements and presence. Angels, also, deeply immersed in the broken world, carrying all its passions, its desires, its senses in their silent voice. In Wallace Stevens's words, "the necessary angel of earth, / Since, in my sight, you see the earth again."[1]

Or, shifting to images familiar from late medieval and Renaissance paintings, I think of bodies just resurrected from the womb of the earth, seeking the words and the language they do not have, yet fully alive in this tentative world of moving encounters. Bodies of flesh, encompassing all, humans and animals, flowers and stones, rivers and landscapes, all old orders lost and forgotten in the flow of the forms and their effects. Reminding, indeed, also of the shamanic travels that are foreclosed to us and accessible, right now, to the imagination alone.[2]

We quickly realize that all this is not about bodies, not about performance, not about "meaning." What exceeds the state of a different time and perception below the forms of assimilation—angels, bodies, the earth—is the participation in figural play, a play that takes shape both outside and in our souls, fully material and fully spiritual. It would be wrong to speak of depth here, of meaning, or of a world that turns into an event. All this, even the all-too-tempting allegories of angels or of resurrected bodies that come as facile allusions to the images we know, are being undone. They are being disrupted, time and again, and replaced by the pull of the movements, the series of impressions, the axes of gaze and sensation, their layering and circulation, in short, by mesmerizing effects of figures and configurations—not figures of life, or figures of anything else, but forms that move perception, affects, images, and concepts in a state of suspension and abandonment.

Thinking of this as the undoing of social, racial, and discursive subjugations in a convergence of flesh and imagination, Audre Lorde's jarringly nominalist disruption in "Poetry Is Not a Luxury" comes to mind: "The white fathers told us, I think therefore I am; and the black mothers in each of us—the poet—whispers in our dreams, I feel therefore I can be free. Poetry coins the language to express and charter this revolutionary awareness and demand, the implementation of that freedom." Lorde writes in a gesture of poetic concretization: "For there are no new ideas. There are only new ways of making them felt, of examining what our ideas really mean (feel like) on Sunday morning at 7 AM, after brunch, during wild love, making war, giving birth; while we suffer the old longings, battle the old warnings and fears of being silent and impotent and alone, while tasting our new possibilities and strengths."[3] The "tasting" of possibilities and strengths in the undoing and remaking of figures from all strands, the rearticulation and recombination of these figures, evokes the ancient idea of *apokatastasis panton*, the return of all things in a new face and in the experience of a different economy of race, gender, and subjectivities. With J. Kameron Carter's notion of "black malpractice" and his rethinking of the "sacred" in dialogue with Georges Bataille and Roger Caillois, I want to speak of an "ek-static threshold before which other, differential and unrepresentable presences, genres or forms of life, unplottable gatherings in representation's colonializing ruins, alternative ways of being, come into view."[4] This does not happen, however, in the form of a "meaning" that could be read, conceived, and interpreted but—recalling Roland Barthes's notion of "emanation" in his essay on photography—in the provocatively antidialectical literalism of Audre Lorde's "making them felt"; in the silence of dance that discards the orders of the theatrical and the performative; and in the magic realism of mesmerizing figures that so blissfully unsettle.

Hunters in the Snow

During the final moments of Andrei Tarkovsky's film *Solaris*, Kris—a psychologist who was once sent to a spaceship to solve the scientific enigma that envelops the cosmonauts' lives and perceptions—walks down a small hill toward a frozen pond. He stops slightly above the plane of ice and looks at it through a crisscross of bare winter branches. We follow the movements of his gaze, its focus put upon us by the work of the camera and framed, I am tempted to say, in a moment of contemplative attention. Memories, associations, and expectations seem to emerge in this moment—lacking, however, all further explanation or exploration. Nothing is explicit here, no memory, no hope, no feeling, no thought. Instead, we move into and stay within the focus on the concrete, the ice and the branches, a focus on the images that does not allow for any abstraction or allegory. Both the mirror of the frozen pond and the crisscross of the branches remain before our eyes in their concrete shape, meaningless, not even enigmatic. They do, however, give shape to our attention, free it from its involvement with itself, and turn it into the encounter that emanates from the things that are seen. They evoke a resonance of figures and remind us of earlier scenes in the film—and, I assume without hesitation, of the words from Paul's first letter to the Corinthians. We see, as he suggests, in no other way than *in speculo in aenigmate*, "in a mirror, darkly," exposed, as in a piece of music, to an encounter that comes from elsewhere—and, in Édouard Glissant's words, in an "opacity . . . considerate of all the threatened and delicious things joining one another (without conjoining, that is, without merging) in the expanse of Relation."[5]

There is no meaning at stake here that supports the relations, just a texture of figures, movements, resonances, and moments of partaking. One of the earlier scenes we are reminded of in this last movement of the film, in this series of never-ending translations of forms, plays in the space station, the main location. A desolate and nearly abandoned place—the living relic of a stellar mission that, at some point, had a defined goal and meaning—it orbits a foreign planet above a mysterious ocean. This vast sea, resonating with the material traces of memories, hopes, and anxieties of the cosmonauts who inhabit the vessel, produces figures that emerge from it and engage the travelers. They disturb the temporal order as much as they recast all experience through these very disturbances, flooding the spaceship with a world of figural appearance.

In a key scene that takes place in what we could call the house of memory in the library and dining room of the vessel, Hari, one of the quasi-phantasmagoric figures conjured by the ocean and a former lover of Kris, is sitting in front of a painting. It is Pieter Brueghel's famous and well-known *Hunters in the Snow*. Here, again, the camera makes us follow the gaze that immerses itself in the image, that follows the hunters, the houses in the background, the skaters on the frozen lake, and the naked branches that cut through the sky. As in the final scene—the frozen pond, the crisscross of branches—and as in Brueghel's painting of the winter landscape itself, no meaning is disclosed. We do not return to a myth or a story, and we do not return to an allegory that could provide consolation and meaning. What happens, alone, is the immersion in a movement within the painting, a movement that establishes a time of its own and unfolds in the effects of the very figures we see.

But what does it mean to speak of immersion? Following the customs of interpretation, we might be tempted to introduce narratives and stories here, allegorical readings, even psychologically and metaphysically thoughtful theories and speculations, building on the knots of figures, of clues, and of events we see. Or we might want to speak of a deeper meaning of the painting and the film. We might be thinking of the relation between early modern times and Tarkovsky's modern melancholy that many interpreters have emphasized or, claiming validity for this observation more broadly, the presentation of what has been called the "human condition" that "speaks" in both the painting and the film.

None of this is entirely wrong. None of this happens, however, in Tarkovsky's installation of Brueghel's painting on the wall of the room in the spaceship. None of this is meant to take place in the way he stages the gaze and the circulation of impressions and our participation in this scene. The only sentence spoken by Hari at the end of her contemplative absorption—"Ia zadumalas'," "I was lost in thought"—paradoxically cuts through all these temptations and desires for meaning. Her comment, "I was lost in thought," does not even hint at a resolution of the enigmatic moment in the customary form of thought or words. It is framed in the form neither of a hermeneutic engagement nor of allegorical meaning or liberating abstraction. Instead, we are led to see her delving into the painting in terms of exposure and absorption, more precisely, of an exposure to the plastic effect of the figures and configurations. Her world, her memory, her affects are nowhere else than in the moving effects of the scenes in the painting: the hunters, the children playing on the ice, the snow, and the houses.

With Walter Benjamin, we can think of this moment as an exposure to "history," a history, in his understanding, that shows itself not from above and from an idealist vantage point but only in the concrete encounter with the material figural forms that already shape our ways of seeing and inhabiting the world. Thus history, in this materialist understanding, reveals itself in that very encounter where we trace the way in which we ourselves have been formed and come to be what we are—sedimented forms of the histories of figuration, open to genealogical reconstruction only in our exposure to these forms.

In another vein, we should also think of these moments and the genealogies that unfold as an exposure to the "human" beyond "the world of Man." Following Sylvia Wynter's and Alexander Weheliye's arguments about the "issue of the genre of 'Man'" that, in Wynter's words, produces all generalizing "filiations,"[6] Hari's immersion in the painting, her exposure to its figures, is to be seen not as a move toward abstraction but into a participation in the multiple forms of the concretely human that give shape to her existence. Thus, no abstract conception, no essence of the human or of freedom is at stake here, but a "figurative truth, the one unwanted by the modern colonial world." In this "epistemic break," which does not restore a universal knowledge of the human, "the existential lived experience of the damned" leads Wynter's black feminist voice to "the charting of new imaginations of freedom" that are, nevertheless, "forever haunted by subjection."[7]

Resonating from afar with these attempts to recast the human in postcolonial voices, the figure of Hari, "lost in thought" and having abandoned all generalizations, is for a moment nothing else than a particular refraction of the figural effects of the painting. She herself, made to appear by the ocean on the foreign planet, her flesh and her presence are, in their irreducible concreteness, the plastic appearance of processes of figuration and the temporalities they produce. The same could be said about the lives of the cosmonauts, their fantasies, their emotions, sensations, and thoughts. In contrast to them, however, Hari is the voice that breaks things open and that makes "Man"—concretely, the cosmonauts and the voices of science—fall apart in the articulation of the very subjugations that produce Man's world. She is the one who, shattering Man's world, makes figures and voices the core of a world that has lost its semblance of unity. It is a world of many faces and things where all concepts fail and where all assimilation is laid bare.

Lars von Trier, using the very same Brueghel painting three decades later in his film *Melancholia*, might have hinted at that plastic effect when he lets a reproduction of the painting go up in flames. He, too, cuts through the hermeneutic desires for resolution, leaving us with nothing else than figures and their effects. Now they are set in the apocalyptic mode of a hopeless white bourgeois world: a rogue planet, expected to destroy the earth; the falling horse, an oblique memory from Tarkovsky's *Solaris*; the landscaped garden; finally, the crisscross of dry branches, again, that form a seemingly protective hut, a network of figures, and a hopeless shelter. The last drop of Tarkovsky's mystical transfiguration of nature, humanity, and history abandoned, nothing is left at the end of *Melancholia*—not even the absorption in the painting that both Tarkovsky and Lars von Trier take as a place of refuge in figural play. Now, in *Melancholia*, it turns into nothing else than the sadness and apocalyptic pleasure of a disheveled aestheticism.

Extension

"Plastic," as I use the term here, refers to a relation between the figures, the things, the landscapes we see and the emergence of landscapes of soul and flesh; to times and spaces that open in coextensive ways in the acts of participation; and, maybe more precisely, to the multiple places where figures give shape to the soul and the soul abandons itself to the effects of the figures in joy, terror, memories and desires, and the innumerable nuances that lie in between. It is a sphere where the distinction of soul and flesh collapses. We might want to call this plastic effect, taking inspiration from Saint Augustine's reflections on the nature of time in his *Confessions*, a "distension of the soul" (*distentio animi*) that underlies all psychic life.[8] This distension has its place nowhere else than in the convolution of figural expressions. Similarly, both in Tarkovsky's and in Lars von Trier's work we are not drawn into the depths of psychological explanation or of metaphysical speculation but into the realm of figural textures and the distensions of living in time. What Tarkovsky foregrounds is a space and a time of perception, a plane of resonances that takes shape in figural ways, that is, in the form of utterly and irreducibly concrete moments that cut through the textures of what is obvious and known. In doing so, in tearing, in disturbing the seemingly familiar, known, and knowable—in the catastrophic break that ends all times just for a moment—things turn into figures, and as figures they produce the participation in disrupting and moving spheres of memory, expression, and possibility. In the catastrophic moments, in Andrei Tarkovsky's undoing of comprehension, and in Lars von Trier's apocalyptic vision of a desolate white bourgeoisie, these are spheres not of the absence of meaning alone. In their expressive character they offer an affirmation that abandoning all meaning, even the meaning of the end, draws attention to the figural force of the voices not heard.

Figures

What we see, feel, and touch in these situations are—even though we might call them by these names—neither objects nor things, nor substances nor essences of any kind. What we see, feel, and live with are figures and their effects, forms that emerge and turn into the shapes of perception, memory, and thought long before we understand anything. Unknown figures ourselves, we might conclude, we are surrounded by figures and the temporal pull of their effects. We often call them things or objects, misleading both ourselves and the world when we construct (and fall into) the trap that we, following a long tradition and the very violence and pleasures of metaphysics, call ontology or ontologies, oriented along the lines of Being, beings, and the being of Man—or, for that matter, the melancholy of its deconstruction and, more recently, the noncorrelationist form of its speculative realist versions in philosophy and theology. In doing so, we cultivate the habits of identifying substances and modes of being when we speak of the real and the imaginary, of the ideal, the immanent and the transcendent, sometimes of Being and beings, or of the One and the multiple. Thus, we register, name, enumerate, describe, and conceptualize things and their places in response to what we feel and experience. Abandoning the disrupting powers of the figural, we produce a world, its parts and relations,[9] as well as, in Western philosophical language, the immanent and the transcendent, the worldly and the divine, the profane and the sacred.

No doubt, all this labor of distinction and abstraction offers its pleasures and truths, its orders of contemplation and comprehension, even its own beauty. It is marked, however, by the terror and violence of subjugation: black and white; men and women; things and animals; nature and culture; the secular and the religious; the animate and the inanimate; west, east, north, and south. Beyond this, and far beyond "being," first and foremost all things touch us and each other. They do so not as things and in the form of objects or subjects, which arrest and fix a world, but as figures that move, emerge in situations, and create ever-new forms. Not as things but as figures do they produce effects, leave marks, imprints, and traces—always locally, materially, sensually. Thus, they open virtual spheres of imagination and of continuous emergence that have their place both inside and outside ourselves and all things. Not as a "thing," however, only as a figure does everything act; deploy force; produce percepts, affects, concepts; and form relations along certain lines—evoking vectors, movements, flows, and constellations of images, sounds, feelings, qualities, and powers that we then give shape to in ontological and epistemological orders.

This sphere of figural play and emergence is, as Jacob Böhme, the seventeenth-century Silesian cobbler and mystic writes, the realm of the imagination—not, however, the imagination in terms of a human faculty alone but of material and spiritual becoming shared by all things. Thus, imagination turns into the name for the unfolding of figures, referring to it as a sphere in-between, beyond the distinctions of human and world, earthly and divine, worldly and heavenly, material and spiritual. Imagination is, according to Böhme, naturally, socially, and cosmically shared; and it forms the common ground of becoming at the intersection of the spiritual and the material in its deeply intertwined, ultimately indistinguishable nature. Spirit, after all, is nothing else than the name for a movement that goes through the figures and of the freedom that—in the figure of its other name: love—annihilates the coercions of "Man," "nature," and "things."

Speaking more casually, consider the chair on the other side of my table, the cup of coffee, the lamp, the keys, and the book. They are things only when we abstract from the figural play of effects they produce and the imagination we share with them; when we abstract from their thick or thin expression that emerges within and around us and that imposes itself on us and on each other in contagious ways. They turn into things and the "real" only when we remove ourselves from the plastic effects, from the bodily textures, the places, the relations, and the particular temporalities that emerge with and beyond us. They turn into things only when we let them recede into a background of utter indifference and withdrawal, when we establish a defined state, a stable, seemingly serious presence or an objectification or commodification that allows us to call them "things." However, the chair, the cup, the lamp are at first never things. They are only things—things invested with essence, meaning, and value—after the figures have produced their playful effects and we, already establishing a distance and producing what we distinguish in terms of the real or the imaginary, quickly abandon them and their interaction in favor of "things," of objects, of orderly language, narration, science, and philosophy. Thus, we conceptualize, analyze, allegorize, and commodify what stands around, what circulates, what emerges and disappears all on its own and in endless movements of interaction. Thus, we abandon what affects; what produces a different circulation of sensation, emotion, and thought; and what, in the words of Audre Lorde that resonate with the medieval mystics, constitutes the "power of the erotic" and the asymmetries of partaking.[10]

At the same time, however, we allude, in weak attempts to save them, often at first in the rhetorical form of enumeration, to the things and objects in their supposed concrete independence. Thus, we make attempts, against all generalizations, to restore a sphere of the real that always escapes us and enable ourselves to speculate about the ungraspable essence of things. Charmingly, we then talk in allusions that evoke a heterogeneous and antinomian sphere of chairs, constellations of stars, limbs, and birds. Or we make these things part of a phenomenology that, abandoning the cosmic liturgy of figure and assimilation,[11] is invested in exploring our own mind and its forms of presence to the world and to itself alone. All these attempts, however, fail at what is at stake here. It is not a return, not the restitution of things and ourselves, not a path of salvation or reconciliation, not a rediscovery of the saturated phenomenon or the forever withdrawing object; nor is it a "newly arisen superior tone in philosophy" (Kant) or the reserve of poetry alone. What is at stake, instead, is the drama of figural play and the dark joy of unknowing that goes with the exposure to it.

Exposure

In our exposure to figures, rhetorical tools form at first the recording devices for that very drama. "Figure," after all, is used most often as a rhetorical term. It refers, as we will see in Erich Auerbach's understanding of the word, above all to the plastic force of shapes and forms. These same devices are also the basis for anything that follows after our very exposure to them, or, what I call here the forms of assimilation: aesthetic experience and pleasure, poetic exploration, scientific analysis and its truth, or philosophical speculation. There can be no question that we need to move on from the figural to the world of similes and of meaning in everyday life, both critically, constructively, and in doing justice. In all cases, however, the return to the figural means a break with our own investment. It disrupts our own hubris, or, in current terms, the so-called anthropocentric perspective of Man. Against this grasp that makes the figures into things and "meaning," the fullness of figures deploys its force in its very concreteness.

This force, in its fundamental asymmetry, goes beyond the confines of hermeneutic appropriation and exploration, metaphysical speculation, and commodification. Restoring a speculative identity of hidden substances or a thought of selves and things in the name of the "real" is in this context—if we look at our own historical moment—nothing else than a nostalgic response to the powers of late capitalism that exhaust and annihilate all substance, replacing it with the quasi-spiritual forms of market value and, more recently, the promise of virtual existence and the ontological conjuration of the real (often with a messianic promise in a lightly concealed Gnostic tone). All these attempts are, if we want, nothing more than expressions of a desire for a reality of things that both embraces and escapes us, being out there, so to speak, in the form of things. This restoration of a metaphysical perspective forecloses, however, the sphere of figural play that is beyond us and reduces it to a language that ascribes time and again essence and substance to objects and things—not least in all the gestures that renaturalize distinctions of gender, race, humans, gods, animals, and nature and culture itself. Abandoning this return to ontologies in favor of figural topology (my argument here) lets us understand essence, substance, and nature as nothing else than the product of metaphysical conceits—conceits that might be necessary for the naturalized forms of inhabiting the world, as well as of freedom and justice, but that are utterly blind to the nonnatural ground and its flow. "Nonnatural" it is, since it cannot be grasped as nature without sacrificing it to the conceptual realm. In opposing the imposition of symmetry by metaphysical and naturalizing gestures, and undermining these in undoing them, the acknowledgment of figural play abandons us to the asymmetry in the encounter with figures. It is, in the rather unfamiliar language of who we call the mystics, the participation by gift of grace or, to put it differently, the silent acknowledgment of the unfinished, never exhaustible character of the figure that encounters us in these moments.

What figures do, before and beyond all this happens, is seemingly simple, utterly contingent, and never finite. We tend to forget about it when we speak of things, of the real, of essence, and of freedom. Figures, above all, produce fields of impression and expression, of vision, touch, smell, hearing, taste, emotions, cognition, and thought. They produce percepts, affects, sensations that circulate—beyond the world of humans as well as within it—like the floating images, the *idola* or *simulacra* Lucretius sees at work when he explains the nature of vision in *De rerum natura* (*On the Nature of Things*). Figures, like the *idola*, at first deploy their plastic force, their form, giving shape to life, to the soul and the flesh, before we know ourselves or anything else, before there is a self and another. It is this plastic force that unfolds an agency that is, without origin, always there and shared in multiple ways.

Nothing forbids us to think of figures affecting the souls of all kinds of stuff in that very same way. After all, even in its conventional medieval understanding, soul is nothing else than the name for the play of matter and form in time. And nothing forbids us to think of soul as exactly that, that very side of us and of all things, that is, the participation in the movements of figural impression, expression, and, in the terms used from Marsilio Ficino to Jacob Böhme and Friedrich Schelling, a cosmic imagination that has its life in the translations that form the life in the flesh. There is no object we could identify here and no subject; no matter and no mind; no perception of anything, just figure, force, affect, and percept. Figures emerge, disrupt, cut, circulate, produce effects, and form textures and temporalities in, between, and beyond us.

That is what happens when you walk down a street, eyes open; when you bite into an apple; when you hear a song. The bifurcations of objects and subjects, of forms of assimilation, of matter and mind, of immanence and transcendence, of faith and reason come about only when we recede from the participation in these textures of figures, when we establish a stable distance from the thresholds of figural play and introduce an orderly pattern of time and space; to put it differently, when we turn into idealists or materialists, nominalists or realists, ascribing identity, difference, substance, and essence. Thus, we arrest the flow of the figural realm of impressions and expressions and establish the determined spheres of us and things, of subjects and objects.

As some medieval and early modern theologians and philosophers argue, this distinction of a sphere of us, of the divine, and of things is nothing else than the signature of human hubris. It is a form of knowledge and of hierarchical systems of knowledge that take themselves—after the mythical exile from paradise and compensating for that very loss—as the convergence and correlation of being and thought. Such ways of knowledge provide us with a philosophical order of worlds and subjects, of conditions of possibility, of ontological and epistemological orders instead of a participation in figural play within the eros and terror of darkness that surround all emergence of forms.

We call the thinkers who express these thoughts about partaking most straightforwardly mystics. They emphasize a thought and an experience of participation where we tend to stay within the consolation and the power of knowledge. What do we know, the mystics ask, putting their emphasis on a radical negative theology, of the identity of what we call "things," of their life, of their ways of existence, communication, and withdrawal? What do we know of ourselves? What of the divine? What of the world? If there is each thing with and in its identity, they answer, it has necessarily, as it were, such identity only within a projected, actual realm of the divine imagination alone and not in the pretentiously enlightened world of the Gnostics or of our tame new forms of it. If there were such an essence of things that we could know, it would be withdrawn into an erotic abyss of divine darkness where it dwells in plenitude above our orders of identity and difference, above the norms of good and evil, above or rather below of what we evoke in terms of world and transcendence. It is not with us, who live in the concreteness of the flesh and in temporal flows and who try to establish order in our own names—and if it is with us, then only in a figural way.

This is the sublime myth of the postlapsarian loss the mystics evoke—only to knowingly abandon it in the play of figures that, in their eyes, so radically transfigures the natural world. Acknowledging the deep sufferings and violence they give testimony to, and the dispersion of beauty and grace in the figures we encounter, the mystics argue not for a return to this lost sphere of a vision of essences, a prelapsarian state, but for a transformation of the world in practices of devotion. Close in their thought to the doctrine of deification in Eastern Orthodox theologies, many of the so-called Western mystics recast the myth in terms of a cosmic arc of creatureliness and never-ending fulfillment, not in the seemingly stable positions of fallen and redeemed existence. Not a saving sublime beauty and truth are at stake here, or the notions of exile and home, or of desert and paradise. What the mystics ask us to acknowledge, instead, is the fact that the vessel is broken, that beauty and terror, peace and violence, consolation and suffering are dispersed in an irreducible multitude of particular figural moments in time and space. And that it is, according to this tradition, our hubris that stands against the fulfillment in the participation within this creaturely dispersion of light.

Breaking the Husk

"This piece of wood," the medieval mystic Eckhart von Hochheim says, pointing at the pulpit during his sermon, "has a rational image in God. It is not merely rational, it is pure reason."[12] Thus, he emphasizes that, far beyond or below the hierarchical orders of identity and difference, each thing in its very singularity and concrete shape is identical with what we ascribe to it in terms of essence. According to these words, when perceived "in God," each thing is not a "thing" but God, virtual and actual in coextensive ways, not caught up in the difference between itself and anything else, while still fully there in its "freedom." We, however, have access to figures alone (the wood of the pulpit, a fly, or the grass in other examples Eckhart uses), and they are divine not in their meaning but in the openness "reason" stands for when it turns into a space of participation. Thinking of "things," "essences," and "identities," both idealist and materialist positions foreclose this radical opening toward the divine forthcoming of figures. They foreclose it in favor of an idolatrous knowledge of the world, of hierarchical orders of subjects and objects, and of Man. In this life, Eckhart postulates, "reason" has to become not a name for an operation that turns the world into things, objects, and concepts, or masters and slaves, but for an opening toward the figural to free itself from its idolatrous state. This is the "reason" Eckhart is talking about, a reason that, as he points out, is "nothing" else than sheer openness to "becoming everything," sheer openness to the multiplicity of the circulations of sensations, affects, and concepts—having thus lost all instrumental character and discursive power. "Above all," Simone Weil writes in a passage that deeply resonates with Eckhart's thoughts, "our thought should be empty, waiting, not seeking anything, but ready to receive in its naked truth the object that is to penetrate it." She calls this "attention," a state of "suspending our thought, leaving it detached" and "empty."[13]

According to Eckhart, the convergence of the virtual and the actual in the exposure to figures—Simone Weil's "attention" to "objects"—is to be seen as the "fullness of time." This is a fullness of time that, in affirming all time in its extension and all figures in their articulation, undermines the world of defined things, of "this and that," of categorical orders of discourse, of substances, essences, and intentional agency. A world of figures emerges thus in the openness reason stands for, that is, as he forcefully argues, in "detachment."[14] Detachment is open toward a different kind of freedom—something a world of things and essences, of objects and subjects, forecloses. The latter, we might add with Eckhart, is nothing else than the name for the acts of submitting to the temptation of idolatry, to the hubris that identifies thought and truth, knowledge and the substance of things and Man. On the other hand, in detached emptiness anything turns into figure, as long as it is afforded rescue from the practice of idolatry, as long as it participates in the coming forth of the world. Nothing, however, is figure as long as it is seen and thought of as "this or that." It is for this reason that, as Søren Kierkegaard writes, the gospel's challenge to live like "the birds" and "the lilies" is not to be understood in terms of a poetic conceit or an allegorical image. Rather, he argues, in this postulate the gospel breaks with both the metaphysical and the allegorical reading, opening literally a space of silence where the figures act and freedom emerges in beauty.[15]

Others have framed this perspective in different ways, thinking about manners of undermining and overthrowing world order. The revolution of language itself is, in the words of the poet Velimir Khlebnikov, to be produced only in a world of words without meaning. Thus, he imagines worlds and words *zaum* (beyond the mind), a play of bare figures, each of them in their very articulation an expansive surface and abyss of expressive fullness.

I am tempted to add other names to form an eclectic list of moments that bring attention to this notion of figure and that forbid eschatological postponement, transcendence, and hermeneutic or metaphysical resolution: Lucretius's exploration of the nature of things in his turn to the concrete, Giordano Bruno's break with scholasticism, Diogenes the Cynic's art of intervention, Saint Francis of Assisi's conversation with birds, Cézanne's paintings of the *Montagne Sainte Victoire*, Belá Balázs's discovery of the new visibility of the world in film, Mark Rothko's engagement with painting in the Houston chapel, some of John Cage's compositions, Chris Marker's *La Jetée* and the "banality" of his cinematographic images. In all these instances—and beyond the specific character of each critical intervention—the challenge of renunciation and ascetic practice, the challenge of infecting language and images with silence, thus drawing attention to the realm of figures, moves through a play of and with forms that undermines the language of essence and things, of immanence and transcendence, and that shifts instead toward spheres of participation and expression, surfaces, configurations, absorbing effects.

What we are asked to acknowledge, then, is sheer surface in a specific way: not surface as the articulation or the expression of something else but surface as form and expression below the threshold of allegory, hermeneutics, and metaphysics. Figures do not mean and do not speak. They act; they circulate; they affect. And surfaces, as figures, are nothing else than the source of all impressions and of the depths that come about in their resonance.

Challenging the habits of listening in *Silence*, John Cage uses the trope of "opening the doors" literally in his performance: "For in this new music nothing takes place but sounds: those that are notated and those that are not. Those that are not notated appear in the written music as silences, opening the doors of the music to the sounds that happen to be in the environment. This openness exists in the fields of modern sculpture and architecture. The glass houses of Mies van der Rohe reflect their environment, presenting to the eye images of clouds, trees, or grass, according to the situation."[16]

Obviously, we can never get rid of the question of meaning and the temptations of hermeneutics, or of phenomenology and metaphysical conceits. John Cage is well aware of it, reiterating the challenge time and again in his works. So does Chris Marker in his films. He reproduces this tension and the temptation of hermeneutics, letting words, images, silences overlay each other relentlessly. Think of *Sans Soleil.* In the end it is the sheer banality of the figure that brings historical concreteness with its pleasure and terror into view and eclipses all discourse. It might, in its evocation of the gift of tears in the last scene of that film, be understood as referring us back to the notion of participation and grace once again.

Voices

These and similar voices, registered in a loose and somewhat accidental way in the previous paragraphs, form the background of what is at the core of this book: voices that draw attention to the figural, raise its claims, play with its power, and try to abandon the reins of meaning without, ultimately, being able to do so. Thus, I argue, the voices I call forth here produce, excavate, and invent possibilities amid and against all powers of discourse and of hermeneutic appropriation, not in plain opposition to it or in forms only of explicit critique. Instead, in gestures of affirmation they turn things around, attract the imagination, and pull it toward the surfaces of the concrete and the abyss of its figural resonances. Speaking in ethical terms, I call these the voices of figural asymmetry. What they postulate is not just an abandonment and an immersion that gives itself to the imagination, with Aristotle's treatise *On the Soul* understood as the material side of the mind where it is fully part of the flow of the world. Rather, in the immersion, they acknowledge in the constructive side of the imagination a critical overcoming of self and hubris and an asymmetry that forms the background of all understanding and discourse. Each figure, each moment of figural encounter, asks us to perform this very abandonment and to let our will and intellect be transformed in this disappropriation. Thus, in focusing on figure, I speak not of nature but of grace; not of justice but of love; not of anything instrumental or even causal but of the asymmetry that characterizes this engagement beyond all normative content and idolatrous order. In this sense, the acknowledgment of this asymmetry, the denaturalization and loss of ourselves, and the analysis of what makes us into subjects that are this and that are all being performed in detachment. Detachment, in opening up this ground of asymmetry, gives space to the figural effects, that is, to the acknowledgment of the fact that figures and effects are there, historically and temporally concrete, and that they can never be grasped in their essence. Resulting in nonnormative forms of doing, this very acknowledgment of asymmetry takes shape in the practice of "virtue" and the flow of "the good" according to Meister Eckhart and the mystics—and, maybe more surprisingly, also to Michel Foucault.[17]

According to the texts that I am discussing here, in giving up on the instrumental powers and pleasures to know and to do, we establish a turn not only of kenotic self-emptying but of rejoining the creaturely flesh and the cosmic imagination in an ethical shape.[18] It is not an ethics of norms but, as the mystics understand it, of recognizing the very asymmetry that comes about in the acts of unknowing—and, as Eckhart puts it, of letting thought itself be shaped by this endless movement of giving up. Not surprisingly, the mystics call this answer to the hubris and pride of knowing "love," supposing the convergence of a kenotic intellect and will in that very acknowledgment beyond good and evil. Knowledge, Eckhart argues, cannot be the place where the good takes shape; and knowing the good would mean a submission to norms. It is only in the self-negation of knowledge, in its becoming empty, that thought turns into the space of circulation where figures display their very effect and the will, in acts of humble self-abnegation, takes shape as the love that pulls the shards of goodness from the abysses of creaturely figural play.

Giordano Bruno, working in a different register and breaking with the discursive order he inherits from scholastic philosophers, presents us with another vision of this very asymmetry. Alluding to Lucretius's image of the emergence of the multitude of the world and to Diogenes the Cynic's break with all *doxa*, he stages a world of perception that is nothing else than an opening to the figures in their many voices. He evokes this, playing with an image drawn from Plato's allegory of the cave, when he opens *Concerning the Cause, Principle, and One* with the following dialogue:

Eliotropio: Like felons used to the darkness, who come up to the light when freed from the depths of some gloomy tower, many trained in common philosophy, and others, will be clutched by fear, seized with astonishment and (unable to stand the new sun of your shining concepts) thoroughly unsettled.

Filoteo: It is not the fault of the light, but of their sight: the more excellent and beautiful the sun, the more hateful and harshly unwelcome it will be to night-witches' eyes.

Eliotropio: In your hope of raising us out of the blind abyss, into the sight of the open, peaceful and tranquil stars that shine with such beautiful variety against the cerulean mantle of heaven, Filoteo, you have picked an uncommon, unusual and difficult venture.

What this opening of the eyes leads to is a new picture of the material world. It is, however, neither a Platonic discovery of a hidden truth behind the movement of things nor an Aristotelian turn toward abstraction but, tearing apart the language of ontology and of hermeneutics alike, the articulation of a multitude of figures that raise their voices, each of them a microcosm that reflects the entire world:

It is clear that the human species displays, in the particularities of its individuals, the variety of all other species together. In each of our individuals, the whole is present more explicitly than in the individuals of other species. Thus, some, as soon as they feel the fresh air, like the bleary-eyed mole, will tunnel straight back down into the earth to seek their natural, inky depths. Others, like night birds, on seeing the vermilion ambassadress of the sun come up in the east, will be forced by the weakness of their eyes to repair to their dingy retreats.

All creatures banished from the presence of the celestial lights and doomed to the eternal chasms, cages and caverns of Pluto—all animals, called by the horn of the fearsome Erynnis, Alecto, will spread their wings and flee headlong to their dwellings. But the animals born to behold the sun, having waited out the hated night, will give thanks to the merciful heavens and, prepared to gain within the globose crystals of their eyes the rays for which they have so long waited and pined, will adore the east, not only with unwonted adoration in their hearts, but with voices and hands. Men will begin to speak when from the east's gilded balcony, handsome Titan has let loose the fiery steeds who cleave the sleepy silence of the moist night. The docile, defenseless and simple sheep flocks will bleat; the horned oxen will bellow, heeded by their rustic ox-herders; and Silenus's quadrupeds will start to bray, frightening the stupid Giants again for the gods' benefit.

Tossing in their muddy beds, the boars will deafen us with their obstinate grunting. Tigers, bears, lions, wolves and the cunning fox poking his head from

> the cave will behold from their high deserts their flat hunting grounds, and will let forth from ferocious breasts their roars, growls, snarls, howls and cries. In the air and on the fronds of branchy trees, the roosters, eagles, peacocks, cranes, doves, blackbirds, crows, sparrows, nightingales, magpies, ravens, cuckoos and cicadas will lose no time responding, re-echoing with their earsplitting chatter. Still further, from their mobile, liquid dominions, the white swans, the many-hued waterfowl, the swift razor-bills, the marsh ducks, the honking geese and the carping frogs will disturb our ears with their din, such that the warm sunlight diffused in the air of our privileged hemisphere will find itself attended, greeted and perhaps plagued by cries as numerous and as varied as are the breaths that drive them out from the hollows of their respective breasts.[19]

There is no question that the metaphysical order that establishes our knowledge of identity and difference is an essential and pleasurable exercise of the mind. It provides us also, as both Kant and Hegel argue in their defense of philosophies of history, with moments of consolation whenever the chaotic disorder and terror of historical events evoke melancholy and despair. It is an exercise, though, that—in its dedication to liberal freedom—overshadows and obliterates the figural flow and reduces the rich and irreducible articulation of the voices Bruno is talking about. It produces, in its ultimate speculative apotheosis, the comprehensive and ultimately arresting analysis of all human naming and conceptualization in Hegel's masterful and beautiful narrative.

I have to confess that I often like this picture of history that Hegel presents, starting—in dialogue with Vico and challenging Kant's critical rearticulation of the postlapsarian framework—with the analysis of figures and forms in movement and, extending it, before modern media theory, to the acknowledgment that figures and the dynamic of assimilation turn into the media that structure and produce historical consciousness in its very unfolding. In this path of history, though—and particularly in the convergence of freedom, negativity, and spiritual perfection—it abandons the voices Bruno tries to mobilize so prominently. In the form of the system, it forecloses and neutralizes our exchange and encounter with them—even in the world of media and endless mediation, a world as figural as any other—and reduces everything to the state of a thing and a historical fact before it might regain its freedom in light of the fullness of spirit at the end of historical time. I also like Marx's gesture of inversion and its vision of a material reconciliation of world and humanity in a revolutionary practice that transforms the world after capitalism has sucked out all essence from it. However, as the young Lukács, Musil, and Adorno write in their reflections on philosophical style, this very form of the philosophical exercises and visions cools down the warmth of the concrete, of the particular, and dries up their wet humors, replacing both with the arid world of conceptual labor and, I want to add, the melancholy that accompanies critique and deconstruction where it discovers its own vain ambition. In opposing these moves, the young Georg Lukács suggests, the very revision of the philosophical style that the form of the essay produces rejoins the language of the mystics. In doing so, the essay turns concepts and words into figures, breathing life into them where it has been lost, by playing with the tensions between the figural, its assimilation, and concepts. Anticipating in these early writings Walter Benjamin's notion of historical materialism and Michel Foucault's use of genealogy, Lukács thus emphasizes that it is in the encounter with the concreteness of figures, in being encountered by the figures, that the historicity of our own lives emerges in the very forms of our sensations, affects, and thoughts.[20]

Possibilities

Before we move into what Lukács and Adorno call the arid and cold places of discourse, conceptualization, and generalization, before we ever get there—and before we fall for the idealist or realist temptations that define the speculative realms of consolation—figures are the sphere of possibilities we inhabit. Neither things nor ideas, they stand on the threshold of the virtual and the actual, or, maybe more precisely, they mark the modes in which the virtual—imagined in the dark and open multitude, the abyss of divine fullness, and the "creolization" of languages—nests in the surface textures of the actual. Figures are, while standing outside the conceptual divide of content and form, always historical, emerging in moments of time, folding the very temporal order anew. As in the craft of making good cheese or sausages, where every gesture restores ages of practice, they are saturated with the materials and relations of all the pasts, undoing and reweaving themselves.

In this movement they tear open the obvious textures and mobilize the asymmetries that make possibilities emerge in everyday life. When the mystics speak of grace and love, they ask us to see these asymmetries differently, to abandon the hubris of self and knowledge, and to let this very abandonment to the figures in modes of partaking shape all circulation of sensation, affect, and thought.

Again, consider the chair on the other side of the table, slightly moved to the side, a scarf thrown over its left arm. The chair and the scarf are not things, nor are they an assemblage of things or of signs. They present us with, absorb us in a figural texture, a configuration of effective moments, shape relations that transcend us and make us part of a world, that act on us, draw us into an irreducible immanence of temporal movements and turn us into a space where these movements are registered in the unfolding of effects. Thus, through the figural, we enter into the sphere of a cosmic imagination where "matter" and "spirit" converge.

Indeed, we might be tempted to start with the invention of a story here, adding narrative content that takes its origin within that texture, with the chair's position and the scarf that has been left behind. We might come up with a story that fills the scene with meaning, a past, and a future; or with a phenomenological exercise that captures a world we encounter and the saturated nature of the phenomena; or a philosophy that ascribes substance to the elements and submits the things to a hierarchy of being, a critique, and possibly a historical and an eschatological vision. Before that, however, we should acknowledge that it is not with the "things," or with the narrative or the philosophical thought, but with the figures that possibilities emerge. The figure is, if we put it in these terms, the entire actual world *in potentia*, the world we participate in, emerging as a flow of voices in a multitude of possibilities long before it "is" or "means" anything. This is the world before being and thought, before identity and difference, before ontology and hermeneutics.

Figure, the form and force of plastic texturings, the irreducible intersection of the virtual and the actual, is thus—once again, in its asymmetry—first and foremost possibility. It is not possibility that awaits a specific realization—not an apple seed that is meant to grow into an apple tree—but possibility as a particular opening toward the virtual multitude of all creation; an opening from the universe toward an irreducible plurality of forms, worlds, and words; an opening where the actual cannot really be distinguished from the virtual since the distinction of form and content breaks down. Thus, at that point, we also cannot think of possibility as something that is folded into the things and that unfolds or as something that is in the world in a state of waiting for realization.

There is, I am compelled to repeat in a somewhat dogmatic tone, no access to the "real" or the "ideal" beyond the figure, the image, the voice, the touch, the smell, the taste. There is no access beyond this recording of possibility in the asymmetry of the actual world. And, to be sure, the figure is nothing that offers access to something else. It is the world, both divine and far from God. Thus, all materialism or realism, in order to be what it suggests, has to become figural, that is, a renunciation of the determining aspects of discourse, of thought and of being, a renunciation of things and the world, of ontology, hermeneutics, and stable subjectivity. We cannot go beyond that figural sphere as long as we do not call for an extraordinary form of revelation—or as long as we do not make revelation itself converge with what emerges from this figural ground. All other claims for access to the particulars of the world are a return: a return to the real or to the myth, to a vision of paradise or to an eschatological promise, akin to the image of the first couple exploring and enjoying the Garden of Eden—or the eternal spring of Ovid's Golden Age—hand in hand in the company of and partaking in the dreams of a loving creator or savior. We are aware, though, made daily aware of the fact of the loss that the myth tells us about, of the disruption of the illusion, of the violence that bears violence, of the dust we are and we will turn into. We are aware, day by day and night by night, of the fact that the vessel is broken and that, graciously, we are left with an art of renunciation that helps pull its shards from the play of figures we inhabit.

This awareness, this openness to the revelatory structure of the figural (the fact that it is all there is), cannot be articulated in terms of being or knowing. Its language, as Dionysius the Areopagite pointed out in his treatises *On the Divine Names* and *On Mystical Theology*, can never be a comprehending, conceptually performed affirmation, not even an affirmation of a knowledge of things in their state of postlapsarian withdrawal. In addressing the unknowable character of God, this unknowability extends to the creation as it presents itself to us. If anything, our words can only be humble praise in the form of hymns,[21] positing the human in the position of an abject enthusiasm that undermines itself time and again in gestures of prayer, a position that, thus acting its freedom, gives itself up to the play and the acknowledgment of the voices and textures of voices that we participate in through the practices of contemplation. While the symbolic paths, the modes of hierarchical ascent, provide the mind with patterns of transformation, they always have to return to this moment of negativity.

Two mythical images, paradise and desert, emerge with this Dionysian language—maybe coming to us from the Syrian landscape that the early hermits inhabited. These are images in which, through which we, often somewhat romantically, try to grasp both the shape and meaning of the world. Before acquiring meaning, however, these images are sheer figures. They form a still life, a *nature morte,* inciting the viewer to read meaning into the figures, to come up with a narrative, to read allegorically, to form traditions as the places where revelation appears: the Garden of Eden or the postrevolutionary world as a time of peace and reconciled cohabitation of all creatures and of a language that is intact and true; the world of dust, suffering, and terror as the place of loss, mortality, time, and mourning; the desert as the place in between. What Dionysius brings into view, however, is not a return to that mythical Eden or, as has been argued, a deconstruction of language that might end with silence in face of an abandoned world and a promise of salvation. Instead, he draws attention to the realm of figuration as a sphere of possibility where, as in the space of an Eastern Orthodox Christian church, light and darkness converge, where the play of figures enacts the very drama of emergence, and where perception turns into participation in that emergence. In a distant response to this and reflecting on that very experience, Nicolaus Cusanus writes: "Possibility itself is called 'Light' by some saints—not perceptible light or rational light or intelligible light but the Light of all things that can give light—since nothing can possibly be brighter or clearer or more beautiful than possibility."[22] It is in the participation in figural emergence, the realm of possibility that is the play of the figures, where, according to this vision, light spreads throughout the creatures.

Touch

There is no book that is not the expression of desire. My long and meandering series of essays articulates a desire for what could also, alluding to Aby Warburg's understanding of figuration,[23] be called a haptic displacement. It does not return to a language of things, essences (however withdrawn), ontology, or identity, or to movements of deconstruction or realist ontology, but it rejoins the moments where touch has been rehabilitated as the most eminent sense—be it in the Franciscan emphasis on touch in the encounter with God and the world, in Johann Gottfried Herder's pronouncement that all aesthetic experience is touch, or in Robert Musil's use of similes as the basis for a language of touch and arousal. Focusing on figure and figuration, the following chapters isolate spheres of perceptual movements and textures that escape thought and being. They respond—and obliquely engage Martin Heidegger's and Jacques Derrida's ontological and deconstructive commentaries on these texts—both to Meister Eckhart's and Angelus Silesius's challenge to live a life "without a why" and to the ethical challenges of a world of strangers without stable community. The notion of the "plastic" forms a link, here, also to the philosophy of media that often takes Marshall McLuhan's observations as a starting point. The haptic, tactile aspect that he discovers in what he calls media is indeed similar to the figural—and so is the anti-Gnostic drive that inspires his writings. This does not, however, turn the figure into a medium but all media into figures. Where they resist and undermine both hermeneutic and metaphysical readings, media are figures insofar as it is their function to give shape to the lives they encounter, most visibly—at least to our eyes—in modern media environments. This encounter with figures, the view of figures also as media, has a long and complicated history that leads us back to contemplative practice. It is this practice that thematizes media and the use of media, but it is also this tradition that resists the temptation to make media or the sphere of affect that goes with them a basis of philosophical anthropology. Instead, it sees both media and affect as part of the figural play we participate in and experiment with when we call this participation "touch."

Not surprisingly, then, many of the texts that appear in this book belong—in generic terms—to theological or devotional traditions and literatures that engage the challenge of figuration, that is, texts that discuss the dissolution of the world of things into figures, referring us to questions of mediation, figuration, exemplarity, artificial means of self-fashioning, and the impossibility to articulate any essence. Or, speaking with Foucault and Bataille, texts that function along lines of "dramatization" in terms not of deconstructive mourning but—with the techniques of meditation they quote—of critique and constructivist pleasure that dismiss both the "real" and "Man" in favor of ascetic withdrawal and divine plenitude—or, to be precise, the fullness of the ungraspable divine that has its place nowhere else than in Nicolaus Cusanus's "possibility," in the voices of the concrete, in the figures that move, and in the acknowledgment of the asymmetry of figures in this dramatization of the construction of meaning, that is, in the only voices of justice and community we can really experience and recognize: the voices that acknowledge the asymmetry of the concrete in the ways suffering and joy affects us and that ask for the abandonment of both the will and understanding to the irreducible figural threshold in what we call generosity and love.

2

Figuration

To the Concrete

In a letter written from his exile in Istanbul in 1939, the German-Jewish scholar of Romance literatures Erich Auerbach wrote to his friend Martin Hellweg: "I would be very happy if you decided to continue your work, and especially if you would use a technique that starts out not from a general problem but from a well-chosen, specific phenomenon [*Einzelphänomen*] that is easy to get a grip on; perhaps a history of a word or an interpretation of a passage. The specific phenomenon cannot be small and concrete enough, and it should never be a concept introduced by us or other scholars but rather something the subject matter itself presents."[1] In this piece of advice Auerbach obliquely talks about his own method, his opposition to generalizations and "spiritualization," and his focus on the concrete and striking moments in a text. One might be tempted to think here of a relation to Walter Benjamin's work. In a similar vein, Benjamin speaks of the written word in terms of an "archive of non-sensual similarity,"[2] where "the correspondences rule" and where he asks us to pay attention to moments of particularity and concreteness.[3] These moments should be perceived in their specific character, not based on forms of generalization that would explain the "similarity" and bring it back into the conceptual fold. Benjamin's theory of the written word thus goes hand in hand with a gesture that identifies "mimesis" and "mimicry" with moments of imitation and participation. These moments underlie and precede language, testifying, in Benjamin's eyes, to a loss at the same time. Auerbach, however, not marked by a suspended messianism and Benjamin's Baroque melancholy, speaks not of a loss here but of the "intensity of evocation" (*Eindringlichkeit der Evokation*) and of "extremely realistic effects."[4] In explaining this, he often relies on Baudelaire's style, calling it "utterly realist" in his vision of a figural world that in adopting prayers and gestures of prayer betrays the "inner structure of a mystic."[5]

As readers of Auerbach's works know, his notion of realism can be deeply irritating. Auerbach has throughout his life been interested in "realism" and "realistic expression" in literature. This engagement, however, much to the chagrin of many of his interpreters, never implied a theory of realism. Instead, it entailed and concentrated on what he called the "concrete," the "strikingly real," and thus also the highly specific and particular moments of attraction in the reading of literature. Recalling at moments the theologian Romano Guardini's philosophy of the concrete and Gershom Scholem's rejection of spiritualism, that point of view is already prominently displayed in Auerbach's early book on Dante, *Dante: Poet of the Secular World*, published in 1929. Beginning with the first pages of this long essay, Auerbach emphasizes that he is interested in one specific aspect of the documents and literary texts he is dealing with: their form and style of presenting events as "immediately evident" in a way that "the question of their probability emerges only in a reflection that follows."[6] Thus, he points out, we are "forced" to "perceive" what the text makes present before we start to think about it and before we engage it in any hermeneutic way. This force lies, as he points out, with the "Gestalt" of the rhetorical figure, not its content or the unlocking of a hermeneutic process. Rather, it coincides with the evocative character in the form of a "lively presence" where the literary source speaks the singular event and expresses it fully. "Expression" (*Ausdruck*), not representation, is the word he uses for this sphere of "immanence."[7] As he points out, "concreteness," "intensity," "sensuality," "affect," "singularity," and "irreducible multiplicity" are the characteristics of this form of evocation through which texts capture the attention and irresistibly shape the mind. This does not mean, however, that the texts mirror the events in a quasi-naïve understanding of realism, that is, in the form of a mimetic assimilation and an absorption of the reader in the pleasure she might feel based on a recognition of similarity between the text and the world outside it. According to Auerbach it is the very rhetorical form in which the texts present the events that gives them a sensual shape and brings the "concrete" before our eyes. Thus, the texts produce the absorption and immersion of the reader in a particular moment. In Dante's writing, Auerbach says, the "real appears with such an intensity" that it is perceived in the imagination "without any interpretation" (*ungedeutet*).[8] "Sensuous reality" and "imagination" are the key words here, pointing to the fact that it is the figural effect that informs the landscape of the soul.

This "concreteness," a concreteness that consists in the striking force of the words, is opposed to two tendencies that Auerbach locates in late antiquity and in medieval thought, "didactic allegory" and "Neoplatonic spiritualism," which, in his view, both "escape" into a realm of "transcendence" and "speculation." Thus, they contribute to a loss of "sensual form" (*sinnliche Gestalt*) and "dampen" and "dull" the "sensual force of creation" in processes of metaphysical speculation and spiritual interpretation, obliterating all engagement with both the historical reality and the very effects of the poetic word.[9]

In his own work with literary texts, Auerbach restores and captures what is being obliterated by these processes of spiritualization, arguing for an understanding of figures that unlocks the experiential effects of the texts. He does so when he focuses on places—and these are the primary topoi in what he discusses as his own method of "historical topology"—where the concrete emerges and where a pre-allegorical and non-spiritual effect of the texts unfolds most visibly. He characterizes this striking force of the concrete in a description of rhetorical effects as "intense," sometimes as "enchanting" or "entangling," always as sensually and affectively captivating—offering thus a phenomenology of the very experience of reading, of rhetorical effects, and of what we can call an experimental poetic empiricism. Time and again he emphasizes the "concrete immediacy" produced by specific literary figures. He understands it in terms of an "event," which is nothing else than an "expression" of and in the world. "The impression" (*Eindruck*), he writes about Dante's expressive style, "is purely sensual" (*ist rein sinnlich*), drawing attention to the "event character" of a poetic style that involves and embeds the reader in sensual, affective, and cognitive moments before any reflection and hermeneutic search for meaning starts.[10] Auerbach speaks thus in his readings of the places, the style, and the forms of language where this happens—often, I want to add, in what we might compare to a kind of material analysis with a specific emphasis on the form of "expression" (*Ausdruck*) and on the formal power of language, the figural that inhabits and suspends all assimilation. No metaphysics of the event, of a pure presence, or of the real is implied here, just attention to the rhetorical force of textual forms and the ways they unfold and produce perception effects.

Figura

To understand this further, we have to go first to Auerbach's essay "*Figura*," published in 1938 during his exile in Istanbul.[11] In this essay Auerbach traces the prehistory of some observations of the book on Dante, especially the figural character of the rhetorical force. In "*Figura*" Auerbach sets up the key difference between the figural and the allegorical, and he finds and reconstructs a notion of figure that cannot be easily reabsorbed into allegory. In fact, he identifies a material, plastic aspect that the notion of figure always encompasses, something that resists and withdraws from the realm of allegory—as well as, he points out, from all spiritualization and abstraction. As he argues, allegory and hermeneutics are, so to speak, always secondary, always a belated interpretive approach that overshadows the concrete, plastic, and sensual aspects of *figura* itself.

According to Auerbach, the use of *figura* in early Christian authors such as Tertullian is essentially, and we could add paradoxically, concrete, anti-allegorical, and anti-spiritualist. These authors do not use the term *figura* to refer to a movement from a literal meaning of the Scriptures to a spiritual meaning that would obliterate the historical concreteness of events as they are presented by the texts. Instead, and sometimes explicitly arguing against these tendencies of spiritualization, *figura* points to the irreducible historicity of the event that is carried forward in its form—and it points to an irreducible aspect in the act of reading. In other words, *figura* is the name for what strikes the reader and shapes the impression.

To support this interpretation of *figura*, Auerbach focuses on the use of the term in a broad range of sources in his analysis of the use of the word. What he observes at first is the fact that *figura* points not to the meaning of an event but to its rhetorical presentation, that is, to what he calls expression. Since *figura* "expresses something living and dynamic, incomplete and playful," Auerbach writes, "it had a graceful sound which fascinated many poets." It refers to the sound and the voice that fascinate, and these point, as he writes, to the "plastic form," often expanding "in the direction of 'statue,' 'image,' 'portrait.'" Once again, he emphasizes the "concrete" and the "sensible." As he argues, the term *figura* keeps this connection with sensible forms—and the work of the potter—also in Cicero's and in Quintilian's classical manuals of rhetoric. There, *figura* stands for rhetorically shaped speech. With regard to Cicero's use of the word, Auerbach writes: "In sum, everything sensible has *figura*."[12]

We might summarize his observations in the following way. *Figura* is the aspect of an event or a thing as it is told, but also the way in which an event or a thing sensually presents itself in perception, not as something that already has meaning but as something that shapes perception, affect, and cognition. This is foregrounded in the rhetorical understanding of *figura*, where the term refers to the shaping of speech that is meant to have certain effects on the mind of the listener, giving form to the life of her soul. *Figura* is not just form; it is form as it emerges with a shaping effect of differential intensity.

It is remarkable that exactly this plastic-concrete aspect of *figura* stays most alive also in the Christian use of the term in the early contexts of figural typology, most prominently for Auerbach in Tertullian's works. As he observes, in Tertullian's rhetoric and style, admired by Baudelaire, Schopenhauer, and Nietzsche alike, "*figura* is something real and historical" that points to something else in the Scriptures that is also "real and historical."[13] This, however, does not mean that the reader has to interpret the event in a spiritual way, moving from a literal-historical to an allegorical meaning and then producing a connection between "events" based on similarities. Typology, the relation between events, is not the product of an interpretive imposition, and there is no conceptual grasp that explains and precedes it. Instead, in the case of Tertullian, the figural is reframed in what Auerbach, making use of a concept from Aristotle's *Rhetoric*, calls Tertullian's "energetic realism," that is, in his lively and evocative retelling of the Scriptures. Based on the rhetorical notion of *energeia*, *figura* is to be seen as the form that carries the energy of the word and shapes a specific form of participation in the reader. Tertullian's literary realism consists thus not in a descriptive mirroring of the real in terms of visual similitude but in the rhetorical capture and production of a lively and living reality—the world not as thing but as concrete figure—that not only affects the readers and shapes their affects and perception but that also brings figures in relation with each other. This happens in the very acts of perception in the reading of the Scriptures, and it happens again, in amplified form, in Tertullian's style. The plastic sensual and historical concreteness—to use Auerbach's words—never moves into the background. Auerbach points out that this is the case even when Tertullian produces figural-typological readings where he sees one pole of the figural pair as prophecy and the other as fulfillment: "There are numerous passages . . . , in which he resists the spiritualizing tendencies of contemporary groups. His realism is even more evident in the way he describes the relationship of the figure to its fulfillment. Sometimes the one and sometimes the other appears to be invested with greater concreteness."[14] Thus, participation in the effects of the figures always entails relation, even before interpretation or spiritualization sets in.

This "concreteness" is the key moment of Tertullian's argument against the Gnostics and against spiritualist readings of the Scriptures that—from Marcion of Sinope to Adolf von Harnack—tend to make the Old Testament superfluous and to focus on the "spiritual message" of the New Testament alone. It is against these positions that, according to Auerbach, Tertullian insists on the specific character of the figural as something that holds the Hebrew Bible and the Gospel together in relations of similarity that do not emerge from interpretation but from the expressive figural form of the texts. Instead of producing a chain of representation, imitation, and understanding, the figural produces a participation—a participation through the *energeia* of the expressive form. This expressive form shapes the very experience of reading and of the life of the soul. In Auerbach's eyes Tertullian's "energetic realism" does nothing else than recapitulate and reinforce the figural realism of the Scriptures themselves.[15] It does so not on the level of an allegorical interpretation or in establishment of a spiritual connection between events. Not an act of interpretation is at stake here but an effect of the text on the reader whose perception is being shaped by singular moments in the act of reading.

The philologist who analyzes these moments of figuration turns thus into a phenomenologist of rhetorical effects who traces the figural force and shape and the formation of figural correlations. As Auerbach observes, these figural moments are always "unfinished" and thus open to forming new connections and networks of resonance. This, I want to add, comes close to ideas of participation in the divine as they have been formulated in neo-Palamist theology.[16] Accordingly, figure is not to be understood in a horizon of causation that characterizes creation but as participation in the divine energies that permeate all creation and that ultimately cannot be thought of in ontological terms. Participation and relation are initiated and made possible through the *energeia* that expresses itself in the figure, while its very essence remains ungraspable and hidden. Thus, we can say that the figure brings creation to expression and into a state of participation that is beyond being and knowing.

According to Auerbach's explanation, a figural typological network is not the product of acts of interpretation or of hermeneutic gestures that uncover a hidden or spiritual sense of the Scriptures. Instead, it arises from the reading of the texts, from the encounter with the Scriptures in their entirety, and it imposes itself on the reader in the form of the "realistic concreteness" of the figures that shape their perception. When Auerbach acknowledges that figural reading entails a "commitment to a certain kind of interpretation,"[17] he acknowledges the necessary investment of the reader. This investment, however, sees itself always confronted with the tension between the veiled character of the figure and the desire for meaning. In Tertullian's case, this means that only the reading of the entire Scriptures, Old Testament and New Testament, Hebrew Bible and Gospel, discloses the figural network of moments that relate to each other. They do not, however, establish a network in a way that is mediated through "meaning." This would imply a practice of spiritualizing hermeneutics. Instead, they emerge as networks—maybe, with Benjamin and Baudelaire, constellations and correspondences—insofar as they form textures based on figural effects and on what Auerbach calls the "energetic realism" of the figural itself. It is only in this form that the concreteness of historical moments is saved against both the allegorical and the spiritualizing impositions of meaning.

History

The work of Giambattista Vico plays a decisive role for Auerbach's understanding of figures and practices of figuration. In his engagement with Vico, from his earliest texts to his late essays, we find additional elements of the understanding of his notion of *figura*—even though he does not make this relation explicit. As Auerbach writes in *Literary Language and Its Public in Late Latin Antiquity and in the Middle Ages*, the fact that Vico understands human nature as essentially historical means that it is shaped through practices of figuration and poetic imagination. This also forms the background of Auerbach's own philological work. He points to Vico's training as a rhetorician, explaining further that the practices of poetic imagination are first and foremost to be recognized as specific practices of figuration. This recognition necessitates, he argues further, not a view from a historical distance or from an external vantage point but a specific engagement of the interpreter with the texts and the use of the figures. Instead of taking on a vantage point outside the text, we are asked to engage the texts in a way that time and again returns to the very experience of the figures in their concreteness and their specific location. We have to do so not as suspicious readers but as readers guided by "generosity" and magnanimity. This attitude of generosity, reflecting the asymmetry of the figures I discussed previously, characterizes a way of reading that understands and loves historical artifacts as testifying to the "existence of humans, as a possibility of ourselves."[18] In regard to this form of reading and perception—generous as opposed to suspicious, and ethical in terms of its acknowledgment of an irreducible asymmetry—Auerbach speaks of a double historical relativism. It extends to the reader as much as it does to the texts, to the sphere of perception as much as to the sphere of figures. It is a relativism, he explains, insofar as it discards the temptation to move from the particular experience of the text into a unifying abstraction outside history; and it is a relativism insofar as it implies a "dramatic" process in which the reader perceives her own exposure to the figures she encounters in the texts.

Auerbach reiterates here the very distinction between spiritualization and figural realism he has established in the "*Figura*" essay. He asks the reader to perceive the very historicity of her mind not from a vantage point above, through abstraction, but in the very exposure to the figural sphere that is found in the text, that forms the mind, and that has left its sediments in the very structure of perception, intuition, and thought. Said differently, in reading we are asked to let ourselves be moved by the figures, and in following the movements we trace the very historicity, the historically shaped form of our own sensations, affects, and thoughts.

Auerbach introduces two significant terms here: "imagination" and "possibility." As he emphasizes with Vico, all figuration draws foremost on the imagination and its very creativity of articulating the historical world in its powers of shaping the mind. In understanding this, he points out, Vico is actually closer to the traditions of rhetoric than we might expect: "He sees in the rhetorical terminology of the schools the remnants of an earlier, concrete, and sensual form of thought that meant to capture the things themselves."[19] Vico, on the threshold between the early modern and the modern, sees "in the rhetorical figures . . . remainders of the originary, concrete, sensual thought." It is on this basis that Auerbach understands the work of the historian and philologist. In the essay "Vico's Contribution to Literary Criticism" he further explains that historicism

> is a difficult and infinite task to understand the particular character of historical forms and their interrelations [i.e., figures and typological relations]—a task that requires . . . a state of mind capable of recreating in itself all varieties of human experience, of rediscovering them in its own "modifications." Each historian (we may also call them, with Vico, a "philologist") has to undertake this task for himself, since historical relativism has a twofold aspect: it concerns the understanding historian as well as the phenomena to be understood. This is an extreme relativism; but we should not fear it.[20]

What Auerbach describes here—resonating with key concerns of Baudelaire and Benjamin and of Nietzsche's notion of genealogy—is a way in which the historian, the philologist, traces the historical world in exposing herself to the effects of the figures, retrieving their power and the ways in which they "modify" the human mind. This notion of modification is another term of Vico's philological history that fascinates Auerbach. While the world of archaic humanity and their minds are shaped by their imaginative creation of figures, the very production of history, the generation of figures, never fully disappears, and it maintains its shaping force. Figuration is thus never primarily representation or the production of meaning but the deployment of figural artifacts that shape the life of the mind in ever-"unfinished" series of movements. This lies at the bottom, so to speak, of all historical creativity, and the philologist traces its productivity underneath all abstraction, spiritualization, and allegoresis in an encounter with the figural character of worlds and texts. As Auerbach points out, Vico "discovered that metaphors and tropes, the artful forms of figured expression that were still flourishing during his time (albeit in completely nominalist form), were the last remaining trace of the sensuous language of the primordial era."[21] What Vico discovered, he writes, is "the principle of a form of intellect that, while lacking the logical powers of understanding, was nevertheless all the richer for its ability to be moved by the senses, to shape these sensory impressions and to give them imaginative form. . . . This is the discovery that lies at the heart of Vico's entire project and that provides, first and foremost, the very architecture of his history of the world."[22]

It is the concrete and sensuous character of these figured expressions that creates the bridge between Auerbach's early work on Dante, his fascination with Vico, and his essay on *figura*, providing us also with a genealogical explanation of his own philological sensibility. Vico's position in this configuration is remarkable, since it is through Vico's notion of the function of figure that we discover how "all possible forms of human life and thinking, as created and experienced by men, must be found in the potentialities of the human mind (*dentro le modificazioni della nostra medesima mente umana*); that therefore we are capable of re-evoking human history from the depth of our own consciousness."[23] Thus, even though as modern people we can "hardly understand" the "very strong sensations" and the "strength of imagination" that we see in the archaic practices of figuration, we as "generous" readers trace their force and their ways of modifying the shape of the life and mind of humans in exposing ourselves to them. Each figure is thus a place through which, in exposing ourselves to its force, we expose ourselves to the experience of our own historicity; and in turn, the rhetorical analysis performs an analysis of the historical modifications of our mind. This, indeed, is Vico's discovery of genealogy. The figural is not just a hypothetical archaic remnant but the force of shaped language and of the shaped world that modifies the life of the mind, the soul, and the flesh. Uncovering it presupposes, Auerbach says, a philology that exercises both a critical stance toward our own forms of allegoresis, spiritualization, and abstraction and a will to exposure, an abandonment in the practice of reading—and, more generally, in the encounter with figures. It is this attitude that characterizes the "historical topology" (as Auerbach calls his method in 1951) that he presents in *Mimesis.* At the center is a focus on topoi, forceful moments of figuration, which then turn into the core of his readings. The starting point of his reading of Racine in *Mimesis* illustrates this. There, he points to the fact that

> the tragic personage is always in a sublime posture, in the foreground, surrounded by utensils, retinue, people, landscape, and universe, as by so many trophies of victory which serve it or are at its disposal. In this posture the tragic person abandons itself to its princely passions. And the most impressive stylistic effects of this sort are those in which whole countries, continents, or even the universe appear as spectator, witness, background, or echo of the princely emotion.[24]

According to Auerbach, we turn into "spectator, witness, background, or echo," reflecting the "princely passions" in the ways in which the figures and their arrangements affect us. Vico thinks history in his focus on figuration as a history of human expression that develops from an archaic beginning through a series of stages—anticipating, at the core, Hegel's speculative view of history and his analysis of the practices of figuration that constitute the life of the spirit in its embodied material history. It is, however, not the emphasis on the archaic beginning and the development that is at the core of Auerbach's interest. James Porter has recently commented on this:

> As for the question why Auerbach dwells so insistently on the earliest moments of Vico's world history, the answer must be in part that he is drawn to the historical trajectory that Vico maps out (and which Auerbach traces in his own way), and in part because he found the role that Vico assigned to the poetic imagination immensely attractive: history works through the poetic imagination as much for Auerbach as it did for Vico. But there are also differences. Auerbach does not "speculate in a fantastical way" as Vico did about mythical prehistory. And Auerbach's view of the imagination is more refined, and more compatible with modern impulses: Montaigne, Baudelaire, and Woolf are as involved as any of Vico's primitive creatures in imagining and in this way creating their respective realities and the kinds of subjectivities that could inhabit them, whether their own or those of the readers they render possible through their writings.[25]

Indeed, it is less the "historical trajectory" Auerbach is fascinated with but more prominently the role of the very movement of the imagination that Vico suggests. In this movement, in its emergence in our imagination, the world is irreducibly figural. In historical time, this produces increasingly thick layers and resonances of figural play that make up our mind. According to Auerbach, only the exposure to the effects of these figures offers access to the historicity of ourselves. In thinking with Vico, Auerbach thinks of history not from a perspective that sets itself up above the events in time but from the perspective of the exposure to the concrete events, their traces, and their forms of rhetorical amplification. This alone allows us to grasp the manners in which our perceptions and thoughts are being continuously woven and transfigured and how we have become what we are. We trace and reanimate the very figures that make up these modifications in our exposure to their effects; that is, we grasp our historicity not in the *understanding* of history but in *participating* in the forces of figures, the *energeia*, that, once sedimented, make us historical beings. As we pierce through the veils of knowledge and the modes of mimetic assimilation, and critically undermine their powers, the exposure to the force of the figures uncovers what makes up the ways of inhabiting these worlds. This, I argue in the following chapters, also allows for an experimentation with figures in a continuous engagement with our own historicity.

3

Reweaving Perception

Figures and Perception

Readers of Auerbach often ignore that a modernist interest in the cultural and anthropological analysis of symbolic and figural modes—from Hermann Usener to Friedrich Nietzsche, Aby Warburg, Ernst Cassirer, and Ludwig Binswanger—is one of the important contexts of his work. These analytical approaches, often articulated in a neo-Kantian vein, are to be seen as parallel with the experimental and critical engagement with rhetorical devices, media, and new modes of writing that explore the formative power of figures and symbolic assemblages in modernist poetics. In this regard, Auerbach's attention to the figural parallels Cassirer's interest in "symbolic forms," Aby Warburg's attempts to think about the afterlife of "pathos formulas," and Friedrich Nietzsche's notion of the penetratingly vivid figures of the Greek gods.[1] All these thinkers analyze the ways in which figures and symbolic forms shape consciousness historically; all understand the cultural production of figures as figural practices that modify the minds and allow for an experimental way of producing perceptual, affective, and cognitive forms; and all use an analysis of style and rhetorical devices to identify these processes. The terms "symbolic form," *figura*, and "pathos formula" draw attention to this.

Auerbach's intervention, insisting on the irreducibly "concrete" and his own "topological" analysis,[2] which is based on concrete and singular literary moments, has to be read as a methodological decision that also reflects this larger intellectual context. In building on concrete figural moments, it sets itself up in opposition to ideological versions of literary history, above all the ones he escaped when he went into exile. In addition, Auerbach's reconstruction of the use of *figura* entails an intimate conversation with both the neo-Kantian philosophies of symbolic forms and modernist poetic experimentation and their interest in the shape and shaping of perception.

At the same time, however, Auerbach's attention to the notion of *figura* in late antiquity also brings into view a particular engagement with figuration that medieval practices of prayer, meditation, and contemplation explore extensively. These practices often reemerge in forms of modernist poetics, particularly in German expressionism. And they played a role, not independently from the movements of modernist literature and art, in the rediscovery of religious practices and the formation of traditions by the French *Nouvelle théologie* during the very same decades when Auerbach published his works.[3]

In light of Auerbach's observation that allegory tends to overshadow the attention to the figural in the Middle Ages, it seems somewhat paradoxical to focus here on medieval practices of contemplative prayer. As I will show, however, prayer and contemplation, an area that Auerbach neglected in his work on *figura* even though in many ways contemplative prayer also shaped Dante's poetics, are a privileged place for the experimentation with figures. In building on Auerbach's work on *figura*, I argue that it allows us to understand a broad range of experimentation with figuration and the production of new affective, sensual, and cognitive states in medieval traditions of prayer. I show that prayer, commonly understood as a medium for a dialogue with the transcendent divine, can be seen as a modification of the order of perception in and of this world. Said differently, I see prayer, meditation, and contemplation as figural practices that address both forms of mimetic assimilation and modes of participation in a highly elaborate and self-conscious way.

What I focus on, then, is a specific aspect in the history of contemplation and mysticism. I foreground a term that is central to a common medieval Christian notion that underlies the understanding of mysticism, "mysticism" as a *cognitio Dei experimentalis*, as an "experiential knowledge of the Divine." In using this formula, I am emphasizing that with regard to sensual, affective, and intellectual forms of mysticism I want to discuss an experiential and, at least at a first and basic level, nondiscursive mode of cognition. This is not to say that the production of experience is necessarily opposed to all discursive knowledge and conceptualization or, for that matter, to hermeneutic engagements with the Scriptures and what is often called the book of nature. However, in relying on practices of figuration, contemplation moves below the discursive and the hermeneutic, shifting in meditation and prayer from the discovery of meaning to forms of mimetic assimilation and to the deployment of figural effects. As part of a path that leads from reading to prayer, these practices can be understood as modes of production of a different kind of awareness and attention. Both are based on techniques and practices that are meant to shape sensation and affects and to make these sensations actually "nest" within and infect the discursive, affective, and sensual orders of our worlds.

This experiential production of a different kind of knowledge presupposes that we think of contemplation not as a technique of approaching and grasping something that is "other" but as a practice invested in participation and the modification and transformation of sensation, affects, and thought. It also presupposes that we see it as a practice of critique—of defamiliarization and deconstruction—where something that is usually hidden in the discursive and affective shapes of ordinary everyday life and its patterns of intelligibility is being reconfigured through a figural practice of utterly absorbing power that eliminates the stable structures of subjects and objects. In this practice the unnamable and unknowable divine, usually imagined and conceptualized as either immanent or transcendent, is experienced as what informs and transforms life—both the soul and the flesh—in the very time of contemplation. What thus affects this new life is obviously not a thing, nor is it in any form an object, but it can only be understood as an excessive moment—a "presence" not "of something" but a presence underneath the distinction of presence and absence, of temporal and atemporal orders—which gives shape to the very experience the mystics aim for in their contemplative practices. As they describe it, this can happen in sensual, affective, or intellectual form. It is articulated and produced through a practice of prayer and contemplation that performs a defamiliarization and critique in gestures of detachment and evokes a transition of agency that happens in the modification of perception. This defamiliarization can be seen as a withdrawal into the cell, the study, or the desert. It is joined by the installation of figures—singing of the Psalms, liturgical music, images, and words of praise—that give shape to a different life within this situation of exile. Although the practices of prayer and contemplation evoke and shape possibilities of sensation, affect, and knowledge, they do so in a way that does not anchor itself in the stability of a subject that stands on its own but in forms of abandonment in which the practitioner exceeds herself in the absorbing power of a new world—often characterized in terms of absorbing love in wonder and admiration,[4] in joy and pleasure—that in and by itself transcends the practice of prayer. This transcendence, I argue, is the absorption into the asymmetrical force of the figure, which in this very asymmetry moves the event from the order of nature to the realm of grace. When I speak of "transcendence" here, we cannot think of it as a presence that arrests time. Instead, in moving away from the temporal axis where we distinguish the "now" and the "then," even the ecstatic moments of contemplative experience turn into a new form of life in time and an affirmation of creaturely life, temporality, and multiplicity.

According to such an understanding of the use of figures in contemplative practice, the person who—akin to Auerbach's view of Dante's poetic practice in his love poetry—stimulates all possible forms of love and suffering in herself will reach a point where the asymmetry of the figures—that is, the sheer affirmation that we call love—takes over and acts through the person. This happens where the defamiliarizing and stimulating figures in the meditative exercise exceed the orderly world of the practitioner and, dramatically set up against the positivity of knowledge and a hermeneutics of the self, disown her in the absorbing forms of *excitatio* or *inflammatio* (arousal or inflammation). Thus, the figures of radically asymmetric love being evoked turn, overwhelmingly, into a new form of perception.

It is the very fact of this experiential absorption in its utter asymmetry—a union in dramatic difference that can take shape in many ways—that is often called mystical. The so-called mystical experience at the very core of the practices of prayer relies on these contemplative techniques, the use of rhetorical devices, in short, the figural practices that are meant to produce this very union in difference and, once again, to pull the practitioner into the sphere of the asymmetry of the figure. Thus, the contemplative practice rearticulates and reweaves the textures of perception, projecting the asymmetry that grounds it—that is, the utterly ungraspable excess called "divine love"—as a constitutive and dramatic tension into the temporal realms of sensation, affect, and thought.

Mimetic Practice

We observe this reweaving of the textures of perception in one of the paradigmatic texts of this tradition. In his *Life of Moses*, the fourth-century Cappadocian theologian Gregory of Nyssa makes an attempt to explain what he sees as the deep paradox and ultimate challenge of the desire for an experience of the unnamable excess of divine goodness and beauty in this life. As he makes abundantly clear when he discusses and interprets the life of Moses, taking Moses who had been granted a vision of God as a model, the human desire to be united with the divine can never become congruent with the imagined and desired fullness. Anticipating a key aspect of Georges Bataille's return to this model in *Inner Experience*,[5] Gregory also emphasizes that the very path toward this fullness of experience cannot be thought of as a "project" but only as a life in never-ending and always-intensifying desire, dramatization, and participation. Instead of illustrating an immediate vision of the divine and providing us with a concrete path toward it, the example of Moses teaches us, according to Gregory, that if we do not want to fall into silence, we always have to rely on mimetic figuration and participation—and on the acknowledgment of the very asymmetry that this practice puts on us. No figure or image can grasp the divine in the form of meaning or representation. No way to the divine can take shape in terms of mimetic assimilation alone. Instead, in its effects the figural, if it is meant to lead to the renewal of the world, must exceed all names and produce a continuous reiteration of the excess of the figural within our very desire. The mimetic practice—words and images directed toward grasping the divine—that recognizes its inability to name and represent affirms this very fact and turns all mimesis and assimilation into participation. In this participation, "humanity in general and individual persons are called to become priests of the cosmos, rendering by their dynamic engagement with the world's order, a degree of divine life, a sacred blessing as it were, to all the fabric of God's created existence."[6] It recognizes that the candle and its light do not "mean" or "represent" the divine light. Instead, it is the recognition of the very fact of the light, the bare figure of light, that affects us and pulls us into the play of light and darkness—and into the convergence of the possibility and the reality of the always unfinished "let there be light." Thus, in Gregory's understanding, "deification . . . is not a posthumous transcending of human nature, but a passing beyond the limits of human nature, in that glorified nature . . . into the radiant fullness of the very purpose of creaturely human being, which is intimate communion with the endless mystery of the Life-Giving Presence."[7]

Consequently, Gregory's explanation of the life of Moses focuses strongly on a liturgical and sacramental transfiguration of the world that remains constant before the restitution of everything in its integrity (*apokatastasis panton*). Upon climbing Mount Sinai, dwelling in "darkness" after gaining access to "the invisible and the incomprehensible . . . beyond all knowledge and comprehension," Moses is "led . . . to the place where his intelligence lets him slip in where God is." There he "sees that tabernacle not made with hands," which Moses, as he learns, will have to show "to those below by means of a material likeness." He has to do so to guide them in their way to the contemplation of true reality and its beauty—"Beauty" and "Being," as Gregory calls the divine in a Greek philosophical vein.[8]

However, the gap could not be larger between the reality of what Moses sees in divine darkness and the practice of a material mimesis he is meant to bring back to his people. As Moses learns, the very mirroring that material mimesis performs—Latin translations speak of *speculatio* and *contemplatio* where I use the term "mirroring"—is the only access to the truth of all things.[9] Gregory, to be sure, is the opposite of a Gnostic who chooses a mental flight into a spiritual realm beyond the earthly landscape of an abandoned creation and exile. Instead, he emphasizes that, as Moses returns from the heights of Mount Sinai, he brings back not only the Tablets of the Law but also an art of figuration that opens ways of "reweaving" our perceptions through material mimesis where conceptual knowledge always fails.[10] Both liturgy and artifacts that form the space of the temple and support the contemplation and reading of the Scriptures are meant to perform this material mimesis. They do so, however, not merely in forms of representations of the moments of divine revelation and in a process of assimilation but also through the production of figures that carry and transform the soul toward the divine in a process of "reweaving" perception and experience. Thus, assimilation turns into participation, sharing in the divine and in the restoration of the cosmos. We might be tempted here to imagine an installation or a stage that is meant to transform the viewers into participants. This stage, on which dark revelation turns into liturgy and tradition, includes all kinds of mimetic figures taken from the Scriptures. It includes objects that are to be used in the liturgy and in contemplation as well as all kinds of vestments, decorations, and sounds, including Bach's cantatas and Aretha Franklin's "Amazing Grace," that fill the space of the temple or church.

For all these mimetic figures theologians have provided us also with allegorical interpretations. However, as both Gregory of Nyssa and Origen of Alexandria make abundantly clear, this mimetic figuration is more than a practice of symbolic representation and of sophisticated allegorical interpretation that opens ways of reading and of a new hermeneutic engagement with things, the world, and God. Instead, below and beyond the practice of hermeneutics and the allegorical interpretation of the Scriptures, material mimesis creates networks of figures and figuration—figures that do not "mean" anything but that move and shape our sensual and affective perception, pulling it into an assimilation with the divine and a participation in divine self-communication. Thus, they produce a tension and asymmetry that break with the naturalized forms of sensation, affect, and thought to produce the emergence of a particular sphere of experiential knowledge and participation.

The fact that Moses "boldly approached the very darkness itself" thus translates into a practice of mimesis that supports a form not of ideal and liberating knowledge (*gnosis*) but of aesthetic experience (*aisthesis*).[11] It translates into a form of participation that transfigures the world in light of beauty and goodness, that is, the sheer affirmation of divine creativity as it is traced in the creaturely itself. Through liturgical transfiguration, the world itself becomes figure, and participation in the figural finds its expression in an ethical and aesthetic transformation. With the support of the *artificium* of material mimesis, this form of *aisthesis* brings forth a different face of things, their figural presence, lost in darkness, and restores the very form of perception that has gone awry in exile and its world order supplements. Thus, material mimesis supports more than a Stoic therapy of the soul, more than a state of tranquility, since the very practice of assimilation and participation transfigures sensation, affects, and thought in a speculative refashioning. In this reconstitution of the world in and through figures, this very practice can, however, in this postlapsarian life, never be more than the production of a growing, ever-more absorbing, and thus also ever-more dramatic intimacy with that very hidden aspect of things and the divine that Moses saw on the mountain.

Reinventing Sensation

The utterly realist character of these theological thoughts, the mechanics that foregrounds the logic and mechanisms of figuration, and the light this throws on our understanding of practices of imitation and their connection to techniques of contemplative transfiguration are striking. Gregory engages in an elaborate mode of material mimesis, of image and object making, that does not end in an allegorical reading of the Scriptures, of liturgy, images, and their symbolically uplifting function alone. Instead, he comes close to Origen, who emphasized the aspect of a speculative and transforming *aisthesis* and the transfiguration of perception that is supported by practices of reading and the installation of liturgical artifacts. Thus, in both Origen and Gregory, speculation is to be seen as an aesthetic experience at the core of the contemplative practice. It is at the core of a contemplative path that is being recast in terms of an experience that brings sensation, affect, and cognition into never-ending participatory circulation and that thus reforms the life of the soul to give it a new shape where all things of the world turn into figures of the ungraspable divine that grounds them. Driven by an ever-intensifying movement of desire—*epektasis* in Gregory of Nyssa—the world emerges anew as a speculative sphere of dispersion, figure, and analogy. If analogy appears here, however, it is in the form of an analogy not of being or of semiosis and hermeneutics but of figural resonance and aesthetic experience. Thus, for example, the light in the space of the liturgy, the flames of the candles, reflected in the gold of the objects, the colors of the liturgical vestments—all this does not function symbolically in terms of mimetic assimilation and meaning alone but as a figural network that resonates with and mirrors the flow of participation and relation when it transforms perception in the contemplative practice. The symbolic in its excess, as it is conceived here, entails and produces this form of participation. As Origen points out, the Scriptures have thus to be read not in light of intellectual understanding alone but in forms of an experience where the figures and tropes are allowed to deploy their rhetorical effects and provide us with a different form of perception, a world seen and experienced in a different way. Read in this way, the Scriptures shape sensation, affects, and thoughts anew and pull us into a drama of figuration, disfiguration, and transfiguration. Thus, and only thus, they liberate the world from the discursive grasp that turns all things into idols and all knowledge into ideology and instrumental thought. In opening up to the figural effects of the Scriptures and in allowing these effects to unfold in sensation and affect, perception at first turns into assimilation in the realm of figural play. However, this exposure to figural play, always resisting the disfiguring grasp of meaning and concept, deepens the fundamental asymmetry between figure and thought. The very excess on the side of the figure—an excess of abundance and beauty—can be captured only in forms of participatory speculation. Only where the soul turns into a pure mirror of the flow of emergence of the world in its multiplicity, in participating in its figural play, does it thus undermine the discursive grasp and allow for worlds to unfold otherwise. Only under these conditions are the "old senses" abandoned and do the "new senses" take shape.

The history of this practice of contemplative reading of the Scriptures, especially in regard to sensation, has often focused on Ignatius of Loyola, the sixteenth-century founder of the Jesuit order, and his *Spiritual Exercises.* The Ignatian model, based on the construction of a mental space and the application of the senses, provides us with a systematic approach to prayer and meditation where the articulation of the Scriptures in forms of sensation and emotion plays a key role. This configuration of a mental space and the application of the senses within that space, was not entirely new, however. It systematized and gave a modern, and more subject-focused, shape to a long tradition of practices that emphasized the formation of the senses and emotional arousal. To understand it, we have to dwell on the history of this practice.

The theological and contemplative tradition I am referring to is centered primarily around the teaching that the experiential knowledge of God through the word of the Scriptures is metaphorically described not only in terms taken from our external sense experience. We do not just speak metaphorically of the sweetness of the divine and the bitterness of hell. Instead, understood more radically, our experience of the divine is, according to Origen and the tradition that follows his teaching, actually based on "five spiritual senses." As I suggest, these spiritual senses cannot be understood as an "alternative" set of senses. Instead, they are to be understood in terms of a reformation of sense perception itself—a reformation based on practices of figuration.[12]

Both a constructivist and phenomenological perspective made the theory of the spiritual senses fascinating not only to medieval and early modern readers but also to the nineteenth-century decadent writers, particularly Joris-Karl Huysmans. It provided them with a model of recasting sensation and with a script for how to move against and beyond nature by means of artificial stimulation of the senses through the construction of theaters of sensual and affective arousal.[13] We are dealing here, in Huysmans and in the theological tradition he is referring to, with a model for the reinvention of sensation that goes beyond and against all naturalist understandings.

This theory of the "five spiritual senses" is usually traced back to its origins in the exegetic practice and theory of Origen of Alexandria, who was probably most famous for his teachings about *apokatastasis*, the eschatological restoration of all things at the end of time. Although, according to him, the inner or spiritual senses do correspond to the five outer senses (and are named in analogous ways), they are not to be seen as analogous or metaphorical alone. Instead, the rhetoric of the inner or spiritual senses and their role in the sensory and affective life of the soul in reading and contemplation opened the possibility for the creation of a new space of "experience," "exploration," and "amplification." I use these three terms because they refer to three aspects of this new experience of the world in light of the Scriptures: an experiential and participatory instead of a conceptual understanding of the excessive pleasures of the divine and its "likeness" in the things, as well as its opposite, the demonic and the "unlikeness"; the exploration of new and unheard-of states of sensation and emotional arousal against the "aridity" of the soul and of everyday life; and finally, a technique of figuration that relies on the amplification of the sensory and affective life through artificial means in prayer, contemplation, and liturgy. This amplification includes the production of feelings of intense desolation, hope and hopelessness, as well as joy, but also of overwhelming sense experience of sweetness or bitterness; and, finally, of intense desire and excessive love that are often seen in terms of an experience of touch.

Ultimately, what is essentially a theory and practice of prayer and contemplation attempts to transcend or, to put it more precisely, inherently transcends the common and universally emphasized disjunction of the "inner" and "outer," of body and soul, in medieval spirituality. It shows that the dualist understanding of inner and outer is misleading since it inscribes an opposition between two realms instead of focusing on the aspect of a transformative practice. Speaking in theological terms, the practice at stake here transforms the everyday world into a sacramental world, where participation replaces instrumental use and the distinction of subjects and objects. The movement at stake can also be characterized as a denaturalization of the senses—the transition from the "literal" and empirical everydayness to a "spiritual" and figural world—and a reconfiguration, a renaturalization, and a return to the intensity of sensory and emotional experience of the world in the form of ever-new aesthetic experience. In this movement, the very literal, concrete, or real is recovered against its abstract status as an object of knowledge and use. This experience of a recovering transfiguration is called "sacramental" by early medieval theologians, and this sacramental world emerges in the specific emphasis on figural practices that shape sensation, affect, and thought in the acts of prayer.

I am well aware that this seems to imply an anachronism since we often hear about the repression of the senses in medieval culture and theology. However, in light of monastic treatises that emphasize *admiratio* (admiration) and *stupor* (wonder) in the face of the sensual experience of the world informed by the reading of the Scriptures,[14] we might indeed want to revise this judgment and think differently about the possibility of a medieval prehistory of Nietzsche's statement about the aesthetic justification of the world. When the world turns into figure in contemplative detachment, it is neither known nor understood at first but experienced in moments of wonder. While maintaining its utterly concrete and particular character, its taste and touch and color, the world in this contemplative transfiguration annihilates all discursive distinction and gives our understanding an entirely new shape.

At first glance, the theory of the inner or spiritual senses is a response to the desire for experience of the divine in light of the impossibility of understanding the divine, that is, of negative theology.[15] It is again in the writings of early Greek theologians, especially Origen and Gregory of Nyssa, where we encounter the attempt to define the relation between man and God in terms not only of an intellectual grasp or of stoic *apatheia* and a controlling repression of sensory and emotional arousal but also of an experience that, as we have seen previously, must be described as sensory transfiguration. Using the Greek term *aisthesis*, Origen indicates that he speaks about an experience that transcends the rational and discursive operations of the intellect. In fact, Origen translates the biblical verse Proverbs 2:5 ("Then shalt thou understand the fear of the Lord, and find the knowledge of God") in a specific way, introducing the term *aisthesis* where other translations, including the Septuagint and the Vulgate, use *gnosis* or *scientia* (knowledge).[16] Thus, Origen emphasizes not only that the Scriptures are the object of each sense of the soul, such as vision for the eyes, sound for the ears, taste for the mouth, scent for the nose, touch for the skin, but also that the experience of the world in light of a specific form of reading the Scriptures acquires a new status. Things, we might say, are no longer seen merely as things and objects of cognition but as things that acquire their experiential qualities through figural resonances within the Scriptures and between the Scriptures and the worlds we are part of. What Origen emphasizes in these passages is the figural side of the Scriptures, the aspect Auerbach grasps with his notion of "energetic realism." Not an abstracting understanding or a spiritualizing allegory is at stake here but the *energeia* that passes through the reading and gives a new life to the ways we inhabit and experience the world. In this context, Origen emphasizes that practice and exercise (*gymnasía*), the continuous returns to the Scriptures in prayer, are key to the constitution of these ever-new moments of experience. Two elements are essential to this practice: first, an intervention that denaturalizes and isolates the realm of sensation and that turns things and events from their status as objects into figures, undermining from within all moments of representation; and second, an intervention that re-creates sensation in terms of intensity by artificial means, that is, by creating the space for the deployment of the *energeia* of the figures in the practice of the recitation of prayers, the singing of the Psalms, the contemplation of images, and the meditation of scriptural verses and scenes.

Movements of Prayer

Many concrete examples of how this art of material mimesis, assimilation, and figural participation is being invented can be found in medieval texts about prayer and contemplation. Throughout the Middle Ages these have been part of a practice of prayer and contemplation in a monastic setting, often with a strong desire to see and taste the divine. The search of monks and nuns for intense experience and overwhelming grace, be it in the form of visions or other experiential states, did not happen without preparation and exercise. Prayer, the "ascent of the mind to God" according to John of Damascus and to a medieval tradition that follows his teaching, is the very technique that prepares and forms the soul, that moves it from reading to contemplation, and that leads it from a state of aridity and desolation into a state where mystical experience, experience of the divine in a transfiguration of affect, sensation, and cognition, had its place and time. Thus, the classic path in prayer from reading to meditation (*lectio* to *meditatio*), from prayer to contemplation (*oratio* to *contemplatio*), could easily be transformed into a model of mystic ascent as we find it in elaborate forms in the later Middle Ages. Consider especially the works of David of Augsburg, Rudolf of Biberach, Henry Suso, and Hendrik Herp, who also exercised a strong influence on the Spanish mystics of the *Siglo de Oro* and on their theories and practices of prayer and contemplation.

Following this tradition, Guigo II the Carthusian writes in his *Scala claustralium* (*The Ladder of Monks*): "Reading looks for the sweetness of the blessed life, meditation finds it, prayer asks for it, and contemplation tastes it" (Beatae vitae dulcedinem lectio inquirit, meditatio invenit, oratio postulat, contemplatio degustat). Or, "You look for it in reading, and you find it in meditation; you knock on the door in prayer, and in contemplation it opens to you" (Quarite legendo, et invenietis meditando; pulsate orando, et aperietur vobis contemplando).[17] Thus, the monastic form of contemplative practice leads from reading to meditation, to contemplation, and to a renewed sensual, affective, and cognitive experience—often expressed in terms of intense love, overwhelming taste of sweetness, and intimate touch.

This, as mentioned earlier, presupposes a specific practice and training. A short twelfth-century treatise on prayer illustrates the basic character of this understanding of prayer and its orientation toward figuration and the production of experiential states—and, more broadly, toward a theory of figural production and a phenomenology of rhetorical effects. As Hugh of Saint Victor demonstrates in his treatise *De virtute orandi* (*On the Power of Prayer*), the practice of prayer is highly informed by rhetorical tradition and training. Prayer, meant to lead into a state of *excitatio* and *inflammatio*, of intense and overwhelming love, is first and foremost an art of arousing affects and emotions that forgets its own intention: "Pure prayer is when from an abundance of devotion, the mind is so enkindled that when it turns to ask something of God it forgets even its petition because of the greatness of His love."[18]

Prayer is to be understood at first in terms of an exercise that arouses the affects in movements of figural stimulation and assimilation. It does so in a way that not only evokes the affect of overwhelming love but also lays out and deploys from the ground of the soul the "innumerable" forms of affects that humans are able to experience. As Hugh points out, the "number of these affects is infinite," making it impossible for him to "count them all."[19] These affects emerge in a practice that moves from a state of unexcited reading or remembering of the sacred texts to moments of intense perception and emotional arousal. The transition to this state of arousal happens in meditation, the "yoke" of the soul, which exercises a shaping force on the ways of perception, assimilating the life of the soul to the effects of the figures and tropes. Meditation produces arousal (*excitatio*) through "frequent mental re-evocation" (*frequens cogitatio*), a process of rumination and mastication that includes sensual and emotional perception as well as a practice of the imagination and of intellectual evaluation of the phenomena that are being created.

In its elementary form, Hugh points out, the practice of prayer starts with enumeration, the construction of lists, and the configuration of tropes drawn from the Scriptures, life experience, lives of saints and martyrs, memory, and other available sources. For example, Hugh states, a list of pains and an enumeration of all possible evils will produce the effect that the soul experiences herself in and through a number of affects of pain and suffering. The more impressive and comprehensive the list, the more the soul "sighs and groans" (*tanto amplius suspirat et gemit*) in an experience of the broad range of affects of suffering.[20] In his discussion of the singing of the Psalms and the effects produced in this practice, Hugh shows how they serve the purpose of weaving rich textures of feelings, assimilating the life of the soul to the text. In a similar way the soul can move herself into a state of admiration, pleasure, and praise when she evokes tropes of divine beauty and happiness.

What Hugh emphasizes in this short treatise is not only the production of specific sites and states of affective experience but also the very transition from one affect to another. Often, he writes, the singing of the Psalms means exactly that, the production of patterns of affects and the transition from one affect to another one, then another one, and so on.

According to Hugh, meditation is a rhetorical practice of evocation with the help of lists, enumerations of words and images, textual configurations, and reconfigurations. It produces textures of affective and sensual arousal that can be savored, experienced, and phenomenologically explored. In addition to the rhetorical device of enumeration, narration is an important tool in the construction of these textures of experience. As many medieval authors demonstrate, biblical narratives such as the *Song of Songs* or the passion of Christ, can serve this purpose as well as the *Lives of Saints*—above all the story of the temptations of Saint Anthony, of the desert fathers, and of Mary Magdalene—or even personal experiences. The function of both the enumeration and the narration does not consist in telling God something he would not know already but in shaping the experiential and the cognitive life of the soul. Affective and sensual assimilation are on this level always joined by an evaluative phenomenology where understanding and reason rejoin figural effects. They do, however, never take the place of its ground.

As Hugh points out, the very function of the rhetorical techniques of enumeration and narration consists in the production of affective states that help overcome the understanding of prayer as a means of petitioning God and of objectifying the relation between man and God. Instead, the forms of prayer he has in mind produce a complex and comprehensive state of dramatic absorption in figural play that can be explored, enjoyed, and suffered—and that then, in the very asymmetry of the figural, makes the intensity of overwhelming love emerge in which a taste of the divine can be savored. In these moments a shift in agency takes place, where human production of affects with the help of material mimesis—the moment of assimilation—turns the unitive absorption into divine love—the moment of participation. In Hugh's texts, this is a state of excess, of partaking beyond all assimilation where love alone reigns. Here, all human agency is shaped by this partaking and disappears in it. No subject or subjectivity remains, just the person that perceives and acts in the flow of the world, shaped by the very asymmetry that figural emergence itself embodies. This, we might be tempted to say after reading Hugh's treatise, is what medieval authors mean when they speak of God as the good that communicates itself. Obviously, there is no "itself" here anymore, only the abandonment to the asymmetry in non-understanding, the submission that turns all production into participation and sharing.

Thus, meditation, the production of a dense texture of both terrifying and consoling affects, opens the drama that entails the elements that since Dionysius the Areopagite have been characterized in terms of purgation, illumination, and contemplative union in an experience of the divine—an experience that a broad range of authors in the later Middle Ages will be speaking about in terms of taste and kiss, the meaningless figures of sharing par excellence.

The most remarkable aspect of Hugh's treatise about prayer is its rhetorical, even technical and mechanical character. It uses the Scriptures, the body of religious texts, and personal experience as an archive of mimetic artifacts that can be mobilized in the practice of meditation in the form of rhetorical stimuli. Based on techniques of amplification—partition, enumeration, narration, construction of lists, rhetorical questions—these stimuli are used to modify the life of the soul and to produce a dense and dramatic texture of sensation and affects. The absorption in sensation and emotions can be fashioned further toward the experience of overwhelming love that forms the ultimate experiential goal of the very practice of prayer. As we see, the production of moments of absorption includes both emotional and sensual states of perception. Together, they form the key elements of a medieval rhetorical practice that serves both prayer and mystical experience. It entails at its core a dramatic engagement with mimesis and an abandonment of all assimilation to participation. While this practice enlists mimetic tools as figures that move, it strips the figures of their mimetic and hermeneutic aspects, abandoning them on the way in order to let go and to let the abandonment in moments of absorption happen. It is this practice that tears the soul from its orderly natural state and transfigures the creaturely world.

Major attempts to systematize this practice of prayer and contemplation can be found in Albert the Great and Bonaventure. Albert relates sight, hearing, and odor to knowledge of truth and to the cognitive intellectual realm; he relates taste and touch to the experience of the good and to the realm of love and will. Inspired by Dionysius the Areopagite, he emphasizes the passivity of this form of experience and the fact that the soul is "suffering" it and that the sensory phenomena are aspects of the reality of this acknowledgment of the divine. Speaking of touch and taste (*tactus* and *sapor*) with regard to the divine, he accentuates the "experiential," purely "receptive," and "passive" character of this kind of perception.[21]

Not surprisingly, the perception of the divine in terms of an experience of taste and touch becomes most significant in Franciscan traditions, in David of Augsburg's *Septem gradus orationis* (*Seven Degrees of Prayer*), in Bonaventure's *Itinerarium mentis ad Deum* (*The Journey of the Mind to God*) and *Breviloquium*, but even more so in Rudolf of Biberach's *De septem itineribus aeternitatis* (*Seven Paths of Eternity*). Other instances where the gustatory and tactile experience is paramount could be added, among those the late medieval works by Peter of Ailly and the *Imitatio Christi* by Thomas a Kempis. *Delectatio* (pleasure) and *suavitas* (sweetness) are the key words these authors use when they discuss the ways by which man can reach the divine in an experiential way, referring time and again to a sensation of taste and touch. Peter of Ailly speaks of the goal "to reach already in this life the pleasures of the eternal rewards in an experiential way, and to taste their sweetness with delight."[22] Rudolf of Biberach, in *De septem itineribus aeternitatis*, uses the following words, largely inspired by Alcher and Bernhard of Clairvaux's, Hugh of Saint Victor's, and Bonaventure's treatment of the inner senses: "Reaching the inner sense of taste, it opens it up toward the tasting of eternal sweetness."[23] In his long treatment of the inner senses, Rudolf makes this experiential aspect very explicit: "This explains why nobody can express this taste. It can only be known through experience, and this is why we have to look for the way in which our mind can reach the experience of this taste."[24]

The eschatological structure of this concept is often obvious, since it is in and through this experience that the senses and affects are supposed to be rehabilitated and transfigured in a way unknown since the loss of paradise. Such experiences can be characterized as an anticipation of eternal bliss and a reconciliation with the ideal existence of humanity beyond the state of sin. However, and more important, these moments of redemption do not refer to a different, spiritual world but nest within the world already now, folding the order of time and modifying our perception *in via* and thinking of human existence in a cosmic arc of possible fulfillments. In the Franciscan tradition, particularly in the nominalist attitudes, this rehabilitation of the senses and experience leads to a new affirmative mode with regard to sensation and affective experience and to an aesthetic affirmation of the world as it is. A large body of Franciscan poetry and science in the later Middle Ages testifies to this. In the Franciscans' eyes, the world here turns into the very play of figures that in their emergence ask for a perception that acknowledges the asymmetry and—in poverty and humility—turns into the place of a sheer acknowledgment of the beauty and the good in the grass, the wolves, and the stars.

Working with a different terminology, we might want to emphasize that this production of intense and ultimately mystical experience of the divine in a participatory mode is not so much an eschatological vision. Rather, it is focused on an immanence of the divine and a practice that uncovers this very immanence in terms of a figural modification of perception. The practice of prayer, in moving from the hermeneutic of the Scriptures to the engagement with figural effects, forms the ground not only of the exploration of experiential possibilities but also of a different sphere of relation where percepts, affects, and thoughts circulate around a focus on loving absorption. They do so in a fashion that, since it never reaches an end, is always dramatic.

Thus far I have emphasized a model of sensory perception that can and indeed must be explained in what we can call constructivist terms. Sensation and affect are produced on the basis of a practice of reading and prayer, of something I have called, following Gregory of Nyssa, the practice of material mimesis. New textures of sensation and affect result from specific rhetorical procedures that are meant to defamiliarize and to liberate from the naïve natural sense experience. These procedures introduce biblical verses, images, artifacts, and music in a specific way into the practice of prayer with the goal that they should produce an arousing effect and evoke an experiential knowledge where the divine and the world converge. Ultimately, this experience is meant to reconstitute—*in via*, in exile, and in human pilgrimage—the lost ways in which Adam and Eve perceived the world and God in nature. Through these forms of affect and sensation an "originary" but always lost—and thus, in grace, an-originary—form of experience is meant to be constituted beyond the limits of nature. We can, however, also understand this practice in terms of an articulation of a horizon where all coming forth of creation in its very historicity and concreteness translates into sensation and affect—establishing a new spontaneity of experience where the distinction of immanence and transcendence collapses in the free coming forth of things and a free encounter with our worlds. This is indeed, speaking in terms of myth, a reformulation of the prelapsarian state and an anticipation of a return of all things in a form of *apokatastasis*. In terms of figural emergence and drama, however, it is also a critique of the reliance on a discursive order of the world and the deconstruction of this very discursive order in acts of defamiliarization and excess. The texts I discuss emphasize that this excess and asymmetry cannot be recovered in a return to myth, that is, to beginnings or to an eschatological anticipation of the end of time, but only through practices that focus on a critique of everyday world perception and the transformation of perception in practices of prayer, contemplation, and abandonment to the flow of emergence. In addition, they do not think of this practice in terms of an individual and subjective redemption and salvation alone but in terms of a cosmic arc within divine dispensation.

This aesthetic view of prayer is shared by the medieval authors I have mentioned. Inheriting Origen's teachings on the significance of the senses and its various interpretations, they stress not primarily the significance of inner experience but even more—especially in the Franciscan tradition—the reconfiguration of perception and the importance of a new production of sensory and emotional experience itself. It is, as we have seen, not an experience *of* the world or *of* God but an experience that dramatically displaces the self in the very abandonment to the figure, thus grounding itself in a participation in the concrete and the particular that exceeds all abstraction.

Dramatization

Often, one particular biblical text plays a major role in this production of a new world of sensation and the transfiguration of perception this entails. It is the *Song of Songs*, used as an exemplary model in the practices of material mimesis and the application of the senses. This text also provides us with a dramatic script. Medieval authors draw from this script both textual figures that serve to evoke specific moments of sensation and a paradigmatic model that allows for a dramatization of sense experience and emotional states, providing a story line for the enactment. We know from the innumerable rewritings of the *Song of Songs* and from complex prayer texts—for example, how the thirteenth-century beguine Mechthild of Magdeburg's *Flowing Light of the Godhead* uses it as a blueprint for the self-fashioning of the life of her soul—that the tropes used in the *Song of Songs* not only evoke sweetness and delight but also bitterness and desolation. The *aisthesis* Mechthild draws from the *Song of Songs* deploys figures in a dramatic evocation of possible experiential states. In this context prayer—understood in Hugh's way—serves as a means to explore the realm of possible sensual experience and to intensify it in ever-new displacements. Mechthild uses the *Song of Songs* as a dramatic script, embedding it in a series of prayers that allow for a rich staging of moments of assimilation, of sensation, and of affective arousal. In doing so, Mechthild of Magdeburg combines in audacious ways the text of the *Song of Songs* with rhetorical elements taken from contemporary love poetry, amplifying further the impact of the text and playing with the aesthetics of sweetness and desolation in adaptations of courtly love lyrics.

In addition to the *Song of Songs,* two other scripts have played a major role and served as blueprints for specific forms of the production of sensation and affects in monastic contexts. The first is a creation narrative, the *Hexameron.* The second is the legend of the temptation of Saint Anthony. The formative influence of these texts is exemplified in two twelfth-century texts, *De quadripertito exercitio cellae* (*On the Fourfold Exercise of the Cell*) by Adam of Dryburgh (Adam Scotus) and *De duplici resurrectione* (*On the Twofold Resurrection*) by Baldwin of Canterbury. Both texts emphasize again—as does Hugh of Saint Victor—that prayer, practiced by monks or nuns in their cells, cannot be understood as a gesture of petitioning or praise alone. Rather, they both point out that prayer has to be seen as a technique that puts the soul in a position in which she can be touched by the text so that she becomes receptive to its rhetorical effects, that is, to emotional and sensual arousal. Baldwin's notion of a twofold resurrection suggests that while "ordinary people" can be content with the resurrection and the experience of the promise of paradise at the end of time, monks know the practice of evoking this experience as a state of emotional and sensual perception in the present. He adds: "Simple mortals are satisfied with one resurrection. We, however, are not satisfied with one resurrection."[25]

In his explanation he invokes musical imagery, imagining the soul as an instrument that resonates (a *psaltherium* or *cithara*) and the senses as the strings that are put in movement through the use of the biblical text in prayer and contemplation. Thus, specific quotes from the creation narrative turn again into figures and elements of material mimesis. These texts produce a melody on the strings of the soul, that is, the senses and the affects. They are used to stimulate the senses, to produce moments of sensation that must be qualified as aesthetic since they are in fact nothing else than the sense experience of the world in the flesh and in light of this figural practice. Meditation on the book of Genesis, the creation narrative, is meant to turn into the shaping of the life of the soul, of sensation and affects, through the very application of the text, which then turns into the medium that transfigures the world itself. As mentioned previously, the words Adam and Baldwin use in this context are *stupor* and *admiratio*, expressing the translation of the creation narrative into wonder, that is, an overwhelming sensual and affective experience of the world.

It is in this overwhelming force of the tropes used here, once again, that we encounter the shift in agency that is constitutive of mystical experience in sensation, affects, and thought. While all practices that we encountered are based on forms of material mimesis that allow for the assimilative production of affective, sensual, and cognitive states, the very absorption into the affect as a form of unity with the divine is and can never be a product of these very practices themselves. In theological terms, we would have to speak of a view that, in transcending the natural force of the practices themselves, finds its core in the logic of grace; in philosophical terms, we would speak of an understanding that abandons the logic of instrumental reason. In fact, the divine here is the excess—if we want, of goodness, of beauty—that the soul experiences in the dramatic return from discourse to figure; from a world of meaning through a world of assimilation to a world of participation; from a world of nature, project, and instrumentality to a world of grace and freedom. What is at stake, ultimately, are a liberation of perception from a corrupted and arid order; a critique of the utilitarian, instrumental, discursive, naturalized modes of attention; and a modification and intensification of perception by means of practices of figuration that acknowledge their utter asymmetry. The facticity of the concrete that turns into figural intensity, however, can never be grasped or exhausted by the practices that shape the life of the soul. It is—with Dionysius the Areopagite, in "brilliant darkness"—the very light of possibility, the inexhaustible realm of possibility that the practices of prayer and contemplation draw on and that takes shape time and again in the reweaving of experience beyond its natural bounds. This very possibility, according to the authors and texts quoted here, cannot be anything but affirmation, gift, grace, or, if we want to use another term, the sheer "darkness" or "nothingness" of the divine as life and creation in everything that opens up to a modified perception in and through the practices and the drama of contemplation. This is the way Meister Eckhart—using another of the available scripts—puts it in his interpretation of Paul's mystical vision on the way to Damascus in Acts 9:8: "I think this text has a fourfold sense. One is that when he rose up from the ground with open eyes, he saw Nothing, and the Nothing was God; for when he saw God he calls that Nothing. The second: when he got up he saw nothing but God. The third: in all things he saw nothing but God. The fourth: when he saw God, he saw all things as nothing."[26]

Visualization

In this practice of transforming perception, the visual registers of figuration play a key role. As Gregory the Great writes in his introduction to the commentary on the *Song of Songs*, the importance of visualization is to be understood in quite concrete and seemingly paradoxical terms.[27] Exactly because the mind is not able to grasp the divine through a literal understanding of the Scriptures and through intellectual cognition, humans have to refer to visual means and ekphrastic illustrations that threaten to turn divine things into idols. Gregory insists, however, that the gaze is literally to be aroused by the visualization of the elements of the *Song of Songs*, the sight of the kisses, the breasts, the hips of the bride, because it is only through this arousal that the mind succeeds in liberating itself from being tied up with the literal meaning of the text and the naïve attachment to the things of this world. The reference to things seen and to the allegorical meaning is made to point not to a hidden meaning but rather to the realm of effects the visible exercises on the soul, moving it beyond all discursive orders. Thus, once again, the visible, the content of ekphrastic production, turns from sign to figure, from meaningful attachment to existential exposure, and from dogmatic to experiential knowledge (*cognitio experimentalis*). This experience entails, however, not a *pathein*, a suffering of the figural effects alone, but an exploration that, in unknowing everything, also moves through all forms of representation and knowing, through abstraction, assimilation, and participation. That very movement with its irreducible character is the main reason why I speak of a phenomenology here, since we do not deal with a form of allegory that uncovers an enigmatic meaning but with a visualization and a process that allow for an exploration of and participation in the figural effects being produced. The transition from the literal to the spiritual is thus not to be understood in terms of an esoteric understanding of the text and its hidden meaning but in terms of a shift that takes place within cognition: a shift from the meaning of the text that can be grasped conceptually to the effect the text has and can have on the soul when she explores it in the practice of visualization. The movement of shifting from knowing to unknowing and from one figural effect to another is in itself temporal, reiterating the process of undoing and reconfiguring the world as we know it in time. From this point of view, the arousing object of vision has no stable meaning or essence in itself. It is deployed with all the possible meanings and effects, in order for the soul to move through them, to undo them, and to end with the excess of the figure in its shaping of the soul—absorbing her ultimately into a drama of love that leads her through the visual space to the divine, through assimilation to participation.

Gregory emphasizes, once again, that the text of the *Song of Songs* should thus not be read in terms of an allegory that could be understood as a mode of symbolic representation put in place of the literal meaning. Rather, the allegorical or spiritual meaning implies a mimetic practice, an assimilation of the mind and the soul through the visualization, and finally a mode of participation that moves and shapes soul and flesh. This evokes a world of both emotions and sensations in the form of an endlessly reiterated exploration of the possible realms of sensory and emotional experience. It is a phenomenological exploration insofar as the soul in the practice of meditative reading guides her awareness, plays with figural effects, experiments with her possible shapes, only to finally abandon the phenomenology for the sake of the figural asymmetry that we call grace, beauty, and justice.

The *Song of Songs* is often used as a kind of blueprint for the visual translation or transference that allows for this specific formation of perception and of a new life. The translation of the word into an object of vision has a seemingly paradoxical effect. It does not produce an object in a literal and thus objectifying sense. Instead, particularly in the icon, the practice of visualization frees up the spiritual meaning of the word not in the form of meaning but in forms of participation. Thus, it transfigures the affective life of the soul, leading—in Gregory's view—from the frigidity of worldly discourse to a state of love.

This practice throws a new and quite fascinating light on the understanding of the relation between the literal and the spiritual sense of the word and the status of visual experience. Following Gregory's exposition, we might want to argue that the literal side of the Scriptures should be privileged. The literal "meaning" is not just a historical sense of the word but any mode of understanding in which nature or scripture gives itself—in its literally "energetic realism"—as a figure, while the spiritual "meaning" consists in nothing else than the unfolding of the rhetorical effects that this shift in the mode of attention and perception produces as a new creaturely life. Paradoxically, what we often call allegory is actually the place where this literalization through visualization happens and where the soul evokes the possibilities of experience that ultimately will purify it and uncover the divine "likeness," that is, the expansive absorbing effect of love in everything.

Monastic practices of visualization often follow this pattern, anticipating the explicit strategies of the spiritual exercises we see in Ignatius of Loyola. Similarly, they include the visualization of hell, of the creaturely world, and, most important, of the passion of Christ where the literal and spiritual distinction entirely collapses in the convergence of assimilation and participation. As we have seen, though, the contemplative practice does not only proscribe the visualization of the word of the Scriptures as a means toward the spiritual understanding of the text that literally becomes a form of life. It also introduces a specific way of understanding vision itself, in terms not primarily of a faculty of perception but in terms of an exploration of the possibilities of sensory and emotional experience and thus of touch.

Medieval visionary literature often builds on this practice of translation of the word in conjunction with the transformation of the space of the church and the liturgy into a theater of experience. Thus, the thirteenth-century Flemish beguine Hadewijch of Antwerp locates her visionary experience in the church and the liturgy. Remembering a visionary experience while sitting in the church, she writes:

> On a certain Pentecost Sunday I had a vision at dawn. Matins were being sung in the church, and I was present. My heart and my veins and all my limbs trembled and quivered with eager desire and, as often occurred with me, such madness and fear beset my mind that it seemed to me I did not content my Beloved, and that my Beloved did not fulfill my desire, so that dying I must go mad, and going mad I must die. On that day my mind was beset so fearfully and

so painfully by desirous love that all my separate limbs threatened to break, and all my separate veins were in travail. The longing in which I then was cannot be expressed by any language or any person I know; and everything I could say about it would be unheard-of to all those who never apprehended Love as something to work for with desire, and whom Love had never acknowledged as hers. I can say this about it: I desired to have full fruition of my Beloved, and to understand and taste him to the full. I desired that his Humanity should to the fullest extent be one in fruition with my humanity, and that mine then should hold its stand and be strong enough to enter into perfection until I content him, who is perfection itself, by purity and unity, and in all things to content him fully in every virtue. To that end I wished he might content me interiorly with his Godhead, in one spirit, and that for me he should be all that he is, without withholding anything from me. For above all the gifts that I ever longed for, I chose this gift: that I should give satisfaction in all great sufferings. For that is the most perfect satisfaction: to grow up in order to be God with God. For this demands suffering, pain, and misery, and living in great new grief of soul: but to let everything come and go without grief, and in this way to experience nothing else but sweet love, embraces, and kisses. In this sense I desired that God gave himself to me, so that I might content him.

As my mind was thus beset with fear, I saw a great eagle flying toward me from the altar, and he said to me: "If you wish to attain oneness, make yourself ready!"

I fell on my knees and my heart beat fearfully, to worship the Beloved with oneness, according to his true dignity; that indeed was impossible for me, as I know well, and as God knows, always to my woe and to my grief.

But the Eagle turned back and spoke: "Just and mighty Lord, now show your great power to unite your oneness in the manner of union with full possession!"

Then the eagle turned round again and said to me: "He who has come, comes again; and to whatever place he never came, he comes not."

Then he came from the altar, showing himself as a Child; and that Child was in the same form as he was in his first three years. He turned toward me, in his right hand took from the ciborium his Body, and in his left hand took a chalice, which seemed to come from the altar, but I do not know where it came from. With that he came in the form and clothing of a Man, as he was on the day when he gave us his Body for the first time; looking like a Human Being and a Man, wonderful, and beautiful, and with glorious face, he came to me as humbly as anyone who wholly belongs to another. Then he gave himself to me in the shape of the Sacrament, in its outward form, as the custom is; and then he gave me to drink in form of the chalice, in form and taste, as the custom is. After that he came himself to me, took me entirely in his arms, and pressed me to him; and all my members felt his in full felicity, in accordance with the desire of my heart and my humanity. So I was outwardly satisfied and fully transported. Also then, for a short while, I had the strength to bear this; but soon, after a short time, I lost that manly beauty outwardly in the sight of his form. I saw him completely come to naught and so fade and all at once dissolve that I could no longer recognize or perceive him outside me, and I could no longer distinguish him within me. Then it was to me as if we were one without difference. It was thus: outwardly, to see, taste, feel, as one can outwardly taste, see, and feel in the reception of the outward Sacrament. So can the Beloved, with the loved one, each wholly receive the other in all full satisfaction of the sight, the hearing, and the passing away of the one in the other.

After that I remained in a passing away in my Beloved, so that I wholly melted away in him and nothing any longer remained to me of myself; and I was changed and taken up in the spirit, and there it was shown me concerning such hours.[28]

I quote this lengthy passage because it shows the ways in which the visionary event is embedded in a transition that moves from the performance of the liturgy through a reference to allegorical symbols to a figural experience of the divine. The starting point is a liturgical moment, Pentecost, and the singing of the matins on that day. This liturgical memory—Pentecost, the soul waiting for the arrival of the spirit, the singing that evokes the desire—leads to a description of the intensity and the character of the beguine's wish for an encounter with the divine, quoting from the repertoire of mystical tropes inspired by the *Song of Songs.* Traversing a path of assimilation, the description of her desire finally gives place to the acts of participation, the play between her and the divine. An eagle, here as in many other cases the allegorical figure of the spiritual messenger, prepares an encounter through which all the symbols of the communion in the Eucharist are transformed into the real presence of Christ in an embodied encounter. The liturgy that represents the text and its message—Pentecost as the moment when the spirit transforms the old world—has become the place where the hidden meaning of the gospel, the union of Christ and the beguine, turns into the literal form of life in the visionary event. The *sensus mysticus,* the mystical or spiritual sense of the Scriptures, thus takes shape in an event that absorbs both the symbolic language of the liturgy and the desire of the beguine for oneness with Christ.

We certainly do not go wrong if we read this visionary text, the play between the soul and Christ, as Hadewijch's interpretation and enactment of the meaning of Pentecost. She refers to the liturgy, to the singing, to the conventional set of liturgical symbols. However, she does this in a very specific way, emphasizing a transition from word to flesh and from flesh to word, from the spiritual to the literal and from the literal to the spiritual. The spiritual desire evoked by the singing in the church leads thus to the literal participation in the divine where the meaning of the liturgical symbols disappears and the figural takes shape in the literal play between Christ and her. This literal encounter, the real presence in the flesh evoked by the symbolic language of the liturgy, finally disappears in the apophatic moment of a unity where all the differences between inward and outward, literal and spiritual, word and flesh disappear. From the perception of the word and the singing the soul moves through the conversion of word and flesh in the encounter with Christ to the sphere where there is nothing other than participation in the divine and the collapse of all distinction of spirit and flesh.

We might argue that the text tells us the story of the perfect absorption of the soul into the hidden and unspeakable meaning of the text, that is, the promised unity with the divine beyond the distinction of word and flesh, spirit and letter. However, the text tells us much more. It brings to our attention that this unity has its place *in via*, in time, nowhere else than in the performance that happens on the visionary stage—a visionary stage that superimposes itself on the liturgy, emphasizing that the true meaning of the word is not to be found in its symbolic representation but in the figuration where it becomes participation and life-shaping form. The transition from the liturgy—the singing, the reading of the word, the Eucharist—to the experience of the divine takes shape in the theater of the imagination in the flesh. Here, the visual enactment, the mise-en-scène of the meaning of the Scripture, is linked to an emotional intensity of the experience that unfolds hand in hand with the visualization. This living image, a *tableau vivant*, is the actual exegesis and reading of the Scriptures and its representation in the space of the church at Pentecost, the day when the spirit was received.

The vision, I argue, is an exemplary instance of such a type of figural reading in terms of Auerbach's notion of "energetic realism," emphasizing the necessity of a performative enactment wherever the hidden, mystical, spiritual sense (*sensus absconditus, mysticus, spiritualis*) of the Scripture is at stake. From this point of view, and from the point of view of the audience of the visionary text, the community of nun and beguine readers, Hadewijch's vision is not a description of her extraordinary experience but a didactic text. It guides and shapes the understanding of the faithful, starting with the situation of the listener in the church and moving on to the person who contemplates the word in the form of a visual allegory and a playful enactment. Thus, the listener in the church is transported from the literal to the allegorical meaning of the text—Christ being the bridegroom of the soul in the exegesis of the *Song of Songs*—then into the realm of figural effects that absorb both the listener and the meaning of the text in the actual and again literal, historical, real encounter of Christ and the soul as bride and bridegroom.

This is a model of reading on which Hadewijch insists in her collection of visions that circulated among medieval beguine readers. It is, on a didactic level, the type of reading her texts try to produce since all of them intend to become examples of figuration, exemplary readings that show and fashion how one has to read and how one should understand the liturgical presence of the Scriptures. In this sense, the beguine is to be seen as a theological author who proposes a specific way of understanding, an alternative practice that establishes a tension between the hermeneutic understanding and the figural reading of the Scriptures. At its center is not the biblical text alone and its memorial presence in the liturgy but the acts of reading and liturgical performance as a repetition and an enactment where the remembering of the Scripture becomes an experience of its hidden meaning, an enactment of the *sensus mysticus* in literal form, and thus participation in the divine. This is the exemplary practice Hadewijch proposes from the perspective of the bride, the racialized and gendered "I am black but beautiful" (Song of Songs 1:5). It is a way of reading where the visual, the image, and the play of figures not only compensate for the otherwise ungraspable meaning of the Scriptures and the visual experience turns into touch but also where her voice emerges in a concreteness that is abject—and often characterized as "hysterical"—in the order of discourse.

4

Imitation

Saint Francis

The assimilation and absorption through visual experience and its transformation into touch can probably best be further studied in the vision of Saint Francis on Mount Alverna. In this vision Francis, who had withdrawn into the mountain desert to pray, sees a seraph with six wings in the form of Christ. This very experience entails his reception of the stigmata. Thomas of Celano's retelling of Francis's vision shows what is at stake in this scene. I am looking at the narrative not as an example of a vision given by the special grace of God but as an illustration of a specific paradigm of visual experience that throws light on the line of thought I have been focusing on in Chapter 3. As Chiara Frugoni has shown in her book on Saint Francis, Thomas of Celano's early biographical narrative, permeated with biblical references and passages, finds a particular path of reconciliation toward other reports of the stigmatization that do not always correspond in the details. Thomas accomplishes this by telling the story twice—once on the occasion of the vision at Alverna and once again on Saint Francis's death—with modifications at crucial passages and with a growing emphasis on the aesthetic quality of the beauty of Francis's body in the eyes of his brothers. Thomas concludes:

> He shone with . . . miraculous beauty before the gaze of his Brothers, and his flesh had become even more white, yet it was wonderful to see, in his hands and feet, not in fact the holes made by the nails, but the nails themselves formed out

of his flesh and still retaining the blackness of iron, and his right side red with blood. These signs of his martyrdom, so far from filling the minds of those who looked on them with revulsion, lent his body great beauty and grace, as little black stones do when inset in a white pavement.[1]

In this retelling of the story, Thomas shows that his concern is not with the identity of Christ and Saint Francis but with the comparison itself, the establishment of the likeness in a material mimesis and an aesthetic experience that produces a convergence of sensation, affect, and thought. Thomas shows this most evidently in his description of the stigmatization. For him, the stigmata embody not so much the wounds of Christ. Instead, they embody the effect of the vision—better, the effect on the observer of the visual translation of the narrative that tells the story of the wounded Christ. Consequently, the appearance of the stigmata in Francis's flesh is not only a particularly privileged sign of his radical assimilation to Christ. In addition, the appearance of the stigmata is in fact related to the specific understanding of the vision itself, in which the saint is completely affected and absorbed by the figure of Christ in form of the seraph.

The stigmatized body is the exemplary figure not of a pious intimacy and imitation or of a particular moment of grace alone but of the very effect of the contemplated image and of a particular medieval practice, which produces the image as a privileged place for the translation of the text of the Scriptures. Similar to what we have seen in Hadewijch's vision, here, too, the experience moves from assimilation to participation. The life of Saint Francis, seen as the perfect imitation of Christ, the act of "nakedly following the naked Christ" (*nudus Christum nudum sequi*) is thereby defined in a very particular way:[2] not only as a representation or legitimizing proof of authenticity but also as a mimetic assimilation, followed by the transformation of the life of the soul and the flesh that turns into participation under the effects of a figure. In Thomas of Celano's legend, the vision is not portrayed as a glance at an object that could be perceived as such and deciphered in its meaning; it is also not just the visual effect of contemplative absorption; rather, it is the space of a transformation that affects the viewer and that has no other meaning than the transfiguration that occurs in the viewer's flesh, beyond his intellect and understanding. The stigmatization in the flesh is in fact the form of understanding the vision. Put differently, the vision and the stigmatization enlighten us in an exemplary way about how we are to think about the effect of the visual experience that explores the precept of the *imitatio Christi*. The meaning of it cannot be expressed or discursively deduced from the text. It lies solely in this very transfiguration. It does not make Saint Francis identical with Christ but allows him to experience his life not only in imitation, in the most radical "as if" that is possible, but in participation that receives its form from Christ. In a relation of absolute difference (manifest as complete incomprehension of what he has seen) and of deepest intimacy and "likeness" with the exemplary model (manifest in the stigmatized flesh), Francis turns into another Christ.

This, too, is more than a description of a historical event. It is, like Hadewijch's visions, a didactic text that addresses the transition from imitation to assimilation and participation. In the legend, Francis is an exemplary case of the very manner by which one is to interact with the Scriptures through a visual translation that figurally arouses the desire and shapes the experience of the soul. In this process of assimilation, however, the visual has to turn into the figural, and it is the partaking in the figure that gives shape to the life of the soul. It produces the collapse of the distinction between immanence and transcendence, as well as the one between vision and touch. This is the lesson of the exemplary figure of the *poverello*, the one who has adopted humility and poverty, abandoning all worldly forms and thus constituting the creature in a new life.

As we know, this very gesture prepares the Franciscan aesthetics of concrete encounters with things in the world as well, resonating in its rhetoric of praise with Origen's reading of Paul and illuminating a specific tradition of visual experience. A tradition, I want to add, that undermines two modern assumptions we still often hear: the status of the visual in medieval visual piety has been mainly symbolic, or it is only a means of supporting affective piety and mysticism. Instead, we learn from Thomas of Celano that the exemplarity of Saint Francis is to be seen in demonstrating the assimilative transformation and participatory transfiguration that Bonaventure, in his *Itinerarium mentis in deum* (*The Soul's Journey into God*), calls "the speculation" of the "poor one in the desert."[3]

Into the Desert

In the year 1965, Luis Buñuel directed the film *Simón del desierto* (*Simon of the Desert*), portraying an ascetic who imitates the life of another saint, the fourth-century Saint Simeon Stylites. Standing for several years and months on a pillar in the desert, Simón practices a most austere form of self-fashioning, attempting to free himself from all natural, social, and historical bonds and staging his existence as an ultimate state of exception within the world. At one point in this short movie, a visiting monk says to the protagonist, "Your asceticism is sublime."

Characterizing the acts of Simón as "sublime," he speaks not only to the impressive spiritual effort of the one who resides on the pillar absorbed in prayer. He also speaks to the aesthetic quality of Simón's performance and to its formal perfection. Asceticism, monastic practice, religious life is—as the monk knows and as the example of Saint Francis who prays on Mount Alverna demonstrates—essentially the imitation of an example in and through acts of prayer. It is the formal repetition and the aesthetic production of an *exemplum*, an exemplary form that, in the assimilation to it, claims to transcend time and history within the very context of the historical world. Buñuel shows us this world, a place of exile in all its poverty, aridity, and cruelty. In this space of exile, detachment, and withdrawal, prayer is the ascetic's act that evokes and realizes the example of sanctity. Responding to the challenge of defamiliarization, the withdrawal into the desert performs an assimilation to an ascetic image, the pillar saint. In the repetitive gestures of prayer, an archive of images connected to this exemplary image is evoked. Buñuel's film is about this repetition of a form, the emulation of the "example of Simeon Stylites," which, in turn, is nothing else than the repetition of the archetypal figure of Christ who exposes himself to the temptations by the devil in the desert—and thus evokes all the images of diabolical temptation the film plays with.

What Buñuel's film depicts—rather than narrates—is the structure of the mechanical reproduction of images of holiness that relies on a tradition of the use of exemplary images going back far beyond the invention of cinema itself. Many elements in Buñuel's filmmaking testify to the fascination with this tradition, a tradition of the imitation and emulation of images of holiness that provides us with a model of image making and figuration in a more general sense.

Simeon and his double Simón represent exemplary imitators in this tradition, figures who in their chosen alienation from everyday life assimilate themselves to exemplary images. The acts of imitation they choose, that is, the isolation from the world in full view of it, evoke in turn a doubling of the world in its figural shape and the production of images of both temptation and holiness. Before the saint succeeds in his attempt to participate fully in the divine, he moves through the drama of figuration and disfiguration that makes his world double. Neither of these worlds has been there before. Both of them emerge only insofar as they are invoked in the acts of the saint who imitates a paradigmatic form that puts itself in an abject position and challenges the world with its seemingly natural face in multiple ways.

It is the saint in his acts of prayer—the core of his practice while standing on the pillar—who thus produces the series of images that start to infect, occupy, and transform the world, turning themselves into the lens that makes the historical nature of his surroundings emerge, not unlike the world in Hieronymus Bosch's famous painting *The Temptation of Saint Anthony*, as the figural realm of abject pleasures, evil seduction, and empty promises. As Simón's reenactment of the exemplary pillar saint shows, the practice of assimilation itself gives the world this double face. It makes the demons appear, which start to inhabit the world and turn it into a landscape of disfiguration. They appear when the figures are taken as forms of true representation of the holy, turning it into an object and thus foreclosing all participation. The man on the pillar, abandoned in prayer, makes prayer the origin of demonic disfiguration wherever it turns into the production of an image of holiness.

In the case of Buñuel's *Simon of the Desert*, the underlying textual, historical, imaginary reference is not only the story of the desert father standing on his pillar but another figure, a figure much more potent in the history of figuration, staging of the body, and—in more general terms—the complicated relationship between control, transgression, temptation, and the imitation of a formal example. I am speaking of the figure of Saint Anthony, a saint well-known through innumerable representations of the legendary scene of him enduring temptations while meditating in the desert. We encounter him, since the late Middle Ages and up to Max Ernst's surrealism, in paintings as he sits and meditates in the middle of a worldly scene that includes monsters of all kinds, lascivious creatures, naked women and men, in short, images of all possible forms of disfiguration and depraved sensuality. This legendary figure provides us with an exemplary script—not that the natural world is full of temptation but that the everyday world turns into a world of disfiguration and violence. It is Anthony's exercise, the specific framework of exemplarity and assimilation, that produces this very scene. Buñuel, who has always been fascinated by the story of Anthony, makes reference to this tradition when he portrays his modern ascetic in the form of the imitator, who in his emulation of an exemplary figure produces the sensual excess of both demonic and divine transgression. These transgressions challenge the everyday in similar ways.

In returning to the exemplary figures of Anthony and Christ in the desert, I find that prayer repeats these images, makes them alive in the imagination, and thus informs both his perception and the face of the world. What Saint Anthony produces is not, as one might think at first, a projection of demonic and holy moments onto the world. Instead, it is a world of disfiguration that necessarily joins all figural assimilation and its sedimentation in forms of representation. Assimilation, when detached from the partaking that acknowledges the utter asymmetry of the figural, produces the monsters that surround the saint and his world. It happens, both inside and outside him, when assimilation is bound by the gestures of mimetic practice alone. Thus, his struggle ultimately consists in challenging assimilation time and again and detaching himself from the images to allow for the participation he desires. His struggle is a never-ending fight with the images he inherits and the images he produces himself. As soon as they are taken for holy, they turn into demons who inhabit the world. The transfiguration itself, thus goes the teaching of the life of the saint, can never be seen as part of this assimilation in natural forms but only as a radical break with nature in an iconoclastic act of partaking.

Buñuel's fascination with the desert saint's immersion in excessive images of divine imploration and sensual temptation has its roots not only in the story of the saint, the surrealist tradition, and its use of dream language. It also points to the fascination of the surrealist and the decadent writers and artists with what we could call the abject forms of Christian sainthood and how these forms challenged the orderly view of "nature" by means of specific technologies of transfiguration.[4] One of the most influential authors in this line of thought is Joris-Karl Huysmans, mainly in his novel *À rebours*, in English translations with the titles *Against the Grain* or *Against Nature*.[5] In his *Studien zur Kritik der Moderne* (*Contributions to a Critique of Modernity*), published in 1894, the Viennese author Hermann Bahr quotes from this novel with an enthusiastic emphasis:

> We have to be able to hallucinate ourselves and to put the dream in place of reality. In the eyes of Jean des Esseintes, the artificial was the most remarkable quality of the human spirit. As he used to say: the time of nature has passed; the nauseating uniformity of her landscapes and heavens has exhausted the patience of the refined spirits.[6]

Referring to Jean des Esseintes, the protagonist of Huysmans's *Against Nature*, Bahr quotes the author of the text when he locates his hero in a "thébaide raffinée, . . . un désert confortable" (a refined Thebais . . . a comfortable desert),[7] thus evoking the very location, the desert of Thebais, where the ancient desert fathers sought refuge in an alternative world structured and produced by ascetic practices and prayer. In the case of Jean des Esseintes, a wealthy nineteenth-century decadent, this practice takes shape in a specific form. Des Esseintes moves into an isolated house in the countryside near Paris and makes this house the instrument of an entirely new world of self-fashioning that relies on the configuration of space, the organization of time, the choice of the furniture and art, the clothes of the servants, and the preparation of his meals. Huysmans himself compares Jean des Esseintes in his change of lifestyle to the monk who takes refuge in his cell in the desert, who removes himself from the world and allows for nothing else than an artificial production of states of mind and intensities of experience within a space clearly defined by architecture, texts, and specific artifacts. It is, indeed, an allegory of the world that has turned into figure. This does not mean, however, that the experience of the world or the intensity of exposure to it would decrease in this context. The contrary proves to be true: the figural simulacra; the production of living images; the artificial evocation of taste, touch, and smell form a sphere of exploration and education of the senses and of the passions in a specific way, meaning that sensation is not understood in the everyday form where it is bound up with the naïve empirical and utilitarian perception of things but rather in a form that allows for ever-new animations of sensation by figural means within specific frameworks of exercise and with specific movements that go back and forth in the sphere of suspension that emerges between the figures and the forms of assimilation.

In Huysmans's text, this takes shape in very concrete forms. Des Esseintes uses all kinds of tools to create his artificial world: aquariums with mechanical fish; images that evoke the bridge of a ship; sextants, compasses, chronographs; timetables and schedules of intercontinental shipping routes. Taken together, these things form a figural space that allows for an experience that removes itself from the natural experience of the world and cultivates an entirely new world of experiential intensity by means that Huysmans compares to the monk's use of images, texts, and scriptural quotes in the practice of prayer. Huysmans writes:

> In this manner, without ever leaving his home, he was able to enjoy the rapidly succeeding, indeed almost simultaneous, sensations of a long voyage; the pleasure of travel—existing as it largely does only in recollection and almost never in the present, at the actual moment when it is taking place—this pleasure he could savor fully, at his ease, without fatigue or worry, in this cabin whose contrived disorder, whose transient character and as it were temporary furnishings corresponded almost exactly with his brief sojourns in it, with the limited time spent on his meals, and which provided a complete contrast with his study, a permanent, orderly, well-established room, fitted out for the solid sustainment of a domestic existence.
>
> Besides, he considered travel to be pointless, believing that the imagination could easily compensate for the vulgar reality of actual experience. In his view, it was possible to fulfill those desires reputed to be the most difficult to satisfy in normal life, by means of a trifling subterfuge, an approximate simulation of the object of those very desires.[8]

This applies not only to taking a virtual cruise but also to travels by train and in general to all forms of lived experience. Jean des Esseintes's artificial world, better, the experience produced by the use of artifacts, seems at first to be a world of radical modernity. It makes use of the most innovative applications of electricity, hydraulics, and photographic reproduction, emphasizing in a decadent fashion the obsolete status of nature and, by way of this, of all naturalist literature. However, the modernist attitude barely hides a *longue durée*, a tradition of the use of technologies of figuration that is to be found in what the text itself hints at when the house of Jean des Esseintes is compared to the cell of the monk and to the desert. With Maurice Barrès, a contemporary of Huysmans and another favorite of the above-mentioned Hermann Bahr, we can follow the trace of this ascetic tradition and of its genuine antinaturalist potential, which is being rediscovered by the decadent authors. In *Un homme libre* (A free man) Barrès writes in 1889:

> If we knew how to produce the exact circumstances for the exercise of our faculties, we would be able to observe how our desires and our soul change and take shape. To create these circumstances, we do not have to use *reason* but a *mechanical method*. We have to surround ourselves with images—images we put between ourselves and the superfluous world and which have a strong impact. As soon as we do this, we push our sensations and emotions from excess to excess.[9]

What the invocation of sensation in this context of a "mechanical method" means is thus not a simple return to a sensualist or materialist ideology. It is neither the return to "nature" nor to an immediate presence, an ontology, a psychology, a phenomenology of first experience, or the "syncopation" of the sublime.[10] Instead, Barrès argues for a practice and technology of the production of sensation that reconfigures the attention to the world and the way in which the world encounters us, not as nature but as excessive play of figures and impressions, of assimilation and participation.

In their textual references, both Huysmans and Barrès—and after them Bahr and Buñuel—point to the tradition of prayer and spiritual exercises that I have portrayed. More specifically, they reevoke the techniques of a "composition of place" (*compositio loci*) and the "application of the senses" (*applicatio sensuum*) that figure in the writings of the founder of the Jesuit order, Ignatius of Loyola.[11] In his *Spiritual Exercises* he writes that these mental techniques are analogous to "taking a walk, traveling on foot, and running,"[12] and they are to be understood as forms of training along the same lines. In prayer and contemplation these techniques shape the body and the soul, providing it ultimately with a new habitus and ethos of the perception of the world. Thus, they help produce specific forms of spontaneity, of sensation, of experience, that have their origin not in nature but in the very practice of the spiritual exercises itself. As I have argued, we must speak of these exercises in terms of training and the production of images that allow for a creative alienation from everyday life;

for the specific intensity of both sensation and passion in assimilation; and for a moment of excess in participation. To do so, the Ignatian method relies on a practice that draws images from the Scriptures and other exemplary narratives, inserts these images as figures in the practice of prayer, and produces a state of sensual and affective absorption that then, in the moment of participation, turns into the perceptual shape of the soul and the flesh in the world.

Joris-Karl Huysmans's novel inherits from this Ignatian method both aspects, the construction of a space and the stimulation of the senses. Probably the most famous passage from the *Spiritual Exercises*, the meditation on hell, illustrates this practice.

Ignatius begins with the composition of place: "Here it will be to see in imagination the length, breadth, and depth of hell." Then he proceeds to the application of the senses:

> The First Point will be to see with the eyes of the imagination the huge fires and, so to speak, the souls within the bodies full of fire.
>
> The Second Point. In my imagination I will hear the wailing, the shrieking, the cries, and the blasphemies against our Lord and all his saints.
>
> The Third Point. By my sense of smell, I will perceive the smoke, the sulphur, the filth, and the rotting things.
>
> The Fourth Point. By my sense of taste, I will experience the bitter flavors of hell: tears, sadness, and the worm of conscience.
>
> The Fifth Point. By my sense of touch, I will feel how the flames touch the souls and burn them.[13]

In following this example, Huysmans constructs the spaces of experience that his protagonist explores, starting with the construction of a space and filling it with the figural stimuli that give a new shape to his senses and affects.

Disfiguration

As we have seen in the examples of Simón and Saint Anthony, this path of reshaping perception through assimilation and excessive participation entails a disfiguration of the world and an acknowledgment that the disfiguration, delving into the abject and disruptive, is a necessary aspect of the practice itself. Again, it is toward the end of the nineteenth century when we find a range of texts and images fascinated with the image of the temptations of the saint that illustrate this aspect. Among those, Gustave Flaubert's *La tentation de saint Antoine* (*The Temptation of Saint Anthony*), published after many revisions in 1874, is the most powerful and significant text. However, it was not well received by readers when it appeared. Barbey d'Aurevilly thought it to be "absolutely incomprehensible." Flaubert's friend Renan called it a "masquerade."[14] For Huysmans, though, it was the only text by Flaubert that is, as he points out, worthy to survive. Finally, Paul Valéry seems to have discovered the significance of the text for a broader audience. Valéry describes it in terms of a "physiology of temptation." He writes:

> It is obvious that all "temptation" results from things we see or things we imagine and the effect they have on us when they evoke a sensation of lack. . . . The devil . . . is nature itself, and temptation is the necessary, evident, and continuous condition of life itself. . . . We live in a lack of stability, through a lack of stability, by a lack of stability. This is the realm of sensibility. . . . What could therefore be more extraordinary and poetic than the attempt to put this irreducible constellation on stage?[15]

Valéry's remarks end with the observation that Flaubert's attempt to do this failed, ultimately, because he was not radical enough, situating the register of temptations within an encyclopedic repertoire and not the interiority of the saint. Thus, Valéry concludes, Flaubert's text ended up being not much more than a collection of diverse moments and a collage, not providing us, as he points out, with a glimpse into the depths of the figure of Saint Anthony.

I am arguing for a different reading. The moments of collage, the encyclopedic texture, the "masquerades" do not have to be understood as a poetic failure. Rather, they present a self-conscious attempt to base the temptations of Saint Anthony not in a sphere of interiority and in the natural depth of a historical character but in the superficiality and formalism of an encyclopedic repertoire and its aesthetic application. This self-conscious reading provides us with the possibility to see the temptations as a practice of masking and shifting masks and of figuration and disfiguration: in other words, as a rhetorical production of excessive sensuality inspired by the saint's life, the practice of contemplative prayer, and the deployment of figural effects in the face of the challenge of moving from mimetic assimilation to participation. The mechanical nature and seemingly superficial artificiality of the text, the most objectionable and despicable quality of Flaubert's *Temptation of Saint Anthony* in the eyes of many of its critics, can thus be seen as a strategy that avoids both the romantic depth of interiority and the tendency toward a rationalist naturalization of temptation, which Valéry seems to invoke. We deal here neither with a hermeneutics of innermost desires nor with a hermeneutics of nature but with a strategy that allows for an analysis of the "temptations of Saint Anthony" in terms of a dynamic of figuration and disfiguration. That is, in terms of a superficial and artificial animation through a set of formal moments, means, and masks that originate not in nature but in the cultural archive and in the encyclopedic repertoire provided by early monastic narratives. Saint Anthony is the one who in prayer returns to the Scriptures and to the narratives of exemplary figuration, who turns away from the world in prayer, and who thus evokes a world of images drawn from the scriptural archive that infects and reshapes the world that surrounds him. In imitating the figure of the follower of Christ, in imitating the figures of all the exemplary followers that precede him, however, he produces at the same time the disfiguration of the world—and the acknowledgment that each act of figuration is necessarily a disfiguration with regard to the participation and transfiguration he is looking for. He recognizes that each moment of assimilation, taken in itself and made into a state of being, obliterates participation and turns into an idol.

Although we can think of Flaubert's experimental text in terms of "physiology"—as Valéry suggests—I want to speak here of phenomenology and a phenomenological exploration of possible sensations and emotional arousal by the means of a multiplication of the figures, masks, and images that can be found in the history of the hagiography of Saint Anthony since its elaboration in the Middle Ages. In other words, we are, once again, dealing with a phenomenology of rhetorical effects. The fact that—in Valéry's view—Flaubert gets lost in a "sea of Scriptures, books, and myths" is not only the specifically modernist character of this text, as Michel Foucault emphasizes in his short reading of it.[16] Rather, Flaubert takes prayer seriously as the basic ascetic practice of citation, reconfiguration, insertion, and deletion of texts and images that the hagiographic tradition provides—a tradition of exercises that, in fact, locates the very origin of the experience of the saint in the highly formalized practices of a figural reading of the Scriptures. In using the term "physiology," we will have to keep this in mind. And indeed, the term is precise insofar as in many lives of saints the phenomenological exploration of possible states of arousal by means of figures is ultimately articulated in terms of a physiology and of a transformation of the flesh and the material world. The site of the effects is always the flesh of the saint and the surrounding world. However, it is never the natural body but rather the flesh as a space of articulation, formation, and transformation.

To understand this better, we have to remind ourselves that the inspiration for Flaubert's *Temptation of Saint Anthony* came from a painting he had seen on a trip to Italy in 1845. In his travel diary, Flaubert notes that he saw a version of Brueghel's painting of the temptation of Saint Anthony in Italy and that the impression it made overshadowed all the other memories of his travel. The painting shows Anthony surrounded by groups of surreal figures of temptation, often interpreted as images of the seven deadly sins and of seductive sensuality. We are used to reading this type of painting as a form of allegorical representation, a form of interiority turned outward and made visible in and through images. However, taking the artificial stimulation of the senses and emotions in contemplative practices into account, we are able to see this in a different light, not in terms of an allegorical representation or a didactics of enlightenment about unbridled inner forces but in terms of an infinite mechanical production and reproduction of states of sensation and affect through the ascetic practice of prayer. The exemplary nature of the temptation of Saint Anthony is thus not to be understood as a reiteration of a Stoic model of control of overwhelming sensuality and passions or as a therapy of the soul along neo-Stoic lines of self-fashioning. Rather, it confronts us with the production of a site and space where the passions and sensuality are configured in a dramatic way that necessarily evokes both the diabolical temptation and the divine transformation, the descent into hell (*descensus ad inferos*) and the ascent into heaven (*ascensus ad Deum*), disfiguration and transfiguration. Thus, in the example of Anthony, figuration is both the figuration in the form of an imitation of Christ that follows his image in similitude and the very disfiguration of the world as the abject place that is to be transformed through this practice of imitation.[17] In addition, each moment of the seemingly successful imitation, each act of following Christ and producing a semblance of his exemplary figure, proves itself in its failure to reach the ideal as a moment of disfiguration that asks for a new transformation. Thus, figuration itself turns into an abyss where all imitation, all gestures of following the figure, all moments of imitation, return into the realm of dissimilitude and drama in the face of the horizon of participation and excessive love.

The script for the dramatic evocation of sensuality and passion is to be found in the practices I have mentioned, in the arousal of an absorbing intensity of sensation, of hearing, seeing, smell, taste, and touch. This arousal is produced by a rhetoric that in the act of prayer draws from the archive of images and texts, which, in turn, take shape as the medium for both the world of diabolical temptation and the world of divine transformation. I am speaking of a dramatic script because it introduces a moment of irreducible tension into the model of sensual stimulation discussed previously. The return to the Scriptures in prayer, that is, the use of citations from the cultural archive for the stimulation of excessive sensation, can in itself never be "pure." It can only be "purified" time and again, acknowledging life as "impure." Thus, it must be dramatic in moving through the abject position of hell, through the disarticulation of nature and the evocation of all possibilities of temptation so that the transfiguration toward the divine excess and the overcoming of all self can take place. The monastic *gymnasía*, training and practice, produces a formal aesthetics of inhabiting the realm of evil—of the abject, transgressive, disarticulate bodies—that necessarily joins the aesthetics of the divine. As I argue, both are antinaturalist, since they both depend on a rhetoric of figural excess that starts with a state of defamiliarization and a reconfiguration through artifacts. This complex engagement with nature is the reason that Ignatius uses the experience of hell in his *Spiritual Exercises*, and it is the reason that Giles of Assisi, one of the early companions of Saint Francis, says that he expects his daily martyrdom when he goes back to his cell to meditate and pray. Both make reference to the dramatic plot drawn from the life of Saint Anthony when they discuss the structure of their life of prayer in the cell. This, to be clear, is the contrary of any Stoic scenario of self-discipline and self-fashioning insofar as it is based not on a repression of inordinate desire, sensation, and passion but on the active evocation of the irreducible conjunction of self and world, the disfiguration that permeates assimilation, and the transfiguration in the participatory excess.

In this training of the hermit, there can no longer be stable interiority or exteriority. Instead, we encounter practices of imitation that allow for the production of certain states of sensation and emotion that always dissolve the conventional borders of self and cosmos. Obviously, in the medieval tradition this dissolution is—demonstrated most prominently by the transfiguration of Saint Francis and emphasized by Erich Auerbach in his notion of mimesis—framed by the ultimate image, the image of the suffering Christ that guides this production. At the same time, however, this paradigmatic image, its irreducible figurality, and its projection into historical time throw the monk or the nun in his or her daily practice back into the imagery of sensual drama time and again, since this is the place the monk or the nun inhabits without ever being able to leave it behind. The excess toward the divine thus always bears the trace of the excess of temptation, as long as we live in time. Giles testifies to this when he speaks of his return to the contemplative exercise in his cell as a return to the battle with demons. Thus, he foregrounds that the effort to transfigure the world into a realm of divine peace and resemblance (the *regio similitudinis*) in its very desire for a stable image necessarily evokes terror and dissemblance, the emergence of dissimilitude (the *regio dissimilitudinis*), the disfiguration that challenges any figuration that attempts to be one with the formal image of salvation. Consequently, the world turns monstrous and is recognized as monstrous when Anthony imitates Christ. It emerges in its unredeemable historicity, in its radical dissimilitude, when the saint challenges it in his efforts and ethos of ideal figuration.

It is not at all surprising that pornographic novels from Pietro Aretino to *Thérèse philosophe* and the Marquis de Sade's *Justine et Juliette* reiterate not only the means of sensual stimulation, images and words inherited from this spiritual tradition, but the very logic of this practice of excess, the ever-new return to assimilation and temptation so that it can be transcended in participatory excess. It would be too facile to speak of parody. Although we might concede that we deal with an inversion of the elements that frame the monastic practice, humility and love, we nevertheless have to acknowledge that both the aesthetics of evil and the antinaturalist emphasis on the excessive and endless refiguration of the senses and passions are shared in a most significant way. In early pornography, as well, the art of dramatic evocation and *gymnasía* is deeply indebted to the script provided by the life of Saint Anthony and to the monastic practice of artificial arousal. As in the life of Saint Anthony and in its decadent refashioning, the moments of transgression do not present themselves as allegories of intensity alone but as moments that have their place within specific frameworks of figural production. They do not present us with a hermeneutics of the self and of hidden desires but with practices of dramatization, evocation, and phenomenological exploration of possible states of arousal beyond the body of social contracts.

Enumeration

The life of Buñuel's Simón and of Flaubert's Anthony is a life of prayer drawn according to exemplary texts and ascetic lives. In and through prayer they give shape to their life, and in prayer the figure of Simón turns into the "sublime" aesthetic existence it is in the eyes of others. Thus, Buñuel refers not only to the historical significance of prayer in the lives of monks and ascetics, but he also points to the importance of the poetics of prayer in a specific aesthetic tradition. Prayer is, as I have shown, intimately connected with the production of exemplary images, with a formal practice of figuration and disfiguration, with a mechanical art of engaging the imagination and affects. As David of Augsburg puts it in his treatise *The Seven Steps of Prayer*, prayer is the very "knocking" on heaven's doors (quoting the "knocking at the door" from Matthew 7:7 and Luke 11:9):

> When he tells us to pray, God does not mean that we should tell him with our words what we wish, since he anyway already knows what we need before we ask him for it. He rather means that we should *knock*. Through knocking we experience how sweet and good he is and thus we love him and join him in love and become one spirit with him.[18]

Said differently, prayer is a practice that—even in the acts of exemplary imitation—has to empty itself of all mimetic content, and anything that humans believe or hope for is not essential to it. Instead, the essence of prayer lies with the act of knocking, the form of repetitive address that produces an experience and thus a realm of qualities that emerge in that very practice. It comes as no surprise, then, that in many medieval mystical and ascetic treatises and texts the practice of prayer is guided by numbers and enumeration, making the act of imitation through prayer an act of elaborate existential repetition and variation. Relevant texts, for example, Mechthild of Magdeburg's *Das fliessende Licht der Gottheit* (*The Flowing Light of the Godhead*), speak of the "four invocations of God," the "five-fold praise of his power," the "seven-fold answer of the soul," and similar arrangements of invocation.[19] Thus, they construct a formal pattern, a schematic approach, that guides the act of prayer and emphasizes a rhythmical element. Simón and Anthony, who both imitate exemplary models of sanctity, are absorbed in this formal act of repetition and variation, of an imitation of the example through the seemingly endless reiteration of the same act of prayer, the endless "knocking" mentioned by David.

Often, the numerical repetition, accumulation of prayers, and acts of penitence have been read and understood in terms of the desire to quantify ascetic efforts and to produce the necessary capital for a personal and universal salvation.[20] And indeed, the thought that through the accumulation of prayers and ascetic acts humans could acquire a trove of grace is one of the important historical aspects of this very practice. This does not, however, explain the significance of numbers, numbering, and enumeration in texts of prayer during the Middle Ages. Other explanations of the role of numbers and numbering in these texts usually refer to medieval numerology or to the symbolism of numbers. Again, this does indeed play a role in certain cases. Often, such a symbolic meaning can be found even in cases that are not as obvious. However, the function of numbers, numbering, and enumeration in prayer goes beyond both the symbolic meaning and the accumulation of grace. Numbering and enumeration acquire a specific role, which is intimately connected with the emergence of images and the absorption through images that Buñuel's and Flaubert's examples of practicing saints present.

In her book, Mechthild of Magdeburg explores the possibilities of the function of numbering in prayer in prominent and exemplary ways. Many of her short texts—prayers, addresses to God, dialogues—contain numbers. In the first chapter of her book, she speaks of "God's Curse in

Eight Things," God's praise "in Ten Things" and "for Five Things," God's caress "in Six Ways," and the return to God "in Six Ways." The rhetorical procedures she relies on in the manufacturing of her texts are *partitio* and *enumeratio*, which in classical rhetoric serve as means of introduction of a series of points that will be treated in the course of a speech. In Mechthild's text, however, enumeration does not have an introductory or explanatory function. Instead, the numbering provides a frame, an underlying formal structure, which in turn serves the purpose to organize a series—and ever-new such series—of scriptural quotes, images, and other elements of her prayer. Speaking of and to God, she writes under the heading "God Caresses the Soul in Six Ways":

> You are my softest pillow,
> My most lovely bed,
> My most intimate repose,
> My deepest longing,
> My most sublime glory.
> You are an allurement to my godhead,
> A thirst for my humanity,
> A stream for my burning.

Then, "The Soul Praises God in Return in Six Ways":

> You are my resplendent mountain,
> A feast for my eyes,
> A loss of myself,
> A tempest in my heart,
> A defeat and retreat of my power,
> My surest protection.[21]

Many of the lines and expressions she uses in these and other similar texts are, once again, drawn from the Scriptures and her readings of the lives of saints. The numbering, however, is hers, and neither is it symbolic nor does it intend to accumulate a trove of grace through the numbers of prayers. Instead, the use of the formal pattern of enumeration allows her to connect figures and tropes, to convey a mechanics that gives shape to her existence, to produce a metonymical structure that holds the metaphors together. The order—one, two, three, four, five—underlies the images with the formal structure, generating a series, allowing for semantic explorations, permutations and variations, rhetorical amplification, and the transformation of the life of her soul into an imitation of exemplary scenes that inform her affects and perception. The contiguity between the elements she uses, however, does not result from the semantic connection between these elements. Instead, it lies with the numbering, the enumeration alone. It provides the mechanics, the formal pattern, David of Augsburg's "knocking," which in turn allows for the iteration and reiteration of images and words drawn from the sources she uses. Thus, she deploys the figural effects of the images and words, their potential to arouse sensually and emotionally, undoing the world as we know it, binding the aesthetic effects through the abstract framework of praying by numbers, and allowing for ever-new metonymical series of substitution and poetic variations in the absorption in prayer. Ultimately, she works through the tension of assimilation and participation, forming a network of similitudes that in their numerical form produce a possible excess in an infinite series of moments of participation.

In their return to models of ascetic exercises, both Buñuel and Flaubert bring the mechanical and material nature of such practices to our attention. They point to the radical formalism of medieval ascetic practices and contemplative prayer, which, I am arguing here, is also at the basis of an important aspect of medieval aesthetic experience. Thus, it does not come as a surprise when Huysmans portrays his protagonist Jean des Esseintes as a reader of Jan Ruusbroec and other medieval devotional authors.[22] In this case, returning to these texts does not stand for a return to a "Platonic" aesthetics of beauty or primarily to a "Christian" aesthetics of salvation but for a rediscovery of medieval practices of prayer, enumeration, and amplification, of figuration and disfiguration that are inspired by a basic model of formal imitation.[23] What we are drawn into with this model—the very practice of prayer—is much more than a gesture of devotion, praise, and submission or a "real presence of the sacred."[24] It is a formal exercise, a mimetic repetition, an art of figuration that is meant to inform the workings of perception, to alienate sensation and emotions, and to immerse them in artificial states that both negate and reveal the natural and historical face of the world. The "sublime" of Simón's asceticism is—and I guess that the monk who watches his example knows this as well as Buñuel, Flaubert, and Origen—as much demonic as it is divine, as much the production of an aesthetics of evil and ugliness as it is the production of good and beauty. And it is not a "syncopation," a radical break with modes of presentation in an absorption into the sublime but an assimilation to all forms of beauty and ugliness, joy and abjection, and joy in abjection, in a movement that runs through all forms of analogies produced through this practice of figuration. In ultimately negating the power of assimilation and in recognizing that all stable representation is demonic, it is the abject position of self-negation—in the cell, in the desert, on the pillar—that comes to stand for the ground of participation and the acknowledgment of the radical asymmetry that it entails.

Delay

Since the emergence of medical psychopathology in the nineteenth century, Christian lives of saints, ascetics, and mystics—particularly Saint Anthony, Hadewijch, Mechthild of Magdeburg, Angela of Foligno, and Teresa of Ávila—have, specifically in their endless joy in abjection and self-negation, often been read as exemplary "masochistic" and "hysterical" narratives. Acts of mimetic assimilation—of mortification, self-mutilation, self-exposure, and radical surrender in a desire for an unreachable fulfillment that dwells in enumeration and delay—lent themselves to views that emphasized such readings. They regularly focused on the "sexual psychopathology" of religious devotion that produces this abject position. Thus, to name just a few examples, moments and episodes from the lives and texts of the Spanish sixteenth-century nun and mystic Teresa of Ávila and of the medieval mystics Hadewijch of Antwerp, Angela of Foligno, and Henry Suso have been interpreted quite regularly in terms of "perverse sexual desire," "hysterical extravagance," and "masochistic" pleasure.[25] What these readings miss is not only the highly experimental character of the scenes of surrender and the elaborate rhetorical structure of their presentation in religious and devotional texts. It is also, and this is maybe more significant, the very cultivation of an art of desire and arousal through the play with figures and forms of assimilation; the art of a highly self-conscious practice of love and joy in participation; and the construction of desire in terms of techniques of delay that escape the modern frameworks of teleological normativity and naturalistic concepts of desire.

Building in part also on a more recent body of works on masochism,[26] I am speaking of an art here since the very term we encounter in the premodern context of this cultivation of love, submission, and suffering is a notion of *artificium*, a basic understanding of religious practice that not only engages "nature" but—as we have seen—intends to reconfigure, transform, and transfigure it. This is the case in medieval techniques both of prayer and meditation and of bodily practices of self-abnegation that are meant to support these techniques and express their necessarily embodied character. Such practices are based on a form that Gilles Deleuze and Félix Guattari called a "conceptual persona,"[27] which in these contexts quite often is identical with the exemplary figure of the saint and the martyr. Saint Anthony, Simón, and Mechthild emulate exemplary lives, saints, and biblical figures. Here, the conceptual persona "simultaneously negotiate[s] the territory of body and thought,"[28] and it forms the basis of the articulation of states of sensual and affective intensities in the religious practices that modern psychopathology calls "masochistic."

I will focus not on the "psychological" character of "masochistic" practices and their genealogy in religious cultures of devotion but on their conceptual, rhetorical, and aesthetic nature; on their form as technologies of the self; images of figural production; material mimesis; and undoing of the natural world that evoke and produce, configure and reconfigure desire and pleasure. They do this in seemingly endless chains of exemplary arrangements of surrender and arousal, figural assimilation, and participatory excess. These arrangements not only imply historical and psychological configurations of power and identity,[29] cruelty and subjectivity,[30] and gendered economies,[31] but more prominently specific aesthetic, sensual, and affective negotiations of desire.

The genealogy of "masochism" is thus, at least in its premodern history, to be seen as a practice of aesthetic embodiment, which is—maybe paradoxically—based on a negation of and a withdrawal from eschatological temporality. Instead of an orientation toward absolute fulfillment or toward its teleological counterpart in modern discourses on "normal sexuality," the figure of the "religious masochist" cultivates an aesthetic—experiential, sensual, emotional, and imaginative—relation to matter and form that transforms the linear structure of time in arrangements of delayed satisfaction and in rhythmical patterns of sensual and affective intensities.

This aesthetic takes shape as a critique of established and accepted teleological forms of desire, religious salvation, or sexuality and as a construction of new configurations of body and soul. It does so, I am arguing, inspired by Chris L. Smith's work on Gilles Deleuze, in "an artisanal mode of production" that complicates the Aristotelian hylomorphic understanding of the relationship between matter and form.[32] In his analysis of Deleuze's thoughts on masochism Smith writes that it is a specific "mobility" that "fosters the deployment of the masochist as the conceptual persona of the critique of hylomorphism" and that "promotes a very different understanding of the form-matter relation than that of hylomorphism."[33] Thus, and in spite of the importance of the imitation of forms and images that I outline later, within the masochistic scenario and the scenario of suffering invented by mystical authors "form does not arrive from a transcendent realm as an 'external act.'" Instead, it "involves an enfolding of both the bodies' material itself and the subsequent acts of working that material."[34]

This enfolding is to be understood in the utterly concrete terms of practices of figuration, which, moving through forms of assimilation, produce the excessive force of participatory experience. In the acts of surrender images of a teleological orientation of desire toward forms of fulfillment are replaced by conceptual, imaginative, and physical practices of assimilation that disperse the intensities of sensation and affect over the body and destroy simple matter-and-form or body-and-soul distinctions—akin to the forms of enumeration in Mechthild's texts—in favor of the inherence of possible forms of arousal, intensity, and pleasure in the indeterminacy of the life of the flesh:

> The body suggests how it wants to be worked: folds in the body are sown; openings tied shut; and taut skin whipped. This is not to isolate or identify folds, openings or taut flesh but rather to disperse the intensity of specific sites to the body as a reconfiguring. It is the differentiation of desire and pleasure that is at stake for the masochist—to swell with desire. Pleasure is aligned with feeling and desire with affect in that pleasure is bound with processes of internality, of constituting a self, where desire is that which exceeds the self. . . . This point is . . . described as the limit-state of supersensualism: a body populated only by intensities, becomings.[35]

In this "cultural state of transmuted sexuality,"[36] nothing else happens than the exploration of virtual forms that inhabit the material of the body and soul and that find their expression in the realm of possibilities that we call "soul" (or, as in the previous quote, the realm of "supersensualism," of "that which exceeds," of that which "swell[s] with desire"). The practices of so-called masochistic surrender and exposure explore a sphere of possibilities that they themselves make emerge in a realm where body and soul can no longer be distinguished. These practices produce, in the very surrender they evoke in the play through figuration and disfiguration, the exposure to the possibilities of pleasure, which, in the very negation of any eschatological fulfillment, turns, when the whippings are being counted, into the pleasure of delay itself, the joy in the abject position where dissolution and affirmation, disfiguration and transfiguration, converge.

The aesthetic that this engenders is nothing else than a rhetoric of endless variation or, to be more precise, of variation that provides pleasure insofar as the masochist figures himself or herself through the establishment of a "conceptual persona" as the seemingly passive site of the production of this endless play of variations and intense figurations, and consequently we should speak here of a culture of arousal and participation instead of a defined form of sexuality. Indeed, sometimes sexual acts can become thematic in these practices; sometimes they are utterly insignificant. The masochist, however, is the embodiment or the incarnation of the rhetorical principle of the pleasure of variation insofar as he or she surrenders to the powers of figuration without putting an end to it. In doing so, the masochist is the exemplary figure in what we could call a phenomenology of figural effects. That is, the exploration of an exposure to means of stimulation that produce and evoke the possibilities of sensation and affect where body and soul fold into each other time and again in this assumption of an abject position.

Surrender

As we know from the life of Teresa of Ávila and from many other lives of saints, ascetics, monks, and nuns, the basic gestures of their taking on this abject position consists in practices of reading, imitation, and figuration. For Teresa, the very act of reading is an act of surrender in and through which she figures herself as a site of desire and figural play. Thus, from the earliest pages, the text of her *El libro de la vida* (*The Life Written by Herself*) is marked by a desire for imitation and martyrdom: the martyrdom of unfulfilled romantic love in her earliest childhood admiration for courtly novels; the martyrdom of Christian love in her desire for the imitation of those who died for the love of Christ; and finally, the martyrdom of her mystic love in the drama of the life she produces in her autobiography. In each case, she abandons herself in giving herself up to the power of figures. At first, Teresa writes, "she was very fond of books of chivalry" and "she became addicted to this reading."[37] More decisive, however, was the reading of the lives of saints:

> I had one brother almost of my own age, whom I loved best. . . . We used to read the lives of the Saints together, and when I read of the martyrdoms which they suffered for the love of God, I used to think that they had bought their entry into God's presence very cheaply. Then I very fervently longed to die like them, not out of any conscious love for Him, but in order to attain as quickly as they had those joys which, as I read, are laid up in Heaven. I used to discuss with my brother ways and means of becoming martyrs, and we agreed to go together to the land of the Moors, begging our way for the love of God, so that we might be beheaded there. I believe that our Lord had given us courage enough even at that tender age, if only we could have seen a way. But our having parents seemed to us a very great hindrance.[38]

In a series of configurations and transformations Teresa explores and proves this love, emphasizing the very fact that her desire takes shape in forms of imitation that turn from chivalric love to the desire "of becoming martyrs," "hermits," and of "pretending to be nuns" during her childhood.[39] What we are dealing with in these passages from Teresa's adolescent memories is at the basis of all the other metamorphoses she describes in her *Life*. The different moments are structured in a way that mirrors the desire for love and for a violent suffering, for battle, for the enactment of and the assimilation to the model provided by the stories of martyrdom. Based on this, the mimetic gesture that inspires her acts of figuring herself will be able to accentuate the fact not that she is a follower or believer but mainly that she, in enacting an abject position, is above anything else a lover of God and thus a witness who follows the example of the martyrs. The martyr is the conceptual persona she wraps herself around, the exemplary image that she submits to and that enables Teresa to generate her world of sensation and affect.

In her *Life*, the violence that qualifies the martyr as an exemplary imitator of Christ at first takes shape in dramatic encounters of temptation, seduction, and deception, on the one hand, and moments of sweet consolation, on the other. These events and encounters, moments in her intense experience of a drama of love, present challenges she will be able to overcome only in suffering a violent symbolic death, the *mors mystica* of her ecstatic experience of the love of God in the abandonment to the absolute asymmetry of the figure of Christ. Once again, assimilation turns into participation. Depicted in form of a visionary experience with a deeply carnal component, this ecstatic suffering of death, the end of her self, is the ultimate moment of unity that has been most memorably—and most theatrically—represented in the sculpture of the ecstatic Teresa created by Gian Lorenzo Bernini in Santa Maria della Vittoria in Rome around 1650. The sculpture is based on the following passage from her *Life*:

> Our Lord was pleased that I should sometimes see a vision of this kind. Beside me, on the left hand, appeared an angel in bodily form, such as I am not in the habit of seeing except very rarely. . . . His face was so aflame that he appeared one of the highest ranks of angels, who seem to be all on fire. They must be of the kind called cherubim, but they do not tell me their names. . . . In his hands I saw a great golden spear, and at the iron tip there appeared to be a point of fire. This he plunged into my heart several times so that it penetrated to my entrails. When he pulled it out, I felt that he took them with it, and left me utterly consumed by the great love of God. The pain was so severe that it made me utter several moans. The sweetness caused by this intense pain is so extreme that one cannot possibly wish it to cease, nor is one's soul then content with anything but God. This is not a physical, but a spiritual pain, though the body has some share in it—even a considerable share. So gentle is this wooing which takes place between God and the soul that if anyone thinks I am lying, I pray God, in His goodness, to grant him some experience of it. Throughout the days that this lasted . . . I had no wish to look or to speak, only to embrace my pain, which was a greater bliss than all created things could give me.[40]

The spear that pierces Teresa's flesh brings together desire and pain, violence and love, and quotes the model of martyrdom as the ultimate moment of authentic faith and love. In her presentation of this scene, the imaginary vision of the Carmelite nun is the perfect simulation of martyrdom. It incorporates the violence in spiritual and bodily ways, and it responds to the fact that martyrdom is not to be experienced in the historically concrete form of literal sacrifice. The mimetic repetition of martyrdom, we conclude after reading the exemplary scenario of her ultimate sacrifice granted by God, has its place only where she succeeds at enacting and writing her life as a simulacrum, a perfect assimilation, and thus to prove the authenticity of her love in the very act of surrender. Both the experience and the act of writing are the place where her desire for literal martyrdom takes shape in the form of a drama that is at the same time spiritual and corporeal.

In the face of this act of transference, in the shift from the historical and factual martyrdom to the simulacrum and the act of writing, the visionary imagination, and the production of her own martyrdom in her experience, we see a virtual martyrdom that she enacts in the figurations of herself. The martyrdom consists of acts of purification and mortification, *purificatio* and *mortificatio*, enacted at the same time on her body and her mind—acts that again produce an exemplary scene of the experience of violent pain and delightful love. In calling this construction a "virtual martyrdom," I argue that this form of experience is to be seen as virtual insofar as it is not to be understood in extensive terms but rather in terms of sheer intensity. This does not mean that the experience of violence and its capacity to testify to the fact of martyrdom is less real. Rather, it is localized in a new way, putting the emphasis not on a literal meaning of the historical fact and the report of martyrdom but on a theatrical space of intense embodiment where the originary violence—the violence experienced by Christ and the martyrs—can take shape and can be figured time and again in actual and concrete scenarios of submission. These scenarios are wrapped around the conceptual persona of the martyr, the central figure, which, in turn, generates ever-new possibilities of figuration. Surrender is the basis of this enactment since only acts of submission open up the space for a participation in love and the recognition of the asymmetry of the divine Teresa is looking for. In offering herself to the divine figure, she creates the empty site that allows for the deployment of the stimuli, the rhetorical means, the scenarios that make her into the martyr of love. This deployment is the function of the *visio imaginativa*, the visionary imagination through which Teresa succeeds at making herself into a simile of the martyrs she attempts to emulate. It ends, here in the scene of violent rapture, when her participation obliterates all forms of assimilation.

Experiment

Once again, in performing this exercise of surrender Saint Teresa follows a tradition of exemplary texts, echoing among other sources the desire of Saint Francis for martyrdom. From that point of view, the experience of her own violent union with God is analogous to the stigmatization of Francis, and we can read Teresa's ecstatic suffering as a specific reenactment of this exemplary scene. It enters a chain of exemplary texts that call for imitation and a refiguration of the moments of surrender. Her *Life* draws from the topoi of surrender that she inherits from the tradition of lives of saints and martyrs, and it also provides the archive of the topoi of surrender with new forms of enactment and figuration. As a document of "masochism," it testifies to the intricate logic of the construction of sites of pleasure and desire, a construction based on the moment of surrender that allows for the deployment of the arts of figuration that produce instances of affective and sensual intensities.

In producing these moments of intensity, Teresa's text cannot be explained in terms of a literary tradition of religious hagiography alone. It is also deeply entrenched in violent traditions of religious practices—practices, I want to emphasize, that go beyond the purely mimetic gestures and acts of symbolic imitation inspired by the reading of hagiographic texts. In her dramatization of the very acts of imitation and participation she points to the fact that the incorporation of the violence experienced by the martyrs is essential to her religious life because—at least in her own eyes—it is only through this incorporation that she turns into a real witness to the asymmetry of love.

Because she is never able to fully reach this moment, the practice she engages in is necessarily a strategy of delay inspired by an eschatological reservation. Not the sudden transition into a state of satisfied and fulfilled desire is at stake here but the love that she intends to cultivate. This love itself, one might say, realizes the very delay of eschatological satisfaction, the active exploration of possible figurations, and the transformation of the world. Although we do indeed encounter moments of fleeting ecstatic union with the divine and of a mystical emphasis on a here and now that fully absorbs her, the text shows otherwise. It produces the conceptual persona of a person who makes herself into the stage for the figuration of martyrdom, for the figuration of suffering, and who thus explores the affective and sensual intensities that this very art of figuration is able to provide. The negation of the eschatological resolution is thus the very condition of possibility that allows her to explore the forces of these processes of figuration, which, in turn, are the only thing that can give shape to the sensations and affects that constitute a love that can be as true as the love of the martyrs. Most explicitly, participation, the end of all assimilation, is presented here as its very condition of possibility. The ultimate absorption in love, akin to Hugh of Saint Victor's state of "pure prayer," turns into the moment that grounds all assimilation.

According to Teresa's *Life*, ascetic suffering, the practice and art of passion, is an evocation of and a return to the realm of aesthetic possibility. Thus, not surprisingly, Gilles Deleuze writes in his essay *From Sacher-Masoch to Masochism*: "It is when the senses take works of art for their objects that they become masochistic for the first time."[41] In Teresa and other mystic or devotional authors of premodern times, we discover the genealogy of this practice with regard to both the work of the senses and the dramatic setup of the sensual, affective, and cognitive life. What they "take for their objects" are indeed "works of art," although not in the modern sense. Instead, they focus on the lives of saints and martyrs to which they surrender in acts of imitation, in other words, in practices of disfiguration and figuration that give shape to the life of the senses and the affects and set percepts, affects, and concepts in ever-new circulation.

The movement at stake in Teresa's practice of submission can be characterized, once again, as a denaturalization of the senses—the transition from the literal and empirical to the spiritual and supernatural—and a reconfiguration and renaturalization, a return to the intensity of sensory and emotional experience of the world beyond meaning and assimilation. This takes place in the form of an aesthetic experience constructed with the help of a specific emphasis on practices of figuration within the scenario of ultimate submission. As I pointed out previously, the devotional theory of the reform of sensation is a response to the desire for experience of the divine in light of the impossibility to understand it, that is, of a radical negative theology. This practice is also the basis for Teresa's imitation of martyrdom. The spiritual martyrdom she cultivates entails the transgression of the natural state of soul and body in acts of utter surrender. These acts form the basis for the deployment of the force of figuration, that is, the force of the rhetorical means that she draws from the texts, the Scriptures, and the lives of saints to produce moments and states of intensity. The site of surrender turns thus into a site of experimentation with the forces of figuration, with the rhetorical stimuli that are available, and with the possibilities of arousal that infect the textures of the world and the flesh.

Rapture

"Rapture," Teresa of Ávila writes in her *Life* about the ultimate state of arousal in the convergence of submission and experimental figuration, "is, as a rule, irresistible. Before you can be warned by a thought or help yourself in any way, it comes as a quick and violent shock; you see and feel this cloud, or this powerful eagle rising and bearing you up on its wings." These "shocks are felt by the soul" and "by the body." In another passage she adds: "There are other times when the impulses are so strong that it can do absolutely nothing. The entire body contracts," while we "play no part, as I have said, in bringing a rapture on."[42]

As we have seen, though, this does not mean that the state of rapture and convulsion is not embedded in a poetics of exemplary images and figures used both to produce it and to describe it. The very key to the notion of passivity that Teresa evokes is to be found in the logic of surrender to the asymmetry of figures that ultimately replaces the idea of martyrdom. Not suffering itself, not the shedding of blood, not the pain is the goal of the practice but the production of a site that makes experimentation with and exploration of sensual and affective intensities possible. Thus, even rapture is not a state of eschatological fulfillment. It is a moment of absorption and participation when body and soul are in "shock," when they converge in this shock, when we "must risk everything," and when "outward" and "inward" become indistinguishable. It is, however, not a final moment in a linear and teleological line that leads from arousal to fulfillment or salvation. Instead, it is discontinuous, fragmented, a state of disturbance that returns into the temporal order of life and gives a new shape to it, folding it differently: "When one comes to one's senses, it sometimes happens, if the rapture has been deep, that for a day or two, or even three, the faculties are so absorbed or in such a state of stupor that they seem no longer to be themselves."[44]

Thus, after rapture has passed, the soul sees and feels itself and the world in a new way:

> The soul perceives man's blindness to the nature of pleasure, and his failure to realize that even in this life it purchases trials and disquiet. What restlessness! What discontent! What useless labor! Not only is the soul aware of the cobwebs that cover it, but the sunlight is so bright that it sees every little speck of dust besides, even the most minute. However hard it may have labored to perfect itself, therefore, once the sun really strikes it, it views itself as most unclean. It is like the water in a glass, which seems quite clear when the sun is not shining on it but, if it does, is seen to be full of tiny specks.[45]

Bare Figure

In this world "full of tiny specks," of "trials and disquiet" in the living flesh, late medieval mystical theology refers to the dramatic correlation of incarnation, imagination, and image.[46] In the writings of Teresa and, above all, Meister Eckhart, Johannes Tauler, and Henry Suso, the incarnation and birth of God is the theological notion and concept that brings all three terms into focus. More precisely, it is the birth of God in the soul, the partaking in the birth of God and in God's death, that is the focus of all creation as figuration, of all coming forth as an image, and of the very nature of God's creativity. This notion of incarnation—the ultimate example of *Ecce homo*—forms the ground for all practices of assimilation and participation. Thus, Eckhart writes: "God's chief aim is giving birth. He is never content till He begets His Son in us. And the soul, too, is in no way content until the Son of God is born in her."

He explains further:

> This [the birth] cannot be received by creatures in which God's image is not found, for the soul's image appertains especially to this eternal birth, which happens truly and especially in the soul, being begotten of the Father in the soul's ground and innermost recesses, into which no image ever shone, or power of the soul was able to look.

And going on with his explanation, Eckhart expresses an overarching tension between image and iconoclasm, imagination (*bilde, bildunge*) and dis-imagination (*entbilden*):

Therefore, you have to be and dwell in the essence and in the ground, and there will God touch you with His simple essence without the intervention of any image. No image represents and signifies itself: it always aims and points to that of which it is the image. . . . And therefore, there must be silence and a stillness, and the Father must speak in that, and give birth to his Son, and perform his works free from all images.[47]

As we can see from these quotations and from many other passages in Eckhart's works, his understanding of the incarnation is intimately linked to the coming forth as an image on the basis of similitude,[48] the very creation of all things, and the overcoming of the fallen state of the creation and of mankind in a form of apophatic dis-imagination. According to Eckhart, only the soul that frees itself from all determination by images and concepts is open to the birth of God and the relation of similitude with all creation that the notion of ground stands for. It is in this convergence of a freedom from images and the incarnation that humanity moves beyond all representational and signifying function of images, beyond all assimilation, and into participation in divine creativity—where all creation comes forth as "free images."

Building on a range of theological traditions and on the strong influence of the negative theology of Dionysius the Areopagite, this formulation of the concept of incarnation is not really surprising. It is, at its core, a reinterpretation of the idea that Mary's soul was ready to give birth to God insofar as she was like an empty, pure mirror (a "speculum sine macula" in Wisdom 7:26). In this immaculate state of mirroring the flow of divine creativity, Mary is seen as the exemplary figure who was able to receive the divine in her flesh and mirror it back into God and into the world. The figure of Mary became thus one of the paradigms for the convergence of incarnation theology and speculative mysticism.[49] On this basis Meister Eckhart puts a main emphasis on the freedom from representational images and on the rebirth as a free image, that is, on the fact that the incarnation—as the birth of God in the soul—is at the same time the apophatic liberation from all representational images,[50] the creation of mankind and the world in God's image, and the restoration of the very coming forth of creation as a "free" image beyond all representation in the pure immanence of divine creativity that the birth of Christ stands for.[51]

It must be emphasized here as well that Eckhart understands the incarnation not primarily as a historical event and as carrying forth an eschatological promise but as something that we could describe as the grounding structure of the soul in relation to itself, the world, and God. Thus, in his theory of the birth of God in the soul, he presents a theory of unity with the divine that thinks of redemption as happening here, now, and at all times. This coming forth of the divine in the form of an ultimate affirmation and unity of all multiplicity has to be uncovered through a praxis that Eckhart understands as "becoming virgin," a notion that he explores in terms of detachment and dis-imagination with a strong focus on the apophatic removal of all images from the discursive and cognitive life of the soul. It is his form of engaging the challenge of abjection and drama, also his way of leaving all assimilation behind. Thus, he writes in a sermon dedicated to a reading of Luke 10:38: "Now note the fact that it has to be a 'virgin' who receives him. 'Virgin' means someone who is free of all alien images, as free in fact as that person was before he or she existed."[52] Explaining this further, Eckhart applies the trope of the virgin to Jesus and develops a new understanding of the convergence between contemplative and active life, between Mary and Martha, and between man and God:

> I say further that the fact that someone is a virgin does not take anything away from the works they have done but rather leaves them free and virginal, unhindered with respect to the highest truth, just as Jesus is empty and free and virginal in himself. We too must be virgins if we are to receive the virginal Jesus since, in the view of the learned, the foundation of union is the meeting of like and like.[53]

For Eckhart, this articulation of a state of virginity is enacted in a practice of detachment, an elimination of images, and a self-emptying of the intellect and will. Intellect turns into the space of abjection, the pure possibility to become everything and to share the divine creativity where soul and intellect are not determined by anything else. Eckhart interprets the incarnation through the prism of the virgin birth in a speculative way, privileging the emphasis on the very freedom of the intellect as the place of pure receptivity, divine participation, and creative unfolding in a spontaneous procession, a mirroring, of non-alienated images in their irreducible diversity.[54] Here, there is neither difference nor indifference between a leaf, a fly, a piece of wood, and God. Nothing is seen through the lens of mimetic assimilation; everything turns into a moment of sheer mirroring and participation.

Eckhart's student Henry Suso, however, and at first glance paradoxically, explains this very path of removal and of rejoining the creativity of the divine ground explicitly in terms of a specific investment of the soul in the world of images. While Eckhart insists on the purely negative and apophatic moves that focus on an engagement with images in which all images, concepts, and words are to be negated to uncover the participation in the birth of God, Suso emphasizes a quite specific engagement with image making and—more generally—practices of figuration. In doing so, Suso draws on Eckhart's negative theology, on his idea of detachment and of the unnamable ground of the soul, but he also reaffirms explicitly both the status of images in the world and of affects and sensations that are to be aroused by the images. Thus, he reevaluates the practices of assimilation. Engaging in a discussion with Meister Eckhart, he turns against the latter's strong intellectualist framing of iconoclasm and explicitly reaffirms a tradition of contemplative prayer and practices of figuration. He does so, possibly arguing against another school of readers of Eckhart, represented by the collection of sermons called *Paradisus anime intelligentis* (Paradise of the intelligent soul).[55]

Thus, in the writings and discussions of some late medieval theologians and mystics, the understanding of the incarnation turns into the very place of a specific evaluation and negotiation of the status of mimetic practices, of images and, as I will demonstrate further based on Suso's writings, of a specific understanding of the role of figuration. "Bare figure," used in this section title, refers not only to the representation of the incarnation in the figure of Christ on the cross but, more specifically, to Suso's attempt to move beyond Eckhart's apophatic challenge and its intellectualist emphasis. Instead of Eckhart's negation of all images, figures, and thoughts in view of a participation of the soul with the divine, Suso is invested in thinking the apophatic move as a key element of the poetics of figuration and imagination itself. To be clear, Suso does not withdraw from Eckhart's radical position when he turns this apophatic move into an essential moment of a transformative figural practice. Rather, in his understanding of the function of images the very act of including the apophatic moment in the practices of figuration makes an attempt to liberate images—and figuration in general—from being bound up with both the representational function and the allegorical meaning, in short, the naturalizing gestures that deprive images of their force. In pursuing this, Suso emphasizes the bareness of figures beyond all hermeneutics, drawing on the facticity and materiality of the incarnation—ultimately, the abject body on the cross, the *Ecce homo*[56]—as the formal ground of figuration itself.[57] We can thus conclude that for Suso the Eckhartian notion of detachment and dis-imagination turns into the core of a practice of figuration and assimilation. As a practice of dis-imagination, however, it does not return to a radical iconoclasm but, time and again, to the enactment of a point zero of the image in disfiguration and in the display of the suffering body of Christ.

Suso must be seen as an outstanding thinker of the problem of the image within the iconoclastic context of Eckhartian mysticism. We have to turn to him to understand what a theory of visual poetics can look like in the late Middle Ages, at least from the perspective of a group of radical Dominican theologians of the fourteenth century. Suso's is just one among many forms of visual poetics that emerge in the time span between Eckhart, Nicolaus Cusanus, and Ignatius of Loyola. With its strong references to Bonaventure, however, it is certainly the one that is intellectually most ambitious and that reflects aspects of significance in other traditions as well, most important, in the Franciscan schools of thought.[58]

As I am arguing here, Suso's emphasis on an engagement with images—in traditional terms, his notion of the movement through images beyond images—is significant in four ways. First, it addresses the question of representation, the critique of images, and the dis-imagination at the center of Eckhart's thought. Second, although it does defend the practical use of images in an allegorical way, it does not return to an exclusively allegorical mode that represents the life of the soul in the form of images inspired by biblical texts. Third, it also does not just present us with images that stand in or form a supplement for something unconceivable and unnamable that we are supposed to grasp or experience in a spiritualizing hermeneutics through the images we use. Fourth, it emphasizes that in the encounter with images as figures we find ourselves in a situation where sensations and affects move beyond allegorical levels of meaning and where perception takes shape before and beyond any hermeneutic engagement. In exactly this regard, the incarnation, the unity of man and God beyond all representation, turns for Suso into the condition of the possibility of a visual poetics that emphasizes the aspect of the bare figure as the ultimate and irreducible moment when the image gives shape to the life of the soul in partaking, making it part of the divine creativity that moves through the encounter of figure, soul, and flesh.

What Suso discusses and develops on the basis of Eckhart's incarnation theology is a highly articulated notion of the image and its reduction to the figural that forms our perception and that carries the soul beyond the realm both of assimilation and hermeneutics. According to Suso, the images produce a sphere where immanence and transcendence cannot be distinguished—a sphere of figural evidence and striking force that, in its utter asymmetry, no longer knows a difference between here and there, archetype and image, since all play with images necessarily moves back and forth beyond negation and position, apophasis and figural effects, assimilation and participation.

To explain his use of images Suso writes in his *Vita*, referring to a response he gave to a question raised by his "spiritual daughter," Elsbeth Stagel:

> His daughter said, "Sir, you have spoken from your own thinking and from sacred scripture very knowledgeably and in keeping with Christian teaching about the mystery of the naked Godhead, about the flowing out and the flowing back of the spirit. Could you outline for me the hidden meanings [the truth of the incarnation and the trinity], as you understand them, by concrete comparisons [*entwerfen mit bildgebender glichnus*]?" He said: "How can one form images of what entails no images or state the manner of something that has no manner (of being), that is beyond all thinking and the human intellect? No matter what one compares it to, it is still a thousand times more unlike than like. But still, so that one may drive out one image with another, I shall now explain it to you through images and by making comparisons, as far as this is possible."[59]

What Suso proposes here and in the following explanations is not just an iconoclastic path that opposes images to a detached state of being free of images and concepts, nor is it a path that leads from images to a state of sheer emptiness. Instead, Suso emphasizes the fact that only a specific animation of the life of the soul through images, comparisons, similes—that is, through the dramatic play with analogy and figure—produces the effect of both overcoming the "natural" power of images, of taking the multiple axes of subjugation into account, and of assimilating the soul to the bare figure of Christ. In this process of figuration—a process that entails the production of paintings as well as ekphrastic language—the assimilation and formation of the soul make her, as promised by the Scriptures, a participant in creation and incarnation by grace.

In Suso's eyes, the uncovering of what is understood as the hidden truth of both the Scriptures and creation does indeed depend on a visual poetics and a practice of assimilation. It is not to be found in refraining from the use of images and in turning to a hidden meaning but in a specific way of producing and using images. In his Latin works Suso speaks here of *figurata locutio* (figural speech), a form of speech that corresponds to the production of imaginative similes (*bildgebende glichnus*). It includes all uses of images, both in writing and in painting.

Often, this has been read as a way in which Suso defends the use of allegories in spiritual pedagogy. In my reading, however, I see Suso as the advocate of a specific poetics of image and figure that builds on theories of contemplation as aesthetic, sensual, and affective experience in order to move from a conceptual mode of spiritual truth to an experiential one or, to put it in different terms, from a representational understanding of images to a figural and experimental one. It finds its basic expression in the statement quoted earlier, that "one may drive out one image with another." Accordingly, images have to be denaturalized, deprived of their arresting status, to recover their force as figures that come forth, undo the modes of subjugation that images and concepts produce, and enact a transfiguration of soul and flesh.

Emphasizing the significance of images and imagination in contemplation, Suso writes in his *Little Book of Eternal Wisdom*:

> A Dominican friar was once standing before a crucifix after matins and was complaining keenly that he was not able to meditate on his [Christ's] torment and suffering (as it deserved), and that he found this especially trying because he had been very deficient in this to that very hour. As he was standing there lamenting, his inner senses were carried off in an unusual manner, and suddenly he was

clearly illumined within thus: "You should perform a hundred *veniae*, each one with its special meditation on my suffering and join to each meditation a petition. Each suffering shall be spiritually impressed upon you, with you repeating this same suffering to the extent you are able." And as he stood there in this illumination and wanted to count them, he found no more than ninety. Then he prayed to God thus: "Dear Lord, you spoke of a hundred, and I can find no more than ninety." Then ten more were pointed out to him, which he had previously practiced in the chapter room before following, as was his practice, his (Christ's) anguished path to death and arriving under this very crucifix. He found that the hundred meditations covered his bitter death very exactly from beginning to end. And when he had begun to practice them as he had been instructed, his previous insensitivity was transformed into heartfelt sweetness.[60]

He was "illuminated" to repeat the image contemplation together with prayers to amplify the rhetorical effect of both the images and the words. This practice—moving from assimilation to participation—transforms "his previous insensitivity . . . into heartfelt sweetness."

Suso continues:

Then he asked whether perhaps anyone else was experiencing this same difficulty of insensitivity and aridity while meditating on [Christ's] dear suffering, the source of all blessedness, so that such a person might also be helped by engaging in this practice and persevering in it until he too might be cured. This is why he wrote down the meditations and did it in German, because this is how they came to him from God.[61]

Suso's pedagogy of meditation and contemplation makes use of images and the work of the imagination not only in terms of a spiritual pedagogy that prepares the apophatic state of being without images that Eckhart postulates. Instead, he foregrounds that the very use of images produces an affective and sensual intensity and relation that open the movement from one image to the other, from the image to its negation and back to the image, and thus to the transfiguration through the image that sweetness and joy indicate. This is, in Suso's understanding, the very becoming-the-image-of-Christ according to the formulation of Galatians 2:20: "I am crucified with Christ: nevertheless I live; yet not I, but Christ liveth in me."

It is in this use of images, which addresses and undoes the modes of subjugation it produces, that one overcomes the "unfree multiplicity" and the old "self":

[One surrenders oneself] in happiness or suffering, in action or omission in such a way that one loses oneself completely and utterly, withdrawing from oneself irreversibly and becoming one in unity with Christ, so that one always acts at his urging and receives all things and views all things in this unity. And this detached self becomes the same form as Christ about whom the scripture by Paul says, "I live, no longer I, Christ lives in me." This is what I call a rightly valued self.[62]

This self is associated with the figure of Mary in an intimate way, emulating once again an image, in this case the image of the Pietà, as its key moment:

O pure and fair Mother, permit me, let me once more bring relief to my heart at the sight of your Love and my Lord, dear Wisdom, before the parting must come and he is carried off from us to the grave. Pure Mother, no matter how profound your sorrow was and how very deeply it may move all hearts, it still seems to me that you should somehow have found joy in lovingly embracing your dead Child. O pure, gentle Lady, I now beg you to lay your tender Child on the lap of my soul, as he looked in death, that I might experience in spirit through contemplation, as far as I can, what you then experienced physically.[63]

To understand the function of images and figures, of imagination and figuration in this process of transfiguration, we have to ask ourselves one more time how exactly Suso conceives of the process of going "through the images beyond the images" in becoming a "pure, bright mirror of the divine,"[64] that is, of the coming forth of the world in the form not of representation or meaning but of figure. In Suso's words: "How can one form images of what entails no images or state the manner of something that has no manner (of being), that is beyond all thinking and the human intellect?" For him, as he explains both in his German *Büchlein der Ewigen Weisheit* (*Little Book of Eternal Wisdom*) and in the parallel Latin *Horologium sapientiae*, images are a necessary element of the path toward the experience of the union with God and the transfiguration that make mankind an integral, non-alienated part of divine creativity. The very network of images, the shifting from positing to negation to repositing of the image as an efficacious figure leads one to "form the suffering of Christ crucified within oneself" so that, in this act of abject disfiguration, "exterior preoccupations disappear" and the soul, having resigned all intentionality, "becomes sensitive to what is supernatural" in the experience of "the constant inward flow of heavenly consolation."[65] The condition of the possibility of the figural efficacy of images is for Suso the incarnation and its relations, the word that becomes flesh in its very facticity, not our knowledge of it. It is the immanence of God in all creation, an immanence that can be brought forth in the life of the soul, in sensation, affect, and cognition through a specific encounter with images. The word that becomes flesh is the image that becomes figure and participation. Thus, images have to bring this very facticity to the foreground without being caught up in an instrumental function, be it representational or hermeneutic. Images are in fact the necessary element in this process of overcoming the very natural, instrumental, representational, and hermeneutic realm, and they do this first and foremost because they produce what Suso calls an *úbernatúrlich enpfintlichkeit* (a supernatural receptivity or sensibility) outside the orders of activity and passivity, transcendence and immanence. This abject position forms the basis for the formation (*in sich bilden*, to form within oneself) of Christ on the cross in the life of the soul.[66]

With Suso, we can thus identify several functions in the operation of the image: first, an allegorical function where images make the spiritual and hidden senses of the Scriptures graspable in forms of evidence through analogy, moving beyond the literal and historical sphere into the realm of the incarnational promise. This opens a sphere of affective and sensual assimilation that in its intensity exceeds the very act of contemplation. Meditation finds its support in a dense network of relations and of series of images deployed in a lively manner throughout the exercise of contemplative prayer. This, however, is not the ultimate moment in the use of images.

Second, and more important, images have an affective and sensual function insofar as they are sensually and emotionally arousing and absorbing. Suso refers to this in his own practice of prayer where he emphasizes that images help him overcome states of aridity and hopelessness. They do this not in view of a specific allegorical meaning but of the ways in which they move the soul and have an immediate impact on the sensual and the affective life, pulling it beyond the limits of understanding into a realm of affective and sensual absorption, acknowledging the bare facticity of suffering. Here, the figure of Christ has lost all meaning. It is nothing else than a moment of participation, the word that has become flesh and that is becoming flesh time and again in the multiplicity of suffering.

Finally, images produce a participation that brings the unity of the divine and the human, of word and flesh in the figure, to the surface. Speaking in a different idiom, we could argue that here the perceptions turn into percepts, the affectations into affect, absorbing the soul entirely into the image and making the figure the only form-giving principle of the life of the soul. The effect of the bare figure, in its exemplary form of Christ on the cross, is in this schema the very key to the transition from the assimilative mode to the emergence of the underlying unity that the image brings forth. The bare figure is also the key to understanding all other images since it foregrounds that understanding with the help of images does not mean to understand what they say, nor does it mean to grasp what they represent. Instead, the very use of the images neutralizes and negates these functions and abandons their force of constituting the "natural" realm in favor of the supernatural transfiguration of life. All images that Suso evokes converge in this experience of a transfiguration through the image where the soul no longer takes on the shape of the image but shares its constitutive ground, the creativity of becoming image both in its active and passive movements. Thus, Suso concludes: "The (ultimate) image is that one should form the suffering of Christ crucified within oneself, his sweet teachings, his gentle conduct, and his pure life, which he led as an example for us to follow, and thus through him press farther within."[67]

For Suso, the allegorical mode in which images represent and express the hidden senses of the Scriptures can be understood only in the participatory mode of the bare figure and concrete facticity. This incarnational form, the movement into the pure coming forth that redeems creation beyond all instrumental function and conceptual understanding, broken into abjection in the face of the world, creates the condition of the possibility to perceive the image as other than a representational tool that helps our conceptual understanding. Instead, the image turns into figure, into an expression of the creation itself, the brokenness that testifies to the monstrosity of subjugation to and of the world, and that brings everything into the spontaneous coming forth from the divine ground where word and flesh collapse. For Suso, this is realized time and again not in a radical step of transcending all images into an empty ground but in a process of image contemplation, of a dramatization where the very meaning and all similitude fall away, and where the image acts as that which gives shape to the life of the soul in an unhindered circulation of percepts, affects, and concepts.

In this, the image itself turns into figure and into the place of divine grace, challenging us to denaturalize our perception and thought and to engage in a practice of shedding our attachments to representation and signification. This dis-imagination that the image in its bare facticity performs on us is to be seen as the very apophatic move in Suso's visual poetics. It is, in spite of its orientation toward the sole image of Christ, a move from image to image that postulates a way beyond the representational and readable function of images. This is the case because a second apophatic move takes place where the image turns into bare figure, that is, the very place where the soul in her contemplation of the image turns into the image itself; where she is absorbed into the image; and where, theologically speaking, she is encountered by the effects of the figure in her abject position, the word that is nothing else than flesh—and becomes one with the figure of Christ and with divine creativity in the very aesthetic experience that the image establishes.

In moving through these steps from allegory to bare figure, Suso's theory of the image prepares a way of understanding aesthetic experience that comes quite close to other late medieval theories of contemplation, for example, the one proposed by Hendrik Herp,[68] but also to the modern notion of aesthetic experience that we will encounter in Herder's attempts to define the aesthetic mode of cognition. In both cases, in Herp's theory of contemplation and in Herder's aesthetics, we also discover the idea that visual experience turns into a plastic and tactile experience, that the visual field of perception turns into a more fundamental horizon of perception where the visual object becomes the plastic form of sensation and affect and then, losing its character as an object, the figural form of the life of the soul itself.

In his visual poetics, Suso describes a similar transition from images that function as objects of contemplation to images that turn into the form-giving principles of the life of the soul. According to him, this has its ground in the very fact that both incarnation and creation establish an identity of word and flesh, an identity that is the condition of possibility to this overcoming of the representational function of images in joy. It does so since it provides us with images that turn into bare figures, figures devoid of all meaning, figures that eliminate all aspects of a "natural" self and a world in favor of a supernatural intensity and an absorption into the divine.

Both in the case of Eckhart and in the case of Suso, we might want to speak of a poetics of dis-figuration that is oriented toward the core of the incarnation, that is, the very fact that in and through the incarnation humans and God are one. The incarnation, the birth of God in the soul, the assimilation of God and man in the regions of dissimilitude of this world, or the divinization of man is to be understood in terms of freeing oneself from all images, words, and concepts that determine our thinking, perceiving, and feeling. This dis-imagination is often expressed in terms of nakedness and bareness, and Eckhart thinks of it as a practice of self-emptying. According to Suso, however, it is not to be understood in terms of a sheer iconoclasm and of self-emptying but of a specific engagement with images that addresses the places of subjugation and—time and again—moves from the allegorical mode, the perception of the image as a carrier of meaning and as a function of representation, to an affective and sensual, and finally a figural mode of engagement. In this mode the figure, both in image and word, becomes bare, meaningless, naked, and tactile. It is what it acts, and thus it encounters us. It reduces us, asking us to acknowledge the utter asymmetry, the ungraspable character of the encounter that most clearly appears to it in view of the suffering flesh. Thus, and particularly in the exemplary figure of the suffering Christ, it reduces the viewer to a state of receptivity where all perception is nothing else than being touched and being shaped by the image that emerges from the abyss of suffering. For Suso, all this—and all visual poetics—is oriented toward one image, the figure of the naked man on the cross. Nothing didactic, nothing that means anything is left at this point, only the challenge of that figure of surrender. It is liberating since it negates all meaning and understanding and asks for nothing else than a movement through images that acknowledges the figural asymmetry in all of them. For humans, however, in this life, *in via*, the moment of ultimate liberation will never be reached. And thus, according to Suso, humans will, in their desire to be free, always depend on a visual poetics that produces both the allegory and the rhetorical effects of figures, only to be turned time and again to the bare figure, the naked face of the suffering human—a face that they cannot grasp conceptually but only reiterate in the encounter that comes from the figure.

Speculation

Henry Suso explores this constellation of figuration and iconoclastic withdrawal further in other places in his works. Often read as an author who argues for a deeply affective mysticism and for a use of figurative speech as a mode of explaining difficult theological matters with the help of allegory, Suso actually does something entirely different. As we have seen, his use of allegory is never to be read in an illustrative or an argumentative mode but consistently as a return to the notion of figure that we find in Auerbach and in the medieval texts about prayer. Along this line, touch, and the privileging of touch as a sense of spiritual intensity, emerges where the allegorical language loses its hermeneutic aspects and turns into a rhetoric of effects. In their touch, the touch of the irreducibly concrete, figures become the place where the distinction of transcendence and immanence loses all significance. This, exactly, is what is also at stake in the tradition of Franciscan art, for example, in Giotto's attention to floral detail and to objects and things of this world. In his paintings the flowers, the grass, the stones are the concrete instances, the points of absorption into the concrete that forms our life, the figures that express moments of participation. And thus, the vision that at first tends to objectify the flowers or the grass turns into joyful perception where beauty, joy, and the language of praise take over and the distinction of transcendence and immanence, word and flesh, desert and paradise collapse.

Henry Suso, in conversation with this Franciscan practice of contemplative attention, expresses a similar take on nature when he discusses the transition from a hermeneutics of nature to a perspective that emphasizes the deployment of figural force. This deployment happens, once again, in a contemplative exercise that deconstructs the spheres of objects and of things to produce a shift from the order of meaning to a modification of perception, that is, in theological terms, from the realm of nature to the realm of grace and from knowledge to participation.

In a remarkable passage in the *Little Book of Eternal Wisdom*—remarkable also as a testimony to the medieval experience of the beauty of nature—Suso writes:

Who shall let me praise worthily in my days the beloved Lord whom my soul loves? O gentle Lord, if only so many pleasant melodies would go forth from my heart as all others played on their strings and as many as there are leaves and blades of grass. All these strains should then be lifted aloft to you in the court of heaven so that from my heart such a blissful, unusual song of praise would arise that might be pleasing to the eyes of your heart and bring joy to all the celestial ranks. Dear Lord, though I am not worthy to praise you, still my soul wishes that the heavens praise you when they shine in their stunning beauty with the splendor of the sun and the countless multitudes of the bright stars in their lofty brilliance. And (let) the pretty meadows (praise you) when, in the delights of summer, decked out with flowers of all kinds, they reflect their natural nobility in beauty that brings pleasure, and (may you be praised by) all the tender thoughts and ardent desires which any pure loving heart ever harbored for you when it was surrounded by the cheerful summer joy of your radiant spirit. . . . When I look at attractive living forms or see pleasing creatures, they say to my heart, "Oh, look how very pleasing he is from whom we flowed forth, from whom all beauty comes!" I traverse the earth and the heavens, the world and the abyss, forest and meadow, mountain and valley: They all cry out to my ears in rich tones of boundless praise of you.[69]

This passage is a meditation on Psalm 33:1: "Sing joyfully to the LORD, you righteous; it is fitting for the upright to praise him." It forms the conclusion of part two of the *Little Book of Eternal Wisdom*. It places "praise" and the moment of pure prayer that is evoked at the end of this very chapter in an abyss of desire, even, in the words of "Eternal Wisdom," an impossibility: "Whoever imagines he is praising me as fully as I deserve is like the one who chases the wind and wants to grab hold of a shadow." In the desire to praise, the soul has to be humble in "contempt for self," in "surrender," and in remaining "constant in this desire till your death," reenacting the meditation of the passion and the transition from image to figure, from word to flesh continuously.[70]

Suso writes, in the voice of the "servant":

And if I could bring back the time lost by all men, make good their wrongdoings and all the dishonor you ever experienced, and could replace this completely with praise and honor, I would willingly do so. And if it were possible, a beautiful song of praise would have to burst forth from me from the lowest depths of hell and it would penetrate hell, the earth, the air and all the heavens before reaching your divine countenance. But if that were impossible, then I would wish to praise you here all the more so that I might enjoy you the more here.[71]

This very last sentence points to something that Suso calls *speculatio*, speculation, and to its relationship with mimetic assimilation. It is in this literal mise-en-abyme of the self that the moment of praise includes both, *imitatio* and *speculatio*, surrendering in the meditation to the suffering of Christ and rejoining first a moment of creaturely bareness in the exercise of *imitatio Christi*, then of creation in speculative participation. Listening to the creature alone, the text emphasizes, is limited; listening to it with the "dearest love" in Christ makes "the heart open and . . . burst forth from it the flaming torch" of praise.[72] This mode of praise is to be understood not in terms of a symbolic representation alone but in terms of a modification of perception that at first, in imitation of the passion, foregrounds receptivity and then in speculation—to be taken literally as a mirroring of the world that becomes figure—restores the things in their fullness.

We find another and more comprehensive iteration of this thought in Suso's *Vita*. There, Suso introduces the notion of speculation, in Middle High German *speculieren*, in a dialogue with his "spiritual daughter" Elsbeth Stagel. The chapter follows a number of explanations about "detachment" (*gelazenheit*), offering a train of thought parallel with the one in the *Little Book of Eternal Wisdom*. Detachment, as it is explained here, entails an imitation that surrenders and loses the self and thus transcends the natural world of attachments in a new, still, and "supernatural life" (*in der stillheit beginnet úbernatúrliches leben*).[73] At this point, the "daughter" asks: "Tell me what is God or where is he or how does he exist. That is to say, how is he one and yet three?" In answering the questions, the text first recapitulates a range of theological and philosophical statements, opening with an affirmation of tropes of negative theology, that all theologians agree that "he is above all thought and intellect." Affirming that the divine "cannot be seen by mortal eye as it is in itself," Suso adds immediately: "One can see it very well in its effects, just as one recognizes a good master by examining his work. As Paul said, 'Creatures are like a mirror in which God is reflected.' And this knowledge is called speculating."[74]

However, working with Romans 1:20, the famous passage about knowing God through the mirror of creation, makes Suso go beyond the trope of the master and his work. What he calls speculation is not the practice of recognizing cause and effect, nor is it a hermeneutical exercise that works through analogies of the divine in the world but a rhetorical practice that produces a picture of the world, a configuration of words and figures, which in turn produce not discursive knowledge but an affective and sensual effect.

Suso explains this in a remarkable passage:

> Let us speculate . . . : Look beyond you and around you to the four corners of the earth, how far, how high the beautiful heavens are in their swift course, and how nobly their Master has adorned them with the seven planets, each of which, except for the moon, is much greater than the whole earth, and how he is glorified by the countless number of bright stars. Oh, the beautiful sun, when it arises cloudless and bright in the summer, what fruits and other good things it gives evenly to the earth! How beautifully the meadows turn green, how leaf and grass surge forth. The pretty flowers laugh. Forest, heath and meadows echo the delightful songs of the nightingale and tiny birds. All the animals that had crept away from the nasty winter come forth, rejoice and join together, just as among humankind young and old are happy with delightful cheerfulness. O gentle God, if you are so lovely in your creatures, how utterly beautiful and lovely you are then in yourself.
>
> Look further, I ask you. Examine the four elements—earth, water, air and fire—and the utter miracle that in them are all sorts of different men, animals, birds, fish and wonders of the sea. Whatever is contained in them all calls out together: "Glory and honor to the unfathomable, marvelous immensity that is in you." . . .
>
> Now, daughter, you have found your God for whom your heart has long been searching. Now look up with eager eyes, with smiling face, with your heart leaping up. . . . From the "speculating" there soon arises in a sensitive person a heartfelt jubilation. Jubilation is a joy the tongue cannot describe, yet it rushes mightily through heart and soul.[75]

This, Suso acknowledges, is a "grace" he received from God repeatedly, and it moves him to speak about this "for the first time" and to tell the "daughter" an "intimate secret that [he has] never told anyone,"[76] that he "often felt as though he were floating in the air and swimming in the deep flow of God's boundless marvels between time and eternity" and being "thus by jubilation transported into God."[77]

The rhetoric of concreteness that we encounter here is what Auerbach calls an "energetic realism." Readers of Suso are indeed struck by the poetic qualities of the text and its emphasis on the natural world. This text is, however, not just the presentation of a picture of nature that in its perfection points to the fact that there must be a master behind the world, its order, and its beauty. Instead, Suso uses the trope of the mirror from Romans 1:20 as the basis for an argument about the production of sensual and affective evidence in and through rhetorical figuration in form of a realism that transforms perception. Instead of the philosophical notion of *analogia entis* we encounter an *analogia pulchritudinis*, an analogy found in aesthetic experience and the rhetoric and poetics that support it. Consequently, we do not find ourselves in the realm of a reading of the book of nature in terms of meaning or in light of the Holy Scriptures but in the realm of a rhetorical deployment of figures that shape perception, sensation, and affect. Analogy and the forms of assimilation do not support an ontological line of thought here. Instead, in our reading of the passage, the text suggests that participation in the form of the *jubilus* is the only place of an encounter with God.

This leads back to the understanding of practices of meditation in twelfth-century monastic devotional theory, particularly in Hugh and in Richard of Saint Victor. In these authors, speculation means the production of a sacramental reality of things that emerges in prayer. In his comprehensive analysis of the notions of image and resemblance in the twelfth century, Robert Javelet writes:

> The word "speculation" is not limited to spiritual introspection. Speculation concerns the spiritual observation of all the simulacrums of nature and grace. It extends to the entire visible world insofar as it resembles the invisible. Speculation is the vision of truth through a mirror, mediated by resemblance. All speculation is sacramental in a general sense.[78]

More recently, Dale M. Coulter adds to this observation:

> *Speculatio* characterizes a mirroring process that may be described as "extraction" rather than abstraction. It is precisely through this process of "extraction" that divine wisdom communicates truth to the human mind, and the human mind comes to participate in that wisdom. This is how the entire created world functions as a "book" that must be read. The inner structure of the human mind is such that it can receive the "forms" of all created things. This happens as

images or forms are impressed upon the memory, which serves as their organizing center. The mental image is itself a reflection of the created object. As such the mind can begin to meditate upon it and to investigate its various features. Investigation of individual features prepares the mind to extract analogies that serve as windows onto other realities. With each "extraction" and connection to another reality, an inner delight occurs that evokes wonder and drives the process onward and upward into the realm of the divine. Affective transformation in and through admiration and wonder fuels cognitive reflection and thus wisdom becomes "sweet" to the soul. Ultimately, a vision of another reality unfolds as divine wisdom intersects with human wisdom, and this vision restores the soul.[79]

In his emphasis on *speculation* and *jubilus*, Suso follows this path of a meditative exercise, and he draws attention to the work of language in the transformation of the world of perception and the perception of the world itself. Suso proceeds in several steps. Imitation of the passion foregrounds in rhetorically effective form the moments of the passion as they are found in the reading of the Gospels. The staging of the passion in meditation produces surrender, abnegation of the self, and detachment (*gelazenheit*), as Suso explains in the chapter of the *Vita* that precedes the chapter on speculation. We might speak here, once again, of the production of a receptivity that is to be seen as an affective attunement, an overcoming of hardness of the soul (*hertikeit*), and an openness toward the word. It is also a deconstruction and a hollowing out of the hermeneutic mode of inhabiting symbolic worlds. Speculation responds to this deconstruction, deploying language rhetorically in a poetics of creation and praise, an enumeration of and a new production of the creation in terms of beauty and love. Theologically speaking, through incarnation and passion (through the enactment of *imitatio* and assimilation in the devotional practice), the soul joins the integrity of creation in its beauty when it joins it in *speculatio*. Praise and joy (*jubilus*), and thus absorbing participation, form the point of convergence for the meditative exercises of both *imitatio* (the reduction to bare figure) and of *speculatio* (the expression of the asymmetry of overwhelming beauty). Both are, in respective ways, material mimetic exercises, but they both focus not only on a representation of key moments of scriptural meditation, that is, passion and creation, but once again on the rhetorical efficacy of the exercise in terms of another point of convergence, the identity of affect and thought, love and intellect. Thus, they produce a state that Suso calls "supernatural." It is a state where nature and grace converge in a human response to nature. In its own movement this response is—as the quoted texts illustrate—nothing else than praise of God in a modification of perception that makes all things sacramental and that turns them into agents of grace. In the act of devotion, always both meditation of passion (suffering receptivity) and speculative praise (exultation in words), this sacramental experience of the world is being produced in the very reception of the words and things as figures, that is, in a poetics of creation that has been purified of all arid conceptual form and that has turned into participation.

An aesthetics of passion and of descent into the abject rejoins here an aesthetics of praise. It does so in the poetic form that transports from a meditation of the passion to speculative praise, to the deep affective and sensual presence of the creation in the moment of *jubilus* and pure prayer, and finally, to the abyss of love. It is in this movement that, as Eckhart, the teacher of Suso, preaches, a fly or a piece of wood is one with God.

What we find in Suso is thus a transformation of the conventional ideas about ways of "reading" the "book of nature." Reading is not the uncovering of the meaning of nature as a mirror of the creator in the medium of prayer and contemplation; nor is it an allegoresis of nature in terms of analogies and similes in light of the Scriptures or a contemplation of the beauty of nature as it testifies to the beauty and goodness of a creator. Instead, it entails a transformation of the very perception of nature that affects reading itself. Reading turns from a hermeneutic act of understanding and meaning seeking to a mode of being touched and of being affected by the very agency, the force of words that carry the force of figures. This is supported by Suso's literary realism (in philosophical terms, a radical nominalism)—a realism that, in the sense of Auerbach's "energetic realism," emphasizes the encounter with particular things and turns their very concreteness into the place of participation in divine grace. In this collapse of distinctions, all perception becomes touch, that is, it opens up toward the agency of the worlds beyond ourselves and the encounters with them. In the new evaluation of the significance of touch that emerges in this contemplative practice, things are nothing else than the concrete and thus always irreducibly asymmetrical, figural expressions that encounter us.

This emphasis also informs the increasing significance of touch in late medieval theories of contemplation, most prominently in Rudolf of

Biberach and Hendrik Herp. Here, touch not only marks the shift from a hermeneutic to a non-hermeneutic attitude toward the world, but it also exceeds all moments that could be described in terms of visual piety and exemplary assimilation. Instead, things of the world turn into figures that testify here and now to the divine neither in the mode of analogous symbolic relation nor in a mode of embodied visionary experience but only in the figural excess, and this excess is called touch. It has its place, as both Rudolf of Biberach and Hendrik Herp explain, in the contemplative exercise that breaks through the hermeneutic order of meaning and the analogy of being, as well as through the order of the visual and its objects. Instead, it points to a modification of perception in the exercise of meditation that turns all things into sacramental reality and into figures that, in the detached abandonment of perception and in the abandonment to their unthought expressivity, communicate nothing else than the grace that shapes their emergence, the gift of becoming that unties them from the places they occupy in the normative order of the world.

5

Framings

Free Spirits

Medieval mystical experiments with figuration have not gone unquestioned, and many of them have been objects of censorship, suppression, and critical reframings. These will be at the center of this chapter. Among them is Suso's critique of the "free spirits." Around 1330, shortly after the official condemnation of a number of sentences of his teacher Meister Eckhart by the church, Henry Suso wrote a short treatise, *The Little Book of Truth.* In this text, which follows the model of a pedagogical dialogue that Suso often uses, he writes that "he asked of eternal Truth that, as far as was possible, it give him the power to distinguish well between people whose goal is a well-ordered simplicity and those who, as they say, aim at unrestrained liberty, and that it teach him what true detachment is, by which he might come to where he ought to be."[1] With this attempt at establishing a correct understanding of "true detachment," and setting this Eckhartian term in opposition to "those" who aim for "unrestrained liberty," Suso presents us with an apology and a defense of the notion of detachment. In opposing the "truly detached" to the ones who aim for "unrestrained liberty," Suso demonstrates that he sees Eckhart's teachings as being misread by some people, the so-called heretics of the "free spirit." Against their antinomian voices, he emphasizes the right use of reason, the authority of the Scriptures, and a "correct" theological and metaphysical understanding of spiritual freedom and detachment. Suso frames the discussion around these terms after Eckhart's death and creates a clear distinction in an area where the discussions about these questions might have been quite complex at the time. Taking on a face that is different from the one I portrayed previously, he draws a distinction that also reacts to one of the central objections to Eckhart's teachings, that with his words he seduced the "unlearned" and opened a path for "wild" interpretations outside the teachings of the church. Adopting what we could call a conservative, "right-Eckhartian" position, he makes an attempt to control "left-Eckhartian" voices, which insist on a libertine reading of detachment that the figure of the wild one represents in Suso's text.

In this treatise Suso also does much more. In exploring the role of figuration and its power of undoing established normative orders further, he participates—I am tempted to say against some aspects of his own teachings that I portrayed previously—in a reinscription of the figural character of detachment into a controllable map of assimilation and hermeneutics. He reacts thus to a broader concern about vernacular teachings, theologies, and "errors" that emerges around 1300—a disciplining concern with errors that are often identified with those who "call themselves little brothers and little sisters of the sect of the free spirit and of voluntary freedom."[2] This designation, quoted here from a letter written by the bishop of Strasbourg on August 13, 1317, identifies a group that, however, never articulates itself as such. As I argue here, it is a "group," a "sect," a "movement" that emerges not from voices that we can historically identify but primarily from the polemics of a heresiological discourse. From this point of view, Suso's intervention can be seen as part of this discourse that seems to focus on "erroneous" teachings and understandings of dogmatic content. In fact, it is not directed primarily at theological errors but at the very practice of allegorical and figural reading, of assimilation and partaking. As we have seen, these new practices have often been promoted most strongly by women.

Behind the layer of errors, a development in the later Middle Ages redefines heresy and heresiology along two lines: the control of hermeneutic engagement with the Scriptures, on the one hand, and of the investment of sensual and affective knowledge in devotional practices, particularly the experience of a unity with the divine and "different forms of life,"[3] on the other hand. To support these axes of discursive control, thus goes the core of my argument, the ecclesiastical censorship develops the phantasm of the free spirits as a group and movement—thus obliterating the multiple voices and giving concise form to a "heresy." In other words, I am not interested here in the heresiological discourses as they develop in the church around matters of correct teaching and so-called errors. These discourses and their institutional logic have been reconstructed exhaustively, be it in the case of the Cathars or Valdensians, of Marguerite Porete, of Meister Eckhart, of the Fratricelli, or of other movements that have had a more or less marginal and marginalized position in the church.[4]

I am also not interested primarily in identifying a transhistorical position of free spirits as critics of culture, power, and economy that can be traced from Diogenes the Cynic to Friedrich Nietzsche and beyond. What I am reconstructing instead is not a specific type of heresy or heterodoxy. Rather, it is a dimension of late medieval heresiology that can be observed most clearly in the case of the so-called free spirits. It is a form of identifying vernacular texts and voices that allegedly spread among beguines and beghards since the thirteenth century. An expression of these voices was, supposedly, also to be recognized in Hieronymus Bosch's *The Garden of Earthly Delights.* As some art historians pointed out, this painting is to be seen as the portrait of an orgiastic ritual of the free spirits.[5] Here, we might add, the mind of the historian meets the construction of medieval heresiology in the production of a phantasm. And it is here as well where the imagination of the historian and the discourse of heresiology trace and often invent the convergence of the so-called free spirits with a spirit of sexual libertinage. Some have drawn a line from the antinomianism of medieval free spirits to the libertines of the seventeenth and eighteenth centuries, thus producing a history of transgression that accompanies cultural and intellectual developments in Western Europe since the Middle Ages. Along this line, Friedrich Nietzsche's "transvaluation of all values" and Georges Bataille's economy of excess (the "accursed share") can indeed be seen as modern articulations of two core arguments that the bishop of Strasbourg had already ascribed to the free spirits in the fourteenth century, a notion of freedom that abolishes all moral norms and normativity and a critique of the economy that allows for a life without work, sustained through "receiving the alms meant for the poor" and "theft" alone, since, as some free spirits supposedly argued, "everything belongs to everybody."[6] It is this radical vision of a genuine and persistent revolutionary antinomian critique that, in his book *Movement of the Free Spirit,* leads to Raoul Vaneigem's emphatic conclusion in 1986:

Either the economy will succeed in submerging the living, or society will rely on the predominance of desires emancipated from their inversion in the market. Either we will all perish in the increasingly debilitating quest for profit and prestige, or the primacy of pleasure will destroy work through creativity, exchange through the gift, guilt through innocence, the will to power through the will to live, anguished satisfaction through the natural rhythm of pleasure and displeasure. . . . A wager is set. . . . The world has merely changed in accordance with the laws of economics. The time has come to create a world in accordance with the harmony of pleasures. In its most original form, the movement of the Free Spirit uses the protoplasmic energy of life as the basis for its magnum opus. . . . This oneiric project, in which everyone will take part, is the only reality that can authorize humanity to turn the world upside-down before it is crushed by its absurdity.[7]

Returning from this late twentieth-century vision to the early fourteenth century, we observe that the censorship of Eckhart's works was actually not focused on what came to be called the movement of the free spirits but, apart from theological questions about the relation between human existence and God, on the question of teaching the "unlearned."[8] Thus, Eckhart's work could be and was seen as part of an increasingly sophisticated body of vernacular texts that opened new hermeneutic paths of reading and interpreting the Scriptures—vernacular texts that inherently, and particularly in the mobilization of women's voices, posed a threat to established and controlled theological teachings.

In the context of German vernacular texts, it is after Eckhart's death, in treatises such as Suso's *Little Book of Truth* and, to use just one example, in the so-called *Treatise of Sister Katrei,*[9] that the question of "true detachment" is raised in terms of the free spirits or of a radical antinomianism. This antinomian position has its ground, as Suso argues in a critical hermeneutical vein, in a misreading both of the gospel and of negative theology. In insisting on the fact that Saint Paul says that "no law is made for the just man" and that "unrestrained liberty" transcends all worldly orders,[10] the fictional free spirit in Suso's text—Suso speaks of the "wild one"—takes on such a position, addressing, beyond all errors, what could be called at first a hermeneutic threat in his free interpretation of detachment and spiritual poverty.

It is to this threat of a wild hermeneutics that Suso turns immediately at the beginning of his treatise:

> He was first directed to the core of holy scripture out of which eternal Truth speaks, that he might seek and gaze upon what the most learned and experienced human beings, to whom God has revealed his hidden wisdom, had spoken about it—as is written in the Latin quotation that begins this book—or what holy Christianity thinks about it, so that he might stay on the secure path of truth.[11]

Reading and interpretation are thus, in a first step, contained within a framework of scriptural theology and authoritative readings that is controlled by theological truth.

However, the free spirit (*daz wilde*, the wild one) in Suso's text takes on a position that is opposed to both. When *daz wilde* appears, the "disciple" asks:

> Where do you come from?
> It said: I never came from anywhere.
> He said: Tell me, what are you?
> It said: I am nothing.
> He said: What do you want?
> It answered and said: I want nothing.
> And he said: This is very strange. Tell me, what is your name?
> It said: I am called the nameless wild one.
> The *disciple* said: You are well named "the wild one" because your words and answers are completely wild. Now tell me something I shall ask you: Where does your wisdom take you?
> It said: To unrestrained liberty.[12]

Not surprisingly, this passage—a classic representation of the voice of a free spirit who is not bound by law and who has abandoned all identifiable positions—reminds us not so much of Eckhart's teachings but of a range of sentences that had been condemned in Marguerite Porete's *Mirror of Simple Souls.* Marguerite, not willing to refrain from distributing her book and from spreading her message, was burned at the stake as a relapsed heretic in 1310.[13] Suso's text, at least in this passage, attacks a reading of Eckhart that might have been shaped by the reception of excerpts from Marguerite, thus creating the most obvious link with a condemned book that was seen as part of the "movement of the free spirit." In her book, Marguerite writes:

> This Soul, says Love, takes account of neither shame nor honor, of neither poverty nor wealth, of neither anxiety nor ease, of neither love nor hate, of neither hell nor paradise. . . . And this Soul, who has become nothing, thus possesses everything, and so possesses nothing; she wills everything and she wills nothing; she knows all and she knows nothing.[14]

Several things are noteworthy in the passages from Suso's *Little Book of Truth* and in the form of his critique: first, the identification of a group of people who aim for "disorderly liberty," and the line he draws from these to both the false prophets of the "Old Testament" who "mixed their false ones in between" the "true signs" that "God" had "worked . . . through Moses" and to those who "when Christ the true Messiah came . . . falsely pretended they were the one."[15] This is a conventional trope in the identification of heresy. Second is the emphasis on a restrictive framework of scriptural reading and traditional interpretation and reasoning as a basis for true discernment. False prophecy, hermeneutic trespassing, and an incorrect interpretation of negative theology are at the core of his call for discernment. This, too, is not surprising. However, it took on a particular significance in the historical context of late medieval vernacular writings. Third, and most remarkably in the context of my argument here, the return to a correct reading of the Scriptures entails a deep and long engagement with Dionysius the Areopagite's negative theology and with the power of allegory and figuration. A Dionysian mode of allegory had, as I have shown previously, been used by Suso himself and in the tradition of beguine writings. They did so to both sustain a strong negative theology—the affirmation that there can be no image and no understanding of God or the soul—and produce a rich archive of allegorical images and figures that entail a strong experiential force in terms of sensation, affects, and vision. As Suso argues in *The Little Book of Truth*, however, negative theology has to be handled rationally,[16] not allowing for forms of speculative thought and allegorization that could work their way through allegories and images to produce a non-conceptual and utterly free world of experiential intensity through a figural practice. In Suso's intervention, the free spirits are, so to speak, censored on these grounds and forced back from their figural play into a sphere of hermeneutics and rational control of all practices of assimilation. Participation, with its inherently antinomian side, is thus recast within a controllable hermeneutic framework. Fourth, based on this, Suso also reframes the dynamics of affect and imagination, not explicitly but in and through the mobilization of a specific type of discernment. In containing the figural effects of allegorical images on the senses and the imagination, in restricting their work in scriptural hermeneutics, he neutralizes forms of speech that tendentially liberate themselves from institutional control. Anticipating Luther's and Kant's arguments against enthusiasm (*Schwärmerei*), Suso frames his defense of Meister Eckhart's idea of detachment in terms of both a hermeneutic control and a theological metaphysics that excludes—at least at this point in his works and in contradiction with other moments in his writings—the sensual, affective, and cognitive excess that characterizes a range of late medieval vernacular writings. Forms of partaking in the divine, forms of thinking of humans in an antinomian multitude of their voices, of thinking the annihilated human as one with the divine, are thus subsumed under a controlling perspective of hermeneutic and rational legitimation that neutralizes the very excess that is often at stake here.

At first glance and for a long time, historians tended to read Suso's critique of the free spirits, as well as the condemnation of Marguerite Porete, as a straightforward model of exclusion and inclusion, that is, an exclusion of heretical radical notions of freedom and the unity of the soul with God and a recasting in terms of theological orthodoxy that avoids the pitfalls of a mystical theology that seems to undermine key distinctions between the human and the divine. Here, I do not focus on the theological positions and questions of dogma that often function as a blueprint for the identification of heretics. Instead, I ask what the free spirits stand for in Suso's text and how their position reflects a larger movement in vernacular engagements with biblical texts and devotional practices. I concentrate on the elements that identify and, as I see it, help construct the very heresy that allows for the emergence of mechanisms of control with a specific heresiological focus in the later Middle Ages. We should think of this focus as the discursive production of a heresy that allows for the maintenance of the stability of an institution and a body of knowledge about the discursive order of access to the divine. What we are dealing with is thus the production of a heresy that is identified along two main axes: one is the spiritual practice and its figural abyss in participation; the other, the phenomenology of rhetorical effects, that is, the production of moments of sensual and affective knowledge through devotional practices of assimilation. At stake here are not differences between theological dogma and heretical opinions ("errors") but practices of knowledge formation and literary production that undermine the stability of a controlled relation between man and God.

It is a legitimate question whether the supposedly radical and explicit defenders of a free spirit and "disorderly libertinage" really existed in any organized form, let alone whether this position can be found in a way that was shared by something we could call a social movement. Increasing skepticism has led to the common opinion that the free spirits might actually never have existed, certainly not in form of a "movement of the free spirit." Instead, they are to be seen as a fiction produced by the papal bull *Ad nostrum* in 1311 and similar documents. Thus, both in Suso and in other late medieval documents the free spirit usually appears as what I would like to call a phantasmatic or a conceptual figure that is meant to neutralize a multitude of voices, some of them highly critical of the institutional church for sure, some of them certainly also what we could call free spirits and libertines in a modern sense. It is a phantasmatic figure that moves beyond the identification of particular, theologically precise points of diverging opinions and possibly heretical teachings. Instead, it produces the imaginary of a radical antinomianism and of a wild hermeneutics that allows for the production of a framework that helps control not primarily specific points of theological teaching but the very imagination in its investment with new forms of engaging the holy Scriptures and devotional practices. Thus, the errors identified in the "movement of the free spirits" can be understood as an identifying pattern that was being deployed to control the very dynamics of vernacular hermeneutics and the investment of a new theological imagination in devotional practices of figural abandonment. Accordingly, "free spirit" is to be read as the name for practices of dispossession, detachment, and liberation that rely on this abandonment.

To illustrate this, I want to discuss two areas in late medieval vernacular devotional writings that seem to form the oblique focus of the identification of free spirits: the wild hermeneutics and the question of participation in the divine that postulates an antinomian form of the circulation of percepts, affects, and concepts. Both are also key moments of critique in Suso's text and in his focus on a specific need for discernment with regard to the question of "true detachment." These two main aspects can also be found in nearly all the documents linked to the free spirits.

As mentioned previously, one of the points of censorship against Meister Eckhart was that he talked to the "unlearned" about things that were deemed to be theologically difficult. This very issue is indeed one that moves to the fore in vernacular texts, particularly in mystical texts since the thirteenth century. Many of these texts have been written by women, and many are part of the beguine culture that forms one of the backgrounds of Eckhart's and Suso's work—as well as of the construction of the "movement of free spirits." What I emphasize, here, however, are, once again, not the disputes about specific exegetical or dogmatic questions but the very character of the engagement with the biblical texts that we encounter in this vernacular tradition and that might have given rise to this culture of suspicion and hermeneutic control. It is this culture of suspicion and hermeneutic control that sought to capture a range of engagements with the Scriptures under the concept of free spirit. To illustrate the practice at stake in these engagements, I return one more time to Mechthild of Magdeburg's *Flowing Light of the Godhead.* Mechthild's text exemplifies this engagement with the Scriptures and the devotional practices, that is, the ways of reading that form the background of the emergence of what will be the identification of free spirits.

Mechthild's book, itself never an object of church censorship, is often classified as "mystical writing," "devotional writing," "spiritual writing," or "wisdom literature." This difficulty to designate a genre, which also characterizes Marguerite's *Mirror of Simple Souls,* is significant. In literary and theological terms it raises the—unresolvable—question of what kind of genre of writing it is, since it complicates Mechthild's own voice along several lines: human and divine voice, woman theologian and male theology, gender and genre, body and soul. We are dealing here with a text that, at least at first glance, does not conform to a conventional notion of religious writings and thus has often been read as an expression of a subjective and private experience of the divine. It does not conform to expectations of an established genre of theological texts (a treatise, a meditation, a prayer) or of literary texts (a narrative, a dialogue, a poem). Instead, a glance into the manuscript shows a surprising richness of literary genres, movements from narrative to dialogue, to short treatise, back to dialogue, to forms of poems and prayers—in short, movements that we might, especially in this situation of the emerging use of the vernacular and in the women's community of writers Mechthild is part of, be tempted to call above all experimental, expressive, and didactic.

The text is in fact experimental in two ways: in experimenting with language and writing and in producing a form of writing that does not represent an ineffable mystical subjectivity but presents us with a pedagogy invested in the shaping of sensation, affect, and thought. Thus, Mechthild often moves from a dogmatic concept to a narrative, to moments of dialogue, and to instances of prayer, bringing dogmatic teaching, practices of assimilation, and modes of participation into an intimate conversation. She does not do so to illustrate theological concepts or grasp them in the form of allegorical images but to argue for and move the reader in a different state of understanding of the very movements between perceptual, affective, and conceptual moments in the life of the soul. What she shows is how experimental writing can recast theology in forms of practices, how it entails a specific focus on language, and how it relates to established forms of devotional practice. Thus, her text makes us aware of the specific use of language in these practices. It does so in focusing through an engagement with a wide range of genres on the figural formation of herself, not on what seems at stake at first glance, so-called religious experience, dogmatic belief, and allegorical representation.

Mechthild of Magdeburg wrote the *Flowing Light of the Godhead* between 1250 and 1280. She started her book while she lived as a beguine in Magdeburg, then finished the last, the seventh, part after she had joined the Cistercian nuns at Helfta in 1272. As pointed out previously, the observation shared by all readers of the *Flowing Light of the Godhead* is something interpreters have called the "idiosyncratic inventiveness" of her book and the shifting genres and styles of writing.[17] The mixed forms she uses, the experiments with forms she is engaged in, are indeed a feature that strikes whoever opens the book and reads through the first couple of pages. Speaking in formal terms, we often move from personal narrative to dialogue or, at the very beginning of the book, from a dialogue between the author and God to a dialogue between personified figures of the soul; from a theological explanation to a narrative with so-called visionary elements; from longer passages to aphoristic statements; from prose to poetry, and so on. What strikes at first glance, as well, is the sophisticated handling of rhetorical devices (allegories, metaphors, paradoxes) and of particular genres and thus the ambitious poetic character of the texts that, indeed, cite and engage a broad range of genres available to the author in her focus on the production of rhetorical effects. All this speaks to an intense interest in variation both in the play with different genres and within the forms of genres themselves, and it speaks to an interest in the use of language that finds one of its expressions in the transitions from prose to verse. Both the citation of established forms and the crossing of boundaries seem indeed programmatic, and so does the way in which she thematizes and complicates her voice.

As we have seen, this crossing of boundaries is well established in the traditions of compositional work that build on the practice of reading, the singing of the Psalms, and meditational and contemplative exercises. What is new in Mechthild's text is its vernacular form, a more intense focus on experimental modes, and the experimentation with voice, gender, and genre and with the modes of assimilation and participation this experimental writing allows. Most remarkably, she draws attention to the tensions between the figural effects and the forms of allegorical assimilation, foregrounding forms of partaking in their break with the language of allegory and dogma.

Reading her writings closely, we observe that they are, in spite of their idiosyncratic originality, deeply rooted in other texts. The frame of reference is not a personal experience but a specific understanding of the very practice of reading the Scriptures. This practice entails vocalization, memorization, and meditation. Anchored in meditative reading, her practice presents itself as a continuous exercise of rewriting. Meditation, quite literally, is a rewriting of the Scriptures, but it is also a reconfiguration not in terms of a hermeneutic alone but also of a deployment of the efficacy of the words. In shifting from the understanding of the Scriptures to the deployment of figural effects, it entails the articulation of an archive of two sets of scriptural figures in a continuous practice of reading and rewriting: narrative scripts and specific tropes of encounter, taken as figures that produce specific effects. Narrative scripts, not surprisingly, comprehend the life of Christ, the *Song of Songs*, the narrative of the annunciation, the descent of Christ into hell, and many others. Tropes of encounter entail the words spoken by the angel to Mary, the kiss, the embrace, the distance from the *Song of Songs*, and many other moments, all drawn from the Scriptures. In addition, Mechthild combines these scripts and figures with tropes from courtly love lyrics, amplifying the scriptural language and giving shape to her own position within this tradition of rewriting the Scriptures in a devotional practice that has been cultivated in medieval monastic circles and that she now gives shape to in the vernacular.

Through her writings, she establishes her own voice in a complex engagement with forms of authorization and power, staging the voice of a woman writing in the vernacular and making use of the language and textual archive available to her. In articulating herself as a writer and in constructing an "I" that speaks here, she moves through this archive and makes that "I" emerge in multiple forms. She presents us, however, not with a hermeneutics of the self or the Scriptures, or with a religious or confessional mode of belief, but with a construction, articulation, and expression that fully rely on the use of the archive of tropes and figures available to her. Mobilizing this archive of tropes and giving shape to it in variations that draw attention to the very use of language seem to be the dominant aspects in this form of writing that transforms scriptural hermeneutics into a vernacular textual practice of figural play and experimentation. Without thematizing it, she establishes her voice on the basis of three scripts that underlie the performance of the spoken word: God speaking to Moses and to the apostle John; the angel speaking to Mary in the annunciation; and the intimate exchange of words in the *Song of Songs*. In combining these moments with elements from courtly love poetry, Mechthild produces a moment of defamiliarization that opens possibilities for a new deployment of the archive of tropes she uses. Thus, the lovers from the *Song of Songs* turn into courtly figures, and the life of her soul turns into a play of voices drawn from biblical and lyrical sources.

It is this gesture of defamiliarization and figural play that anticipates what will also be at the core of the notion of "free spirits"—not in terms of a fantastic freedom, however, but of a specific engagement with texts and traditions. The transformation of scriptural hermeneutics in a figural rewriting along the lines of biblical scenarios actually constitutes the very freedom that undermines dogmatic authority and the control that Suso finds missing in the articulation of the position of the wild one. The absorption into the play of the figures, the articulation of her human existence through these figures, and the abandonment to participation in a play that brings love and understanding together in this absorption have replaced the authoritative voice of learned hermeneutics.

My second observation focuses on the production of affective intimacy. In Mechthild, the use of scriptural tropes stands not in the service of an exegetical perspective, a question of dogma, or an explicit ethical transformation in normative terms. While these aspects do indeed play a role, they are strategically subordinated to a pragmatic function, the deployment of the scripts and tropes as devices that shape both Mechthild's perception and the acting in the world that is meant to flow from it. Rewriting scriptural scenes thus serves the purpose of establishing an "I" that speaks and a dispossession of that very "I" that stages itself as a figural effect of the Scriptures. Positing the "I" and the very writing she produces entails what we can call a specific, technically speaking, an indexical relation to several contexts: her position as a reader in a tradition of reading that sees itself as a life-forming rewriting of the text; as a woman reader who addresses the question of authority and authorization; and as an annihilated self where the texts of the Scriptures deploy their force of shaping perception and ethical action along the lines of biblical scenes that take shape in the beguine's life in love and suffering.

As I have mentioned, for a long time, this text and similar ones have been read either in terms of a psychology of experience (a medieval woman talking about her mystical encounters with the divine); in terms of a pathology of desire (especially in the nineteenth century in picturing a hysterical woman drowning in the intensity of her desire); in hermeneutical terms as a form of scriptural exegesis (an ambitious laywoman adopting authority in a highly controlled field of religious speech); or as a socially marginal writing that practices forms of transgression that, in turn, can be seen as both generating and reflecting on new types of gendered subjectivity. What the latter position already draws attention to is an emphasis on the practice of writing as one to be read not in hermeneutic terms but in terms of a generative experimentation—an experimentation with authoritative, subjugating, and subject-forming power—that mobilizes specific linguistic archives and reconfigures these in contextually sophisticated ways, thus undermining a model of subject formation that relies on normative rules and authoritative exegesis. Mechthild transforms this very model in her experiments and in the way she uses and stages the use of language in tensions between assimilation and participation.

This practice of engaging the Scriptures, I want to add, might indeed have looked "wild" from the point of view that Suso sets up to create a framework for the control of the free spirit. What I want to emphasize here, however, is not that Mechthild is a "free spirit." It is above all the observation that the practices of Mechthild and other vernacular authors are more deeply invested in forms of life than in a hermeneutics or a dogmatic understanding of the relation between the soul and the divine. She demonstrates that what we call the genre of "religious" or "devotional" texts and artifacts in fact folds scriptural hermeneutics into a figural practice, that is, a contextually saturated form in which the artifact does not transport meaning alone but primarily shapes perception and the life of the reader. In this sense the devotional text performs a radical critique of everydayness, a radical defamiliarization, and an abandonment of stable subject positions. It is an expression of critique that cannot be criticized itself, except through a movement that attacks this style of devotion and adopts a hermeneutical norm and a concurrent metaphysical perspective, as Suso does in his *Little Book of Truth*.

Mechthild's text and similar devotional artifacts are, at first glance, inspired rewritings of moments drawn from the Scriptures, from the liturgy, from lives of saints. They simply consist of rhetorical steps, invention and enumeration, the search for figures, the construction of lists, the use of repetition and rhetorical questions, and the configuration of tropes drawn from the Scriptures, from life experience, from lives of saints and martyrs, from memory, and from other available sources. In the meditational exercise and in the practice of writing, the very construction of such lists presents the soul with a picture, with a series of figures that all have a specific effect on perception, on affect and sensation, and on thought. As we have seen, these effects can be further amplified through repetition, rhetorical questions, and narrative scripts that help unfold the power of the figures. In her exercise of meditative writing, Mechthild relies on these practices of figuration and rhetorical amplification, allowing for the production of a broad range of effects. At the same time, Mechthild's use of the Scriptures emphasizes strategies that strip the figures from the meaning and from the intention-bound nature of the devotional exercise. Extracted from the archive, liberated from their immediate context and from intentions, the figures and tropes then serve the production of an affective and sensual space that is open toward the effects of the language and new forms of contextualization.

Most remarkably, this practice above all means attention to language and voice. To communicate with God, the unnamable and the unimaginable, the affective and sensual forms of meditative prayer treat tropes not primarily as images, symbols, or concepts provided by the biblical text but as artifacts that can be used in specific ways, not to represent the divine but to produce the absorption in patterns of sensation, affect, and concept. Thus, I argue, we have to speak of a circulation of percepts, affects, and concepts that is being enacted in forms of participation against an established model of subject formation. These moments of absorption and participation are explicitly present in Mechthild's texts when she points out that the result of the practice is supposed to be a new and different kind of knowing herself and thus a new ethical shape of the person. With the help of these figures, drawn from an archive of available topoi both in the Scriptures and in the erotic language of courtly literature, the soul alienates herself from a defined "old" state, the subjugation to the world and its powers, creating instead the compositional exercise of meditation and writing that allows for the production of a "new" state. It is this state that the rhetorical figures and the textual work are meant to produce and explore, forming a new relational, sensual, affective, and cognitive landscape of the soul. And, one has to add, it is the apophatic core, the unnamable center of participation, that allows for the radically experimental tone that characterizes these texts and their necessarily antinomian position. Not surprisingly, beyond the "wild" hermeneutics that does not submit to the voices of authority, Suso draws attention to this last point when he speaks of the misreading of negative theology by the wild one. Quite close to the position of the latter, Mechthild makes clear that ethical self-formation is not to be seen in terms of norms but in terms of a constitutive asymmetry, the drama of love mediated through the practices of assimilation and participation. In stating this, she replaces authoritative scriptural hermeneutics with an experimental rewriting of tradition. The rewriting is a practice that explicitly draws attention to the use of figures and that experiments with textual composition in view of a reform of the life of the soul; and her composition follows the logic of what is otherwise seen as an exercise of meditation, which in turn is characterized not primarily by a turn toward a "spiritual meaning" but toward a deployment of the text in forms of figures. In assimilation and participation, this practice gives a new form to the spheres of sensation, affect, and cognition. Thus, the texts turn from an investment in scriptural hermeneutics to an economy of rhetorical effects that cannot be contained by authoritative exegesis, and the "spirit" turns into the production of new forms of life.

The "devotional" character of Mechthild's text consists in the function that it has for its readers. It asks the reader to shift continuously from the perspective of a hermeneutical engagement to one that allows for the deployment of the efficacy of the text—something that, in formalist terms, entails a practice of defamiliarization; in theological terms, a movement back and forth between an apophatic and a cataphatic mode. This practice breaks with the established patterns of speaking and perception insofar as it mobilizes the rhetorical force of language and its effects, setting assimilation and allegoresis up against participation and the concrete. Thus, instead of following the path of established readings and the submission to correct teachings, these texts engage the circulation of percepts, affects, and concepts in a highly self-conscious—and, indeed, free-spirited—way, producing in the processes a kind of experimental empiricism of the word of God. Drawing on an archive of figures and scripts, they rewrite and reconfigure the chosen elements along a line not primarily of semantic intent but also of rhetorical effect, turning all experience into an experience of figures. While we might speak of defamiliarization at first, both in the moves that isolate certain elements from their usual contexts and in recombining them with unusual contexts, the writing is, at the same time, invested in a phenomenology of rhetorical effects, an exploration of the ways in which the use of language makes subjectivities and ethical formations emerge beyond all imposed normativity.

Maybe surprisingly, the seemingly unconventional and provocative text written by Mechthild is indeed very close to more conventional, ritualized forms of religious life, liturgical forms of prayer, meditation, and song. However, breaking with everyday uses of language and norms of reading, she gives power back to the Scriptures as the device that is meant to give a new form to life. She engages this practice of rewriting in a way that necessarily questions the powers that control this process and the authority that threatens to discredit her voice as the one that animates the text. Thus, she prepares the aspects of a vernacular engagement with the biblical text that Suso will try to reframe in his attempt to control the identification of Eckhart's idea of detachment with the teachings of the "wild one."

The phantasm of the "heresy of the free spirit," represented here by the voice of the wild one, focuses exactly on the hardly controllable possibilities of this type of experimental engagement with the Scriptures and of ethical formation, as it is coming to the fore in the condemnation of Marguerite Porete's *Mirror of Simple Souls* and in Suso's portrait of "disorderly freedom." It is thus not surprising that one hundred years later Jean Gerson does not primarily criticize the very content of mystical devotion and of the production of experience that I am discussing here but the fact that devotional practices open a new space of hardly controllable textual production, spiritual pedagogy, and dissemination. In his eyes, the dangerous aspect of this new devotional tradition in the vernacular is not the content of the teachings but the proliferation and the "insatiable desire to talk" about these things.[18]

He writes this in his *De probatione spirituum* (*On the Testing of the Spirits*), a treatise that like many others addresses the question of the discernment of spirits. The growing number of such treatises in the later Middle Ages—authored by Henry of Friemar, Peter of Ailly, Henry of Langenstein, and Denys the Carthusian—testifies to the increasing need to control this form of experiential spirituality and to an emphasis on the control of hermeneutic engagements. In Gerson's eyes, the conversation and proliferation speak to an increasing invasion of the public sphere by devotional practices that foreground the transition from a hermeneutic focus on meaning to the figural production of experience. Not surprisingly, ecclesiastical authorities react to this experiential turn with a number of treatises on the topic of the discernment of spirits in vernacular languages.[19] Thus, the late medieval church produces the type of heresiological identification that seems to be concerned with specific religious or theological ideas but that in fact tries to cope—as we saw in Suso's *Little Book of Truth*—with the effects of a specific form of the vernacularizing of theological discourses and scriptural exegesis. It is in the process of this vernacularizing that the practices of figural assimilation and participation, up to this point framed by a monastic practice of discernment of spirits and ecclesiastical control, enter a new space of lay piety.

This can also be observed in a more active engagement of the imagination in scriptural exegesis, particularly the investment of the imagination in the rhetoric of meditative rewriting of the Scriptures and the strategies of affective arousal. Speaking in a different vocabulary, we could argue that at the core of the heresiological discourse is not so much—and rarely only—the question of correct teaching, that is, a discursive control along the lines of theological dogma, but the control of the "wild" circulation of percepts, affects, and concepts as it emerges in vernacular texts, challenging both moral normativity and the ecclesiastical control of scriptural exegesis. Against this, Mechthild and Marguerite show in their use of language both explicitly and implicitly—and coinciding here formally with the supposed antinomian libertinage of the free spirits—that participation in the asymmetry of love, as it is deployed in their texts, destroys all normative order and sets free. The critique of this antinomian moment mobilizes the authoritative voice of control. It makes an attempt to control the vernacular use of the Scriptures with a particular focus on the liberating figural and iconoclastic abandonment. "Detachment," Suso thus suggests in his *Little Book of Truth*, has to be framed by both scriptural authority and a correct understanding of negative theology. The critique of free spirits reframes the figural practices, the dynamic tension between figuration and assimilation, and thus also the teaching of "detachment" within a disciplined hermeneutics.

Framing Mysticism

The history of mystical texts and notions of detachment has been told in many ways. Often, the historiography of the topic has focused either on key motifs in the thought of medieval mystics, the poetic form and language, and the reception from the sixteenth to the twentieth centuries, or on modern intellectual paradigms and their relations to medieval mysticism. Typical examples of the latter can be found in the ways in which Heidegger and Derrida make use of the notion of detachment, connecting Meister Eckhart's iconoclasm with questions of twentieth-century philosophy and the challenges of post-metaphysical thought.[20] Countless other examples could be added here, illustrating the engagement with medieval mystical traditions: Georges Bataille's references to medieval mystics, especially to Angela of Foligno, in the part of his *Summa Atheologica* where he discussed "inner experience"; Pierre Klossowski's use of extended quotes from Eckhart's German and Latin works in his *Roberte ce soir*; and Ingeborg Bachmann's, Paul Celan's, and Robert Musil's use of quotations from mystical writings in their texts;[21] or, to mention a more recent example, John Cage's poem for Marcel Duchamp and Meister Eckhart, written shortly before his death.[22]

In addition, some intellectual paradigms and paradigm shifts in modernity have been understood in relation to medieval mystical texts. The most famous case is Hegel's encounter with Eckhart's vernacular sermons. The legend goes that Hegel exclaimed enthusiastically that "there we have what we were looking for!,"[23] when Franz von Baader showed him a collection of Meister Eckhart's German sermons. And this—in turn—led Hegel and his interpreters to speak of Eckhart's mysticism as an anticipation of modern concepts of subjectivity.[24]

One of the most recent references to medieval mysticism and its iconoclastic core can be found in Derrida's engagement with questions of negative theology. He did so first in the lecture "How to Avoid Speaking."[25] In a later text, *On the Name*, Derrida indicates that sixteenth- and seventeenth-century texts play an important mediating role in his reading of medieval sources. Here, Derrida extensively quotes not only the fourteenth-century Eckhart but, more prominently, Angelus Silesius, possibly emphasizing the fact that Silesius, an early modern writer, functions as a link between medieval mystical tropes and their modern adaptations.[26] Without acknowledging it explicitly, Derrida picks up on a line of thought that has been prepared by Martin Heidegger. In *Der Satz vom Grund* (*The Principle of Reason*), a series of lectures given in 1955–1956 and published in 1957, Heidegger quotes Angelus Silesius's verses:

> The rose is without a why: it blooms because it blooms,
> It pays no attention to itself, asks not whether it is seen.[27]

Heidegger explains:

> The verses are found in the first book of the spiritual poetry of Angelus Silesius, which is entitled *The Cherubic Wanderer: Sensual Description of the Four Final Things*. The work first appeared in 1657. The verses carry the number 289 with the heading "Without Why." Angelus Silesius, whose given name was Johann Scheffler, *doctor philosophiae et medicinae*, by profession a medical doctor, lived from 1624 to 1677 in Silesia.

To this short historical note Heidegger adds:

> Leibniz . . . was a younger contemporary of Angelus Silesius and was familiar with *The Cherubic Wanderer*. Leibniz often speaks in his writings and letters of Angelus Silesius. Thus, in a letter to Paccius on January 28, 1695 he once wrote: "With every mystic there are a few places that are extraordinarily clever, full of difficult metaphors and virtually inclining to Godlessness, just as I have sometimes seen in the German—otherwise beautiful—poems of a certain man who is called Johannes Angelus Silesius. . . .
>
> And in his *Lectures on Aesthetics*, Hegel says the following:
>
> Now the pantheistic unity, raised up in relation to *the subject* that senses *itself* in this unity with God and God as this presence in subjective consciousness, would in general yield the *mystic* as it has come to be formed in this subjective manner even within Christianity. As an example I will only cite Angelus Silesius, who with the greatest cleverness and depth of intuition and sensibility has spoken with a wonderfully mystical power of description about the substantial existence of God in things and the unification of the self with God and of God with human subjectivity.

Heidegger concludes:

> The judgments of Leibniz and Hegel about Angelus Silesius are only intended to briefly allude to the fact that the words cited from "Without Why" stem from an influential source. But one might immediately point out that this source is indeed mystical and poetic. The one as well as the other belong equally little in thinking. Certainly not *in* thinking, but perhaps *before* thinking. Leibniz and Hegel, whose thinking it is difficult to surpass in sobriety and rigor, testify to this.[28]

I will not venture into an exegesis of Heidegger's engagement with mysticism or into the larger question of mysticism and subjectivity evoked by

Heidegger's quote from Hegel's *Lectures on Aesthetics.* Rather, I want to draw attention to the importance of early modern sources in this engagement with mysticism and to the function of these sources with regard to the specific character of its survival—of what I call mystical tropes and their specific articulation of a tension between figuration, assimilation, and partaking—in a seemingly secular modernity. It is significant, then, that in Hegel, Leibniz, and Heidegger, the mystical tradition is not only associated with a specific language—something we can speak of with Hans Blumenberg in terms of a historical metaphorology and of *Umbesetzung* (resignification)[29]—but also, and quite prominently, with a specific emphasis on sensation and perception, in other words, something we can speak of in terms of experience. This might not come as a surprise since references to mystical traditions in modernity often seem to be associated with commonsense understandings of romantic turns and forms of a "return" to premodern concepts of immediacy, spontaneity, and spiritual unity.

In the following, I argue that Martin Heidegger's reference to the "poetic" nature of Silesius's thought hides something that is essential in early modern reworkings and the recasting of medieval mystical sources, a very specific emphasis not so much on "subjectivity" or on a "romantic turn" but on something we might call a poetics or poiesis of experience. In my understanding the specificity of this emphasis on experience is not to be seen in the fact that it is—as Heidegger puts it, with and against Immanuel Kant—"before thinking" or that it represents a poetic adaptation of medieval mystical texts but that it provides us with models of an experimental poetic understanding of experience and sensation that draws on the techniques of figuration portrayed in earlier chapters. As I argued in the previous section, the genealogy of these models is intimately linked with a tension that emerges in the late Middle Ages and finds its expression in the attempts to neutralize the so-called free spirits. As I want to show here further, a second line of neutralization can be observed in ways of instituting a secular order and a disjunction of the secular and the spiritual that are introduced by Martin Luther. Thus, in early modern times mystical tropes come to be increasingly projected into the new epistemological space of a private spiritual and aesthetic experience. This projection transposes the mystical language from its medieval anchoring in practices of reading the Scriptures and makes it available to a series of transformations from the sixteenth to the twentieth centuries, leading to Heidegger's identification of the mystical with something that is "before thinking"—which, I want to add after the previous explorations, is not at all the case in medieval discourses about the "experiential knowledge of the divine."[30] There, as I have shown, it is to be seen as a transfiguration of thinking in a practice that always entails a circulation of sensations, affects, and thought.

To explore this transposition, I return first to Martin Luther and his critique of the most mystical of the sixteenth-century reformers, the radical spiritualists. In this critique we observe a framing of inspired and mystical readings that is important for the shift that turns medieval practices of mystical experience into the "subjective" or "religious" experience invoked by Hegel, Leibniz, and others. After Luther and his critical intervention—an intervention that isolates inspired reading from the newly instituted secular realm—the mysticism that in the Middle Ages is located in contexts of devotional practices of reading takes shape as a model for the experience of the self and the world. Rewritten as a form of cosmopoiesis and poetic self-fashioning under the pressure of Luther's institution of the secular order and Kant's critique, the references to medieval mystical traditions thus serve specific purposes in modernity. These purposes are not determined by nostalgia and esoteric inclinations—although this sometimes plays a role as well—but they fit into a structure of the modern poetic elaboration of possibilities and possible worlds, testifying both to the power of the institution of the secular in Luther's works and its capacity to conceal its theological origin. I outline this shift, focusing on the importance of Luther's arguments for an irreducible secular order, on one of the ways in which mystical tropes figure in the post-Reformation world, and finally on Kant's reiteration and elaboration of Luther's distinction between the secular and spiritual realms. It is this focus on the control of hermeneutics and its reconfiguration in terms of subjectivity that is, in my view, a much deeper shift than the one we usually connect with the emergence of late medieval "nominalism." At the same time, I portray neither the nominalist nor the subjective turn in terms of loss. What is at stake, instead, is a reconfiguration that both addresses and further deploys key aspects of the medieval practices of reading, meditation, and prayer. With the nominalist intervention, its focus lies on the irreducibly concrete; with the subjectivizing intervention, its focus recasts the dramatic structure of assimilation and participation that figural practices entail.

Remarkably, most of the modern engagements with medieval mysticism find themselves outside the common forms—ecstatic union and suffering, inspired speech, intense emotion and sensation—that frame the use of mystical tropes during the Middle Ages, as well as the context of monastic practice, especially prayer, meditation, liturgy, and the reading and rewriting of the Scriptures in the community of monks and nuns. As I have shown, medieval mysticism, particularly in its specific emphasis on the circulation of percepts, affects, and concepts, cannot be adequately understood outside this framework, and mysticism can in many ways be described in terms of a figural practice that engages participation and assimilation at the limits of scriptural hermeneutics. From William of Saint Thierry and Hugh of Saint Victor to Hadewijch of Antwerp, Mechthild of Magdeburg, Meister Eckhart, and many other late medieval mystics, mystical experience has its place in the context of regulated forms of reading, preaching, and prayer, above all the reading of the Scriptures and the liturgical formats that enact, recall, and perform aspects of the Scriptures. Mystical experience—understood as *cognitio Dei experimentalis* (experiential knowledge of God) based on figural partaking—is thus embedded in a specific culture of prayer and contemplation, most often a monastic one, and for a long time it is determined by a specific language, Latin. Speaking of a hermeneutical framework here means to acknowledge that the experience in question is evoked and produced through a set of practices exercised in view of an understanding of textual traditions and a rhetorical amplification of this understanding that often takes shape in the form of intense sensation and emotion. As I argued previously, the challenge to hermeneutics lies in the emphasis on the figural and in a logic of participation that runs up against assimilation. The pedagogy that supports these practices can be found in treatises that are part of a larger monastic culture and its emphasis on experiential piety. Within the monastic culture, the production of such moments of ecstatic experience is accompanied by the subtle and elaborate practices of a "discernment of spirits," that is, again, a phenomenological approach and evaluation of the validity of the moments of experiential intensity and the absorption in love.[31] This discernment has its place exactly on the threshold of hermeneutics, assimilation, and participatory abandonment, since it tries to explore and evaluate what happens to the soul in the practice of prayer and contemplation. The very evolution of the practices of discernment testifies to the line of control that I laid out in the preceding section. From a phenomenology of rhetorical effects—an evaluation of devotional experience in terms of sweetness and bitterness, beauty and ugliness, humility and pride—we move to the institution of a hermeneutic control in Suso and increasingly to a semiotic control that identifies the signs of the divine and the demonic in early modernity.

As I have argued, during the later Middle Ages a number of texts dealing with mystical experience and written in vernacular languages support a transformation that tends to dissolve the institutional and hermeneutical framework in which medieval mysticism subsists. It can be traced back to books such as Hadewijch's *Poems in Stanzas* and *Visions*, Mechthild of Magdeburg's *Flowing Light of the Godhead*, and Marguerite Porete's *Mirror of Simple Souls*, all written in vernacular languages for communities of readers that are not part of traditional monastic orders.[32] Instead, the writings of these women are at the core of the formation of new communities, often, as in the case of beguine communities, forming alternatives to traditional monasteries. As we have seen in the case of Mechthild of Magdeburg's *Flowing Light of the Godhead*, she relies on the translation of hermeneutic reading into figural practices, a shared emphasis on devotional experience that challenges the worldly order, and the continuous production of vernacular writings that circulate within and between new social groups. The attempts to keep these voices under control can be seen in reactions of the church against some of the late medieval beguine movements and in the works of fourteenth- and fifteenth-century theologians who criticize some aspects of vernacular mysticism and try to enforce the practice of "discernment of spirits" beyond the traditional context of monastic discipline, focusing increasingly on beguine and lay religious practices. As mentioned previously, Henry of Friemar, Henry of Langenstein, Peter of Ailly, Jean Gerson, and Denys the Carthusian are key figures in the elaboration of theological responses to the developments of vernacular mysticism.[33]

The major impact of the shift and transformation I am interested in here, however, becomes most visible only in Martin Luther's works. In his writings, the issue turns out to be much larger than in earlier attempts to control and frame mystical practices and texts. At stake here is the very question of containment of the meaning of the Scriptures. Luther addressed this in his polemical exchanges with the radical reformers, that is, the groups of anabaptists and social revolutionaries who also made use of the new possibilities offered by the printing press in the sixteenth century.[34] At the center of these polemical exchanges—exchanges that often happened in the form of so-called *Flugschriften* or pamphlets—we can identify the problem of who is entitled and justified to propose and publicly defend a specific reading of the Scriptures, which was often an "inspired," "mystical," or "prophetic" reading of the biblical text. It is in this move against the mystical and inspired readers of the Scriptures—a move that parallels his critique of Dionysius the Areopagite's negative theology and of figural practices in the Catholic Church—that Luther introduces the concept of the "secular" as a new corrective. Luther's concept of the secular replaces the medieval, essentially phenomenological practice of the "discernment of spirits"—applied on a case-by-case basis to evaluate the effects and texts produced by spiritual practices—through a normative framework that, in spite of and concomitant with the turn of the individual believer toward a highly self-centered reading of the Scriptures, is meant to limit the possibilities of scriptural exegesis, particularly the transitions from letter to image and from image to excessive and absorbing figure. Participation and assimilation cannot be produced in and through a play with figures in meditation, Luther argues, but they have to be conceived of only in terms of grace and the word.

In his critique of the anabaptists and other "enthusiasts" (*Schwärmer*), Luther's arguments against their readings of the Scriptures perform a very specific move. Luther produces a notion of the "secular" not as a realm that is subordinated to the "religious," absolutely disassociated from it, or opposed to it, or primarily as a realm that is an outward expression of the inner faith of the believer—as explained in Luther's *Freedom of a Christian* and analyzed by Max Weber in *The Protestant Ethic and the "Spirit" of Capitalism*. Instead, the "secular" forms an institutional frame that is meant to contain and limit the use that can be made of the Scriptures and of scriptural exegesis. The secular order (*weltliche oberkeit oder ampt* or *des welltlichen regiments werck*, the office of secular order, as opposed to the *predig ampt*, the office of preaching, exegesis, and interpretation) is not only meant to distinguish humans from animals and submit them to the civilizing force of law (*rechte*) and reason (*vernunfft*),[35] but to form the core of a pedagogy that censors the reach of scriptural inspiration and the texts that are allowed to circulate. In an essay on the schooling of children Luther writes: "In the office of preaching Christ acts through his spirit. However, in the secular realm we have to act on the basis of reason (where the laws have their origin, as well), since God has subjected the temporal powers and the material world to reason, and he has not sent the holy spirit to interfere with it."[36] As I observe later, Luther here does not operate on the basis of a distinction between faith and reason. Instead, he establishes and justifies the secular order as a social and pedagogical institution that is meant to control the ways in which the Bible can be read and staged as a source for inspiration. While he makes the biblical text available in the vernacular, translating it into German and into the language of all possible readers, he introduces the secular order as an institution that limits the engagement of the reader with the biblical text, containing the exegetical practice and the inspired hermeneutics within the borders of the *predig ampt*, that is, the function of preaching. Thus, Luther—reminding us of Suso's intervention against wild hermeneutics—contains the formation of legitimate communities of readers as well, limiting the act of reading to the "freedom of a Christian," within the "inner man" and a contained religious community alone.[37] With this step, Luther not only neutralizes the possibilities for a life that takes its shape under the figural effects as they were deployed in the Catholic tradition of prayer and contemplation in forms of assimilation and participation; he also neutralizes the effects of the "word alone" when it tends to disturb the "worldly order."

I want to explain this further with an example. In 1524 Luther wrote a letter to the dukes of Saxony against the radical reformers of Allstett. It goes under the title "Von dem auffrurischen geyst" (On the revolutionary spirit).[38] In this letter, he attacks the social and revolutionary tendencies in the reform movement (in Luther's words, "those who want to change the world with their fists"). "To overthrow the secular powers and to be masters of this world themselves" makes up their political and religious program.[39] What they are acting on, he argues, is not a hermeneutically correct, that is, appropriately controlled, reading of the Scriptures but an "inspired" or "enthusiastic" reading, an uncontrolled and uncontrollable scriptural hermeneutics that leads the revolutionaries to form a new community and overthrow the existing social order. This inspired, mystical, radically eschatological, and—speaking from Luther's point of view—wild reading is often at the origin of what we call *Flugschriften*,[40] a genre of printed pamphlets that circulated among groups of reformers and informed radical communities.[41] In the case of one of Luther's enemies, the anabaptist Thomas Müntzer, this form of reading the Scriptures links prophetic dreams and divine communication in the holy spirit with a community of interlocutors that explicitly competes with the "secular authorities" (*weltliche obrigkeyt*) and enacts a mystical eschatology, emphasizing the political relevance of an egalitarian biblical message. Consequently, and based on the figure of prophetic dreams, Müntzer draws the conclusion from the biblical text that the message of the gospel is to be understood in terms of profound social change and an eschatology that projects the day of judgment into historical time.[42] His actions, Müntzer claims, are nothing else than participation in God's work in the world.

Luther argues against the position of Müntzer and the radical reformers; quoting John 18:36 ("his kingdom is not from this world"), he emphasizes that a correct biblical teaching and exegetical practice have to be contained by the institution of the secular order, an order that a correct reading of the Scriptures must draw from the divine word itself. In "Temporal Authority: To What Extent It Should Be Obeyed" he thus writes, summarizing his references to biblical passages and pointing to the irreducible status of the secular law: "The law of this temporal sword has existed from the beginning of the world. For when Cain slew his brother Abel, he was in such great terror of being killed in turn that God even placed a special prohibition on it and suspended the sword for his sake, so that no one was to slay him. He would not have had this fear if he had not seen and heard from Adam that murderers are to be slain."[43] Therefore, the institution of justice as a secular practice and as a prerogative of worldly authority that asks for subjection has, according to Luther, its foundation in the correct reading of the Scriptures. It forms the divine corrective that prevents the hermeneutical engagement with the text from turning into a practice that could form inspired communities of readers who might compete with the established structures of social hierarchy and seek their own justice beyond norms. As Luther argues also in his treatise "The Freedom of a Christian," freedom and faith are to be correlated with the inner, spiritual man, while the "outer," worldly man is to be seen as a subject of the worldly order.[44]

What Luther responds to in his critique of the radical reformers is not just a local problem of social rebellion during the 1520s. It is, as we have seen in the discussion of the framing of free spirits, a larger problem that arose within and at the margins of the church and late medieval religious culture since the thirteenth century, mainly when writings in vernacular languages started to offer their own readings of biblical texts, often in ways that we call inspired or mystical—and that I characterized as a specific turn to figural reading. The problem that church censorship tried to address at several fourteenth- and fifteenth-century councils lies, however, less with issues of social justice or the so-called inspired or mystical character of such texts and the increasingly common use of mystical tropes of unity, divinization, ecstatic suffering, and visionary experience. As I have shown, it appears more prominently where vernacular texts start to circulate and to produce a realm of communication about a reading of the Scriptures in the vernacular that threatens the authorized exegesis of the canonical texts.

In defining the "secular," Luther draws the consequences from the strategy of framing mystical hermeneutics—building on the fourteenth- and fifteenth-century critique of free spirits—that focused on the formation of communities of readers and interpreters of the Scriptures. He does so, however, not in terms of the traditional practices of "discernment of spirits" and hermeneutic control itself but in a way that foregrounds the disjunction between the secular realm (the realm of worldly powers) and the realm of a supposedly unmediated sphere of spirit, faith, and freedom. This disjunction, Luther argues, has its ground in the divine order itself, an order established in grace and faith through the Scriptures. This very order of the world invalidates certain readings and grants social stability in the temporal realm of a postlapsarian state. What we might conclude, then, is the following: Luther evokes and defines the "secular," what he calls the "outer" man, and the "worldly authorities" (*weltliche Obrigkeit*) from within the control of hermeneutics, inheriting and transforming a late medieval practice of "discernment of spirits" and establishing a normative frame, which has the function of restricting the realm of legitimate readings of the biblical text. In doing so, he builds on changes already under way in the evolution of the practices of discernment. These practices turn from a phenomenology of pride and humility in monastic texts, to an evaluation of correct and permissible readings in vernacular mysticism, and finally to a semiotics of the divine and the demonic in the late Middle Ages, represented most prominently by Heinrich Kramer's *Malleus Maleficarum* (*The Hammer of Witches*) from 1486. Luther, finally, articulates it in terms of social order and a critique of "enthusiasts."

In Luther's model, the secular is, however, not seen as free from the "religious." Far from that, the secular is the normative limit Luther draws from his reading of the Scriptures, mainly Paul's letter to the Romans, chapter 13, as the means to control the hermeneutical possibilities and the enthusiastic abandonment to the Scriptures that radical reformers explore. The secular order is in Luther's view the frame that excludes spiritual enthusiasm, the law that knows the signs and that the Scriptures themselves produce to limit the hermeneutic possibilities and to control the use of mystical tropes with their specific liberating and antinomian claims. The normative character of the secular order forms from now on the limit of "religious" communication. It is dictated, as Luther would have it, by the divine revelation through the biblical text itself.

The secular is thus a principle of inclusion and exclusion. It establishes itself as the universal order of the social world in its temporal state, defining a rational economy of governance and subjection that conceals its origin, the exclusion of specific hermeneutical possibilities and their force in community formation. The abyss of the figural can no longer function as a source of inspiration of practices of assimilation, which, in turn, motivate "wild" voices and possibilities of antinomian excess. As a normative framework that validates and invalidates certain readings of the Scriptures, the abyss of "grace alone" and "faith alone" replaces the phenomenological approach to practices of assimilation and participation that had been cultivated by monks, nuns, laymen, and church authorities in the form of the "discernment of spirits."

In the following I pursue two lines of interpretation. The first points back toward the late Middle Ages, the problem of mystical texts as it was addressed in the fourteenth and fifteenth centuries, and the fate of mystical experience after Luther. A second one offers a short comment on the relation between the harshest critic of mysticism in modernity, Immanuel Kant, and Luther's distinction between the secular and the spiritual.

Luther's arguments against the radical reformers can be seen in a larger context of issues that emerged when vernacular religious texts started to circulate in the late Middle Ages. As we observe in council documents and writings, for example, in texts written by the fifteenth-century theologian Jean Gerson, the main problem between the church and so-called heretical movements was not that the doctrinal positions in their writings were sometimes seen as unorthodox, heretical, or questionable by the church authorities. Rather, it was the fact that "conversation," as Gerson writes, "a delirious wish to talk" accompanied the propagation of such vernacular texts and their ambitions.[45] Much of this must be seen as part of a new order of communication that actually leads toward and that is part of what we call the Reformation. From this point of view, Luther's intervention forms an attempt to contain this "wish to talk" about the Scriptures, to limit the realm of justified readings, and to control the formation of social communities with their own readings and enactments of canonical texts. It is at this point when he introduces the secular order as the essential corrective, using it as the new institutional and normative context that replaces the practices of church censorship and of "discernment of the spirits," which used to be exercised by the Catholic Church through a set of defined practices. In Luther's text, the newly established authority of the secular has replaced the specific character of censoring practices of the Catholic Church, defining the limits of what is and is not permissible communication and hermeneutics in terms of a universalized "secular regime" (*weltliches Regiment*) that is detached from "the gospel, from conscience, and from grace."[46] Thus, the secular can be seen as the public realm that turns "wild animals" into "men,"[47] and it controls the ways in which religious communities are allowed to form and communicate based on their readings of the Scriptures. Or, to put it in more general terms, the secular establishes itself as a paradigm of rationality that dismisses "inspired" readings of the canonical texts and the claims of participation in the divine whenever they threaten it. It institutes a correlation of hermeneutics and subjectivity, on the one hand (the reader of the Scriptures lives in faith and saving grace), and of hermeneutic and rational normativity, on the other (the reader is isolated from figural modes of assimilation and participation and the revolutionary enthusiasm that the Scriptures might evoke).

This situation can, as many have shown before me, also be read in terms of media politics. We should remind ourselves that Luther finds himself in a paradoxical position. It is with and around Luther that printed culture expands in a hitherto unknown way. With him the production of a mass of printed pamphlets sets in, and there can be no doubt that the success of the Reformation depended in some part on the effects of the circulation of such texts. They address issues of church politics, theology and dogmatics, but also social issues, and they continue the proliferation of vernacular texts that goes back to the thirteenth century. Questions of iconoclasm, childhood baptism, begging and poverty, the interpretation of the Eucharist and other sacraments appear at the center of these pamphlets, and the printing of the pamphlets turns into a stage where all the polemical issues between the parties are fought. This proliferation of a public discussion of theological questions represents exactly what fifteenth-century church authorities were already afraid of at the Council of Constance when they warned against the inclinations of too many people to discuss the Bible and their religious experience in vernacular languages, particularly in using the tropes of mystical language. The possibilities offered by the printing press to produce pamphlets led to an intensification of these conversations and to an inflation of polemical positions that claimed to represent alternative readings of the biblical text. Many voices had predicted this evolution. Jean Gerson was concerned that the books and pamphlets in vernacular languages would produce confusion and heresy, and later a Nürnberg decree states:

> Pay attention to prevent and control the pest of printed books, the translations of the Holy Scriptures, since these translations undermine the authority of the church and true faith, they create confusion in the Holy Church, lead to the condemnation of the souls and destroy both the worldly and spiritual order. . . . You have to be opposed to this in the beginning, before the distribution of German books leads from a spark of error to a conflagration.[48]

It can be argued that the medium of the printing press itself made it impossible to prevent the consequences, the outbreak of the "fire" of the

Reformation, of the multiplication of opinions and of errors. In Luther's reaction, in his attempts to contain this multiplication of standpoints, lies also one of the origins of the projection of mystical tropes into a new realm. Removing them from authorized hermeneutics and thus setting them free—so to speak—for their use in a new epistemological realm prepares both revisions of orthodox Lutheranism, particularly later in pietism, and the transition into the sphere of aesthetic experience that I discuss later. Luther's position is paradoxical. He profits from the possibilities of the new medium of printed pamphlets to create a new community, church hierarchy and hermeneutic authority, that supports the Reformation. In doing so, he relies on a new focus on interiority and the encounter with the word of the Scriptures that, as many have argued before me, relies on late medieval mystical voices. However, he restricts the very danger that the multiplication of these voices and the printed pamphlets pose in his eyes, the unleashing of competing interpretations of the biblical texts and their message, and thus a potential disturbance of the worldly order. He draws the consequences, the isolation of the secular order from radical interpretations of the Bible, foremost in and through the famous distinction he makes when he, relying on Paul's letter to the Romans, discusses the specific "freedom" of the believer. Declaring that a Christian is "free inside" and "bound outside," that Christians are free in their faith and in the reading of the Scriptures but bound in their very exegetical practice by the worldly order that has been instated by God, stands in his eyes on theological and biblical grounds. At the same time, this forms the setup for a sharp distinction between the spiritual and secular realms that allows for a censorship that can be exercised against the distribution of the new media and voices insofar as they threaten to destabilize this very distinction.

Beyond this, I want to point to another aspect of Luther's intervention. As we have seen, Luther invalidates the legitimacy of the radical political and spiritualist hermeneutics practiced by Thomas Müntzer and others. He suppresses the possibility of drawing political consequences from the mystical readings of the Scriptures that try to enact a revolutionary eschatology of universal equality and justice. In doing so, Luther draws in his own work, especially through his edition of the late medieval *Theologia Germanica* (*Theologia Deutsch*),[49] on the very same vernacular tradition of mysticism. This puts a strong emphasis on the importance of the individual act of reading the Scriptures and on the presence of the spirit in this very act. However, he removes this act of reading from the medieval framework of liturgy, monastic practice, and contemplative reading with its mystical tropes and the figural registers of rhetorical amplification that I portrayed earlier. Thus, he prepares—quite paradoxically—the ground for a new way of reading the mystical texts that early modern readers inherit from the medieval tradition. Devoid of their liturgical and hermeneutical embeddedness, as well as a diverse devotional culture, they are now stripped of all para-scriptural means that support the figural amplification in contexts of the production of devotional experience. Devoid also of a politico-eschatological meaning, these texts and the mystical practices of prayer and contemplation turn into something new, the basis for what we could call an experimental poetic mysticism that is explored in many forms from the sixteenth to the twentieth century. Since this experimental poetic mysticism has its place—in spite of many political and religious conflicts—no longer necessarily within or against an authorized hermeneutics or within a devotional register of figural practices, and since its subversive political and eschatological powers have been neutralized through the distinction of the secular and spiritual, the mystical tropes are thus set free to be used in a different realm. It is a realm that we can call an experiential supplement to the spiritual freedom of a Christian that, according to Luther, is to be found in the correct reading of the Scriptures alone. Luther himself does not explore this and, in fact, is highly critical of any kind of use of mystical tropes to support and produce mystical experiences that might result from the reading of Scriptures. In extracting these tropes from the possibilities of authoritative reading, he makes them available for a new use, which in Baroque mysticism will take the form not primarily of a hermeneutical practice that explores figural asymmetries but also of a poetics of self-fashioning that is often meant to bridge the abyss between the secular order of submission and, in Michel de Certeau's description, a marginal practice of the freedom in faith.[50]

Many of the forms in which mystical tropes will be adopted subsequently are indeed "poetic," as Heidegger suggests in the passage quoted previously, relegating, as I argue in the next chapter, early modern modes of knowledge characterized by emblematic tensions to an area "before thought." Angelus Silesius is only one example. Katharina Regina von Greiffenberg is another author who fits this new paradigm,[51] and a reading of their works shows how exactly they make use of common figures of thought and experience from medieval mysticism in their poetry. It opens up a new field of variations around questions of hermeneutics, tensions of figural production, and authorized speech—variations that we observe throughout the seventeenth and early eighteenth centuries. Thus, they reconfigure the use of mystical tropes in response to Luther's institution of the secular and in terms of an experimental use and a constructivist understanding of experience. Heidegger, I think, does not do justice to this when he calls it (merely) "poetic," mainly because he does not take into account the projection of the mystical tropes into an epistemological realm where experience, perception, and knowledge take shape in certain forms that—in foregrounding the suspension of ontology in the tension between figures and assimilation—would undermine his approach.

No doubt, what I call the experimental and constructivist understanding of experience has been well prepared by the medieval mystics themselves and the attention they draw to the significance of figural practices. As I have shown, they use quotes from the Scriptures, passages from the *Song of Songs*, and moments of the liturgy throughout the year as rhetorical means to produce certain effects and to construct modes of assimilation and participation. These effects include strong emotions, sensations, and what is often portrayed in the form of stages of an experience of a unity with God and the world. In many cases medieval authors do this with the acknowledged and highly self-conscious intent to produce an anticipated eschatological state, often described in terms of a "foretaste of heaven." This entails a rhetoric, a style of phenomenology, and even a mechanics that are used methodically to evoke certain effects and to enact aspects of ecstatic suffering, vision, passion, and divine unity under the sign of a desired eschatological reconciliation or, maybe better, a collapse of the distinction between immanence and transcendence. Figure, turning into figure, and participation in the divine stand for this very collapse.

After Luther's critique of these ascetic and rhetorical practices, and devoid of their monastic and liturgical framings, such practices do not entirely disappear. Instead, they resurface and become available to an experimental poetics of both the self and the world, evoking time and again the intent of producing a "foretaste of things to come." Their position shifts, however, and they now increasingly locate this "foretaste" in a subjective perception and experience. Increasingly, they also lose the revolutionary meaning the experience of a "foretaste of heaven" had for Thomas Müntzer.[52]

The experience is also no longer—as in Hadewijch's and Mechthild's writings—located primarily in visionary events that happen within the frameworks of the liturgy or the reading of the Scriptures. Instead, the experience finds itself located in the perception of the world and in the rhetorical construction of relations between the material world and the self. In Katharina von Greiffenberg's poetry, nature in its concrete forms turns into the figure and the playing ground for the use of such tropes, enacting a new order of communication where the self experiments with the possibilities of sensual and emotional intensity drawn from mystical tropes and with possibilities of experiencing the world in light of them. Thus, her poetry reflects one of the lines that can be drawn from Paracelsus to Johann Arndt, to Jacob Böhme and to the pietists, to Nicolaus Zinzendorf and Susanna Katharina von Klettenberg, Goethe's "beautiful soul." Along this line, not so much the figural production of an experience of the Scriptures and of nature in light of the Scriptures moves into the foreground but the production and intensification of a specific experience of nature and of sensual experience as an experiential supplement to an abstract concept of faith.

Not surprisingly, the imagination now plays a more explicit and growing role in this tradition that increasingly foregrounds subjective experience. At the same time, however, a cosmopoetic understanding of the imagination moves to the fore. In the multiple intersections with alchemical and hermetic traditions characteristic of the sixteenth- and seventeenth-century use of mystical tropes, they turn into what makes mind and nature converge. It is significant that this experience of the world is still mediated through meditational practices, through the use of scriptural quotes and images that inform and shape the imagination and thus give form to the experience of the world. In other words, the foretaste of heaven and the intimacy with Christ that medieval mystics found in their enactment of the Scriptures and of the liturgy, this very foretaste now takes shape in the form of experiential modes of perception still produced on the basis of the Scriptures but in a more pronounced poetic mode. In this mode, poetic figuration meets the cosmopoetic imagination in forms that make both converge. On the one hand, a more clearly delineated anthropocentric and subject-centered focus emerges. On the other, culminating in Charles Baudelaire's poem "Correspondances," poetic figuration and cosmopoetic imagination go hand in hand and make all stable positions collapse. Here, the adaptation of mystical language is still not just allegory and illustration but a figural practice that shapes perception and the knowledge of the world. However, while this practice has its place outside the strictly hermeneutical and figural settings of medieval devotional practice, it now turns into a model for self-fashioning that folds the circulation of sensation, affect, and thought more pronouncedly around a monadic singularity of the self. It shows itself most often in the tension between a cosmic imagination and a melancholic desire to rejoin it.

Again, a quote from Silesius can illustrate this. In a conclusive aphorism he writes:

> Freund es ist auch genug. Jm fall du mehr wilt lesen,
> So geh und werde selbst die Schrift und selbst das Wesen.
> (Friend, let this be enough; if you wish to read beyond,
> Go and become yourself the writ and yourself the essence.)[53]

This act—"become yourself the writ"—now stands outside the medieval framework of liturgy and reading and its claims. It takes shape as an application of mystical tropes that produces ever-new forms of experience on the basis of rhetorical experiments. The "science of saints" turns into an "experimental science" (Jean-Jacques Surin),[54] an art of figuration of the life of the soul in its conversation with itself, a community, and the world.[55] It is an art of figuration that makes use of the mystical tropes inherited from medieval mysticism. However, it projects these tropes into a practice of writing and conversation that has transformed their participatory claims and reconfigures them in the mode of an "emblematic tension." Contained by the limits set up by Luther and running up against these limits, they form an experiential sphere that in modernity often is seen as aesthetic, subjective, and poetic alone.

The radical pietist Susanna Katharina von Klettenberg points out how she understands this very process of producing an experiential sphere against the Lutheran orthodoxy in a letter to Johann Heinrich Lavater dated January 9, 1774. She defends the thought that the "imagination," "when filled with such images," enables us to experience "true beatitude" (*réelle Seeligkeit*) in this life.[56] She points out that the imagination, informed by "images" drawn from the Scriptures and other, mostly mystical sources, is the mediator between the self, nature, and the divine. The imagination, now isolated in this function, is the faculty and medium of experience insofar as it provides a sensual, emotional, and intellectual space of assimilation; and insofar as it allows this very experience to be produced through the practices of giving shape to the imagination and to anticipate an eschatological state, this is "real beatitude" here and now. Significantly, this eschatological state has its place not in visionary experience of the divine word that unlocks the participatory circulation of percepts, affects, and concepts. Instead, it is the multiplicity in the experience of the world that is informed by the practice of the imagination and that in its resonance with an inherited mystical language turns into a pedagogy of perception.

Again, I want to emphasize that for Angelus Silesius, Katharina Regina von Greiffenberg, and Susanna Katharina von Klettenberg, the mystical tropes they use are detached from the medieval scriptural and monastic framework and projected into a new epistemological space. There, they serve not only the production of specific sensual and emotional experience but also the constitution of a specific knowledge of the world and the self. It is characteristic for this knowledge that it attempts to unite the interior and the exterior, imagination and perception, sensuality and spirit, addressing issues of the convertibility and reversibility of Luther's "inner" and "outer man," of the effects of the world on the self and the self on the world in processes of perception and cognition. And it is characteristic that this unification of interior and exterior, this construction of moments of convergence, depends heavily on the specific use of mystical tropes that are meant to shape the imagination. Thus, they transpose the eschatological goal of a union with the divine, the figural partaking, into something Susanna Katharina von Klettenberg calls *Lebenskunst*, an "art of living." It has its ground in an art of perception shaped by the use of mystical tropes as figures—as figures, however, that are detached from the hermeneutical frame of the Scriptures and from the medieval tension between the figural and the hermeneutical. Concreteness and particularity still characterize the figural. It is set up, however, along a new line, the transformation of nature in the imagination. Thus, "nature" is, in response to the neutralization of the wild possibilities of scriptural hermeneutics, being established as the defining horizon of things. Figures no longer gain their transformative force from within a tension with scripture and scripture-based gestures of a reinvention of nature but from within a focus on nature. As I show in the next chapter, a new emblematic form of thought and perception and a new understanding of relations between interior and exterior are one of the expressions of this shift.

The Romantic poet Novalis reflects on it when he writes:

> We have two sense systems which, however different they appear, are yet entwined extremely closely with one another. One system is called the body, one the soul. The former is dependent on external stimuli, whose essence we call nature or the external world. The latter originally is dependent on the essence of inner stimuli that we call spirit, or the world of spirits. Usually, this last system stands in a nexus of association with the other system—and is affected by it. Nevertheless, frequent traces of a converse relation are to be found, and one soon notices that both systems ought actually to stand in perfect reciprocal relation to one another, in which, while each of them is affected by its world, they should create harmony. . . . In short, both worlds, like both systems, are to create free harmony, not disharmony or monotony.[57]

It appears that Novalis describes body and soul, the senses, the emotions and reason in terms quite typical of Romanticism and German idealism. In fact, however, Novalis draws here on a terminology and use of mystical tropes that come to him through the pietist tradition. In particular, where the specific concepts of "inner" and "outer" are concerned, Novalis builds on this, foregrounding the idea of a "converse relation" of interiority and exteriority and a desire for a new configuration of this relation. What Novalis inherits, mediated through the pietist literature about the topic, is the idea of an artificial and rhetorical stimulation and formation of the senses. And, last, he inherits the idea of an eschatological reconciliation, a collapse of the distinction of immanence and transcendence that is projected into the realm of perception. In the passage just quoted, its expression is to be found in the idea of a "free harmony" between the "two systems," the inner and the outer, where both systems interact and affect each other in a different state of perception and knowledge.

For Novalis, as well as for the free spirit and radical pietist Susanna Katharina von Klettenberg, the application of mystical tropes does not produce an experience of the divine alone. It also deploys figures as means of a reformation of perception and experience, introducing a moment of eschatological resolution expressed in terms that recall Jacob Böhme and his models of cosmopoiesis and emblematic monadology. I come back to this in the next chapter.

Against Enthusiasm

Building on Immanuel Kant, we might be tempted to argue that such poetic and speculative adaptations of mystical tropes and practices of figuration from Jacob Böhme and Angelus Silesius to Novalis are "a pretension of philosophy," born out of "natural laziness," and dedicated to "listening and enjoying the oracular voices from within." It is, in Kant's terms, philosophy that is caught up in *Anschauung* (intuition, also contemplation or representation) and in the opinion that its inspiration is drawn immediately from the divine.[58] This seems particularly true in a world where the engagement with formative figural practices seems entirely removed from the authorizing sphere of scriptural hermeneutics. Shying away from the "labor" of true philosophy—that is, the work of the concept and its limits—mysticism is thus identified with a *salto mortale* in an entirely naturalized world, an undue preference for "emotion," and "the mistuning of heads into exaltation."[59] This exclusion of mystical inspiration and enthusiasm from philosophy is not only technical and dogmatic. Beyond that, it builds on Luther's arguments that focused on social control and the restriction of radical, inspired hermeneutics as well as figural ascetic practice. The "exalted philosopher" endangers the integrity of the social body, Kant writes, both through the "tone" of his discourse and through the formation of "clubs" that undermine its coherence. The ambition of the inspired philosopher and the community he evokes endangers the "modicum" and "humility" that ideally should result from the "critique of his own reason."[60]

With his arguments Immanuel Kant places the legitimate use of mystical tropes exclusively within the language of poetry (in Heidegger's terms, "before thought"). Moreover, he also reinforces Luther's institution of the secular in terms of reason itself, obliterating the very origin of a distinction that is also at the basis of his "An Answer to the Question: What Is Enlightenment?" While Luther argued that the institution of the secular (the "worldly regiment," the realm of "law," "reason," and the submission of the "outer man") has its origin in the Scriptures, limiting the scope of reading and hermeneutics, and while he placed true freedom only in the "inner man," Kant argues that reason itself is the source of both submission and freedom. Excluding inspired speech and the use of mystical tropes in scriptural hermeneutics from the scope of the practice of reason, Kant rewrites Luther's distinction between the spiritual work of the preacher and the secular regiment in terms of the exercise of reason itself and of a distinction between its "public" and "private" use. In the most famous passage from "What Is Enlightenment?" he writes:

> The *public* use of one's reason must always be free, and it alone can bring about enlightenment among mankind; the *private use* of reason may, however, often be very narrowly restricted, without otherwise hindering the progress of enlightenment. By the public use of one's own reason I understand the use that anyone as a *scholar* makes of reason before the entire *literate world.* I call the private use of reason that which a person may make in a *civic post* or office that has been entrusted to him.[61]

In accepting this, he argues further, "Only a ruler who is himself enlightened and has no dread of shadows, yet who likewise has a well-disciplined, numerous army to guarantee public peace, can say what no republic may dare: "*Argue as much as you want and about what you want, but obey!*"[62]

Kant's image of an ever-increasing enlightenment and of an enlightened society is thus bound up with a distinction that replaces Luther's freedom of the "inner man" by "complete freedom in religious matters" and the "public use" of reason in the form of argument. However, Luther's concept of the "outer man" and his submission to the "worldly regiment" reappears in the shape of the submission to "duty" in the "private" use of reason. What Kant inherits from Luther's distinction between the secular and the religious spheres, however, is not only the fact that he shelters the realm of "duty" from the realm of "freedom," the realm of the "worldly regiment" from the realm of "argument." In light of his remarks about the relation between the legitimate practice of reason and the use of mystical tropes (the "oracular voices," *die Stimme eines Orakels*, and *allerlei*

Auslegungen, "all kinds of interpretations"),[63] he also shelters the interaction between the spheres of duty and free argument from the uncontrollable interference of "inspired" speech. As a practice of reason, both its public and private use are qualified as such only insofar as reason, in the reduction to its two naturalized aspects, "public use" and "private use," excludes its other, that is, inspired, enthusiastic speech and wild hermeneutics. It is thus no accident that Kant takes his examples in "What Is Enlightenment?" mostly from "religious matters." No "emergence from self-imposed immaturity" can happen, as he argues, where reason falls back into "enthusiasm" and where it thus disqualifies itself from the "spirit of freedom" that enables it to enter into a public argument with "governments that misunderstand their own function."[64]

Mystical speech, its tropes, figures, and precritical practices of reading are thus excluded from the "prosaic" private and public use of reason.[65] They are extracted from their power to claim authority in worldly and private matters and redefined as "an aesthetic mode of representation." Thus, in Kant's view, they gain validity as representations and objects of sensation and emotion only "after" the conceptual labor of reason.

To illustrate this, he discusses the image of Isis:

> The veiled goddess before whom we of both parties bend our knees is the moral law in us, in its inviolable majesty. We do indeed perceive her voice and also understand very well her command. But when we are listening, we are in doubt whether it comes from man, from the perfected power of his own reason, or whether it comes from another, whose essence is unknown to us and speaks to man through this, his own reason. At bottom we would perhaps do better to rise above and spare ourselves research into this matter; since such research is only speculative and since what obliges us (objectively) to act remains always the same, one may place one or the other principle down as foundation. But the didactic procedure of bringing the moral law within us into clear concepts according to a logical methodology is the only authentically *philosophical* one, whereas the procedure whereby the law is personified and reason's moral bidding is made into a veiled Isis (even if we attribute to her no other properties than those discovered according to the method above), is an *aesthetic* mode of representing precisely the same object; one can doubtless use this mode of representation backward, after the first procedure has already purified the principles, in order to enliven those ideas by a sensible, albeit only analogical, presentation, and yet one always runs the danger of falling into an exalting vision [*schwärmerische Vision*], which

is the death of philosophy. To be able to *intimate* that goddess would therefore be an expression that means nothing more than to be led to concepts of duty by moral *feeling* before one could have *clarified* the principles on which this feeling depends; such an intimation of a law, as soon as methodical treatment lets it pass into clear insight, is the authentic occupation of philosophy without which the expression of reason would be the voice of an *oracle* that is exposed to all sorts of interpretations.

"At bottom," Kant adds in a footnote, "all philosophy is indeed prosaic; and the suggestion that we should now start to philosophize poetically would be just as welcome as the suggestion that a businessman should in the future no longer write his account books in prose but rather in verse."[66]

The exclusion of the "oracle" and of "all sorts of interpretations" means not only that all hermeneutical practices cannot be open to ascetic figural production and transfiguration (Luther's argument) but that they now have to be subordinated to the prior clarification of principles, that is, the exercise of reason, which, through a hermeneutic framing, then also subordinates all powers of figuration (now reserved for the territory of the aesthetic alone). It is this philosophical practice of clarification itself—maintained up to today in distinctions between "aesthetic" and "religious" experience—that ultimately redefines Luther's principle of distinction between the secular and spiritual realms, which, in turn, abolishes and replaces the medieval practice of an art of discernment of spirits. Visions, inspirations, ecstatic experiences that claimed to be valid readings and figural translations of the Scriptures and of the world in the context of medieval contemplative practices are now—after Kant—qualified as "aesthetic representation" alone, as aesthetic pleasure or as images used to illustrate concepts and ideas, devoid of all claims to different truth. They have thus been turned into "poetic" speech, into mere rhetoric and analogy, the place of the tension of figure and assimilation now relegated to the poetic imagination and the work of the artist. Thus, they are justified only as forms of illustration and presentation, and they can be true only on the basis of a preliminary clarification of principles within reason itself. This transformation into "aesthetic objects" further neutralizes what Luther tried to contain with his institution of the secular, obliterating its origin in Luther's reading of the Scriptures and defining it as a sphere of refuge for the mystical tropes that have lost their critical power. In modernity, it will thus be the function of poetry to recover not the spiritual truth of these tropes but a realm of possibility of thought and experience in the form of a circulation of percepts, affects, and concepts that has been cultivated in devotional practices but exiled by Luther's and Kant's interventions.

Speaking in terms of discernment, we have moved from a phenomenology of rhetorical effects (the evaluation of exemplary assimilation in affect and sensation that we encountered in medieval contemplative practices) to a framework of hermeneutic authorization (Suso's identification of correct reading in his critique of free spirits), a semiotics of the demonic and divine (in late medieval treatises on the discernment of spirits), a neutralization of inspired speech (in Luther's critique of figural devotional practices and his notion of faith-based "religion"), and finally an entirely naturalized clarification of rational principles of discernment (in Kant's critique of enthusiasm).

6

Monadic Transcriptions

Emblematic Tensions

Recent attempts to think about how we might know "nature" and the world differently from the "objectifying" notions of modern thought have often returned to pre-Kantian, premodern modes of knowing and relating. Often, they entail three conceptual elements or three moments of fascination with the "premodern": the rediscovery of something we could call a shared ground of embodied knowing (as opposed to a post-Cartesian and Kantian anthropocentric, "correlationist" epistemology and a hierarchical naturalized order of representation and signification); the rediscovery of analogy or similitude as an organizing principle that also takes on the shape and name of "sympathy"; and a complex reference to something early modern thinkers called, rather enigmatically, the "signature of things."

In all these instances, the fascination lies with a relation between figure, simile, and concept that is not being neutralized and controlled along the lines of framing I followed in the previous chapter. Instead of recalling modes of allegorical or analogical thinking, I want to draw attention to this correlation, what I call the emblematic tension, that dominates early modern thought, the production of artifacts, and the experience of the world. This tension is established—most prominently in the form of the emblem itself—in a pattern where an abstract concept is joined by a figure or image, which, in turn, is complemented by a short text. Often, the text, called a "subscription" in relation to an image, can be read in terms of an allegorical exploration of the meaning of the image. Thus, in fabricating an emblem, an abstract notion or a virtue is not explained in a straightforward way and through the use of an illustrating example. Instead, in the popular collections of emblems that dominate sixteenth- and seventeenth-century culture, the abstract and universalizing concept—called a "motto"—is related to a figure (*pictura*), which then is explored in a short text, sonnet, or commentary.

What is important is that none of these elements can stand alone. Inheriting the discourse of negative theology, the emblem problematizes concepts and acknowledges their finite character. Inheriting the Franciscan, nominalist, and empiricist emphasis on the irreducibility of the particular, the emblem thus breaks the abstract motto down into the concretely figural. Inheriting the medieval, then the sixteenth-century Ignatian tradition of spiritual exercises, it articulates—in the subscription—the irreducibility of the tension between abstract concept, concrete figure, and modes of sensual and affective assimilation. Thus, the emblem foregrounds and reiterates the tension produced in the relations of concepts, figures, and modes of assimilation. Neither of these three moments forms an end point in itself. Instead, they all remain in the unresolved and irresolvable state of what I call emblematic tension. In a circular movement, the concept refers to the figure, the figure to the subscription, the subscription back to the concept and the figure. In insisting on this movement, the emblem resists both Kant's critical epistemology and Hegel's dialectical resolution.

This explains that the figural, located during the Middle Ages so prominently in the convergence of practices of prayer, the experience of reading, and the transformation of the perception of the world in light of the Scriptures, moves now more prominently to the core of an emblematic mode that generates a new experience of the world. Thus, the emblem becomes a ubiquitous artifact and a mode of knowing during the long sixteenth and seventeenth centuries—and it lingers in modern times, often relegated to "poetic" modes and practices of critical intervention until today. As Walter Benjamin argued, one of the key aspects of this early modern epistemology is that it lays the historically concrete bare and exposes it to the experience in forms of allegories that—as he sees it, following a Romantic trope—have lost their grounding in the supposedly coherent theological horizon of the Middle Ages. Thus, he argues, these allegories exist only as "ruins."[1] Beyond Benjamin's foregrounding of the melancholic side of a perpetual loss, however, and in leaving us with constellations of concepts, figures, and forms of sensual, affective, and hermeneutic assimilation, emblems are not just allegories—taken in Benjamin's sense—but also ever-new instantiations of an emblematic tension. In the emblematic form, the figural can be reduced neither to the conceptual nor to the allegorical; and knowing can never escape the circle that the emblem establishes. In mobilizing this horizon, the emblem opens ever-new worlds of experience, affect, and concept, pulling us into the figural and empirical, on the one hand, and producing the overwhelming richness of images and words, allegories, and concepts, on the other. It is this abyss of figural play that Enlightenment thinkers in their attempts to clarify the conditions of possibility of knowledge, to determine natural and rational relations, and to offer a natural and rational poetics will be highly critical of when they speak of the Baroque modes that overwhelm the mind.[2]

Figure and Ground

In *The Order of Things*, Michel Foucault has famously referred to a key aspect of this premodern episteme in notions of resemblance, opposing it to the modern epistemes of representation and signification. More recently, other thinkers returned to this early modern episteme, acknowledged and more often unacknowledged, also in the voices of new forms of materialism. This is, to consider just one example, the case in the writings of Karen Barad, particularly in her notion of an agential realism and of what she calls "Transmaterialities."[3] Strikingly, but maybe not surprisingly, she uses an image that seems to be in intimate conversation with Jacob Böhme, as she brings together Foucault's notion of the episteme of resemblance with what I see as the emblematic tension that emerges from its figural core. She does so to grasp the "imagining" that is going on in nature, in matter, and that she observes in the event of lightning and thunderstorms:

> Lightning is a reaching toward, an arcing dis/juncture, a striking response to charged yearnings.

A dark sky. Deep darkness, without a glimmer of light to settle the eye. Out of the blue, tenuous electrical sketches scribbled with liquid light appear/disappear faster than the human eye can detect. Flashes of potential, hints of possible lines of connection alight now and again. Desire builds, as the air crackles with anticipation. Lightning bolts are born of such charged yearnings. Branching expressions of prolonged longing, barely visible filamentary gestures, disjointed tentative luminous doodlings—each faint excitation of this desiring field is a contingent and suggestive inkling of the light show yet to come. No continuous path from sky to ground can satisfy its wild imaginings, its insistence on experimenting with different possible ways to connect, playing at all matter of errant wanderings in a virtual exploration of diverse forms of coupling and dis/connected alliance. Against a dark sky it is possible to catch glimmers of the wild energetics of indeterminacies in action. . . .

Matter is promiscuous and inventive in its agential wanderings: one might even dare say, imaginative. Imaginings, at least in the scientific imagination, are clearly material.[4]

What this passage and its emphasis on "imaginings" remind us of is, above all, the philosophy of Jacob Böhme and his notion of the emergence of figures from the "ground"—as well as the strong resonances of Böhme's thoughts in Schelling's philosophy of nature.

"Ground" is indeed a key word in the history of medieval and early modern German mysticism that reemerges with great impact in Baroque thought, forming a backdrop for the elaboration of emblematic tensions between figural effects, forms of assimilation, and the reference to concepts. It is in the history of medieval mystical literature where we encounter both the term "ground" in the vernacular for the first time and the speculative exploration of its meanings and use. "Ground," "abyss," "unground" (*Grund, Abgrund, Ungrund*), but also "ground of the soul" (*Seelengrund, fundus animae*) are terms that emerge from this history and give shape to a specific understanding of the relation of figure and ground, of the dynamic emergence of the figure from the ground, and of the way in which figures reflect this very emergence in forms of expression. Following the medieval speculative explorations in the use of the terms, the notions of ground and of the ground of the soul also turn into conceptual tools in early modern and modern contexts. To name just one instance, which I discuss later, both Baumgarten and Herder refer to the notion of the ground of the soul in their attempts to understand and characterize aesthetic experience. In their eyes, this very notion does not just anchor aesthetic experience in some kind of "mystical" or "spiritual" experience—and it would be entirely wrong to speak of an "influence" of medieval and early modern mystics on these two thinkers. Instead, they are to be seen as making use of and recontextualizing a specific trope that emerges in mystical speculation. Thus, I suggest, they use the term to draw attention to a specific relation between figure and ground and to think about the effects of figures on the life of the soul. In this relation, ground is defined conceptually in terms of possibility and plasticity; figure, in terms of any concrete agency that, emerging in its expressive force, informs and gives shape sensually, emotionally, and cognitively to that ground, anchoring a chain of assimilations and making it collapse—or fold back into the figural—at the same time. As it did for the mystics before them, the undetermined ground that the notion of ground of the soul indicates takes plastic shape in the encounter with the figure. As Baumgarten and Herder describe aesthetic experience, in the contemplation of a work of art we are moving away from seeing a "thing" as an "object." Instead, the ground of the soul takes on a new shape, resonating with the figure that affects it and tracing in its own shape the forces that are at stake in the emergence of the figure itself. The imagination of the viewer rejoins the imagination of the artist that is embodied in the figure. Similarly, in Karen Barad's description of a thunderstorm, the imagination—in what, in fact, is an aesthetic experience—rejoins the cosmic imagination that is at work here. As I point out in my engagement with Böhme later, in his understanding this imagination is in each case formally and even materially the same, human and nonhuman, cosmic and divine.

What is at play here is a very specific view of the soul. Looking at it from the point of view of medieval understandings of the soul, particularly in the mystical tradition, we have to keep a particular application of negative theology in mind. It is, once again, most clearly articulated by Meister Eckhart, who argues that since God is ungraspable and imageless, the soul, made in God's image and as a point of convergence between man and God, is equally ungraspable and undetermined. Thus, a wide range of texts that deal with contemplation and contemplative experience point out that God and the ground of the soul are identical in being "nothing" and—as they add—the very possibility to be everything. At the same time, God, understood as the fullness of everything, is mirrored in the soul that liberates itself from discursive determinations and "returns" into its "ground" or "ground without ground." Thus, in the very undoing of determinacy soul is the point of convergence of the possibility and the actuality of everything.

From this point of view, "soul" names in everything both its particular form and the open ground on which this form emerges and that gives it the possibility "to be everything." The soul is that very movement, and it is a movement that *in via* cannot come to an end. According to this, ground and abyss are the horizon of utter possibility where things emerge in processes of mirroring reduplication and reinscription. In the language of theology, they are created, coming forth, being recognized as good and beautiful in their figural emergence, and thus fold back into God. As I have observed in medieval treatises, contemplation restores this perspective, producing an aesthetic experience, "admiration" and "wonder," in the fullness of sensation and affect. Each thing, not as an object but as a figure that is freed from its thingness and objecthood in the contemplative practice, is a particular form of expression of this original, ungraspable fullness. Each thing, not thought of as "thing" but perceived in its emergence as a figure, mirrors the whole of creation in a particular place, time, and way. Thus goes what we can call a mystical monadology, centered around the idea that through the perception of the figure in its very particular concreteness we perceive the whole world, its very origin and fullness fully folded into that figure and active in our perception: that is, in modes of assimilation and of conceptualization, which, in turn, realize their finitude in the acknowledgment of the utter asymmetry of the figural that lays at their ground. To illustrate this, some early modern authors make use of the image of a world of mirrors and the different cuts of mirroring glass. Akin to the form in which each concrete mirror or piece of glass or crystal vessel reflects the world according to the way in which it is cut, our perception of figures—that is, the things beyond or below their thinghood and objecthood—is the place where the whole world is mirrored. It is mirrored according to the form of receptivity, the way it is cut, and the way in which it allows for the enfolded character of the figure to unfold its effects. The ideal and empty ground of the soul, the mirror that is pure, allows for the fullness, reflected in each figure, to unfold in the soul and to mirror everything, that is, to be all the actual and possible "imaginings" in this very moment. The mirroring itself is the partaking that allows for all the possibilities of assimilation, forming the ground that reflects all figures. It does so since the soul in the form of an empty mirror never imposes a defining nature on things in this figural perception. Thus, the very perception is never to be understood in terms of assimilation and representation alone but in terms of expression or coming forth of the figure in the free flow of mirroring that, time and again, makes all assimilation and conceptualization collapse. Following this line of thought, we have to understand the ground of the soul as a dark and undetermined place of possibility where the soul in perception becomes everything.

Emergence

It is on the basis of these observations that I want to discuss an aspect of what we call Baroque mysticism, the way in which it conceives of figuration as a form of expression that in its expressivity reflects and traces both its emergence from a dark ground—both creaturely and divine—and its formative effects in relation to its environment. I focus on a specific notion of monadology that underlies some early modern understandings of expression.

Access to this mode of monadology can be found also in Baroque forms of theatricality, most prominently represented in the German Baroque plays Walter Benjamin wrote about in *The Origin of the German Trauerspiel.* In one of these plays, Daniel Casper von Lohenstein's *Sophonisbe*, the key protagonist emerges onstage with the following words:

> Masinissa:
> Guilt swarms round as round light will swarm the moth.
> He springs the trap himself who treaties breaks and troth.
> So Sophonisba falls and Syphax's hope is shivered,
> Since she the breach and peace conceived, and he delivered.
> Now you can figure on the fingers of one hand:
> If you deserve of us that we assistance lend,
> That we your crackling house to save from flames endeavor,
> Your town in dire straits from gore and gutting sever.
> The stinger of the bee is too its honey duct.

Who feels offense will have from vengeance far more sucked
Than sugar in his heart, for sweet is without rival
What fervor cools. No dew so sparks the snail's revival
As to insulted men the blood of foes lands zest.
With this reviving balm the heavens have me blest.[5]

This is one of the moments when—in the eyes of its Enlightenment critics—Baroque drama seems to be utterly puzzling, stuck in and overwhelmed by its enthusiastic use of images, allegories, emblematic constructions, and archival erudition. Read closely, however, it is much more than that. In this moment of appearance onstage, all enveloped in emblematic figments, the emerging figure presents itself and the drama that emerges as a place of inscription, as deeply shaped by a set of emblematic tensions between figure and assimilation, and as deeply unstable in its figural emergence from the ground of possibilities. Moreover, the figure in its appearance is actually not overdetermined by the images; instead, it is in its expression the convergence of the efficacy of all the images that configure its coming forth at that moment. They confirm its very historicity; better, they constitute its historicity. And they form the dark ground in front of which the figure takes shape in its articulation and expressivity. The figure is in itself nothing else than a reflection of dramatic emergence, tracing in this particular moment all the constitutive elements that provide it with its form. The emblematic moments, combining words and images, address time and again the very tension between hermeneutics, assimilation, and figuration, between allegorical meaning and figural effect in these movements of emergence.

It is in response to this form of theatricalization of emergence that we have to draw attention to a specific transformation of the mystical language that happens in Baroque mysticism. In addition to the self-fashioning and to the new poetic language that mystical tropes support, we observe the growing importance of a cosmopoetic imagination. It nearly entirely replaces the hermeneutic horizon of contemplation, which was key in medieval mysticism and figural practice. This is most visible in the works of Jacob Böhme. Others have read Böhme's mysticism in terms of a return to a Gnostic narrative of cosmic fall and salvation. Instead, I propose a model of cosmopoetic theatricalization that transforms and gives a new shape to the tension between ground and figure. As Böhme transforms the medieval paradigm, he amplifies the drama of figural emergence, drawing attention not to the figure alone but to the figure as a place of never-ending transcription and transformation in endless imaginings. Thus, the figure—each thing in its particular form as it encounters us—that in the language of the mystics has been seen as a monad, as a particular mirroring of the world as a whole, now turns into a place of dramatic cosmic production—and of a permanent crisis. According to Böhme, in its emergence the figure transcribes and expresses its very production with all the breaks, violence, desires, and qualities that unfold in this process.

Instead of an ontology that puts an emphasis on being and individual substances we encounter a world of articulation where each thing reflects the whole world both as a mirror, insofar as it is passive and receptive, and as a machine and organism that processes all the elements that constitute its articulation in a dramatic form. Pushing this point a bit further, we can speak of a horizontal line of emerging figural networks in a flow of multitudes where everything shares both in the dramatic (self-) expression of everything else but also in the reparative labor that responds to the violence of the ongoing drama. As Böhme emphasizes repeatedly, we live—together with everything else—in and through the sound of this machine, processing everything in forms of our participation in the soundscapes—the resounding echoes (*Hall*)—of this drama.

Böhme thus articulates the outline of a model of a permanent crisis of emergence, drawing attention to something that is also characteristic for German Baroque tragic drama. Shifting from Böhme's cosmopoetic perspective to the historical viewpoint of the tragic dramas, the scenes of most plays present the emerging persons not as stable figures but as crossing points of figural moments, images, and multiple transcriptions. These images present what the person in the historical moment embodies. They are the forces that make the figures emerge as this or that person in this particular historical moment. Such images might be read as rhetorical artifacts, as the display of erudite memory—or, with Benjamin, as the ruins of a divinely contained medieval allegory that now has been lost—but they are more than that. They do more than represent things. Instead, they fold the entire world and its history, to put it succinctly, into the particular moment of emergence that is coequal with its representation, enveloping everything that is going to happen onstage in a texture of figural relations. Each person appears thus as a monad, reflecting and refracting in its particular form all the lights that shine on him or her from the past; and each person emerges from an ungraspable ground, takes shape as a particular reflection of the entire world and its history through its self-expression. Since the images never succeed at doing justice to a state, at stabilizing its position, at fully delimiting a border between the dark ground and the figure itself, everything stays in a state of a crisis of emerging and representation.

Monadic Transcriptions

To explain this process of emergence, a notion of monadic transcription seems most useful. I will explain this with Jacob Böhme's treatise *The Signature of Things*. Emphasizing the moment of dramatic emergence of all things, Böhme writes in his prophetic and often enigmatic style:

> 1. Seeing then there are so many and diverse forms, that the one always produces and affords out of its property a will different in one from another, we herein understand the contrariety and combat in the Being of all beings, how that one does oppose, poison, and kill another, that is overcome its essence, and the spirit of the essence, and introduces it into another form, whence sickness and pains arise, when one essence destroys another. . . . 4. For the eternal nature has produced nothing in its desire, except a likeness out of itself; and if there were not an everlasting mixing, there would be an eternal peace in nature, but so nature would not be revealed and made manifest, in the combat it becomes manifest; so that each thing elevates itself, and would get out of the combat into the still rest, and so it runs to and fro, and thereby only awakens and stirs up the combat.[6]

The "combat" Böhme talks about here is the dramatic coming forth of all things, of figures from the ground. Remarkably, the very "likeness" that characterizes all that emerges from "the nothing," the "stillness," the "rest," is absorbed not into stable and graspable substances but into endless series of transcriptions. In its emergence, each thing is a figure that expresses, in terms of likeness, the whole, and, in terms of combat, the particularization and antagonism. Each figure carries forth the "will of liberty," that is, the free production in the form of a multiplicity of figurations; and it turns, in its very emergence as a figure and transcribing it into the openness of receptivity, into the "desire" that marks its very particularity. In its manifestation "the will," genuinely free according to Böhme, turns into a world of figures that time and again transcribes the process of emergence in a particular way, that is, in the particularity of the expression that emerges from the ground.

One more passage illustrates the dramatic figural formalism that is so characteristic of Böhme—and that makes his texts so hard to understand:

> 9. For in the nothing the will would not be manifest to itself, wherefore we know that the will seeks itself, and finds itself in itself, and its seeking is a desire, and its finding is the essence of the desire, wherein the will finds itself. . . . 12. For in itself before the desire is the liberty, viz. the nothing, and the will may not be a nothing, for it desires to manifest in the nothing; and yet not manifestation can be effected, except only through the essence of the desire; and the more the reconceived will desires manifestation, the more strongly and eagerly the desire draws into itself, and makes in itself three forms, viz. the desire, which is astringent, and makes hardness, for it is an enclosing, when coldness arises, and the attraction causes compunction, and stirring in the hardness, an enmity against the attracted hardness; the attraction is the second form, and a cause of motion and life, and stirs itself in the astringency and hardness, which the hardness, viz. the enclosing, cannot endure, and therefore it attracts more eagerly to hold the compunction, and yet the compunction is thereby only the stronger. 13. Thus the compunction willeth upwards, and whirls crossways, and yet cannot effect it, for the hardness, viz. the desire stays and detains it, and therefore it stands like a triangle, and transverted orb, which (seeing it cannot remove from the place) becomes wheeling, whence arises the mixture in the desire, viz. the essence, or multiplicity of the desire; for the turning makes a continual confusion and contrition, whence the anguish, viz. the pain, the third form (or sting of sense) arises.[7]

I read this long and exhausting passage (which many philosophers, including Hegel and Schelling, who admired Böhme, would certainly have liked) to illustrate the dramatic nature of Böhme's theory of the emergence of things—but also to show how his very perspective abandons an ontological point of view in favor of a dramaturgy of emerging qualities in a process of all-encompassing imagination. Focusing on the transition from nothing to something, from the ground of darkness to the emergence of figures, Böhme identifies the "will" as a first moment in which the dark background, "nothing," "stillness," and "rest," breaks and turns into manifestation and multiplicity. Reading Böhme's explanation of this process in terms of a theory of emanation, that is, of the unfolding of the One into a multiplicity of beings, would imply that we read his language here as a metaphorical deployment of illustrative images that allegorize the process of unfolding from an originary One to the multiplicity of things in the world. This, however, does not do justice to Böhme's very notion of unfolding, which, as it turns out, is to be understood both in terms of the concrete qualities that he brings into play in this passage and in terms of his understanding of imagination. What is striking about this passage is the fact that Böhme's "voluntarism" dissolves the language of "being" and turns everything into a deployment of qualities and their physical, sensual, and affective aspects. In other words, his analysis does not revert to a complex picture of metaphors that illustrate a Neoplatonic model of emanation and return. Instead, it takes figuration in its qualitative concreteness as imagining, as the concrete process of becoming where sensual, affective, and cognitive moments are at work coextensively. The German language offers a series of composite words that are being used here: *Bildung, Einbildung, Überbildung, Entbildung* (formation, information, transformation, deformation)—and in Böhme's language, following a tradition that goes back to Meister Eckhart, each of these terms applies to each thing all the time. Figure is what emerges and what produces moments of assimilation and dissimilation, of transfiguration and transformation, of a process of expressive unfolding that has no end.

Thus, in his understanding of "creation," every moment of emergence is a moment that is nothing else than the sensual, affective, and cognitive qualities that are expressed in it, the assimilations and disassimilations that are produced by the figures. And the qualities, however abstract, are nowhere else than in the expressions that constitute the worlds we encounter and live in. These expressions are monadic insofar as each of them expresses the whole world in a particular form, folds it into a figural emergence, and thus enacts a particular moment in a cosmic drama that mirrors its entirety in its always unstable coming forth from the ground.

The cosmic coming forth folds into these expressions—in its constitution being nothing else than the image of imagining in its expressivity—all the aspects of the process of manifestation in their dramatic interaction. "Folding," the concept that Gilles Deleuze used in his book on the Baroque and also in his attempt to understand the monadology of Gottfried Wilhelm Leibniz, is to be seen as a key notion to understand Böhme as well. Each thing, each figure that emerges from the dark ground is indeed nothing else than a particular folding of the forces, qualities, and antagonistic combats that are always at stake in this process.

A passage where Böhme discusses the functions of the elements Sulphur, Mercury, and Sal helps explain further what I mean by transcription. Drawing also on practices of alchemy, he writes:

35. The desire of the dark world is after the manifestation, viz. after the outward world, to attract and draw the same essentiality into it, and thereby to satisfy its wrathful hunger; and the desire of the outward world is after the essence or life, which arises from the pain and anguish. 36. Its desire in itself is the wonder of eternity, a mystery, or mirror, or what is comprehended of the first will to nature. 37. The outward world's desire is Sulphur, Mercury, and Sal; for such an essence it is in itself, viz. a hunger after itself, and is also its own satisfying; for Sul desires Phur, and Phur desires Mercury, and both these desire Sal; for Sal is their son, which they hatch in their desire, and afterwards becomes their habitation, and also food. 38. Each desire desires only the essentiality of salt according to its property; for salt is diverse; one part is sharpness of cold, and one part sharpness of heat; also one part brimstone; and one part salniter from Mercury. 39. These properties are in one another as one, but they sever themselves, each dwelling in itself; for they are of a different essence, and when one enters into another, then there is enmity, and a flagrat. A similitude whereof we may apprehend in thunder and lightning, which comes to pass when the great Anguish, viz. the mother of all salts, understand the third form of nature, impresses itself; which come to pass from the aspect of the sun, which stirs up the hot fire's form, so that it is penetrative, as the property of fire is; and when it reaches the salniter, then it enkindles itself; and the salniter is in itself the great flagrat in Mercury, viz. the flash, or compunction, which enters into the coldness, so also into the cold sharpness of the sal-spirit; this coldness is exceedingly dismayed at the flash of the fire, and in a trice wraps or folds up itself in itself, whence arises the thunder-clap (or the tempestuous flash, which gives a stroke in the flagrat) and the flagrat goes downwards, for it is heavy by reason of the coldness, and the sal-nitrous spirits light by reason of the fire, which [spirit] carries the thunder of sound sideways, as is to be heard in tempest and thunder; presently thereupon comes the wind or spirit out of all the four forms one against another, for they are all four enkindled in the penetrating flagrat; whereupon follows hail and rain; the hail folds itself together in the coldness, in the property of the cold salt-spirit; for the wrath attracts to

itself, and turns the water to ice, and the water arises from the meekness, viz. from the desire of the light, for it is the essentiality of the meekness; this the cold salt-spirit congeals into drops, and distils it upon the earth, for before the congelation it is only as a mist, or steam, or as a vapor, or damp. 40. Thus we see this ground very exactly and properly in thunder and lightning.[8]

To understand these passages and elaborations—which bring us back to Karen Barad's observations in face of a thunderstorm—we have to listen to them conceptually and pictorially at the same time. They present a conceptual understanding, but they transcribe this conceptual understanding in processes of both cosmic and human imagining, folding both back into cosmic figural emergence. In this process alone we understand things as figures in their productivity—and thus, abandoning a stable configuration of knowing subjects and known objects, we participate in their and our cosmic formation, open to the forms of transcription that inform all things in their emergence.

The Signature of Things

Böhme focuses on the aspects of emergence and transcription when he discusses the "signature of things," pointing again to the dramatic incongruency and emblematic tension that characterize all expression. This tension has to be taken into account in our understanding of what early modern thinkers call *signatura rerum*, that is, in Jacob Böhme's words, the basis of all knowledge:

ALL whatever is spoken, written, or taught of God, without the Knowledge of the Signature is dumb and void of Understanding; for it proceeds only from an historical Conjecture, from the Mouth of another, wherein the Spirit without Knowledge is dumb, but if the Spirit opens to him the Signature, then he understands the Speech of another; and further he understands how the Spirit has manifested and revealed itself (out of the Essence through the Principle) in the Sound with the Voice. For though I see one to speak, teach, preach, and write of God, and though I hear and read the same, yet this is not sufficient for me to understand him; but if his Sound and Spirit out of his Signature and Similitude enter into my own Similitude, and imprint his Similitude into mine, then I may understand him really and fundamentally, be it either spoken or written, if he has the Hammer that can strike my Bell.[9]

"Signature" is not a hidden writing to be read in terms of meaning. It is the reality of expression as it shapes perception, the presence and the effect of the figure that emerges and enters into dramatic relations with everything else in this emergence. It is, in simple terms, the place where our imagination in the encounter with the world rejoins all the formative moments, the violence, the desire, of each thing—without relating to it as a subject does to an object but in a state of "similitude." It is the way in which figures encounter us and inform our imagination, making it a place where the cosmos unfolds and where we are part of its unfolding.

In a recent attempt to explore this notion of "similitude" and to explain his own historiographical method, Giorgio Agamben has returned to Foucault's notion of the "paradigm" and to the significance of the idea of the *signatura rerum* that plays an important role in Foucault's understanding of the "Renaissance episteme" in *The Order of Things*. While Foucault emphasizes the role of resemblances in premodern epistemologies, making it the key to our understanding of its specific character, he also, according to Agamben, refrains from defining "the concept of signature, which for him resolves into resemblance." Agamben adds: "However, there is a motif in his definition of the Renaissance episteme that only needs to be elaborated to identify the proper site and function of signatures."[10] This motif is to be found, he points out, in the distinction between a semiology, that is, the recognition of signs, and a hermeneutics that elaborates and excavates the meaning of signs; and it is, according to Agamben and Foucault, exactly in the incongruency between the two that the signatures have their proper place. Thus, signatures seem to form the web of resemblances that becomes "visible only in the network of signs that crosses the world from one end to another."[11]

According to Böhme, however, "signatures" cannot be fully exhausted either by a semiology or a hermeneutics. They articulate a point of resistance precisely insofar as the signature, in Agamben's summary of Foucault, "refers to the resemblance between the sign and its designated thing."[12] In Foucault's words, "A signature adheres to the sign in the sense that it indicates, by means of the sign making, the code with which it has to be deciphered."[13]

While both Foucault and Agamben point to a decisive moment in the notion of signature, the fact that signatures cannot be exhausted either by a semiological or hermeneutical understanding alone, they ignore what for both Paracelsus and Jacob Böhme, the two most prominent authors who write about the *signatura rerum*, is at the core of the signature. Indeed, in the latter's understanding, signs "do not speak unless signatures make them speak."[14] Signatures, however, exceed both the hermeneutic and the semiotic realms. They are, so to speak, figural moments—or, to use in modified form one of Walter Benjamin's observations, "ruins" of a world of prelapsarian integrity and of a medieval Christian universalism that, as he wrote in a somewhat too schematic manner, medieval allegory had been trying to conserve.

To explain the figural character, we have to return to how Böhme conceives of the signature of things. If I understand him correctly, the signature of things cannot be thought of in terms of semiology or of hermeneutics. Instead, it has to be conceived in the form of a break with the chains of signification. It is a break where things and words and images return to moments of efficacy that can be traced only by the imagination. Or, to use the German terminology of the texts, they return to *Bildung* and *Einbildung*, "formation" and "information," in their figural form. The solution to the problem of the discrepancy between semiology and hermeneutics is thus not a step into either epistemology or ontology, even though we can indeed speak of "passions of being" here or of existence as "a transcendental dissemination in passions, that is, in signatures."[15] While this is the case, the notions of *Bildung* and *Einbildung* refrain from establishing such a metaphysical perspective. Nothing here is about applying an epistemological code that establishes similitude or, for that matter, a normative rule to establish sympathy.

Instead, everything stays with the moments of figuration and formation, the processes of monadic transcription that absorb the imagination and pull it into a realm of heteronomy and multiplicity. What Böhme postulates are not seemingly stable monadic moments of identity but processes of an always liminal emergence that produce signatures in their imaginative self-expression—in the expression that affects us at each moment and that is traced in the unfolding of our imagination, which thus rejoins the workings of the cosmic imagination. Signatures can thus not be read in a semiological or hermeneutic way or in terms of an incongruency between them. Instead, they are visible only to a practice of thought that in itself returns to its material constitution in processes of figuration that break with the dominance of both. Signatures are figural effects on the imagination that make the imagination resonate with the figures in their emergence. And the mark of the signature, that is, what Böhme calls "signature," is the effect on the imagination, the mark on the imagination that lets itself be touched. Not surprisingly, the trope Böhme uses most consistently is music, pointing to the fact that ultimately all the affectability of the imagination resolves itself in the sound, song, and play of the strings of the soul. It is, ultimately, in this form that the imagination turns into the place where materially the formation of all creation is being traced. Moving beyond semiology and hermeneutics, allowing for the gap and the tension between the plastic emergence and the sphere of meaning to appear, means, in Böhme's understanding, that in returning to the processes of figuration our imagination materially rejoins the multiplicity and the multiplication of things, peoples, languages, and, as he foregrounds, the sounds that accompany all this. Imagination rejoins, in each moment of being marked by the effects of a figure, the very emergence of figure from darkness before or underneath its deployment of meaning or, returning to the appearance of figures on the Baroque stage, the emergence of a figure that expresses its own form as what is being nothing else than the dramatic effect of the figures that make it emerge in its particularity.

At the same time, we see that Böhme's speculative understanding of this process is deeply indebted to forms of prayer and contemplative exercise. They offer models for what is at stake here, a practice of detachment that allows for the figures to deploy their effects on the life of the soul, producing and encountering a free circulation of perception, affects, and concepts in their dramatic unfolding. However, in its emphasis on processes of figuration, Böhme's thought is also deeply indebted to dramatic models of a cosmopoetics that, in privileging the imagination, breaks with ontological concepts of the emanation of being and beings. Böhme explores this deployment of a drama of forces in terms of an actual drama between the semiotic, the hermeneutic, and the figural. In the emergence of the figures from the ground of darkness that gives plastic shape to the imagination, unlocking both the semiotic and the hermeneutic spheres, the spheres of meaning and reasoning are deconstructed continuously. In reducing these spheres to the *signatura*, that is, to the figural effect of things, words, and images, imagination is open in two directions: in the direction of things that leave their plastic marks and in the direction of the mind that moves back and forth between these marks of an imaginative *aisthesis*, an aesthetic experience that unfolds from the ground of the soul in figures, and forms of assimilation.

Aesthetic Experience

Alexander Gottlieb Baumgarten, the founder and inventor of the modern philosophical discipline of aesthetics in the mid-eighteenth century, makes a surprising reference to this same notion of the ground of the soul, the *fundus animae.* At first glance, surprisingly, he points out that he wants to call our attention to a basic concept that "many people, even philosophers, ignore nowadays." Baumgarten writes this in his *Metaphysica* of 1751.[16] The very context of the thought, however, is his elaboration of the modern meaning of "aesthetics" as a theory of "sensible cognition." "Aesthetica," Baumgarten writes in a famous sentence of his *Aesthetica*, "est scientia cognitionis sensitivae" (Aesthetics . . . is the science of sensible cognition).[17] Aesthetics is not primarily a realm of knowledge concerned with normative questions of beauty but—and this will be true for Herder as well—with questions of cognition, experience, and sensation, in short, with the *aisthesis* of things that used to be called "lower gnoseology."

How, then, does the notion of the ground of the soul play a role in this new science?[18] How is it that this key term from the vocabulary of medieval and early modern theology and mysticism returns in the context of one of the most modern questions and quests, the understanding of aesthetic experience and sensation? And why is it that Herder, with Kant arguably one of the "crucial protagonists of the transformation of aesthetics after Baumgarten,"[19] returns to this same figure of thought, emphasizing a common element in his and Baumgarten's project and giving even more prominence to the ground of the soul?[20]

In short, we could say, at this point in the eighteenth century—and quite surprisingly—a mystical trope enters the stage again, seemingly from a different direction, the new discourse about aesthetics and sensual knowledge, and thus challenges us to ask what the use of this figure of thought implies. As I show here, the references to the ground of the soul in Baumgarten and Herder testify not only, as it is often phrased in general terms, to a pietist element in the thought of these two thinkers. Beyond that, and more important, an inquiry into the use of the notion of a ground of the soul will help explicate the seemingly secular concept of aesthetic experience in Baumgarten and Herder and its indebtedness to a mystical image of the soul as a realm of possibility, as well as to the tension between figure and forms of assimilation. The inquiry into the ground of the soul will also help us understand one of the most significant turns in Herder's thought about aesthetic experience, his attempt to privilege the sense of touch in the constitution of aesthetic experience.

As is well known, Herder considers the sense of touch to be the highest of all our senses. This has often been understood in terms of a rehabilitation of touch in a historical context that predominantly and quite conventionally puts vision at the top of a hierarchy of the senses. While Herder indeed rehabilitates the sense of touch, he actually does more than that. He turns touch not only into a specific sense that, in an Aristotelian vein, is the foundation of all sensation but also into something that figures as the very sphere of possibility for the deployment of all effects of sensation and aesthetic experience. In aesthetic experience, one might summarize Herder's position, all sensation turns into touch—and touch encompasses virtually all sensation. Or, to put it differently, touch is the aspect of sensation and the life of the soul that constitutes the realm of possibility: the possibility to become everything in sensation, to take shape in sensation, and to experience what I am calling the plasticity of the soul in its relations with itself and the world. Touch is the place where the soul takes shape in an experience that is made possible by the very openness, darkness, and potentiality that has its foundation in the ground of the soul. Touch is the name of the plasticity of the soul, of its very ability to take shape aesthetically from its ground and of the possibility to dwell in sensual pleasure as a place that is open to the circulation of percepts, affects, and thoughts.

Baumgarten refers to the ground of the soul both in his *Metaphysica* and in his *Aesthetica*. In the latter he introduces the notion of the ground of the soul in a chapter on "aesthetic enthusiasm."[21] In the original Latin he speaks of the "impetus aestheticus" and the "pulcra mentis incitatio, inflammatioque, . . . ecstasis, furor, enthousiasmós, pneuma theou" (the beautiful arousal of the soul, its inflammation, . . . ecstasy, furor, enthusiasm, divine spirit or inspiration). This arousable character of the soul, he says, is a fundamental quality required for the "felix aestheticus" and aesthetic experience.[22]

Experience, to be clear, means here the way in which the soul takes shape under the sensual influences that awaken the "lower faculties of the soul," that is, the faculties that have been "lying dead." When I say the soul "takes shape," I use the term here in a somewhat Aristotelian way, thinking of the soul as a realm of potentialities that are brought into emergence and into form in specific interactions with the world. Beyond Aristotle, however, the notion of the ground of the soul points to a different concept of possibility and potentiality, which has been elaborated in the history of late medieval mysticism, especially in the writings of Meister Eckhart and his followers. As we have seen, in this tradition the ground is often understood as a pure and empty mirror,[23] a realm of utter possibility to "be" or "become everything" in breaking through the intentional, instrumental, teleological, and rational order of the world and to experience the world in light of the divine. This model of an "empty" soul ultimately undermines the Aristotelian idea of faculties or potentialities of the soul, emphasizing instead its nothingness and emptiness. Under the condition of the breakthrough in "enthusiasm," Baumgarten writes, the ground of the soul, in itself nothing other than the possibility to be everything, rises up, is aroused, and informs the higher faculties in unexpected ways, shaping the whole apparatus of perception, including the senses and the affects.[24] In this ecstatic reduction, in this aesthetic experience, body and soul affect each other mutually, and the soul—better, the collapse of the distinction of soul and body—takes on a new shape and appears as something new. "Compare this," Baumgarten writes to illustrate this moment, to the experience and the pleasure of *otium* (leisure) during a pleasurable walk. When the spirit "leaves behind all sorrow," when the soul leaves behind the hardship of work and of business, and when it moves without plans and goals along a pleasant alley of blooming trees, it opens freely to aesthetic perception and pleasure. This way of being encountered by the world, Baumgarten concludes, "is possibly the experience of the Helicon, the dream of Parnassus,"[25] which now figurally informs the soul and the body, giving shape to it in a way that we call aesthetic experience.

Since many philosophers, Baumgarten writes further in these passages of his *Aesthetica*, "ignore" the ground of the soul, people usually point to the "gods" and a model of divine gifts when they try to identify the origin of this extraordinary state of experience. They usually do so, he adds, in evoking "the poets" and their divine "inspiration." Baumgarten himself, however, introduces the term *fundus animae*, the "ground of the soul" instead, indicating that he draws on a tradition that, as he argues, "is currently ignored by the philosophers."[26] He thus points to a tradition that puts the emphasis on the immanence of the divine principle, on the collapse of the distinction between immanence and transcendence, and on the soul as the very ground of possibility that is virtually everything in sensation, imagination, and affect.

Commentators have noted that Baumgarten connects the notion of the ground of the soul in his *Metaphysics* with ideas he inherits from Leibniz.[27] Thus, he writes that the whole universe is darkly present in the ground of the soul, which can be understood as a complex of "dark perceptions."[28] At the same time, however, Baumgarten values this realm of "dark perceptions" quite differently, turning it into the foundation of all our perceptions and sensations and the basis for aesthetic experience. All sensations, he says, are true at this level, and he connects this argument with a stronger emphasis on the life of the senses, departing on this point significantly from both Gottfried Wilhelm Leibniz and Christian Wolff. In the sensual world that arises from the darkness of the ground of the soul lie both the "sensuality" and the specificity, the "poetic nature" of the aesthetic experience and the very value and shape things acquire in this experience. The ground of the soul is not only the virtual ground and basis of perception and representation but the very possibility of the soul to take shape in relation to the figures of this world in ways of aesthetic enthusiasm.

As I have pointed out, Baumgarten's argument and his introduction of the notion of the ground of the soul go beyond his allusions to Leibniz. We are dealing here with a reference to a trope that has a long history in German mysticism, where the Latin concept of a *fundus animae*, the image of an innermost intimacy between man and God that goes back to writings of early Christian theologians, is translated as *Grund der Seele* (ground of the soul). This tradition reaches from Meister Eckhart's

German sermons to the writings of Johannes Tauler, to Valentin Weigel, and finally to Teerstegen and other authors of pietist spirituality. There can be no question that Baumgarten knew at least some of the relevant texts. The fact that he polemically points to the "ignorance of the philosophers" indicates that he is aware of the fact that he uses a term that has its origin in a different discourse—a discourse where the ground of the soul acquired a very specific significance.

As I have argued, starting with Meister Eckhart, we encounter in mystical theories of the soul a strong emphasis on the difference between the ground of the soul and the faculties of the soul. While the faculties are understood as determined in their nature, as forms of assimilation ranging from the lower ones, including the vegetative system and sensation, to the highest ones, intellect, will, and memory, the ground of the soul itself is seen as undetermined. In this undetermined way, in this "freedom," Eckhart points out, the ground of the soul is to be seen as a structural moment of identity between the divine and the human.[29] In terms of Eckhart's strong emphasis on apophatic thought this means that the ground of the soul is also a realm of "darkness." It is nothing we can describe, and negative theology since Dionysius the Areopagite forbids us to talk about it as it forbids us to talk about the divine. At the same time, Eckhart explains further, in its very darkness, freedom, and divine nature the ground of the soul is also the possibility to "become everything" and to be everything[30]—a quality Leibniz will ascribe to the realm of "obscure perceptions," which for Baumgarten constitute the ground of the soul and make it an ineffable mirror of the universe containing every possible experience.[31]

When Baumgarten speaks of the ground of the soul in terms of a *regnum tenebrarum* (the reign of darkness) and an ineffable "complex" of "dark perceptions,"[32] he inherits and quotes this application of negative theology not only with regard to the divine but also with regard to the human soul and its ground. Johannes Tauler, a fourteenth-century German mystic who was widely read in the sixteenth and seventeenth centuries, is probably the author who has most deeply marked this characterization of the ground of the soul. He speaks in one of his sermons of a "silent, sleeping, divine . . . darkness," emphasizing the fact that we cannot really name the ground of the soul since it escapes language and conceptualization in the same way the divine does. In multiple places he calls it an "abyss," a place of indefinite possibility, and it is in the divine darkness of this "boundless abyss" where in his view the image, the experience, and the birth of the divine have their place:[33] "The abyss that is created draws the uncreated abyss into itself, and the two abysses become a single one, a pure divine being, so that the spirit is lost in God's Spirit. It is drowned in the bottomless sea."[34] In a reference to the Neoplatonist Proclus, Tauler also introduces the motif of divine mania, evoking a notion that is close to Baumgarten's "enthusiasm." Proclus, Tauler says, "calls it sleep, silence, and divine furor,"[35] and he mentions that within ourselves from this divine abyss we are longing for an experience of divine pleasure and plenitude beyond reason and understanding.

There are three important elements that accompany the discourse about the ground of the soul from Eckhart up to the pietist authors of the eighteenth century: the first is its receptivity and openness; the second its ability to become everything and to perceive everything in light of divine pleasure; and the third its character as a mirror that makes the soul a realm of reflection of the pure figural and experiential quality of everything and every event in light of the divine. According to late medieval authors, in the ground of the soul everything appears in its state of fullness, not in the state of worldly corruption and instrumentality but in the freedom and pleasure that reminds of Baumgarten's promenade in the alley of trees where the soul gets absorbed in its own "Parnassian" experience of itself and the world.

Touch and Feeling

As I argued before, an additional element appears in some late medieval mystical treatises in this context of "Parnassian" experience, namely, an emphasis on touch and the inversion of the traditional hierarchy of the senses. Hendrik Herp, who together with Tauler was widely read in the sixteenth and seventeenth centuries, portrays touch as the sense that most intimately reflects what is at stake in the concept of the ground of the soul, the indeterminacy, possibility, and intimacy where inside and outside converge in an event of overwhelming sensation and experience. Herp develops his argument in the context of his discussion of the role of sensation in prayer and contemplation.[36] Building on the tradition of spiritual *aisthesis* that, as we have seen, goes back to the church fathers and especially Origen, Herp teaches that in prayer all the senses are being activated; that the soul takes on a new shape in this very experience; and that it is absorbed in experiences of sweetness and bitterness, light and darkness, pleasure and abandon. In spiritual vision, he argues, the relation between an object and a subject is still stable and static, while in touch this relation disappears and the soul itself takes shape in the very experience it makes when it is absorbed in affection or divine enthusiasm. Not vision that always sees something and somebody is the sense that is privileged here. It is the tactile experience instead, where the soul is being absorbed by perception and where it takes shape, losing itself sensually and emotionally under the effects of this perception. To phrase this differently and more pointedly, in touch, the sensation that accompanies all other sensation, the ground of the soul arises and takes shape. In the very practices of prayer and contemplation it is being sculpted in forms and figures that lie hidden in this very ground of possible experience and that are brought forth when it is encountered by the figures of the world.

As I have shown, medieval theologians present in their theories of prayer an approach to sensation that we would nowadays call phenomenological since it does not focus on individual faculties and organs of perception but on the phenomena and events that emerge in the soul as a sphere of virtuality and possibility. This is the level where spiritual experience during the reading of the Scriptures and the contemplation of the world turns into aesthetic experience, that is, an experience of the effect of word and image in terms of absorption in sensation and affect. According to this, the reader of the *Song of Songs* does not just read the dramatic poem to remember the story or to understand its literal and allegorical meaning. Instead, the reader allows the poem to deploy its figural effects in terms of an assimilation in sensation, vision and hearing, smell and touch, and to let herself be absorbed and aroused in divine experience. Thus, the poem turns into the figure that encounters the contemplative and deploys the figural effects in the empty spot of her abandonment. The notion of the ground of the soul, the aspect of the soul that transcends all specific and determined sensation within each sensation, is the basis of this notion of freedom and possibility that allows the reader to engage in the contemplative process and to deploy it with the help of words and artifacts. Touching the divine is at the same time its lowest and highest moment, the realm where the soul accomplishes an experience of fruition and pleasure that arises from its ground of virtual plenitude and includes all sensation, imagination, and emotions.[37]

As I have pointed out, Herder is famous for his rehabilitation of touch—in German *Gefühl*, that is, "feeling" and "touch."[38] When he thinks about touch, he does so, as do Hendrik Herp and other medieval authors, in connection with the ground of the soul, the *fundus animae*. An instance where he addresses the issue are his reflections and elaborations on aesthetics. For Herder, too, the ground of the soul is not just a negative counterpart of our discursive and intellectual activity and knowledge. It constitutes a complex intersection of sensuality, affect, perception, feeling, and imagination and thus forms the basis for an alternative way of cognition where the dualism of soul and body, spirit and matter, is being replaced by a monism of sensual experience, of figuration and assimilation.

The difference between Baumgarten and Herder lies not only with the fact that Herder puts an even stronger emphasis on the notion of the ground of the soul and on it being both the origin of the soul and of all experience,[39] but also with Herder's tendency to naturalize this very notion. While the mystics point to the open receptivity of the ground of the soul, to its aspects of sheer virtuality, to its function as a monadic mirror of God and creatures, to its unity with God, Herder turns it into the place of perception of the whole cosmos (*des ganzen Weltalls*) in the embodied soul. When Herder mentions that all mankind, that each human being is born as a *dunkel fühlende Auster* (a darkly feeling and perceiving oyster), he emphasizes a naturalizing aspect of his notion of the ground of the soul even more strongly in terms of a horizon of emergence for all possible worlds in the relation between the ground of the soul and the world it is part of.[40]

In this regard, Herder's notion of the soul resonates with the elements of contemporary philosophy of nature and aspects of French sensualism from which he draws. However, he never entirely covers up the provenience of the mystical trope of the ground of the soul. Thus, he writes in his *Metakritik der sogenannten Transzendental-Ästhetik* (Metacritique of the so-called transcendental aesthetics) that "nothingness in nothingness" reveals itself "in the dark ground of the soul of the mystics" (das Nichts im Nichts . . . offenbaret sich im dunklen Seelengrund der Mystiker) in order to become the "only possible condition of the revelation of the sensual as well as the comprehensible world."[41] In other words, the ground of the soul is not only the natural and generic ground of our becoming and of all our abilities that he grasps in the image of the oyster; it is also the "dark ground" of all our feelings, and it is "the dark ground of the soul of the mystics," the nothingness and the abyss that we find in Tauler and—much closer to Herder but not equally naturalized, yet—in Baroque mysticism and pietist thought.

On this basis Herder figures and reconfigures the sense of touch in a new way, as correlation between the "darkness" of the ground of the soul and its very expression in feeling and touch, that is, in the way the soul takes shape in perception.

The emphasis on touch in Herder's thought has been extensively analyzed, and one important context is certainly the discussion of touch in French philosophy, especially by the Abbé de Gandillac. In my focus on the notion of the ground of the soul, I am adding one aspect that has been ignored: in rehabilitating touch, Herder rehabilitates a notion of "darkness" and of the mystical tropes that go with it. One of the most beautiful passages that lets us understand what Herder means in his turn toward touch can be found in his attempt to portray and characterize what happens to a viewer who observes a sculpture. The example he chooses is—not surprisingly—Winkelmann, the "thoughtful observer of the Vatican Apollo":

> Didn't Winkelmann have to destroy the very properties of the object of his contemplation, i.e., all the properties and qualities that make our visual perception, namely color, surface, angle of view? And didn't he have to give his eyes seemingly a new sense, namely feeling? And wasn't the sense that he used [the eye] a reduction and replacement of a more originary sense? A sense that was open to the proper or essential effect of art? Now let's suppose he [the viewer] reaches this sense? His engaged viewing, his obvious touching and feeling transport the beautiful in its form and shape into the imagination, giving it to the imagination in an embodied way . . . and thus the effect happens: the beautiful body is perceived as a body . . . the imagination becomes active and engaged, and the imagination speaks as if she felt and touched: speaks of pleasant fullness, of admirable curves, of beautiful roundness, of soft aspects, of the moving marble that is brought to

life by the touching hand. These are all feelings! Why feelings? And why feelings that are *not* metaphors? They are experiences. The eye that started to collect them wasn't eye anymore when it collected; the eye turned into hand . . . perception into immediate touch. The imagination speaks feelings and touch.[42]

In this difficult passage Herder describes—following Winkelmann's gaze—the transformation of the eye into an organ of feeling and touch, the transformation from perception as observation to perception as exposure and participation. For Herder this happens literally, not metaphorically. He does not describe ways in which the eye, as we sometimes say, touches a surface or a body, using the notion of touch to express the intensity of seeing. Instead, he describes a transformation that happens while we see and observe, a transformation in which the eye loses its specificity, the determinate ways of looking at form, surface, color, shape, and perspective. In this transformation the eye turns into touch and the visual is "reduced," as he writes, to the tactile, which is the very ground of possibility of all sensation and feeling and which takes shape in aesthetic experience. It is touch that is encountered by the sculpted figure, that moves along its surfaces, and that in moving along is absorbed in the very perception, making the experience one of the effects of the sculpture in the soul and of a relation between the soul and the object. In this moment, perception turns into partaking, into an engagement of the imagination and the affects that immediately arise from touch. But, to be clear, it is not the visual that is reduced or diminished by touch. The paradigm of visuality, often seen as the highest faculty among the senses, is here presented as *Verkürzung*, as an "abbreviation" and representation, as a reduced version of perception, which replaces a more originary and more comprehensive sense and sensation.

We see this more comprehensive form of sensation appear where the language of the viewer—in the quoted example, Winkelmann observing a statue, analyzed by Herder in a wonderful phenomenological way—betrays that he has already moved on, that he has left the visual behind, that in his experience he is forced to move on from the visual to the realm of touch and feeling. It is important, to take Herder's argument seriously, that we are not dealing with metaphorical language here. He does not present us with an allegorical or metaphorical explanation of the act of viewing and the ways in which emotions and affects are involved in it and in which they are seduced by the object. What happens instead is to be described as a kind of transfiguration of seeing into touch whereby the ground of the soul is being aroused in the experience of the sculpture and where something new takes shape in this experience—a new figure, a new soul, and a new sphere of experience. The eye sees determined, limited, defined shapes, forms, and colors, thus constituting a determined thing and object of experience. Touch, however, appears as a moment of liberating dissimilation from this determination, as a reminiscence of something, and as the level of experience where object and subject, sculpture and viewer, collapse in a slow temporal process of aesthetic experience.

Inka Mülder-Bach has analyzed the passages where Herder discusses this transfiguration, among them the passage just quoted, and she speaks here of an "eroticizing processuality."[43] Touch implies an erotic as well as a temporal unfolding in which the experience of the darkness of touch and the animation of senses, affects, and imagination take shape—or, to put it in different terms, a temporal process in which the soul takes shape and forms the place of such an experience. This produces a scene of reciprocity, thus the notion of erotic, where—as Herder writes—"the 'warm, creating hand,' the organ of artistic creation, turns into the organ of the very reception of the work of art."[44] The plasticity of the ground of the soul, its receptivity and openness, is informed by the effects of the statue and takes shape in a tactile exchange with it. The "tactile" is the name for this experience that deconstructs the objectivity of vision and its plane of reification to allow for the statue to fully deploy its effects on the soul, to act on the soul, and to unfold in forms of shared experience. Through this process the soul is increasingly absorbed in the very experience of the effects that take place in this exchange between the viewer and the sculpture. They transform the encounter from seeing to touch.

I want to emphasize that both aspects, the "eroticizing processuality" and the tactile reciprocity, should be linked to the mystical use of the notion of the ground of the soul. It is this moment of being touched that makes all the elements of perception emerge—the erotic, the desire, the imagination, the emotions, and the relational nature of the soul. It does so beyond understanding, in darkness and silence. What happens is—reminding us again of the monastic treatises on contemplation—a "string play," an arousal of the soul and of all its potentials in forms of assimilation, letting it take shape in an experience that we call aesthetic, but also reducing it to the very fact of the encounter with the figure that underlies all assimilation. It is, as the quote illustrates, a form of cognition unified not through an act of rational intervention but through the "spirit" that dwells in this darkness and that emerges from it in the very moments of aesthetic relation.

With these observations Herder rehabilitates "the sense of touch and feeling that has been so decidedly repressed and obliterated by vision."[45] Subsequently, discourses on touch in modernity tend to focus on the reevaluation of touch as a form of original and originary sensuality that has been overshadowed and obliterated by the predominance of vision. Thus, touch seems to stand for a primal presence, an immediacy, and a fusion of object and subject. In the context of Herder's thought, however, this is, I believe, not the dominant thought. Indeed, Herder does speak of touch as a forgotten sense. This sense takes shape, however, not only as a forgotten form of presence or an obliterated ground of all sensual experience. Instead, he offers an alternative understanding of his focus on touch as a sphere of modality and relation that escapes the hierarchical order of the senses and accompanies and encompasses all forms of perception. In his recourse to touch, Herder constructs a critical position that does not set up an opposition only between touch and vision. Herder's rehabilitation of the "darkest sense" and his emphasis on the connection between touch and the dark ground of the soul make touch part and foundation of all sensation. Touch is the connection of sensation with the very plasticity of the ground of the soul, and it stands for the temporal process in which aesthetic experience takes shape in all forms of sensation, imagination, and affect. Thus, touch is not opposed to the other senses but the very nature of sensation since it is in touch that all the other modes of sensation move back into the ground of the soul and gain the fullness of experience that characterizes the aesthetic in Herder's and Baumgarten's view. Touch is the place where the world turns from object to figure. Where the eye moves along the object, where it is affected and absorbed by particular moments, it actually turns into feeling and touch, not because feeling and touch are more "authentic" or "primal" but because touch is the very possibility of being affected and absorbed by the figure in the temporal experience that we call perception.

Religious and philosophical authors, going back to Aristotle and including medieval theories of prayer and contemplation, speak of touch not only in terms of a specific sense and its organ but also in terms of a ground of sensation that accompanies all sense experience and perception. Touch and reflections on touch can thus be seen in the context of an art of experience in which the soul takes shape. Touch, one might want to say, is the nondetermined sense and thus the sense that can be everything. Mystical darkness, the night of the soul, and the very ground of the soul evoked by Herder and Baumgarten, then, do not function as a negative image opposed to visual shape, conceptual grasp, and rational understanding. Instead, they form the virtual basis of all possible experiential intensity that is not preframed by reason and that can be explored in aesthetic enthusiasm.

In both Baumgarten and Herder the notion of the ground of the soul has obviously lost some or all of the theological significance that is so prominent in late medieval and early modern texts. However, what stays alive and what is made more prominent are at least four things: the image of an undetermined and open structure of the soul (if we do not conceive of it in terms of a set of determined faculties but in terms of "dark ground" of all experience and perception); the understanding of the ground as a realm of possibility and plasticity of the soul that takes shape in a temporal process of exchange; the notion that the ecstatic, enthusiastic experience arises from this ground of possibility; and, especially with Herder, the elaboration of the structure of this experience in terms of touch, which, as the ground of the sensation, is the place of indeterminacy, openness, and possibility to be virtually everything. Thus, I am arguing here, the references to the mystical trope of the ground of the soul do not indicate a "religious" turn or a "'religious" reminiscence in Baumgarten's and Herder's thought—although that might be the case as well—but an attempt to retrieve something contemporary philosophy did indeed, as Baumgarten points out, not have a term for, the plasticity of the soul and its utter freedom to take shape in an aesthetic experience of a world that turns from object into figure, from thing into monad. With this, both Baumgarten and Herder also undermine the modern distinction between the "secular" and the "religious" that Luther established.

Dance

In his reflections on aesthetic experience, Johann Gottfried Herder also discusses dance, the production of moving figures in space and time. It is an art of figuration that affects and touches both the performer and the perceiver. As we have seen, Herder is invested in a very specific understanding of touch, and he brings to our attention that touch is not just one sense among others but the very sensation that forms the ground of all sensuous perception and affect. What Herder analyzes is the intimate connection between touch and sculpture and, to speak in broader terms, between touch and figure or, even more broadly, touch and the art of figuration with its sensual, emotional, and cognitive assimilations.

In a short sketch, "Von der Bildhauerkunst fürs Gefühl" (On the art of sculpture in view of feeling), written in 1769, Herder observes:

> When our dance will change, when it isn't anymore the play of little feet and the forced bending of breasts and hips that we call grace, then the body will be able to speak. Now everything is forced into one thing: little feet and their movements, the shielded hips, the forced grace—it is all there is, and the dance is all gothic.[46]

What "gothic" refers to in this eighteenth-century context is an obscure, confused, and contrived form of expression.[47] Instead of this "forced" form of articulation, Herder is searching for a way in which the body starts to speak and, maybe better, to turn into a figure of evocation, relation, expression, perception, and experience. Herder raises the very same issue and question with regard to sculpture when he writes at the beginning of the same essay: "A statue has to live; her flesh has to come alive; her face has to speak. We have to believe that we are touching her, that she becomes warm under our hands. We have to see her standing before us and to feel that she is speaking to us." He continues: "Thus, the eye moves into the tips of our fingers and we forget the cold surface and the comparison to painting. We do not see anymore. Instead, we feel tender skin, a round knee, the pleasant cheek, the beautiful breast and hip, in short, the beauty of the body."[48]

But how, then, should we imagine the body in expression, the dance that is not caught up in the "gothic" small movements of the "little feet" and the "forced grace," the dance that takes shape in sculptural figures to produce an experience that is unique and at the same time the basis for all other experience, including emotions, sensation, and cognition? In reading the passages where Herder discusses this transfiguration, among them the passage quoted earlier, we might want to speak again of an "eroticizing processuality" since touch implies an erotic in its spatiotemporal unfolding. Through this process the soul is increasingly absorbed in the very experience of the effects that take place in this exchange between the viewer and the figures in motion—to the point that the life of the soul can no longer be distinguished from the liveliness that the figures deploy.

What Herder has in mind is neither in the figures alone nor in the soul alone. It is in the movement that embraces both and that produces the absorption in sensation, affect, and cognition. In another passage about a classical Greek statue he writes:

> A spirit has poured itself into the statue, guided the hand of the artist, held the work of art and made it one. Whoever stood next to the famous statue of the hermaphrodite (to use a most difficult example) and who didn't feel how Bacchic dream and hermaphroditism reign in every trembling and curvature of the body, in everything he touches and doesn't touch—to whomever, who didn't feel the torture of sweet thoughts and voluptuousness like a fire that inflames his body, who didn't perceive involuntarily the resonances and consonances of this play of chords, neither my words nor any words can explain this. It is the very nature of a sculpture that she speaks to us as an act since she is all mankind and living body. It is the character of a sculpture that she captivates and pierces our being, and that she arouses the chords of human compassion.[49]

This moment of being touched makes all the elements of perception emerge, the erotic, desire, imagination, emotions, and the fundamentally relational nature of the empty soul. It does so beyond words, in darkness and silence below the horizon of meaning. What happens is an arousal of the soul and of all its potential to resonate through figures in space and time, letting it take shape in an experience that we call aesthetic. In his discussion of dance, Herder does not focus on a formally defined social practice, for example, the Baroque courtly dance. Instead, for him, dance can be, can become that very art of figuration, an exemplary cultivation of the realm of possibilities that we call soul, that is, affective possibilities, sensual possibilities, and cognitive possibilities. It can be the very art of figuration that is free of allegory and metaphor in order to be nothing else than a play with figures and their effects in and on our empty plane of perception. Dance is thus a realm of figuration before meaning emerges, before we identify pictures, images, and allegories. It is a realm of figural play that Herder identifies with touch or, better, that he identifies with a transition from the visual to the tactile—a transition that escapes both intention and meaning, and a transition that time and again opens a field of emergence.

According to this, dance is the enactment of the emblematic tension freed from its third pole, the concept. It is figure and assimilation set free, partaking outside "gothic" norms. Thus, figures in motion elicit possibilities and produce perception events, sensation events, affect events in time and space. Depending on the specific situation they can indeed represent something, can acquire meaning, can give birth to allegorical forms. Strictly speaking, however, as figures they do not represent anything, and they do not have meaning. They are just figures in movement on a background of darkness, a screen of possibilities and interactions, a screen or plane of touch and being touched. Thus, they do not represent events; they constitute events. Figures in movement, bodies in movement are not media and they are not embodied forms of meaning and ideas—although this can indeed be the case as well. For our purpose, however, it is important to be aware of this difference. They are places, spatial moments and movements, configurations, transfigurations, and disfigurations where touch unfolds. And ever again we become aware of the fact that the visual, our gaze, turns into touch, into sensation, emotion, cognition. The visual, which is there without doubt, loses its dominant aspect: we do not look at the dancer and his or her figurations as an object, we do not look at each other in dancing as objects—but we are getting caught up in moments of absorption that happen before our eyes and express themselves on a plane of perception where touch and being touched converge in perceptions, sensations, affects.

Arguing in a comparable vein, John Cage returns to the notion of the ground of the soul—with explicit references to Meister Eckhart—in his writings and interviews. In his Darmstadt lectures on "Composition as Process" (1958), Cage constructs an intimate relationship between the "function of the performer," his acts of "giving form," and "the Ground of Meister Eckhart."[50] In bringing together the acts of "giving form" with a specific notion of "indeterminacy," Cage also views the ground of the soul as a horizon of possibility, a realm of darkness, "from which all impermanencies flow and to which they return."[51] He does so in a way that is experimental, transposing the relation between figuration and the ground of the soul into a realm of aesthetic creation and experience where "the outcome" can never be "foreseen." In turning away, Cage writes, "from himself and his ego-sense of separation from other beings and things," both the performer and the listener or viewer "faces the Ground of Meister Eckhart" and "does what is to be done, not splitting his mind in two, not separating it from his body, which is kept ready for direct and instantaneous contact with his instrument."[52] What results from this cannot be fixed in time. It is the product of a correlation between an art of figuration and a horizon of possibility where an experimental play explores forms of cognition, perception, and affect. According to Cage, this experimental play is to be found in dance, in the relation between "clarity of rhythmic structure" and "grace," which form "a duality":

> Together they have a relation like that of body and soul. Clarity is cold, mathematical, inhuman, but basic and earthy. Grace is warm, incalculable, human, opposed to clarity, and like the air. Grace is not here used to mean prettiness; it is used to mean the play with and against the clarity of the rhythmic structure. The two are always together in the best works of the time arts, endlessly, and life-givingly, opposed to each other.[53]

In this quote Cage reflects, from an entirely different point of view, on the question of grace that Herder raised two hundred years earlier. Like Herder, Cage makes use of the trope of the ground of the soul to think about dance and grace. Beyond "forced grace" and "prettiness," dance turns into the art of figuration that evokes—"life-givingly" for Cage and as a body that "speaks" for Herder—not specific meanings but a realm of possibilities of sensation, affect, and cognition. For both, the *chiffre* that points to this realm is the ground of the soul, and for both it is dance that produces the experimental figures that make these possibilities emerge from the darkness of the ground in temporal shapes of perception, of joyfully touching and being touched, and in forms that are nothing else than endless monadic transcriptions in aesthetic experience.

7

Modernist Moments

Against Nature

Joris-Karl Huysmans begins his novel *Against Nature* with the following epigraph: "I must rejoice beyond the confines of time . . . though the world be repelled by my joy, and in its coarseness know not what I mean."[1] This quote from Jan Ruusbroec's *The Spiritual Espousals* evokes a moment of mystical experience in overwhelming joy.[2] The moment of joy Huysmans makes reference to, a mystical absorption into the divine, is alien to the ordinary world and will forever be unknown to it. Its trace, however, reemerges in the experience of the decadent protagonist of Huysmans's novel, Jean des Esseintes, who reproduces the very alienation from the world in his retreat from it and the very joy of the mystic in his artful enactment of, and in his experimentation with, moments of intense aesthetic experience.

One of these moments is to be found in Jean des Esseintes's contemplation of the books that stand in his library. After the works of Charles Baudelaire, for whom his "admiration . . . was boundless,"[3] des Esseintes reviews a number of Catholic writers, among others Ernest Hello, the nineteenth-century translator of Ruusbroec's work into French. Huysmans writes: "Des Esseintes felt drawn to this unbalanced yet subtle mind; no fusion had been achieved between the skilled psychologist and the pious pedant, and it was these jarring collisions, these very incongruities that formed the essence of Hello's personality."[4]

Among other things, Ernest Hello was the translator and commentator of medieval mystics, of "Angela da Foligno's *Visions*, a book flowing with unparalleled inanity," and "of the selected works of Jan van Ruysbroeck the Blessed, a thirteenth century mystic, whose prose offered an incomprehensible but appealing amalgam of mysterious ecstasy, sentimental effusions, and scathing outbursts."[5] Like Baudelaire, "close to those frontiers which are the dwelling-place of aberrations of the mind," Hello had—according to Huysmans's protagonist—uncovered or rediscovered "the tetanus of mysticism,"[6] and he prepared the readings that fascinated Jean des Esseintes most, the ones from a medieval mystical tradition that gave him the joy he was looking for.

Huysmans's fascination with the mystics and the rediscovery of medieval mysticism in the nineteenth century does not, however, lie primarily with mystical theology or with anything the mystics believed or taught in dogmatic or theological terms. Instead, it lies with the experiences they produced and explored in their contemplative practices, with the very language and texture of their discourse, and with the practices of figuration and sensual and affective assimilation. In the eyes of Jean des Esseintes—and of the author Huysmans—the essence of mysticism is to be found in what the mystical writers shared with Baudelaire, the fact that he "had gone further" than any other poet, that "he had descended to the very bottom of the inexhaustible mine, had journeyed along abandoned or uncharted tunnels, eventually reaching those regions of the soul in which the nightmare growths of human thought flourish."[7]

Thus, Huysmans puts a form of rhetoric and poetic practice at the center of his engagement with medieval mysticism—a rhetoric and poetic practice that can be understood in terms of a literary and spiritual exercise at the same time. It is an exercise that focuses—to use the words of Georges Bataille, who will follow Huysmans's line of thought and his admiration for Angela of Foligno—on the "possible," on pushing the "limits of the possible,"[8] and on exploring those very limits of human experience. In fact, many of the moments of pleasurable experience in Jean des Esseintes's life are conceived in ways that follow this tradition. They are inspired by Ignatius of Loyola, his spiritual exercises,[9] and the medieval practices of contemplation and the production of mystical experience that lie at the basis of the Ignatian model of reading and contemplation.

A Sense of Possibility

As it was for Georges Bataille, whose references to medieval mystical traditions in his book *Inner Experience* resonate deeply with the quoted passages from Huysmans's *Against Nature*, the focus of this figural poetics of experience does not consist in the construction of a body of knowledge but in an experiential exploration that goes from "knowledge" and "values" to "non-knowledge" and intensities "unknown" to this world.[10] Bataille writes:

> For some time now, the only philosophy which lives—that of the German school—tended to make of the highest knowledge an extension of inner experience. But this *phenomenology* lends to knowledge the value of a goal which one attains through experience. This is an ill-assorted match: the measure given to experience is at once too much and not great enough. Those who provide this place for it must feel that it overflows, by an immense "possible," the use to which they limit themselves. What appears to preserve philosophy is the little acuity of the experience from which the phenomenologists set out. This lack of balance does not weather the putting into play of experience proceeding to the end of the possible, when going to the end means at least this: that the limit, which is knowledge as a goal, be crossed.[11]

Quoting the mystical tropes of "darkness," of "non-knowledge," and of "unknowing," Bataille evokes in these lines a specific kind of phenomenology. It is not the type of philosophical phenomenology known to us from early twentieth-century German thought alone but a phenomenology that emerges in mystical texts that explore and "cross" the limits of knowledge, opening up the "uncharted" territory that is also the realm of Huysmans's fascination. In Bataille's view, the mystical texts do so in response to the challenges of negative theology, focusing on the very practices that allow for the production of experience and for a phenomenology of experience where knowledge fails and always has to fail. Thus, the production of experience moves to center stage, as it does in the late medieval author Bataille loves most, Angela of Foligno.[12] This production of experiential moments happens, however, not in the form of an experience that allows for us to "know" something and to build a body of knowledge (something Thomas Aquinas and his *Summa theologiae* stand for in Bataille's ironic juxtaposition of Thomas and Angela) but as a practice of phenomenological exploration that acknowledges the impossibility to know and that moves the boundaries of the possible time and again from within this utter acknowledgment of finitude and "nakedness." According to Bataille, this takes place in exemplary form in Angela of Foligno's *Liber de vere fidelium experientia* (*The Book of the True Believers' Experience*), a text that he puts in opposition to the work of Thomas Aquinas and other scholastic theologians.[13]

Dionysius the Areopagite, whom Bataille quotes in this context as well, also forms here a starting point of this rhetoric of experience. Dionysius's treatises *Mystical Theology* and *Divine Names* are both the inspiration for the strong notion of apophatic speech—the "joy unknown to the world" in Huysmans's and the "non-knowledge" in Bataille's words—and for cataphatic speech, for a poetics of praise and abandonment, an experimental poetics of affirmation and negation, and an erotic and poetics of pushing the limits of the possible that allows for the production and exploration of ever-new experiential states. These states—moments of utter absorption in many guises, thus often associated with erotic excess—compensate for the impossibility of knowing the divine (or, with Nietzsche, any kind of absolute truth) and provide an experiential "voyage to the end of the possible of man."[14] In foregrounding the possible and in setting it up against the real and the world of "projects," Bataille's refusal of an ordinary take on phenomenology reiterates the tension between figures and forms of assimilation. Ultimately, it is not the latter that is at the center of his interest here, not the sphere of experience in its phenomenological qualities but the threshold function of the figural that makes this experiential richness and its absorbing qualities; the realm of possibilities emerges as break, transgression, and disruption. The erotic vignettes that Bataille produces throughout his work reiterate this time and again, opposing the excess to the forms of assimilation. The limit position, "the possible of man," has thus moved into the place of the abstract "motto" in what I called an emblematic tension in the previous chapter. "The possible" could be the title above the erotic story and above *Inner Experience.* In its unspeakable nature, however, it is the empty spot, the abyss—some would say, the abyss of desire as an index of possibilities—that hovers underneath the tension between the figural and the forms of assimilation in sensation, affect, and thought.

Essayism

As I mentioned in the Preface, in the first part of his essayistic novel, *The Man without Qualities*, Robert Musil introduces the notion of a "sense of possibility," suggesting that the emergence of possibility within our actual world of determined meaning is in basic ways connected to rhetorical practices of figuration that undermine set frames of meaning. Beyond his interest in theories of perception, Musil was familiar with traditions of contemplative mysticism, drawing on the works of Martin Buber and the experimental psychologist Carl Girgensohn, who studied the effects of prayer in psychic life.[15] Informed by these texts, Musil's own notion of the use of similes, analogies, and comparisons builds on the figural disruption, the effects of rhetorical devices, and the forms of sensual, affective, and cognitive assimilation.

In the fourth chapter of *The Man without Qualities*, still within the first part of the book that is called "A Sort of Introduction," Musil writes:

> To pass freely through open doors, it is necessary to respect the fact that they have solid frames. This principle, by which the old professor [Ulrich's father] had always lived, is simply a requisite of the sense of reality. But if there is a sense of reality, and no one will doubt that it has its justification for existing, then there must also be something we call a sense of possibility.

He then continues:

> Whoever has it does not say, for instance: Here this or that has happened, will happen, must happen; but he invents: Here this or that might, could, or ought to happen. If he is told that something is the way it is, he will think: Well, it could probably just as well be otherwise. So the sense of possibility could be defined outright as the ability to conceive of everything there might be just as well, and to attach no more importance to what is than to what is not. The consequences of so creative a disposition can be remarkable, and may, regrettably, often make what people admire seem wrong, and what is taboo permissible, or, also, make both a matter of indifference. Such possibilists are said to inhabit a more delicate medium, a hazy medium of mist, fantasy, daydreams, and the subjunctive mood. Children who show this tendency are dealt with firmly and warned that such persons are cranks, dreamers, weaklings, know-it-alls, or troublemakers. Such fools are also called idealists by those who wish to praise them. But all this clearly applies only to their weak subspecies, those who cannot comprehend reality or who, in their melancholic condition, avoid it. These are people in whom

the lack of reality is a real deficiency. But the possible includes not only the fantasies of people with weak nerves but also the as yet unawakened intentions of God. A possible experience or truth is not the same as an actual experience or truth minus its "reality value" but has—according to its partisans, at least—something quite divine about it, a fire, a readiness to build and a conscious utopianism that does not shrink from reality but sees it as a project, something yet to be invented.[16]

What Musil anticipates in this passage is not only something he will reflect on later when he discusses his idea of a "utopia of essayism." More than that, it is something that characterizes his style of writing and that is to be realized in it. That is, the very production of possibility takes place not in thinking of what might be possible but instead in a specific use of comparisons, similes, and endless rows of figures that disrupt the textures of the real; replace other figures time and again; and open a sphere of variation, enumeration, incongruency, and analogy. This practice makes emerge a realm of possibility that nests in what is conventionally defined as the real, producing new worlds out of the old ones and modifying the life of the soul in the play with the efficacy of figures.

The "utopias of essayism," Musil writes later in the novel about his style, are "much the same as possibilities." They are results of a practice of figuration that disentangles things and words from their restraints, that gets rid of the preconceived qualities and conceptual and semantic determination, that undoes established textures and worlds. Thus, the sense of possibility does not produce a concrete utopian thought. Instead, it consists in a use of figures that time and again disturbs and modifies patterns of perception in drawing attention to the concrete figures and their disruptive force. This allows the writer, as Musil points out, to perform a kind of work that is quite similar to what happens "when a scientist observes the change of an element within a compound and draws his conclusions." In other words, the "utopia of essayism" is to be seen as the practice and the result of an "experiment, . . . in which the possible change of an element may be observed, along with the effects of such a change on the compound phenomenon we call life." Thus, it is allowed "to exert its exemplary influence on everything it touches." A "paradoxical interplay of exactitude and indefiniteness" is the consequence of this experiment, the utopian state itself, or, if we think in terms of literature, the "essayism" and the essayistic exploration that Musil's own work embodies.[17] His novel is not essayistic insofar as it includes what we could call reflective theorizing passages but insofar as it deploys things, events, and concepts as figures that disrupt and constitute characters and relations, evoking time and again possibilities and experimental openings where we expect semantic closure.

The essayistic novel is the medium, the very space in which thought and language experiment on themselves and with themselves in figural ways that reproduce the tension between figural effects and hermeneutics we find in Auerbach. What Musil is interested in is not a realm of hermeneutic possibilities but, as he explains in "Das Theorem der menschlichen Gestaltlosigkeit" ("The Theorem of Human Formlessness"), the formative power and function of figures. It is, similar to what we have seen in my reading of Auerbach and Vico, the efficacy of figures in modifying the life of the mind and the soul. A good page of prose, Musil writes, is at first not a message that can be understood but nothing else than the production of "arousal," of a disruption, based on figural effects, that entails chains of assimilation. It is a sensual and affective stimulation of the mind through the artful production of a configuration of elements that shape perception. This is nothing else than what Auerbach has in mind when he speaks of "intensity." Thus, Musil's text, his essayism, explores "exactitude" in and through words and elaborates from within this engagement a world of possibilities and new relations between words, things, and concepts. It destabilizes fixed qualities and allows for new configurations. The utopian state is a state of rhetorical invention and play; of configurations of words, figures, and things; and of emerging relations. It is not and is never a state of redemption, stability, or identity. Instead, it is a state that is open to the experimental figural empiricism Musil develops in his construction of scenes of interaction. We can think of many scenes in his novels that function along these lines—neither illustrating the effects of figures, nor representing these effects, but experimenting with their force to produce states of perception, feeling, and cognition. Thus functions the beginning of the novel with its setting of atmospheric pressure systems, movements in streets, the rhythm and vibration of the city, the cars in movement, the accident of the car, the word *Bremsweg* (braking distance) itself in the first scene. All these elements are deployed in terms not of meaning alone but of the ways in which they disrupt and shape the protagonists that appear. Similarly, in another scene I referred to earlier, the first words and gestures exchanged between Ulrich and Diotima are to be read as the display of an experimental setting of figural moments that draw our attention not so much to what they mean but to what plastic effects they deploy and how they unfold a realm of possible correlations and configurations that the protagonists are not aware of and that the novel further explores in other figural constellations.

As I mentioned in the Introduction, Robert Musil played with an expression that had been coined by Meister Eckhart in the very title of his novel *The Man without Qualities.* In many of his sermons Eckhart speaks of "human without qualities" (*mensch âne eigenschaften*), creating a term and a concept for an ideal that embodies specific aspects of detachment, freedom, and salvation. Musil's reference to Eckhart in his great and unfinished novel does not end there, however. In addition, he inserted in his text a series of quotes and excerpts from Meister Eckhart, whom he had read in a number of anthologies and in the translation published by Herman Büttner in two volumes between 1903 and 1909.

Büttner's edition of Eckhart's works was highly popular during the first decades of the twentieth century. It has been studied by everybody in the German-speaking intellectual world of the time, including Georg Simmel, Max Weber, Karl Mannheim, and Martin Buber, but also Ernst Bloch, Georg Lukács, and Belá Balázs. As one of the many reflections of this interest in the "mystical tradition" and in Meister Eckhart, one might point to an intense and heated discussion that erupted after Ernst Troeltsch's presentation on the emergence of modernity at the First Convention of German Sociologists. The conversation focused on the relation between "mystical traditions and the genesis of the modern world." Karl Mannheim was part of this. And when he met Georg Lukács for the first time, they discussed Lukács's plan to write an "essay on mysticism." At this point, Lukács had already translated some Eckhart texts, and he later wrote an essay deeply inspired by his reading of Eckhart with the title "Über die Armut am Geiste" ("On Poverty in Spirit," published 1912). Among the readers of Eckhart's writings was also Béla Balázs, an author known today mainly through his book on film, *Der sichtbare Mensch, oder die Kultur des Films* (*Visible Man, or the Culture of Film*), published in

Vienna in 1924. He played a key role for Musil and his engagement with Eckhart as well, since it is Musil who writes a review of Balázs's book that evokes the specific relationship between the culture of film, its aesthetic, and the convergence of mystical experience and utopian thought as Musil understands it.

We might be tempted to discuss this interest in Eckhart and his writings, and more generally the interest in the mystical tradition, in terms of a fashion that took hold of a large part of intellectual life of the early twentieth century. It is indeed a surprising and fascinating phenomenon of reception, bringing rather difficult and sometimes quite esoteric medieval texts back into the realm of early twentieth-century culture, philosophy, and intellectual conversation. My interest here lies, however, not with this fascination, not with the nostalgia, the so-called irrationalism and the esoteric inclinations that might have motivated this renaissance of mystical literature in the contexts of early twentieth-century cultural criticism. Nor does it lie with a universalizing notion of "mystical experience" that shaped twentieth-century scholarship in the study of religion.[18] Instead, I want to foreground the innovative side of the use Musil makes in some of his quite fragmented references to Eckhart, in which he explores the possibilities of how to read Eckhart and of how to deploy a specific critical and utopian discourse on the basis of his engagement with Eckhart's texts—an engagement that, in its attention to the practices of figuration and the asymmetry of the figural, sustains the formation of an aesthetic and ethic of possibilities.

Attention to notions of possibility emerges in the context of readings of Eckhart in the early twentieth century as a key term, resonating—beyond Musil's text—with a short note in Lukács's *Heidelberger Notizen* written between 1910 and 1913. There, Lukács speaks in the middle of a large body of excerpts surprisingly and rather enigmatically of "Eckeharts Lehre von der Möglichkeit" (Eckhart's teaching about possibility). Unfortunately, he does not give us more than this quick note: "Vgl. Eckeharts Lehre von der Möglichkeit und seine Christusauffassung" (Compare Eckhart's teaching on possibility and his understanding of Christ). Unfortunately, it also will never be known whether Musil and Lukács discussed this or something along these lines when they met in Balázs's apartment in Vienna during the years Balázs spent there mainly as a film critic. What we know, for sure, however, is that Lukács's later thought turned toward a rather different concept of utopia and a moral rigorism that seems radically opposed to Musil's own utopian thought.

The configuration of a "philosophy of possibility" is the cornerstone of Musil's project. It also forms, and this will be the link to Belá Balázs's book, the core of Musil's engagement with his theory of film when he wrote his review of it in 1925 under the title "Ansätze zu neuer Ästhetik. Bemerkungen über eine Dramaturgie des Films" ("Toward a New Aesthetic: Observations on a Dramaturgy of Film").

The passage quoted previously from Musil's *Man without Qualities* reflects all the elements important in the elaboration of his notion of possibility. What appears in this passage is not only the reference to the "unawakened intentions of God," the "divine" character of a "conscious utopianism," the allusion to the image of the holy fool, and the conjunction of "creativity" and "birth" that connects this text with Eckhart's thought but the very notion of "possibility" itself as it is introduced by Musil in a chapter that ends with a consideration of "being without qualities." It is this notion of "possibility" that Musil quotes from a sermon by Eckhart, reconfiguring its meaning in view of a non-messianic, ethically refined, and—as Musil calls it—essayistic "utopia of precision."

The humans engaged in this "utopia of precision," he writes, "would be full of the paradoxical interplay of exactitude and indefiniteness," and thus the "stable internal conditions guaranteed by a system of morality have little value for a man whose imagination is geared to change."[19] "Ultimately," he continues, "when the demand for the greatest and most exact fulfillment is transferred from the intellectual realm to that of the passions, it becomes evident . . . that the passions disappear and that in their place arises something like a primordial fire of goodness."[20] Thus, "the pallid resemblance of actions to virtues would disappear from the image of life; in their place we would have these virtues' intoxicating fusion in holiness."[21]

What then, we might want to ask, is the connection between this image of an absorbing holiness, a free-spirited ethics beyond morality and norms, a "conscious utopianism," and the notion of possibility; and how does Musil reconfigure Eckhart's thought? This is indeed not a return to or a recovery of an "irrational mysticism," as one often reads, but an exploration into the territory of rationality and "exactitude" that engages Eckhart's text in substantial ways. To explain this, I return to Musil's "utopia of essayism," as he calls it in his novel. The essay is the medium that imitates a quasi-alchemistic practice "to dissolve and coagulate" (*solve et coagula*) in a space where thought explores its exactitude in and through words and elaborates from within this exactitude a world of possibilities and new relations between figures, figural effects, meanings, and concepts. This world, according to Musil, includes not only thought but also sensation and emotion in the interaction with things, the world, animals, and people.

All this might at first glance seem quite far from Eckhart's writings, although many of his sermons can indeed be read, especially in Büttner's translation, as essayistic in style. However, I want to suggest that Musil does not only refer to key elements in Eckhart's theological discourse, picking up some vague ideas of unity and of an ethics beyond bourgeois normativity and morality, but that he reconfigures the quotes he uses in view of his utopian essayism.

The very notion of "possibility" appears in Eckhart's so-called speculative mysticism as the concept that motivates and determines its critical character. It is also a concept that he uses to reinterpret the tradition of negative theology. The "nothingness" of the divine, divine "darkness," Eckhart points out, can be "called . . . a possibility or receptivity"—a possibility and receptivity that can be traced in our intellect itself. Thus, he does not argue for a radical iconoclasm and a seemingly irrational flight into mystical unity but for an intellectual engagement, a thought of exactitude and an exactitude of thought that realize and recognize their own finitude. The very desire that moves thought finds its expression in an exploration of possibilities, since "the soul never comes to rest until she is filled with the fullness of her reality; exactly like matter never rests until everything is fulfilled that lies in her possibility." And Eckhart continues, according to Büttner's translation: "Our life on this earth is meant to become aware of God and all things in the mode of pure possibility."[22]

As Eckhart argues, this does not mean that thought and reason have to be left behind. Rather, thought that engages with itself discovers its own discursive character and thus acknowledges that in its discursive form it determines itself in a seemingly stable order of reality. Every word and every sentence are, as far as they represent knowledge of an object or a concept, the very structure that deprives this object and the viewer of their freedom, enclosing them in the world of "qualities." In acknowledging this, reason discovers itself as the place of an immanent freedom when it explores itself, and it does this exactly insofar as it sees itself as an ever-new realm of possibility. In realizing, in acknowledging, its own finitude, reason becomes for Eckhart the place of an elaboration of possibility.

This notion of mysticism never entails an abandonment of reason but an engagement with it that liberates it from its determined shape and opens up this realm of possibility. Key terms such as "detachment" (*Gelassenheit* or *Abgeschiedenheit* or *Bildlosigkeit* in German) refer to this intellectual practice that, as Eckhart argues, liberates not only thought but also all the things that otherwise get caught up in the order imposed on them by reason. As he states in a passage that is important in view of Musil's reading of his work, a person who could see "a fly or a piece of wood" without the order imposed on it—and thus as a figure in this realm of possibilities—would not need a sermon or even the Scriptures. This person would see it *âne eigenschaft* (without quality), *sunder warumbe* (without a why)—not as something, not as this or that, but in a moment where intellect and love, reason, sensation, and affect converge, where the human mind grasps the infinite and the unsayable in and through the irreducible particularity of the "piece of wood"—and of every other thing it sees and encounters. In his conclusion of the short essay he writes on Balázs, Musil calls this moment *Schau*, "vision," and he connects it with the very experience of film: "In this vision film uncovers . . . the infinite and ineffable character of all beings—as if put under glass, so that we can watch it."[23]

Here, my reading of Eckhart seems to be inflected by Musil already. And indeed, this is what Musil makes us do when we read his text. He forces or seduces us to follow the path of his essayistic engagement with the texts and quotes he uses; the disruptions they produce, the figural effects and forms of assimilation; the conversations that develop around these quotes; and the voices that engage with them throughout his novel. In his reconfiguration of Eckhart's notion of possibility in conjunction with his notion of the "experiment," he thus translates his own readings, fashioning these readings into a realm of possibility from which the "utopia of essayism" emerges. What he projects here, however, is not just this. It is a fascinating reading of Eckhart that takes into account an underestimated element in his thought, the intricate connection between a liberation of the intellect that emerges when it sees itself as a realm of possibility and the attention to a presence of a world of things and images, that is, to figures in their disruptive force. What Musil observes and what he inserts in his text is this relation of the intellect as the realm of possibility in its engagement with images, similes, and things. What he cuts out, one might add, is quite often "God"—while he nevertheless retains the moments of the "infinite" and "unnamable" that are characteristic marks of both Musil's and Eckhart's texts. And in both, the "infinite" takes shape as a realm of possibilities that opens up when things, images, and words are set free by the empty intellect that turns to the figural in its concreteness and asymmetry, thus exploring and undermining the ways in which all things and words affect our assimilative emotions, senses, and thoughts.

Later in Musil's novel, Agathe's and Ulrich's adventure itself, the encounter between the siblings that dissolves all norms, is characterized in terms that return to this point and emphasize the very moment of attention to the particular for both the reader and the protagonists:

> When she now spoke to Ulrich he had not even noticed how long the interruption had lasted. But whoever has not already picked up the clues to what was going on between this brother and sister should lay this account aside, for it depicts an adventure of which he will never be able to approve: a journey to the edge of the possible, which led past—and perhaps not always past—the dangers of the impossible and unnatural, even of the repugnant: a "borderline case," as Ulrich later called it, of limited and special validity, reminiscent of the freedom with which mathematics sometimes resorts to the absurd in order to arrive at the truth. He and Agathe happened upon a path that had much in common with the business of the possessed by God, but they walked it without piety, without believing in God or the soul, nor even in the beyond or reincarnation. They had come upon it as people of this world and pursued it as such—this was remarkable about it.[24]

It is again the negativity of negative theology that characterizes this very moment: "some tissue of habit tears," the "purposeful, practical connotations" have "suddenly" been "lost," and "what is left on the pictorial plane might best be called an ocean swell of sensations that rises and falls, breathes and shimmers, as though it filled your whole field of view without a horizon."[25] Building on this, Ulrich continues his conversation with Agathe, describing the visual impression of a herd of grazing cattle:

Of course, there are still countless individual perceptions contained within it: colors, horns, movements, smells, and all the details of reality; but none of them are acknowledged any longer, even if they should still be recognized. Let me put it this way: the details no longer have their egoism, which they use to capture our attention, but they're all linked with each other in a familiar, literally "inward" way.[26]

Once again, at first glance, this passage seems to be nothing more than a reminiscence of vaguely characterized mystical feelings and a somewhat indistinct sentiment. This, however, would underestimate the analytical sharpness that characterizes the conversation between Agathe and Ulrich as it unfolds. It is the conversation itself that brings out the possibilities of thought, and it is the conversation that brings us back to the role of the attention to the particular and the asymmetry of the figure in this utopian language. If we deal with mysticism here—and again, the pages are interspersed with quotes from Eckhart and others—it is a mysticism without the imaginary of salvation or the absolute presence of a mystical moment in unmediated experience. Instead, the "suddenness" is seen in terms of what could be called the moments of emergence, of absorbing figural disruption and relation that subvert the real critically, liberating it from its orderly nature and transforming it into the realm of an ethical encounter in the realm of the possible that is full of particularities and has gotten rid of all normative constraints. Consequently, the conversation between Agathe and Ulrich turns from the aesthetic toward the ethical, transforming the utopian essayism into an exploration of its ethical implications. Here again, Musil inserts several quotes from Eckhart's works into the conversation, for example, when Agathe says, "One possesses nothing in the world, one holds on to nothing, one is not held by anything." She thus refers to a state beyond "good and evil," a state where, as Ulrich responds, "one slips away from a life of inessentials" and where "everything enters into a new relationship with everything else." He adds:

I would almost go so far as to say into a nonrelationship. For it's an entirely unknown one, of which we have no experience, and all other relationships are blotted out. But despite its obscurity, this one is so distinct that its existence is undeniable. It's strong, but impalpably strong. One might put it this way:

ordinarily, we look at something, and our gaze is like a fine wire or taut thread with two supports—one being the eye and the other what it sees, and there's some such great support structure for every second that passes; but at this particular second, on the contrary, it is rather as though something painfully sweet were pulling our eye beams apart.[27]

To this, Musil adds two other Eckhart references. First, in Ulrich's voice: "They say that nothing can happen in that condition which is not in harmony with it." Then, in Agathe's voice, adding some thoughts about this state of being: "A good person makes everything that touches him good, no matter what others may do to him; the instant it enters his sphere it becomes transformed."[28]

The moment they evoke is part of the conversation itself, and it is part of their own exploration of the possibilities of their relation to each other. It is at the same time, however, the moment when an ethics of attention emerges. This ethics builds on the quotes from Eckhart's sermons, devoid of their theological background, to articulate what emerges from the encounter with the particular and the harmony that establishes itself with it. It is an ethics that builds on the asymmetry of the figural and that, in allowing for its disruptive and absorbing force, undermines the violence imposed on things and the world by the "sense of reality."

Visible Man

As mentioned previously, Musil develops some of his most important thoughts about this role of the figure and its tension with forms of assimilation in his review of Béla Balázs's book *Visible Man*. Balázs's key argument in this essay on film—he is speaking of silent film in 1924—is that film gives us something to see that has been obliterated by the hegemonic power of words. It is not just another form of theater or pantomime, as some critics would have it, but something entirely different. Its force lies in what he calls the physiognomic character, the face not only of humans but also of things, animals, landscapes, teacups, bridges, gestures, and everything else that surrounds us. And it has the power to move us through these images, selecting them, combining them, reconfiguring them, and thus of elaborating ever-new possibilities of figuration and effects that lie in the face of things, glances, and gestures. As Balázs points out, "The images should not mean thoughts but form and evoke thoughts—thoughts that emerge as consequences, not as symbols or ideograms, which have already taken shape in the image."[29] Using the term "physiognomy," which he inherits from Goethe and Lavater, Balázs does not imply a predefined meaning or character of the things we see. Instead, he focuses on the "visible gesture," the specific surface and superficiality that is able to liberate possibilities of signification, emotion, and sensation—possibilities that have been obscured by the predominance of the word in modern culture and that are able to recast the world in its very visibility. Even the word itself, Balázs argues later in his defense of the presence of sound in film, appears in a new visibility and audibility, together with a "rediscovery of our acoustic environments." "Film," he writes, "is an art of the surface" that embodies, and Balázs uses the Middle High German verb from Eckhart's texts here, "das *wesen* der Materie" (the *being* of matter), adding "a useful old verb!"[30] In its reduction to surface, to the living face of things and faces, it offers a time-affirming phenomenology of possibilities that emerge from figures and move us along. So, for example, in the face of Asta Nielsen in a silent film that Balázs describes:

> There is a film where Asta Nielsen looks through a window, observing someone approaching her house. A deadly fear, a petrified terror appears on her face. Then, slowly, she realizes that she has been wrong and that the person who is approaching doesn't mean something unhappy but the greatest happiness instead. And slowly, moving through the scale of possibilities, her expression changes from terror to a timid doubt, to uncertain hope, finally to careful joy and to ecstatic happiness. We watch her face for about twenty meters in close-up. We observe each trait of her face, the movements around her eyes and mouth, the changes that take place. What we see during those minutes is an organic *history of the evolution of her feelings* [die organische *Entwicklungsgeschichte ihrer Gefühle*] and nothing else. This is the story we see.[31]

Both Musil's and Balázs's emphasis on the surface of things, the face of things and faces, the discovery of the visual that might undermine the predominance of the word in the modern world, has sometimes been explained in terms of a discourse of *Aufmerksamkeit*, "attention," and of discussions about the nature and media of perception in the early twentieth century. This reference does indeed explain key aspects of it. It does not, however, exhaust the problem, nor does it explain Musil's statements about the "mysticism of film" in his review of Balázs's book. Musil speaks here of "the face of things and their awakening in the stillness of the image," and he points out: "What is extraordinary is that a book on the practice of film reaches this point at all, and touches quite consciously on the border between these two worlds," that is, "the normal condition of our relationship to the world, to people, and to ourselves" and a "positive, causal, mechanical way of thinking," on the one hand, and the sensible, affective, and experiential condition, on the other. In "this world there is neither measure nor precision, neither purpose nor cause; good and evil simply fall away, without any pretense of superiority, and in place of all these relations enters a secret rising and ebbing of our being with that of things and other people. It is in this condition that the image of each object becomes not a practical goal, but a wordless experience."[32] The very muteness of things makes the things visible; the very muteness of faces transports sensation, affects, and cognition. This leads back to the thought of possibility or, maybe better, the emergence of possibilities in the realm of visibility that has gotten rid of the word that frames and determines the face of the world.

"Visible Possibilities" is a subtitle in Béla Balázs's essay, and the "theory of film" itself is for Musil a genre that points toward the possibilities of a new aesthetic and ethic that are analogous to his understanding of the work of the essay. It is something he also discovers in Balázs's "style," which he characterizes in the following words: "The ingenious style, which creates an atmosphere that immediately relates each impression to many others, and above all the clear, profound, ordered layering of this atmosphere—these are personal qualities of Balázs the writer." Balázs is the scientist, the "anatomist and biologist" of film that brings out "experientially and scientifically" an "unexpected paradigm."[33] The key term in this paradigm is for Musil as well the "only-visible," an abstraction that "is just as much a matter of increase in impression as a reduction." Thus, he argues against the "concepts of purposeless beauty or of beautiful illusion," which "have something of a holiday mood about them," in favor of a "negation of real life," which, in turn, can be compared to the "special attitude toward things that . . . [Lucien Lévy-Bruhl, in his *Les fonctions mentales des sociétés primitives*] calls participation."[34]

This brings us back to the notion of partaking. What we see are not things we know but things that are experimentally set free in a realm of possibilities, that move emotionally and intellectually, thus allowing us and forcing us to follow the ways in which they deploy themselves, their realms of meaning, and their relations with each other. "Precisely this," Musil writes, "allows us some hope that film will contribute to a new culture of the senses" and of emotions through the excitement it produces when the words are silenced. It is there in literature as well, since "even on a page of prose deserving of the name, one can recognize that a general excitement [*Erregung*] is communicated *before* the meaning."[35] The silent film, however, brings it to the surface, opening up the space of possibilities that tends to be obliterated by the word, evoking not only the particular and its face but also the world of intensities where the particular evokes new relations and thus allows for the exploration of new possibilities of relations between things and between things and viewers that have not been thought and experienced before. As Musil points out, these new relations change both the things and the viewers, liberating them for a moment from a discursive regime and thus opening up a horizon of new aesthetic and ethic relations that he calls utopian.

I do not want to again summarize here Musil's engagement with Eckhart's thought. It is too manifold, and it follows the very law of Musil's essayism, that is, the multiplication of perspectives and the layering of readings he tends to work with. There is one point, however, I want to emphasize: the transformation of some elements Musil draws from Eckhart into what could be called an "art of attention" and a "weak utopianism." Thus, Musil turns Eckhart's mysticism into a figure of reflection about attention and about the intellectual, affective, and sensual engagement with the figures that things, people, the world always are. He does not discard the theological context of Eckhart's thought entirely, but he frames its critical potential in view of an experimental attitude that is able to set free possibilities of interaction, perception, and relation that have not been observed before. The fact that he values Balázs's theory of film in this context is part of this elaboration of a "conscious utopianism." As Musil emphasizes, Balázs's book is exactly that, a "theory," a movement of the mind, a contemplative exercise that exposes itself to a figure, the silent movie, and that traces its own movements, affects, and concepts in the form of the essay.

In his review of Balázs's book, Siegfried Kracauer expressed his doubts about the character of this utopian discourse, ending with the critical and dogmatic statement: "The new visibility of man that is presented to us in film is in fact the contrary of a turn toward true concreteness. Instead, it is the confirmation and conservation of the bad rationality of capitalist thought. Only insight and language can bring radical change."[36] Against this critique and in his defense of Balázs's emphasis on the "visibility of man," Musil participates in the same discussion about "change" (*Umschwung*). Inspired by Balázs and Eckhart, he offers an intriguing reformulation of "conscious utopianism" as an art of the elaboration of the possible. What Kracauer does not see, we might say, is the fact that the film does not "represent" or "illustrate" (*veranschaulicht*) the new visibility of man but that it is—in figural analogy with the utopian essayism—an experimental form in which possibilities are explored in correspondence with the ways in which they are set free in figural play.

Thus, we find ourselves, once again, at the point that Auerbach recovers from early rhetorical and theological thoughts about the plasticity of the figures, drawing attention to a tension between the energy of the figure and its meaning and exploring ways in which the realm of new possible configurations can be seen not in terms of hidden meaning but as a result of practices of figuration that modify the experiential landscape of perception and relation before it is understood.

8 

Holy Fools

At the Limits of the Possible

I return to the beginning of this book and to the phenomenology and experience Georges Bataille and Joris-Karl Huysmans refer to when they talk about mysticism. What I tried to portray here in a number of more or less elaborate descriptions of historical moments are a few aspects of a genealogy of notions of figuration, of abandonment to the asymmetry of the figural, and of a phenomenology of rhetorical effects. When Huysmans speaks of the "frontier," Bataille of the "limits of the possible," and Musil of a "sense of possibility," they bring to our attention that the form of awareness and immersion mystical practices ask for is based on a set of figural practices and that, in fact, these practices produce certain forms and configurations of intense experience, exploring the tension between the unspeakable "dark brilliance" of the figure and the forms of sensual, affective, and intellectual assimilation. Thus, they also evoke a specific aspect of a medieval tradition of spiritual exercises, an aspect that I call a phenomenology of rhetorical effects, which, in turn, leads to a new conception of the circulation of sensation, affect, and thought. As I have argued, this phenomenology forms an element of meditative prayer and of certain techniques of contemplative reading—and of looking at the world—that focuses on the shaping of the life of the soul and the animation of its experiential possibilities in disruptive encounters with and in partaking of the figural face of the world in its concrete particularity.

Thus, worlds turn into figures, liberated from the reign of discourse and undoing it time and again. Meditative prayer and contemplation use rhetorical techniques to evoke the figural and produce sensual and emotional states of experience, doing so in sharpened awareness for the irreducible tension between figural effects and all forms of assimilation, be they sensual, affective, or conceptual. Late medieval mystics make extensive use of these techniques, also experimenting with them increasingly beyond the borders of the regulated life-forms of monastic communities. Thus, they prepare the field for later uses of this technique both in experimental mystical poetics of the Baroque and in the conception of notions of aesthetic experience in the eighteenth century. In all these cases we encounter the type of phenomenology Bataille and Huysmans are asking for and returning to, a phenomenology of rhetorical effects invested in an alienation from the world of discursive order, instrumental reason, and calculated project; in an abandonment to figural play and the dramatic challenge it raises in disarticulating the subjugation to world orders and its production of subjects; in addressing thus the "limits of the possible" and in crossing these limits in dispossession and in reconfigurations of experiential textures against the imposed stability of the world. In exposing humans to the limits of the possible, these techniques open a sphere that ultimately abandons the phenomenological perspective, even the phenomenology of rhetorical effects. They rejoin, in arguing for an abandonment that is most radical in being "without a why," a different form of circulation of sensation, affect, and thought. They become—most prominently and explicitly probably with Jacob Böhme and his readers up to today—part of an imagination and cosmopoiesis where humans find their ethical position not in an affirmation of norms but within the willful acknowledgment of a constitutive asymmetry, the detached abandonment to processes that make everything emerge and flow. Figure and figural realism, drawing attention not to ontological or epistemological orders but to the striking force of figures, make this asymmetry emerge in the insistence on the irreducibility of the concrete, the flesh, the multitude of movements. In always moving along these limits, in always evoking an excessive asymmetry, in tying each moment of perception to a surplus of possibility, they share, taking shape in perception, what is the good that comes to them in that very collapse of transcendence and immanence that figures establish. To cultivate this asymmetry and its ethical root in the attitude of abandonment can, however, be nothing else than a bunch of foolish acts in the eyes of the onto-hierarchical views of Man. Musil calls attention to it when he quips that, when talking about the people with a sense of possibility, we often call them "children" and "fools."

Throwing Nuts

I end where I started: the sense of possibility and the figure of the "fool for Christ's sake"; figures, figuration, and the challenge of turning observation of the world into specific forms of partaking in its ungraspable flow, in the language of its dreams, and in detachment. In her defense of the performance of Pussy Riot activists in the Moscow Cathedral of Christ the Saviour on February 21, 2012, Nadezhda Tolokonnikova, one of them, calls the members of her group "jokers, jesters, holy fools." In playing with that image and with the prayer to Mary, asking the Theotokos to chase away Putin, she draws attention not only to an ironic form of intervention—the comedy that is a characteristic of the performance of cynics and holy fools since late antiquity[1]—but also to the critical and parrhesiastic nature of gestures of madness that challenge the ontological and epistemological norms of the world of Man and its hierarchies. There can be nothing more foolish, asymmetrical, and true than begging the Mother of God to liberate the protesters from political oppression. Nevertheless, the Cathedral of Christ the Saviour must be the place to foolishly do so and to free the imagination and dreams that go with it.

In addition to the holy fools of the orthodox churches—the ones Tolokonnikova is evoking in the explanation of her actions—we might want to think here again of the gesture of Saint Francis, the son of a merchant who undresses in front of people on the city square, turning the challenge of spiritual poverty into a literal moment of rejoining the creature in its bare, living, expressive flesh. Figuring himself as the *poverello* (the poor one) and the *pazzo* (the crazy one), he does not take refuge in dogmatic teachings about sainthood and contemplation, but he turns, in the practice of his life, all things into figures, into concrete moments that evoke suffering and praise, abjection and joy.

There is, however, no sentimentality and no illusion of happiness in these gestures. Instead, they introduce a different language that, in its claim to freedom from the world of suffering, abuse, and coercion, locates this very freedom in the acts of the fool who acknowledges, once again, the fundamental asymmetry that characterizes the relations between the divine and the world, the experience of beauty and suffering and ontological and epistemological world orders. In answering Pope Gregory's suggestions to adopt one of the established monastic rules, Francis consequently answers that God "called me" and "showed me" a "path of simplicity," and he concludes that no one should tell him to follow the rules of "Saint Augustine, nor Saint Bernard, nor Saint Benedict." Instead, he foregrounds that God wanted him to be a *novellus pazzus in mundo* (a new fool in the world).[2] What this brings into view is what is called a Franciscan spirituality with its specific emphasis on the concrete in its asymmetrical fullness, the beauty of the sun and the stars, the human and nonhuman animals, the plants, the rivers and landscapes. More than that, in its emphasis on what we can call a nominalist, empiricist, realist, even materialist turn, it is also a profound resistance against all *doxa* and positive knowledge of God and the world. Thus, his critical intervention, radically concrete in spirit and a crazy call for humility, poverty, and simplicity, never relies on normative orders. Instead, in the very imitation of Christ that will shape his flesh and mark it as the very space of understanding the divine, he practices something that is akin to the way Judith Butler characterizes Michel Foucault's notion of Enlightenment critique as an "art that suspends ontology and brings us into the suspension of disbelief."[3] No doubt, for Francis this very art that suspends ontology, epistemology, and our notions of freedom has its ground in the exemplary figure of the suffering Christ, while for Foucault, Baudelaire and the figure of the dandy, the flaneur, and the artist come into view. They do so also as exemplary figures. For Francis, the "originary freedom," the freedom Foucault speaks about with a postmodern hesitation and reservation, is thus grounded in the "foolish" following of Christ in the flesh. Not surprisingly, though, Foucault ends his own comments on "critique" in an oblique moment and tone, and with some irony, when he postpones a possible answer to this challenge of an "originary freedom" and speaks of it as "both part of, and not part of philosophy," pointing to the fact that "this matrix of critical attitude in the Western world must be sought out in religious attitudes" and that "one of the first great forms of revolt in the West was mysticism."[4] Francis addresses this moment of an ungraspable origin—of nonphilosophy, and, as Foucault remarks, of an ethical and aesthetic transfiguration of "the will"—in the very gesture of his foolishness. It is in Francis's foolishness that both ontological and epistemological orders are abandoned in "the will" that takes shape when he turns toward the asymmetry of creaturely existence in its concrete figural presence, that is, in how he is being encountered by the creatures that surround him and by their expressive forms devoid of all meaning. It is this formation of the will in the abandonment of the impositions of discourse, both free and turned toward the excess in the expression of surrounding figures, that is unidentifiably foolish in terms of norms and concepts.

This does not mean, however, that foolishness produces a clean cut with normative orders. Instead, it forms a specific address that opens the sphere of figural play. In the eyes of both Saint Francis and Foucault's figure of "Baudelairean modernity," the "self delimits itself, and decides on the material for its self-making, but the delimitation that the self performs takes place through norms which are, indisputably, already in place."[5] This entails, as Foucault points out in terms of the specific modernity of Baudelaire's vision, the fact that "he transfigures that world" in an "exercise of extreme attention to what is real" and confronts it in a "practice of liberty that simultaneously respects this reality and violates it."[6]

Far from trying to ignore all the historical differences that might make Baudelaire's modernism incompatible with the devotional attitude of Saint Francis, I nevertheless want to draw attention to these structural similitudes, particularly the fact of living in a threshold position. Quoting from Baudelaire's *The Painter of Modern Life*, Foucault points to moments I have emphasized in portraying the history of devotional practices, the fact that in these practices "'natural' things become 'more than natural,' 'beautiful' things become 'more than beautiful,' and individual objects appear 'endowed with an impulsive life like the soul of [their] creator.'"[7] This transfiguration of the natural world into a supernatural world, this form of inhabiting a limit position and addressing it both in undoing the positive knowledge about the world and of challenging it in drawing on figures of possibility and the play with sensation, affect, and thought, is at stake also in the foolish practice of Saint Francis. For both Francis and Baudelaire, it is a normative order, tradition, and specific hermeneutic establishment of the self that is being addressed through acts of exposing these norms and of undoing them. And in both Francis and Baudelaire a figural realism is the place that opens the possibilities of transforming the world in new forms of assimilation, invention, and variation. The creaturely figures in Saint Francis's praise of sun and moon fulfill thus a function that is analogous to the non-classicist take on colors and things in Eugène Delacroix's paintings that Baudelaire praises in his *Salon de 1859*. Both Francis and Delacroix undo normative ontological and epistemological orders, the paradigms of being and the conditions of possibility of knowing, and open the space of representation to the very excess of the figural. It is in this openness and "brilliant darkness" that for both Baudelaire and the Franciscan tradition, imagination is reestablished in its own right as the place where this excess takes shape. This entails, I want to add once again, a notion of inhabiting the limits of the possible in a way that does not claim that "freedom is to be found in the abyss of potentiality" (Agamben) and is thus relegated "to a terrain of utter abjection outside the iron grip of humanity, thereby disavowing how the ether of the flesh represents both a perpetual potentiality and actuality in Man's kingdom, only enveloping some subjects more than others."[8] Instead, the shift in the notion of possibility that is articulated in the position of Francis and that I have reconstructed throughout this book affirms, in Alexander Weheliye's words, "the flesh in its opulent and hieroglyphic freedom," a "freedom and humanity conjured from the vantage point of the flesh and not based on its abrogation."[9]

Along these lines, the figure of the homeless and cosmopolitan Diogenes the Cynic comes to mind as an exemplary image shared by all three, Nadia's "holy fool," Saint Francis's *pazzo*, and Foucault's "critic" who takes on a "*limit-attitude*" in and "through a historical ontology of ourselves."[10] In the exemplary figure of the fool, however, the "historical ontology," the analysis of the forces and powers that subjugate within this world at each historical moment, moves from within such an ontology, going beyond and challenging it in bringing forth the flesh of the world and its expressive articulations. The gestures of the fool thus break with the world of things and ontological and epistemological orders. The fool does so—also going beyond Foucault's characterization of Enlightenment critique and resonating with the figure of Foucault that Hervé Guibert calls "Muzil" in his *To the Friend Who Did Not Save My Life*—in a gesture of impoverishment that Eckhart, focusing on the self-emptying of the intellect, calls detachment, and Francis, focusing on the self-emptying of the will, calls the foolishness of love. Medieval mystics, as we have seen, join both perspectives when they foreground the practices of figuration as a place where the abandonment of ontology and epistemology, of all naming in detachment, rejoins the fullness of the world as it expresses itself in the very asymmetry of the figures that encounter us.

Closer maybe to Nadia Tolokonnikova's "jester" might be the figure of Simeon the Holy Fool, who, in the gesture of dragging a dead dog behind himself, quotes and refers to the very performance pieces of the Cynics and to their emblematic animal. As Leontius of Neapolis reports, after Simeon had "spent twenty-nine years in the desert practicing every asceticism and mortification, in cold and in heat, enduring many and unutterable temptations from the Devil and conquering them, and had arrived at a high level (of virtue),"[11] he returned to the life in society and the city. In conjoining "two prototypes, Diogenes and Christ,"[12] Leontius, writing this vita of a holy fool, testifies to the way in which "Cynic material was absorbed into the ascetic tradition."[13] It was absorbed into it not only as an exemplary paradigm that finds one of its expressions in the Franciscan tradition, turning the Cynic into a pre-Christian saint and example of poverty. Beyond that, it makes the very gesture of the Cynic, the performance of undoing the world of *doxa*, the core of a transfiguration of the perception of the world.

Thus, Leontius's story of Simeon goes:

> As was said above, after spending three days in the holy places, he arrived in the city of Emesa. The manner of his entry into the city was as follows: When the famous Symeon found a dead dog on a dunghill outside the city, he loosened the rope belt he was wearing, and tied it to the dog's foot. He dragged the dog as he ran and entered the gate, where there was a children's school nearby. When the children saw him, they began to cry, "Hey, a crazy abba!" And they set about to run after him and box him on the ears.
>
> On the next day, which was Sunday, he took nuts, and entering the church at the beginning of the liturgy, he threw the nuts and put out the candles. When

they hurried to run after him, he went up to the pulpit, and from there he pelted the women with nuts. With great trouble, they chased after him, and while he was going out, he overturned the tables of the pastry chefs, who (nearly) beat him to death. Seeing himself crushed by the blows, he said to himself, "Poor Symeon, if things like this keep happening, you won't live for a week in these people's hands."

According to God's plan, a phouska-seller saw him, who did not know that he was playing the fool. And he said to him (for he seemed to be sane), "Would you like, my lord abba, instead of wandering about, to be set up to sell lupines?" And he said, "Yes." When he set him up one day, Symeon began to give everything away to people and to eat, himself, insatiably, for he had not eaten the whole week. The phouska-seller's wife said to her husband, "Where did you find us this abba? If he eats like this, it's no use trying to sell anything! For while I observed him, he ate about a pot full of lupines." But they did not know that he had given away all the rest of the pots to fellow monks and others—the beans, the lentil soup, the desert fruits, all of it. They thought that he had sold it. When they opened the cash box and did not find a single cent, they beat him and fired him, and pulled his beard. When evening fell he wanted to burn incense. Now he had not departed from them that evening, but slept there outside their door. And not finding a shard of pottery, he put his hand in the oven and filled it with live coals and burned incense. Because God wished to save the phouska-seller, for he was a heretic of the Acephalic Severian sect, his wife saw Symeon burning incense in his hand and was very frightened and said, "Good God! Abba Symeon, are you burning incense in your hand?" And when the monk heard this, he pretended to be burned and was shaking the coals in his hand and threw them into the old cloak which he wore, and said to her, "And if you do not want it in my hand, see I will burn incense in my cloak." And as in the presence of the Lord who preserved the bush [Ex 3:2] and the unburnt boys [Dn 3:19–23], neither the saint nor his cloak were burned by the coals. And the manner in which the phouska-seller and his wife were saved will be told in another chapter.

It was also the saint's practice, whenever he did something miraculous, to leave that neighborhood immediately, until the deed which he had done was forgotten. He hurried on immediately elsewhere to do something inappropriate, so that he might thereby hide his perfection.

Once he earned his food carrying hot water in a tavern. The tavern keeper was heartless, and he often gave Symeon no food at all, although he had great business, thanks to the Fool. For when the townspeople were ready for a diversion, they said to each other, "Let's go have a drink where the Fool is." One day a snake came in, drank from one of the jars of wine, vomited his venom in it and left. Abba Symeon was not inside; instead he was dancing outside with the members of a circus faction. When the saint came into the tavern, he saw the wine jar, upon which "Death" had been written invisibly. Immediately he understood what had happened to it, and lifting up a piece of wood, he broke the jar in pieces, since it was full. His master took the wood out of his hand, beat him with it until he was exhausted, and chased him away. The next morning, Abba Symeon came and hid himself behind the tavern door. And behold! The snake came to drink again. And the tavern keeper saw it and took the same piece of wood in order to kill it. But his blow missed, and he broke all the wine jars and cups. Then the Fool burst in and said to the tavern keeper, "What is it, stupid? See, I am not the only one who is clumsy." Then the tavern keeper understood that Abba Symeon had broken the wine jar for the same reason. And he was edified and considered Symeon to be holy.

Thereupon the saint wanted to destroy his edification, so that the tavern keeper would not expose him. One day when the tavern keeper's wife was asleep alone and the tavern keeper was selling wine, Abba Symeon approached her and pretended to undress. The woman screamed, and when her husband came in, she said to him, "Throw this thrice cursed man out! He wanted to rape me." And punching him with his fists, he carried him out of the shop and into the icy cold. Now there was a mighty storm and it was raining. And from that moment, not only did the tavern keeper think that he was beside himself, but if he heard someone else saying, "Perhaps Abba Symeon pretends to be like this," immediately he answered, "He is completely possessed. I know, and no one can persuade me otherwise. He tried to rape my wife. And he eats meat as if he's godless." For without tasting bread all week, the righteous one often ate meat. No one knew about his fasting, since he ate meat in front of everybody in order to deceive them.

It was entirely as if Symeon had no body, and he paid no attention to what might be judged disgraceful conduct either by human convention or by nature. Often, indeed, when his belly sought to do its private function, immediately, and without blushing, he squatted in the marketplace, wherever he found himself, in front of everyone, wishing to persuade (others) by this that he did this because he had lost his natural sense. For guarded, as I have often said, by the power of the Holy Spirit which dwelt within him, he was above the burning which is from the Devil and was not harmed by it at all. One day, when the aforementioned virtuous John, the friend of God who narrated this life for us, saw him mortified from his asceticism (for it was the time after Easter and he had passed all of Lent without food), he felt both pity and amazement at the indescribable austerity of Symeon's regimen, although he lived in the city and associated with women and men. And wanting him to refresh his body, John said to him playfully, "Come take a bath, Fool!" And Symeon said to him, laughing, "Yes, let's go, let's go!" And with these words, he stripped off his garment and placed it on his head, wrapping it around like a turban. And Deacon John said to him, "Put it back on, brother, for truly if you are going to walk around naked, I won't go with you." Abba Symeon said to him, "Go away, idiot, I'm all ready. If you won't come, see, I'll go a little ahead of you." And leaving him, he kept a little ahead. However, there were two baths next to each other, one for men and one for women. The Fool ignored the men's and rushed willingly into the women's. Deacon John cried out to him, "Where are you going, Fool? Wait, that's the women's!" The wonderful one turned and said to him, "Go away, you idiot, there's hot and cold water here, and there's hot and cold water there, and it doesn't matter at all whether (I use) this one or that." And he ran and entered into the midst of the women, as in the presence of the Lord of glory. The women rushed against him, beat him, and threw him out. The God-loving deacon (John) asked him, when he told him his whole life, "For God's sake, father, how did you feel when you entered into the women's bath?" He said, "Believe me, child, just as a piece of wood goes with other pieces of wood, thus was I there. For I felt neither that I had a body nor that I had entered among bodies, but the whole of my mind was on God's work, and I did not part from Him." Some of his deeds the righteous one did out of compassion for the salvation of humans, and others he did to hide his way of life.[14]

Simeon, "to hide his way of life," turns here both into the figure of a fool and—like the Franciscan *ioculatores*, the "jokers"—into a figure of joyous possibility to whom the earth in its very multitude of faces, voices, sufferings, and bliss—as in Tarkovsky's *Andrei Rublev*—appears sanctified. It is, paradoxically, the fool who expresses the will at the core of this ethics of transfiguration, that is, the abandonment to the world that Audre Lord points to in the lines quoted earlier. The fool turns into the flesh that, in its suffering and joy, is open to the very acknowledgment of both abuse and injustice, as well as the figures of pleasure in their excessive asymmetry. Thus, he moves through the articulations of ordinary life, the norms, the customs, the habits, and the metaphysical assumptions, only to undo them and to bring into view what exceeds this very grasp in the figural concreteness of creaturely life and a new play with all modes of assimilation.

Returning here to Tarkovsky, another one of the protagonists in my first chapter, we might say that this is the role played—in an exemplary fashion, quoted in Lars von Trier's *Melancholia*—by the horses in his films. They do not symbolize or mean anything. They just stand and move, fall and die, calling attention to their figural presence. Obviously, we want to know more, but we are left with this call to inhabit the limits of the possible and to turn it, in the very acknowledgment of the asymmetry of the figure, into the excessive flow that the exemplary way of the holy fool, a key figure also in *Andrei Rublev*, reveals. What it reveals is nothing normative but, as in the eye of Benjamin's flaneur and his "love at last sight,"[15] what gives itself beyond the human in all its possibilities—perceived in the flow that emerges from nowhere else than the foolish abandonment to the concrete world of figures and the joy of playing with them.

Acknowledgments

In its production over the last ten years, this book has profited from many friends, interlocutors, and institutions. UC Berkeley has provided me with necessary sabbatical leave. The Wissenschaftskolleg Berlin has supported the project with a year of fellowship in Berlin. Invitations by colleagues, among them Birgit Meyer, Tanja Michalsky, Cornelia Zumbusch, and Christian Kiening, have given me the opportunity to present ideas and concepts. I thank Klaus Krüger and Peter Geimer for their invitation to the Kolleg-Forschergrupper BildEvidenz. The collaboration with Anja Lemke during the last five years, supported by the Anneliese Maier Prize from the Humboldt Foundation, offered opportunities for conversations with colleagues and students in workshops and summer schools, providing me with much-needed inspiration. Students in a seminar I taught at the invitation of Princeton University as a Stewart Fellow; participants at a seminar I taught as a Fellow of the School for Criticism and Theory at Cornell University; Hent de Vries, my faculty colleagues at the School for Criticism and Theory, and the students in my seminar; and graduate students in my Berkeley seminars have helped me in developing my ideas. An invitation to give the Conway Lectures at the University of Notre Dame has allowed me to develop my reading of Mechthild of Magdeburg further. I thank all of them for their support. Alex Dubilet, David Marno, and the collaborators in our Prayer Research Group at UC Berkeley have been invaluable interlocutors in exploring the history of prayer. Stefania Pandolfo, Nir Feinberg, Brent Eng, and Alex Dubilet were the first readers of this manuscript. Their input has been essential in many of the thoughts I develop here. Special thanks go to Brent, Nir, and Alex; and to Jessica Ruffin who has been a wonderful first copyeditor. I am grateful to Eric Santner and to an anonymous reader of this manuscript for their suggestions. And, above all, I thank Karen Feldman for being, apart from many other things, a challenging and inspiring interlocutor.

In writing the last lines of this book, I dedicate it to the memory of Saba Mahmood, remembering a long walk on Stinson Beach where we talked about our projects and where I tried to explain to her where the core of my work on mysticism and modernity lies.

Parts of Chapters 4 to 7 of this book build on essays that have been published in the following journals and collections:

"The Logic of Arousal: St. Francis of Assisi, Teresa of Avila, and *Thérèse Philosophe*," *Qui Parle* 13, no. 2 (2003): 1–18. Copyright 2003, Duke University Press. All rights reserved. Republished by permission of the publisher. www.dukeupress.edu.

"Inner Senses—Outer Senses: The Practice of Emotions in Medieval Mysticism," in *Codierung von Emotionen im Mittelalter / Emotions and Sensibilities in the Middle Ages*, edited by Stephen Jaeger and Ingrid Kasten (Berlin: De Gruyter, 2003), 3–15.

"Scripture, Vision, Performance: Visionary Texts and Medieval Religious Drama," in *Visual Culture and the German Middle Ages*, edited by Kathryn Starkey and Horst Wenzel (New York: Palgrave Macmillan, 2005), 207–219.

"Praying by Numbers: An Essay on Medieval Aesthetics," *Representations* 104 (2008): 73–92.

"'A Sense of Possibility': Robert Musil, Meister Eckhart, and the 'Culture of Film,'" in *Religion: Beyond a Concept*, edited by Hent de Vries (New York: Fordham University Press, 2008), 739–749.

"Mysticism, Modernity, and the Invention of Aesthetic Experience," *Representations* 105 (2009): 37–60.

"The Plasticity of the Soul: Mystical Darkness, Touch, and Aesthetic Experience," *Modern Language Notes* 125 (2010): 536–551. Copyright © Johns Hopkins University Press. Published with permission by Johns Hopkins University Press.

"Divine Suffering—Divine Pleasure: Martyrdom, Sensuality, and the Art of Delay," *Figurationen* 12, no. 1 (2011): 67–79.

"The Rhetoric of Mysticism: From Contemplative Practice to Aesthetic Experiment," in *Mysticism and Reform, 1400–1700*, edited by Sarah

Poor and Nigel Smith (Notre Dame, IN: University of Notre Dame Press, 2015), 353–379.

"Figure, Plasticity, Affect," in *Touching and Being Touched: Kinesthesia and Empathy in Dance and Movement*, edited by Gabriele Brandstetter, Gerko Egert, and Sabine Zubarik (Berlin: De Gruyter, 2013), 23–34.

"The Art of Prayer: Conversions of Interiority and Exteriority in Medieval Contemplative Practice," in *Rethinking Emotion: Interiority and Exteriority in Premodern, Modern, and Contemporary Thought*, edited by Rüdiger Campe and Julia Weber (Berlin: De Gruyter, 2014), 58–71.

"The Poetics of the Image in Late Medieval Mysticism," in *Image and Incarnation: The Early Modern Doctrine of the Pictorial Image*, edited by Lee Palmer Wandel and Walter S. Melion (Leiden: Brill, 2015), 173–186.

"Mimesis," in "Notes from the Field: Mimesis," by Dexter Dalwood, Suzanne Preston Blier, Daniela Bohde, Helen C. Evans, Sarah E. Fraser, Thomas Habinek, Tom Huhn, Jeanette Kohl, Niklaus Largier, Peter Mack, and Alex Potts, *Art Bulletin* 95, no. 2 (2014): 207–208.

"The Media of Sensation," in *The Anthropology of Catholicism: A Companion Reader*, edited by Valentina Napolitano, Maya Mayblin, and Kristin Norget (Berkeley: University of California Press, 2017), 316–325.

I thank the publishers for the permission to draw from these essays.

Notes

INTRODUCTION

1. Alfred North Whitehead, *Science and the Modern World* (New York: Free Press, 1967), 191.

2. Robert Musil, "Der deutsche Mensch als Symptom," in *Gesammelte Werke in neun Bänden*, ed. Adolf Frisé (Reinbek: Rowohlt, 1978), 8:1368, 1374 (my trans.). English translation: "The German as Symptom," in *Precision and Soul: Essays and Addresses*, ed. and trans. Burton Pike and David S. Luft (Chicago: University of Chicago Press, 1990), 157, 163.

3. Marcel Proust, *In Search of Lost Time*, vol. 2: *Within a Budding Grove*, trans. C. K. Scott Moncrieff and Terence Kilmartin, rev. D. J. Enright (New York: Modern Library, 1992), 318.

4. Robert Musil, *The Man without Qualities*, trans. Sophie Wilkins (New York: Knopf, 1995), 11.

5. Musil, *The Man without Qualities*, 11–12.

6. Erich Auerbach, *Dante als Dichter der irdischen Welt*, ed. Kurt Flasch (Berlin: De Gruyter, 2001), 21–22 (my trans.)

7. Musil, *The Man without Qualities*, 10.

CHAPTER 1

1. Wallace Stevens, *Collected Poetry and Prose*, ed. Frank Kermode and Joan Richardson (New York: Library of America, 1997), 549.

2. Compare Charles Stépanoff, *Voyager dans l'invisible: Techniques chamaniques de l'imagination* (Paris: La Découverte, 2019); Stefania Pandolfo, *Knot of the Soul: Madness, Psychoanalysis, Islam* (Chicago: University of Chicago Press, 2018); Jonathan Garb, *Shamanic Trance in Modern Kabbalah* (Chicago: University of Chicago Press, 2011).

3. Audre Lorde, "Poetry Is Not a Luxury," in *Sister Outsider: Essays and Speeches* (Berkeley, CA: Crossing Press, 2007), 76. I thank Rahma Haji for bringing Lorde's thoughts about figuration and possibility to my attention.

4. J. Kameron Carter, "Black Malpractice (A Poetics of the Sacred)," *Social Text* 37, no. 2 (2019): 74.

5. Édouard Glissant, *Poetics of Relation*, trans. Betsy Wing (Ann Arbor: University of Michigan Press, 1997), 62.

6. Glissant, *Poetics of Relation*, 61–62; Sylvia Wynter, "Beyond the World of Man: Glissant and the New Discourse of the Antilles," *World Literature Today* 63 (1989): 637–658; Alexander Weheliye, "After Man," *American Literary History* 20 (2008): 321–336.

7. Tendayi Sithole, *The Black Register* (New York: Polity, 2020), 47–48, 58–60.

8. Augustine of Hippo, *Confessions* XI, xxvi, trans. William Watts (Cambridge, MA: Harvard University Press, 1988), 2:268–274.

9. For the notion of "ontologies," see Philippe Descola, "Presence, Attachment, Origin: Ontologies of 'Incarnates,'" in *A Companion to the Anthropology of Religion*, ed. Janice Boddy and Michael Lambek (Oxford: Wiley Blackwell, 2013), 35–49. While Descola speaks of "figuration" as "the public instauration of an invisible quality through a speech act or an image," I focus on the "figural" as what suspends "ontologies." Compare Peter Skafish, "The Descola Variations: The Ontological Geography of *Beyond Nature and Culture*," *Qui Parle* 25 (2016): 65–93, for a discussion of Descola's use of "ontology" and a comparison with Viveiros de Castro's "perspectivism."

10. Audre Lorde, "Uses of the Erotic: The Erotic as Power," in *Sister Outsider*, 103–114.

11. For a discussion of the idea of "cosmic liturgy," see Willemien Otten, *Thinking Nature and the Nature of Thinking: From Eriugena to Emerson* (Stanford, CA: Stanford University Press, 2020), 52–78.

12. Meister Eckhart, *The Essential Sermons, Commentaries, Treatises, and Defense*, trans. and introd. Edmund Colledge and Bernard McGinn (New York: Paulist Press, 1986), 193.

13. Simone Weil, "Reflections on the Right Use of School Studies with a View to the Love of God," in *Waiting for God*, trans. Emma Craufurd (New York: HarperCollins, 1951), 62.

14. See, for example, Meister Eckhart's *Counsels on Discernment*, in *The Essential Sermons, Commentaries, Treatises, and Defense*, 251–254. For a discussion of the notion of detachment, compare Meister Eckhart, *Werke*, ed. Niklaus Largier (Frankfurt: Deutscher Klassiker Verlag, 1993), 1:318, and commentary.

15. Søren Kierkegaard, *The Lily of the Field and the Bird of the Air: Three Godly Discourses*, trans. Bruce H. Kirmmse (Princeton, NJ: Princeton University Press, 2016), 9–38.

16. John Cage, *Silence: Lectures and Writings* (Hanover, NH: Wesleyan University Press, 1961), 7–8.

17. Meister Eckhart, *The Essential Sermons*, 209–210; Eckhart, *Werke*, 1:755–758; Michel Foucault, "What Is Critique?," in *The Politics of Truth*, ed. Sylvère Lotringer and Lysa Hochroth (New York: Semiotext(e), 1997), 25. Compare also Judith Butler, "What Is Critique? An Essay on Foucault's Virtue," in *The Political*, ed. David Ingram (Malden, MA: Blackwell, 2002), 212–226.

18. See Alex Dubilet, *The Self-Emptying Subject: Kenosis and Immanence, Medieval to Modern* (New York: Fordham University Press, 2018).

19. Giordano Bruno, *Cause, Principle, and Unity, and Essays on Magic*, ed. Richard J. Blackwell and Robert de Lucca (Cambridge: Cambridge University Press, 2004), 15–16.

20. Georg Lukács, *Soul and Form*, ed. John T. Sanders and Katie Terzakis, trans. Anna Bostock, introd. Judith Butler (New York: Columbia University Press, 2010), 24.

21. Victor V. Bychkov, "The Symbolology of Dionysius the Areopagite," *Russian Studies in Philosophy* 51 (2012): 29–30.

22. Nicolaus Cusanus, *De apice theoriae. Die höchste Stufe der Betrachtung*, ed. Hans Gerhard Senger (Hamburg: Meiner, 1986), 8. English translation quoted from Johannes Hoff, *The Analogical Turn: Rethinking Modernity with Nicholas of Cusa* (Grand Rapids, MI: B. Eerdmans, 2013), 21.

23. Aby Warburg, *Werke*, ed. Martin Treml, Sigrid Weigel, and Perdita Ladwig (Frankfurt: Suhrkamp, 2018), 587.

CHAPTER 2

1. Erich Auerbach et al., "Scholarship in Times of Extremes: Letters of Erich Auerbach (1933–46), on the Fiftieth Anniversary of His Death," *PMLA* 122 (2007): 756.

2. Walter Benjamin, "Doctrine of the Similar," in *Selected Writings*, ed. Michael W. Jennings, Howard Eiland, and Gary Smith (Cambridge, MA: Harvard University Press, 2005), vol. 2, part 2, 698.

3. Walter Benjamin, "On the Image of Proust," in *Selected Writings*, vol. 2, part 1, 244.

4. Erich Auerbach, *Gesammelte Aufsätze zur Romanischen Philologie* (Bern: Francke, 1967), 278 (my trans.).

5. Auerbach, *Gesammelte Aufsätze*, 285 (my trans.).

6. Erich Auerbach, *Dante als Dichter*, 6 (my trans.).

7. Auerbach, *Dante als Dichter*, 11–15 (my trans.).

8. Auerbach, *Dante als Dichter*, 77 (my trans.).

9. Auerbach, *Dante als Dichter*, 23–27 (my trans.).

10. Auerbach, *Dante als Dichter*, 58–59 (my trans.).

11. For a recent comprehensive reading of this essay, see James Porter, "Disfigurations: Erich Auerbach's Theory of Figura," *Critical Inquiry* 44 (2017): 80–113. While I largely agree with Porter's reading of the text and his emphasis on the supersessionist character of *one side* of what Auerbach emphasizes, the transformation of the Old Testament "from a book of laws and a national history of Israel into a series of figures of Christ and of Redemption" (95), I am focusing here on the *other side*, the realist affirmation of the historically concrete event that the notion of *figura* supports. It is no coincidence that Auerbach starts his analysis with the realist aspects of Tertullian's "materialist" theology that emphasizes carnal creaturely reality (see Jean Daniélou, *Les origines du Christianisme Latin* [Paris: Cerf, 1978], 280–282).

12. Erich Auerbach, "*Figura*," in *Time, History, and Literature: Selected Essays of Erich Auerbach*, ed. James Porter, trans. Jane Newman (Princeton, NJ: Princeton University Press, 2014), 65–71. Translations have been modified slightly according to the German text (Erich Auerbach, "*Figura*," in *Gesammelte Aufsätze*, 55–59).

13. Auerbach, "*Figura*," in *Time, History, and Literature*, 79.

14. Auerbach, "*Figura*," in *Time, History, and Literature*, 81.

15. Compare Hayden White's notion of a figural realism ("Auerbach's Literary History: Figural Causation and Modernist Historicism," in *Figural Realism: Studies in the Mimesis Effect* [Baltimore: Johns Hopkins University Press, 1999], 92–97) and his discussion of Primo Levi and Dante in "Figural Realism in Witness Literature," *Parallax* 10 (2004): 113–124. My reading of the figure and the figural differs from White's in my emphasis on the tensions between the figure and the forms of assimilation.

16. Jeffrey D. Finch, "Neo-Palamism, Divinizing Grace, and the Breach between East and West," in *Partakers of Divine Nature: The History and Development of Deification in the Christian Traditions*, ed. Michael J. Christensen and Jeffery A. Wittung (Madison, WI: Fairleigh Dickinson University Press, 2007), 236–240.

17. Auerbach, "*Figura*," in *Time, History, and Literature*, 79–80.

18. Erich Auerbach, *Literatursprache und Publikum in der lateinischen Spätantike und im Mittelalter* (Bern: Francke, 1958), 14 (my trans.).

19. Auerbach, *Literatursprache*, 16.

20. Erich Auerbach, "Vico's Contribution to Literary Criticism," in *Time, History, and Literature*, 7.

21. Erich Auerbach, "Vico and Herder," in *Time, History, and Literature*, 21.

22. Erich Auerbach, "Vico and the Idea of Philology," in *Time, History, and Literature*, 27.

23. Erich Auerbach, "Vico and Aesthetic Historism," in *Time, History, and Literature*, 40.

24. Erich Auerbach, *Mimesis: The Representation of Reality in Western Literature,* trans. Willard R. Trask (Princeton, NJ: Princeton University Press, 2003), 374–375.

25. James Porter, "Introduction," in Auerbach, *Time, History, and Literature,* xxxii–xxxiii.

CHAPTER 3

1. Compare Warburg, *Werke,* 176–184; Ernst Cassirer, "The Concept of Symbolic Form in the Construction of the Human Sciences," in *The Warburg Years: Essays on Language, Art, Myth, and Technology,* trans. and introd. S. G. Lofts with A. Calgagno (New Haven, CT: Yale University Press, 2013), 72–100; Friedrich Nietzsche, *The Birth of Tragedy,* ed. Raymond Geuss and Ronald Speirs, trans. Ronald Speirs (Cambridge: Cambridge University Press, 1999), 25.

2. In *Vier Untersuchungen zur Geschichte der französischen Bildung* (Bern: Francke, 1951), 7, Erich Auerbach speaks of his method in terms of a "historical topology" that focuses on "conditions of emergence" and "directions of effects."

3. Compare Hans Boersma, *Nouvelle Théologie and Sacramental Ontology: A Return to Mystery* (Oxford: Oxford University Press, 2009).

4. For a discussion of admiration and its role in thought, see Hent de Vries, *Miracles et métaphysique* (Paris: Puf, 2019), 43–49.

5. Compare Amy Hollywood, *Sensible Ecstasy: Mysticism, Sexual Difference, and the Demands of History* (Chicago: University of Chicago Press, 2002), 60–110.

6. J. A. McGuckin, "The Strategic Adaptation of Deification," in Christensen and Wittung, *Partakers of Divine Nature,* 107.

7. McGuckin, "The Strategic Adaptation," 109.

8. Gregory of Nyssa, *The Life of Moses,* trans. Abraham J. Malherbe and Everett Ferguson (New York: Paulist Press, 1978), 91–94.

9. Gregory of Nyssa, *The Life of Moses,* 41–44, 94–106.

10. Gregory of Nyssa, *The Life of Moses,* 104.

11. I am using the terms that Origen introduces when he discusses the "inner senses." Compare the literature in note 12.

12. Compare Mariette Canévet, "Sens spirituels," in *Dictionnaire de spiritualité ascétique et mystique* (Paris: Cerf, 1989), 13:598–617; Karl Rahner, "La doctrine des 'sens spirituels' au Moyen-Age, en particulier chez Bonaventure," *Revue d'ascétique et de mystique* 14 (1933): 263–299; Karl Rahner, "Le début d'une doctrine des cinq sens spirituels chez Origène," *Revue d'ascétique et de mystique* 13 (1932): 113–145; Hans Urs von Balthasar, *Herrlichkeit. Eine theologische Ästhetik* (Einsiedeln, Switzerland: Johannes, 1961–1969), 1:352–367; Niklaus Largier, "Medieval Mysticism," in *The Oxford Handbook of Religion and Emotion,* ed. John Corrigan (Oxford: Oxford University Press, 2008), 364–379; Paul L. Gavrilyuk and Sarah

Coakley, eds., *The Spiritual Senses: Perceiving God in Western Christianity* (Cambridge: Cambridge University Press, 2012).

13. Compare William of Saint Thierry, *Epistola ad fratres de Monte Dei*, ed. Jean Déchanet (Paris: Cerf, 2004), 170.

14. See Baldwin of Canterbury, "Tractatus de duplici resurrectione," in *Patrologia Latina*, ed. Jean-Paul Migne (Paris: Migne, 1855), 204:429–442.

15. Compare Albert the Great, *Commentarii in tertium librum sententiarum* III d. 13 a. 4, in Opera Omnia, ed. Stephanus Borgnet (Paris: Vivès, 1894), 28:240.

16. Origen, *Commentaire sur le Cantique des Cantiques* II 9, 12, ed. Luc Brésard, Henri Crouzel, and Marcel Borret (Paris: Cerf, 1991), 442.

17. Guigo II the Carthusian, "Scala claustralium, sive tractatus de modo orandi," in *Patrologia Latina*, ed. Jean-Paul Migne (Paris: Migne, 1862), 184:476 (my trans.). See also Guigo II the Carthusian, *Lettre sur la vie contemplative (L'échelle des moines). Douze méditations*, intr. and ed. Edmund Colledge and James Walsh (Paris: Cerf, 2001), 81–87.

18. Hugh of Saint Victor, "De virtute orandi," in *L'œuvre de Hugues de Saint-Victor*, ed. and trans. P. Sicard, H. B. Feiss, D. Poirel, and H. Rochais (Turnhout, Belgium: Brepols, 1997), 1:136; Hugh of Saint Victor, "On the Power of Prayer," in *Writings on the Spiritual Life: A Selection of Works of Hugh, Adam, Achard, Richard, Walter, and Godfrey of St Victor*, ed. Christopher P. Evans (Hyde Park, NY: New City Press, 2014), 334.

19. Hugh of Saint Victor, "De virtute orandi," 152; "On the Power of Prayer," 341.

20. Hugh of Saint Victor, "De virtute orandi," 130; "On the Power of Prayer," 332.

21. Albert the Great, *Commentarii* III d. 13 a. 4, 28:240: "Si autem objicitur contra hos duos sensus, quod sensus est vis cognitiva: istud autem non ordinatur ad apprehendere, sed potius ad affici: dicendum, quod est cognitio per modum receptionis quasi ab extra: et est cognitio experimentalis, sicut dicit Dionysius quod Hierotheus patiendo divina, didicit divina: et haec cognitio est per gustum et tactum spirituales." See also Albert the Great, *De caelestis hierarchia*, in Opera Omnia, ed. Stephanus Borgnet (Paris: Vivès, 1890–1899), vol. 14, ch. 15, 5.

22. Peter of Ailly, *Compendium contemplationis*, in *Opuscula Spiritualia* (Douai, France: apud Viduam Marci Wyon, 1634), 134.

23. Rudolf of Biberach, *De septem itineribus aeternitatis. Nachdruck der Ausgabe von Peltier 1866 mit einer Einleitung in die lateinische Überlieferung und Corrigenda zum Text*, ed. Margot Schmidt (Stuttgart-Bad Cannstatt: Frommann-Holzboog, 1985), ch. VI, dist. V, 467.

24. Rudolf of Biberach, *De septem itineribus aeternitatis*, ch. VI, dist. V, 467.

25. Baldwin of Canterbury, "Tractatus de duplici resurrectione," 429.

26. Meister Eckhart, *Meister Eckhart: Teacher and Preacher,* trans. Bernard McGinn (New York: Paulist Press, 1981), 320; Eckhart, *Werke,* 2:65.

27. Gregory the Great, *Gregory the Great on the Song of Songs,* trans. Mark DelCogliano (Collegeville, MN: Liturgical Press, 2012), prol. 1–4, 109–110.

28. Hadewijch, *The Complete Works,* trans. Columba Hart (New York: Paulist Press, 1980), 280–282.

CHAPTER 4

1. Thomas of Celano, *Vita prima S. Francisci Assisiensis,* ed. PP Collegii S. Bonaventurae (Florence: Collegium S. Bonaventura, 1926), lib. I, pars II, cap. 3, nn. 94–95, 101–103, and cap. 9, n. 113, 125–126.

2. For a history of this adage, see Jean Châtillon, "Nudum Christum Nudus Sequere," in *S. Bonaventura 1274–1974* (Grottaferrata [Rome]: Collegio S. Bonaventura, 1974), 4:719–772; Réginald Grégoire, "L'adage ascétique "Nudus nudum Christum sequi," in *Studi storici in onore di Ottorino Bertolini* (Pisa: Pacini, 1972), 1:395–409; Franco Mormando, "'Nudus nudum Christum sequi': The Franciscans and Differing Interpretations of Male Nakedness in Fifteenth Century Italy," *Fifteenth-Century Studies* 33 (2008): 171–197.

3. Bonaventure, "Itinerarium mentis in Deum," in *Opera theologica selecta,* ed. Augustinus Sépinski, 5:182 (Florence: Collegium s. Bonaventurae, 1964); Bonaventure, "The Soul's Journey into God," in *The Soul's Journey into God; The Tree of Life; The Life of Saint Francis,* trans. and introd. Ewert Cousins, pref. Ignatius Brady, O.F.M. (Mahwah, NJ: Paulist Press, 1978), 59.

4. Luis Buñuel, *My Last Sigh,* trans. Abigail Israel (Minneapolis: University of Minnesota Press, 2003), 8–18.

5. Buñuel also wrote a film script based on Huysmans's novel *Là-bas*: Luis Buñuel, *Là-bas: Guión cinematográfico de Luis Buñuel y J.-C. Carrière, basado en la novela homónima de J.-K. Huysmans* (Teruel, Spain: Instituto de Estudios Turolenses, 1990).

6. Hermann Bahr, *Studien zur Kritik der Moderne* (Frankfurt: Rütten and Loening, 1894), 23: "Es kommt vor allem auf das Vermögen an, den Geist auf einen einzigen Punkt zu sammeln, sich selber zu halluciniren und den Traum an die Stelle der Wirklichkeit zu setzen. Das Künstliche erschien dem *des Esseintes* als das eigentliche auszeichnende Merkmal des menschlichen Genies. Wie er zu sagen pflegte: die Zeit der Natur ist vorbei; die ekelhafte Einförmigkeit ihrere Landschaften und ihrer Himmel hat die aufmerksame Geduld der Raffinirten endlich erschöpft."

7. Joris-Karl Huysmans, *À rebours,* ed. Marc Fumaroli (Paris: Gallimard, 1977), 84.

8. Joris-Karl Huysmans, *Against Nature*, trans. Margaret Mauldon (Oxford: Oxford University Press, 1998), 18–19.

9. Maurice Barrès, *Un homme libre*, ed. Ida-Marie Frandon (Paris: Imprimerie Nationale, 1988), 105–106: "Si nous savions varier avec minutie les circonstances où nous plaçons nos facultés, nous verrions aussitôt nos désirs (qui ne sont que les besoins de nos facultés) changer au point que notre âme en paraîtra transformée. Et pour nous créer ces milieux, il ne s'agit pas d'user de raisonnements mais d'une méthode mécanique, nous nous envelopperons d'images appropriées, et d'un effet puissant, nous les interposerons entre nôtre âme et le monde extérieur si néfaste. Bientôt, sûrs de notre procédé, nous pousserons avec clairvoyance nos émotions d'excès en excès."

10. Jean Luc Nancy, "The Sublime Offering," in *Of the Sublime: Presence in Question. Essays by Jean-Francois Courtine, Michel Deguy, Eliane Escoubas, Philippe Lacoue-Labarthe, Jean-Francois Lyotard, Louis Marin, Jean-Luc Nancy, and Jacob Rogozinski*, trans. Jeffrey S. Librett (Albany: State University of New York Press, 1993), 35–37.

11. For a short comment on Huysmans's references to Ignatius, see Marc Fumaroli's notes in Huysmans, *À rebours*, 394.

12. Ignatius of Loyola, *Spiritual Exercises and Selected Works*, ed. Parmananda Divarkar and Edward J. Malatesta (New York: Paulist Press, 1991), 121.

13. Ignatius of Loyola, *Spiritual Exercises*, 141.

14. Quoted from the introduction by Jacques Suffel in Gustave Flaubert, *La tentation de saint Antoine*, ed. Jacques Suffel (Paris: Flammarion, 1967), 20–21. For a reconstruction of Flaubert's sources, see Jean Seznec, *Nouvelles études sur "La tentation de saint Antoine"* (London: Warburg Institute, 1949).

15. Paul Valéry, "La tentation de (saint) Flaubert," in *Variété V* (Paris: Gallimard, 1982), 205–206 (my trans.): "Flaubert a été comme enivré par l'accessoire aux dépens du principal. Il a subi le divertissement des décors, des contrastes, des précisions 'amusantes' de détails, cueillis ça et là dans des livres peu ou mal fréquentés: donc, Antoine lui-même (mais un Antoine qui succombe), il a perdu son âme. . . . En ne s'inquiétant pas sur toute chose d'animer puissamment son héros, il a négligé la substance même de son thème: il n'a pas entendu l'appel à la profondeur. De quoi s'agissait-il? De rien de moins que de figurer ce qu'on pourrait nommer la physiologie de la tentation, toute cette mécanique essentielle dans laquelle les couleurs, les saveurs, le chaud et le froid, le silence et le bruit, le vrai et le faux, le bien et le mal jouent le rôle de forces et s'établissent en nous en forme d'antagonismes toujours imminents. . . . Je ne doute pas que Flaubert ait eu conscience de la profondeur de son sujet; mais on dirait qu'il a eu peur d'y plonger jusqu'à ce point où tout ce qui peut s'apprendre ne compte plus. . . . Il s'est donc égaré dans trop de livres et de mythes; il y a perdu la pensée stratégique, je veux dire l'unité de sa composition qui ne pouvait résider que dans un Antoine dont Satan eût été l'une des âmes."

16. Michel Foucault, *Dits et écrits* (Paris: Gallimard, 1994), 1:297: "Ce lieu nouveau des fantasmes, ce n'est plus la nuit, le sommeil de la raison, le vide incertain ouvert devant le désir: c'est au contraire la veille, l'attention inlassable, le zèle érudit, l'attention aux aguets. Le chimérique désormais naît de la surface noire et blanc des signes imprimés, du volume fermé et poussiéreux qui s'ouvre sur un envol de mots oubliés. . . . L'imaginaire se loge entre le livre et la lampe. On ne porte plus le fantastique dans son coeur; on ne l'attend pas non plus des incongruités de la nature; on le puise à l'exactitude du savoir; sa richesse est en attente dans le document. Pour rêver, il ne faut pas fermer les yeux, il faut lire. La vraie image est connaissance."

17. Most medieval manuals of prayer could be used to illustrate this. See William of Saint Thierry, *Epistola ad fratres de Monte Dei*, 170: "Hoc enim modo cellarum incolae saepe descendunt ad infernum. Sicut enim assidue contemplando revisere amant gaudia caelestia, ut ardentius ea appetant; sic et dolores inferni, ut horreant et refugiant." Compare also Adam of Dryburgh, "Liber de quadripertito exercitio cellae," in *Patrologia Latina*, ed. Jean-Paul Migne (Paris: Migne, 1880), 153:840; William of St. Thierry, *Meditativae orationes*, ed. Jacques Hourlier (Paris: Cerf, 1985), 124, 136.

18. David of Augsburg, "Septem gradus orationis," ed. Jacques Heerinckx, *Revue d'ascétique et de mystique* 14 (1933): 161.

19. Mechthild of Magdeburg, *The Flowing Light of the Godhead*, trans. Frank Tobin (New York: Paulist Press, 1998), 45–48.

20. For a comprehensive study, see Angenendt et al., "Gezählte Frömmigkeit," *Frühmittelalterliche Studien* 29 (1995): 1–71.

21. Mechthild of Magdeburg, *The Flowing Light of the Godhead*, 48.

22. See Huysmans, *Against Nature*, 115–133, where Ruusbroec figures alongside Charles Baudelaire.

23. Not surprisingly, Prudentius's *Psychomachia*, which forms one of the backgrounds of Mechthild's texts and her allegories of personification, is also part of des Esseintes's readings. See Huysmans, *Against Nature*, 30.

24. Compare the discussion of Hans Belting, *Bild und Kult: Eine Geschichte des Bildes vor dem Zeitalter der Kunst* (Munich: Beck, 1990), in Hans Robert Jauss, "Über religiöse und ästhetische Erfahrung. Zur Debatte um Hans Beltings 'Bild und Kult' und George Steiners 'Von realer Gegenwart,'" *Merkur* 45 (1991): 934–946.

25. An early example can be found in Karl A. Fetzer, *Der Flagellantismus und die Jesuitenbeichte: Historisch-psychologische Geschichte der Geisselungsinstitute, Klosterzüchtigungen und Beichtstuhlverirrungen aller Zeiten* (Leipzig: J. Scheible, 1834). See also Niklaus Largier, *In Praise of the Whip: A Cultural History of Arousal* (New York: Zone Books, 2007), 222–241, 425–455. For a critique of the psychoanalytic reading of masochism, see Gilles Deleuze, "Coldness and Cruelty," in *Masochism*, trans. Jean McNeil (New York: Zone Books, 1989), 7–138.

26. For an overview, see Frida Beckman and Charlie Blake, "Shadows of Cruelty: Sadism, Masochism, and the Philosophical Muse. Part One," *Angelaki* 14, no. 3 (2009): 1–9, and Part Two, *Angelaki* 15, no. 1 (2010): 1–12.

27. Gilles Deleuze and Félix Guattari, *What Is Philosophy?* (New York: Columbia University Press, 1994), 69.

28. Chris L. Smith, "Text and Deployment of the Masochist," *Angelaki* 14, no. 3 (2009): 48.

29. Compare Judith Butler, *The Psychic Life of Power: Theories in Subjection* (Stanford, CA: Stanford University Press, 1997).

30. See Gilles Deleuze, "Mysticism and Masochism," in *Desert Islands and Other Texts, 1953–1974*, trans. Mark Taormina (New York: Semiotext(e), 2004), 131–136.

31. Compare Kaja Silverman, *Male Subjectivity at the Margins* (New York: Routledge, 1992); John Noyes, *The Mastery of Submission: Inventions of Masochism* (Ithaca, NY: Cornell University Press, 1997).

32. Beckman and Blake, "Shadows of Cruelty," Part One, 6.

33. Smith, "Text and Deployment," 49.

34. Smith, "Text and Deployment," 50.

35. Smith, "Text and Deployment," 50–51.

36. Deleuze, "Coldness and Cruelty," 69.

37. Teresa of Ávila, *The Life of Saint Teresa of Ávila by Herself* (London: Penguin, 1957), 26.

38. Teresa of Ávila, *The Life*, 24.

39. Teresa of Ávila, *The Life*, 24.

40. Teresa of Ávila, *The Life*, 210.

41. Deleuze, "Coldness and Cruelty," 126.

42. Teresa of Ávila, *The Life*, 136, 139.

43. Teresa of Ávila, *The Life*, 136.

44. Teresa of Ávila, *The Life*, 143–144.

45. Teresa of Ávila, *The Life*, 146.

46. For a comprehensive overview, see Bernard McGinn, *The Harvest of Mysticism in Medieval Germany* (New York: Herder, 2005).

47. Meister Eckhart, *German Sermons and Treatises*, trans. Maurice O'C. Walshe (London: 1979–1985), 2:157–162; Eckhart, *Werke*, 1:132–141.

48. Alois Haas, *Sermo mysticus* (Freiburg: Universitätsverlag, 1979), 209–237.

49. See Niklaus Largier, *Spekulative Sinnlichkeit: Kontemplation und Spekulation im Mittelalter* (Zürich: Chronos, 2018).

50. Meister Eckhart, *Selected Writings*, trans. Oliver Davies (London: Penguin Books, 1994), 158.

51. For a discussion of Eckhart's notion of immanence, compare Dubilet, *The Self-Emptying Subject*, 60–91.

52. Eckhart, *Selected Writings*, 158.

53. Eckhart, *Selected Writings*, 159.

54. For two opposing interpretations of the procession of images in Eckhart, compare Kurt Flasch, "Procedere ut imago. Das Hervorgehen des Intellekts aus seinem göttlichen Grund bei Meister Dietrich, Meister Eckhart und Berthold von Moosburg," in *Abendländische Mystik im Mittelalter*, ed. Kurt Ruh (Stuttgart: Metzler, 1986), 125–134; and Niklaus Largier, "Negativität, Möglichkeit, Freiheit: Zur Differenz zwischen der Philosophie Dietrichs von Freiberg und Meister Eckharts," in *Dietrich von Freiberg: Neue Perspektiven seiner Philosophie, Theologie und Naturwissenschaft*, ed. Karl-Heinz Kandler and Burkhard Mojsisch (Amsterdam: B. R. Grüner, 1999), 149–168.

55. Compare Niklaus Largier, "Kontextualisierung als Interpretation. Gottesgeburt und *speculatio* im *Paradisus anime intelligentis*," in *Meister Eckhart in Erfurt*, ed. Andreas Speer and Lydia Wegener (Berlin: De Gruyter, 2005), 298–313.

56. Alois Haas, *Kunst rechter Gelassenheit: Themen und Schwerpunkte von Heinrich Seuses Mystik* (Bern: Lang, 1995), 149–178.

57. Compare Largier, "Allegorie und Figur. Figuraler Realismus bei Heinrich Seuse und Erich Auerbach," *Paragrana* 21 (2012): 36–46.

58. For a comprehensive study, see Karnes, *Imagination, Meditation, and Cognition in the Middle Ages* (Chicago: University of Chicago Press, 2011).

59. Henry Suso, *The Exemplar, with Two German Sermons*, ed. and trans. Frank Tobin (New York: Paulist Press, 1989), 200–201.

60. Suso, *The Exemplar*, 207.

61. Suso, *The Exemplar*, 207–208.

62. Suso, *The Exemplar*, 314.

63. Suso, *The Exemplar*, 265.

64. Suso, *The Exemplar*, 266.

65. Suso, *The Exemplar*, 202.

66. Suso, *The Exemplar*, 202.

67. Suso, *The Exemplar*, 202.

68. Largier, "Tactus. Le sens du toucher et la volupté au Moyen Age," *Micrologus* 13 (2004): 233–249.

69. Suso, *The Exemplar*, 286–287.

70. Suso, *The Exemplar*, 287–289.

71. Suso, *The Exemplar*, 289.

72. Suso, *The Exemplar*, 293.

73. Henry Suso, *Deutsche Schriften*, ed. Karl Bihlmeyer (Stuttgart: Kohlhammer, 1907; repr.: Frankfurt: Minerva, 1961), 170, 1–2; Suso, *The Exemplar*, 186.

74. Suso, *The Exemplar*, 187.

75. Suso, *The Exemplar*, 187–188.

76. Suso, *Deutsche Schriften*, 173, 15–16.

77. Suso, *The Exemplar*, 188–189.

78. Robert Javelet, *Image et ressemblance au XIIe siècle. De saint Anselme à Alain de Lille* (Paris: Letouzey et Ané, 1967), 377: "Le mot 'spéculation' n'est pas réservé à l'introspection spirituelle: la spéculation concerne l'observation spirituelle de tous les simulacres de la nature et de la grâce. Elle embrasse tout le monde visible en tant qu'il ressemble à l'invisible. La spéculation, c'est la vision de la vérité par le moyen d'un miroir, par la médiation des ressemblances. Toute spéculation est sacramentelle au sens large."

79. Dale M. Coulter, "Contemplation as 'Speculation' in the 12th Century," in *From Knowledge to Beatitude: St. Victor, Twelfth-Century Scholars, and Beyond*, ed. E. Ann Matter and Lesley Smith (Notre Dame, IN: Notre Dame University Press, 2013), 224.

CHAPTER 5

1. Suso, *The Exemplar*, 308.

2. Eric Mangin, "La lettre du 13 août 1317 écrite par l'éveque de Strasbourg," *Revue des Sciences Religieuses* 75 (2001): 533. For a history of the "free spirits," see Guarnieri, "Il movimento del Libero spirito dalle origini al secolo XVI," *Archivio italiano per la storia della pietà* 4 (1965): 353–499; Robert Lerner, *The Heresy of the Free Spirit in the Later Middle Ages* (Berkeley: University of California Press, 1972); Raoul Vaneigem, *The Movement of the Free Spirit: General Considerations and Firsthand Testimony concerning Some Brief Flowerings of Life in the Middle Ages, the Renaissance and, Incidentally, Our Own Time* (New York: Zone Books, 1994).

3. Mangin, "La lettre," 533.

4. For a recent overview of approaches, compare Michael D. Bailey and Sean L. Field, eds. *Late Medieval Heresy: New Perspectives. Studies in Honor of Robert E. Lerner* (York, UK: York Medieval Press, 2018). For Eckhart and Suso, see Fiorella Retucci, "On a Dangerous Trail: Henry Suso and the Condemnations of Meister Eckhart," in *A Companion to Meister Eckhart*, ed. Jeremiah Hackett (Leiden: Brill, 2012), 587–606.

5. See James Snyder, *Hieronymus Bosch* (New York: Excalibur Books, 1977), 100.

6. Mangin, "La lettre," 534.

7. Vaneigem, *The Movement of the Free Spirit*, 254–255.

8. Henry Suso, *Das Buch der Wahrheit*, ed. Loris Sturlese and Rüdiger Blumrich (Hamburg: Meiner, 1993), 66. Compare Sturlese, "Einleitung," in Suso, *Das Buch der Wahrheit*, xxi–lxiii.

9. Franz-Josef Schweitzer, *Der Freiheitsbegriff der deutschen Mystik: Seine Beziehung zur Ketzerei der "Brüder und Schwestern vom Freien Geist," mit besonderer Rücksicht auf den pseudoeckhartischen Traktat "Schwester Katrei"* (Frankfurt: Lang, 1981); see also Barbara Newman, *From Virile Woman to WomanChrist: Studies in Medieval Religion and Literature* (Philadelphia: University of Pennsylvania Press, 1995), 172–181.

10. Suso, *The Exemplar*, 330.

11. Suso, *The Exemplar*, 308.

12. Suso, *The Exemplar*, 326.

13. See Bernard McGinn, *The Flowering of Mysticism* (New York: Herder, 1998), 244–265.

14. Marguerite Porete, *The Mirror of Simple Souls*, trans. Ellen Babinsky (New York: Paulist Press, 1993), 84–85.

15. Suso, *The Exemplar*, 308.

16. Suso, *The Exemplar*, 308–315. Compare Walter Senner, "Meister Eckhart's Life, Training, Career, and Trial," in *A Companion to Meister Eckhart*, ed. Jermiah Hackett (Leiden: Brill, 2012), 45–83; McGinn, *The Harvest of Mysticism*, 103–107; Sturlese, "Einleitung," in Suso, *Das Buch der Wahrheit*, xxi–xxviii.

17. McGinn, *The Flowering of Mysticism*, 226–227.

18. Jean Gerson, "De probatione spirituum," in *Oeuvres complètes*, ed. Palémon Glorieux (Paris: Desclée, 1973), 9:184.

19. Compare Niklaus Largier, "Rhetorik des Begehrens: Die 'Unterscheidung der Geister' als Paradigma mittelalterlicher Subjektivität," in *Inszenierungen von Subjektivität in der Literatur des Mittelalters*, ed. Martin Baisch (Königstein, Germany: Helmer, 2005), 249–270; Niklaus Largier, "Die Phänomenologie rhetorischer Effekte und die Kontrolle religiöser Kommunikation," in *Literarische und religiöse Kommunikation in Mittelalter und Früher Neuzeit. DFG-Symposion 2006*, ed. Peter Strohschneider (Stuttgart: Metzler, 2009), 953–968.

20. Martin Heidegger, *Discourse on Thinking: A Translation of Gelassenheit*, trans. John M. Anderson and E. Hans Freund (New York: Harper and Row, 1966); Jacques Derrida, *On the Name*, trans. David Wood, John P. Leavey, and Ian McLeod (Stanford, CA: Stanford University Press, 1995), 73–74.

21. Pierre Klossowski, *Roberte ce Soir; and, The Revocation of the Edict of Nantes*, trans. Austryn Wainhouse (Chicago: Dalkey Archive Press, 2002); Ingeborg Bachmann, "The Thirtieth Year," in *The Thirtieth Year: Stories by Ingeborg Bachmann*, trans. Michael Bullock (New York: Knopf, 1987), 18–55; for Paul Celan, compare the poem "Du sei wie Du" in *Lichtzwang*, in *Gesammelte Werke*, ed. Stefan Reichert and Beda Allemann (Frankfurt: Suhrkamp, 1986), 2:327. For Musil's quotes from Eckhart's writings in his novel *The Man without Qualities*, see Brigitte Spreitzer, "Meister Musil: Eckharts deutsche Predigten als zentrale

Quelle des Romans 'Der Mann ohne Eigenschaften,'" *Zeitschrift für deutsche Philologie* 119 (2000): 564–588.

22. Published in Émilie Zum Brunn, ed., *Voici Maître Eckhart* (Grenoble: Jérôme Millon, 1998), 430.

23. Günther Nicolin, ed., *Hegel in Berichten seiner Zeitgenossen* (Hamburg: Meiner, 1970), 261.

24. Compare Donata Schoeller, *Gottesgeburt und Selbstbewusstsein: Denken der Einheit bei Meister Eckhart und G. W. F. Hegel* (Hildesheim: Morus, 1992).

25. Jacques Derrida, "How to Avoid Speaking: Denials," trans. Ken Frieden, in *Languages of the Unsayable: The Play of Negativity in Literature and Literary Theory*, ed. Sanford Budick and Wolfgang Iser (New York: Columbia University Press, 1989), 3–70.

26. Derrida, *On the Name*, 74–85. For a discussion of Heidegger's and Derrida's engagement with Angelus Silesius, see Hent de Vries, *Philosophy and the Turn to Religion* (Baltimore: Johns Hopkins University Press, 2019), chaps. 4, 5.

27. Quoted after Heidegger, *The Principle of Reason*, trans. Reginald Lilly (Bloomington: Indiana University Press, 1991), 35.

28. Heidegger, *The Principle of Reason*, 35.

29. Hans Blumenberg, *Theorie der Unbegrifflichkeit*, ed. Anselm Haverkamp (Frankfurt: Suhrkamp, 2007), 28.

30. Compare the discussions about the relationship between love and reason in the thirteenth century, examined by Bernard McGinn, "Love, Knowledge, and Mystical Union: Twelfth to Sixteenth Centuries," *Church History* 56 (1987): 7–24.

31. For a recent treatment of this topic, see Rosalynn Voaden, *God's Words, Women's Voices: The Discernment of Spirits in the Writing of Late-Medieval Women Visionaries* (Woodbridge, Suffolk, UK: Boydell and Brewer, 1999); Nancy Caciola, *Discerning Spirits: Divine and Demonic Possession in the Middle Ages* (Ithaca, NY: Cornell University Press, 2003); Carol Thysell, *The Pleasure of Discernment: Marguerite de Navarre as Theologian* (Oxford: Oxford University Press, 2000).

32. See Bernard McGinn, ed., *Meister Eckhart and the Beguine Mystics: Hadewijch of Brabant, Mechthild of Magdeburg, and Marguerite Porete* (New York: Continuum, 1997); Bernard McGinn, "The Four Female Evangelists of the Thirteenth Century: The Invention of Authority," in *Deutsche Mystik im abendländischen Zusammenhang. Neu erschlossene Texte, neue methodische Ansätze, neue theoretische Konzepte. Kolloquium Kloster Fischingen, 1998*, ed. Walter Haug and Wolfram Schneider-Lastin (Tübingen: Niemeyer, 2000), 175–194.

33. See Robert G. Warnock, "'Von den vier Einsprüchen'—Die volkssprachliche Überlieferung," in *Der Traktat Heinrichs von Friemar über die Unterscheidung der Geister. Lateinisch-mittelhochdeutsche Textausgabe mit Untersuchungen*,

ed. Robert G. Warnock and Adolar Zumkeller (Würzburg: Augustinus, 1977), 39–145.

34. For an overview, compare Michael Giesecke, *Der Buchdruck in der frühen Neuzeit: Eine historisch Fallstudie über die Durchsetzung neuer Informations- und Kommunikationstechnologien* (Frankfurt: Suhrkamp, 1991).

35. Martin Luther, *D. Martin Luthers Werke: Kritische Gesamtausgabe* (Weimar: Hermann Böhlau, 1883–2009), vol. 30, part II, 555, 562; vol. 40, part I, 208.

36. Luther, *D. Martin Luthers Werke*, vol. 30, part II, 562 (my trans.): "Denn jm predig ampt thuts Christus fast gar durch seinen geist, Aber jnn welltlichem reich mus man aus der vernunfft (da her die Rechte auch komen sind) handeln, denn Got hat der vernunfft unterworffen solch zeitlich regiment und leiblich wesen, Gene. 2 [1 Moses 2:19], und nicht den heiligen geist vom himel dazu gesand."

37. Martin Luther, "The Freedom of a Christian," in *Martin Luther's Basic Theological Writings*, ed. Timothy F. Lull and William R. Russell (Minneapolis, MN: Augsburg Fortress Publishers, 2012), 403–427.

38. Luther, *D. Martin Luthers Werke*, 15:210–221. Compare Alois Haas, *Der Kampf um den Heiligen Geist: Luther und die Schwärmer* (Freiburg: Universitätsverlag, 1997).

39. Luther, *D. Martin Luthers Werke*, 15:213, 217–218.

40. For a collection of these texts, see Karl Simon, ed., *Deutsche Flugschriften zur Reformation (1520–1525)* (Stuttgart: Reclam, 1980).

41. See G. H. Williams, *Spiritual and Anabaptist Writers: Documents Illustrative of the Radical Reformation* (London: Westminster John Knox Press, 1957); Heinold Fast, *Der linke Flügel der Reformation: Glaubenszeugnisse der Täufer, Spiritualisten, Schwärmer und Antitrinitarier* (Bremen: C. Schünemann, 1962).

42. See Thomas Müntzer, "Auslegung des anderen Unterschieds Danielis," in *Schriften und Briefe: Kritische Gesamtausgabe*, ed. Günther Franz (Gütersloh, Germany: Gütersloher Verlagshaus Gerd Mohn, 1968), 241–263.

43. Martin Luther, "Temporal Authority: To What Extent It Should Be Obeyed," in *Martin Luther's Basic Theological Writings*, 431.

44. Luther, "The Freedom of a Christian," 421–422. For a recent treatment of Luther's doctrine of two kingdoms, see Volker Mantey, *Zwei Schwerter—Zwei Reiche: Martin Luthers Zwei-Reiche-Lehre vor ihrem spätmittelalterlichen Hintergrund* (Tübingen: Mohr Siebeck, 2005); Per Frostin, *Luther's Two Kingdoms Doctrine* (Lund: Lund University Press, 1994).

45. Gerson, "De probatione spirituum," 184.

46. Luther, *D. Martin Luthers Werke*, vol. 40, part I, 208.

47. Luther, *D. Martin Luthers Werke*, vol. 30, part II, 555.

48. Quoted in Giesecke, *Der Buchdruck*, 176–177.

49. Luther edited this text for the first time in 1518. See Wolfgang von Hinten, ed., *Der Franckforter (Theologia Deutsch): Kritische Textausgabe* (Munich: Artemis, 1982). For Luther's relationship to mystical traditions, compare Alois Haas, *Gottleiden—Gottlieben: Zur volkssprachlichen Mystik im Mittelalter* (Frankfurt: Insel, 1989), 264–294; and Gerhard Müller, *Die Mystik oder das Wort? Zur Geschichte eines Spannungsverhältnisses* (Stuttgart: Akademie der Wissenschaften und der Literatur, 1999).

50. Michel de Certeau, *The Mystic Fable*, trans. Michael B. Smith, 2 vols. (Chicago: University of Chicago Press, 1992, 2015), 1:161–163.

51. Hans-Georg Kemper, *Deutsche Lyrik der frühen Neuzeit* (Tübingen: Niemeyer, 1987–1991), 3:245–78.

52. See Müntzer, "Auslegung."

53. Angelus Silesius, *Der Cherubinische Wandersmann*, ed. Louise Gnädinger (Stuttgart: Reclam, 1984), 49. I follow the translation by John P. Leavey in Derrida, *On the Name*, 41.

54. See Certeau, *The Mystic Fable*, 1:179–187.

55. For a discussion of the rhetorical aspects of this shift, compare Marc Fumaroli, *L'école du silence: Le sentiment des images au XVIIe siècle* (Paris: Flammarion, 1994).

56. Burkhard Dohm, "Radikalpietistin und 'schöne Seele': Susanna Katharina von Klettenberg," in *Goethe und der Pietismus*, ed. Hans-Georg Kemper and Hans Schneider (Tübingen: Niemeyer, 2001), 117.

57. Novalis, *Philosophical Writings*, ed. Margaret M. Stoljar (Albany: State University of New York Press, 1997), 61.

58. Immanuel Kant, "Von einem neuerdings erhobenen vornehmen Ton in der Philosophie," in *Werke*, ed. Wilhelm Weischedel (Frankfurt: Insel, 1964), 3:377–378; Immanuel Kant, "On a Newly Arisen Superior Tone in Philosophy," in *Raising the Tone of Philosophy: Late Essays by Immanuel Kant, Transformative Critique by Jacques Derrida*, ed. Peter Fenves (Baltimore: Johns Hopkins University Press, 1993), 51–52.

59. Kant, "Von einem neuerdings erhobenen vornehmen Ton," 386; "On a Newly Arisen Superior Tone," 62.

60. Kant, "Von einem neuerdings erhobenen vornehmen Ton," 393; "On a Newly Arisen Superior Tone," 61–62.

61. Immanuel Kant, "Beantwortung der Frage: Was ist Aufklärung?," in *Werke*, ed. Wilhelm Weischedel (Frankfurt: Insel, 1964), 6:55; Immanuel Kant, "An Answer to the Question: What Is Enlightenment?," in *Perpetual Peace and Other Essays*, trans. Ted Humphrey (Indianapolis: Hackett, 1983), 42.

62. Kant, "Was ist Aufklärung?," 61; "What Is Enlightenment?," 45.

63. Kant, "Von einem neuerdings erhobenen vornehmen Ton," 396; "On a Newly Arisen Superior Tone," 61–65.

64. Kant, "Was ist Aufklärung?," 60; "What Is Enlightenment?," 45.

65. Kant, "Von einem neuerdings erhobenen vornehmen Ton," 397; "On a Newly Arisen Superior Tone," 72.

66. Kant, "Von einem neuerdings erhobenen vornehmen Ton," 397; "On a Newly Arisen Superior Tone," 71–72.

CHAPTER 6

1. Walter Benjamin, *The Origin of the German Trauerspiel*, trans. Howard Eiland (Cambridge, MA: Harvard University Press, 2019), 194.

2. Compare Johann Jakob Bodmer and Johann Jakob Breitinger, *Schriften zur Literatur*, ed. Volker Meid (Stuttgart: Reclam, 2014), 59–61.

3. Karen Barad, "Transmaterialities: Trans*/Matter/Realities and Queer Political Imaginings," *GLQ: A Journal of Lesbian and Gay Studies* 21 (2015): 387–422.

4. Barad, "Transmaterialities," 387.

5. Daniel Casper von Lohenstein, *Sophonisbe*, ed. Rolf Tarot (Stuttgart: Reclam, 1985), 141.

6. Jacob Böhme, *The Signature of All Things, and Other Writings*, trans. Clifford Bax (London: Clarke, 1969), 13; Jacob Böhme, *De signatura rerum*, in *Werke*, ed. Ferdinand van Ingen (Frankfurt: Deutscher Klassiker Verlag, 1997), 519–520.

7. Böhme, *The Signature of All Things*, 14–15; *De signatura rerum*, 522–522.

8. Böhme, *The Signature of All Things*, 20; *De signatura rerum*, 529.

9. Böhme, *The Signature of All Things*, 9; *De signatura rerum*, 514.

10. Giorgio Agamben, *The Signature of All Things: On Method*, trans. Luca D'Isanto with Kevin Attell (New York: Zone Books, 2009), 58.

11. Michel Foucault, *The Order of Things* (New York: Vintage Books, 1966), 29.

12. Agamben, *The Signature of All Things*, 59.

13. Foucault, *The Order of Things*, 30.

14. Agamben, *The Signature of All Things*, 31.

15. Agamben, *The Signature of All Things*, 66.

16. Alexander Gottlieb Baumgarten, *Metaphysica* (Halle: Hemmerde, 1779; repr.: Hildesheim: Olms, 1982), § 511: "Hic anime fundus . . . a multis adhuc ignoretur, etiam philosophis."

17. Alexander Gottlieb Baumgarten, *Aesthetica*, ed. Dagmar Mirbach (Hamburg: Meiner, 2007), §1: "Aesthetica (theoria liberalium artium, gnoseologia inferior, ars pulcre cogitandi, ars analogi rationis) est scientia cognitionis sensitivae."

18. See the discussion of the meaning of *grunt* in Eckhart and Tauler in McGinn, *The Harvest of Mysticism*, 83–93, 118–124, 254–264.

19. Angelica Nuzzo, "Kant and Herder on Baumgarten's *Aesthetica*," *Journal of the History of Philosophy* 44 (2006): 577.

20. Herder emphasizes, "[dass] in dem Grunde der Seele unsere Stärke als Menschen besteht." See *Werke in zehn Bänden*, ed. Hans Dietrich Irmscher (Frankfurt: Deutscher Klassiker Verlag, 1991), 1:665.

21. Baumgarten, *Aesthetica*, 62–76.

22. Baumgarten, *Aesthetica*, 62.

23. See Niklaus Largier, "Spiegelungen: Fragmente einer Geschichte der Spekulation," *Zeitschrift für Germanistik*, n.s., 3 (1999), 617–625.

24. Baumgarten, *Aesthetica*, 64.

25. Baumgarten, *Aesthetica*, 66.

26. Baumgarten, *Aesthetica*, 65.

27. See Dagmar Mirbach, "Einführung," in Baumgarten, *Aesthetica*, xxxii–xliv.

28. Baumgarten, *Metaphysica*, §511: "Sunt in anima perceptiones obscurae.... Harum complexus fundus animae dicitur."

29. For references in Eckhart's works, see the commentary in Eckhart, *Werke*, 1:763–772.

30. For Eckhart's specific emphasis on "possibility," compare Largier, "Negativität, Möglichkeit, Freiheit."

31. Compare Baumgarten, *Metaphysica*, § 518 and § 511; and Gottfried Wilhelm Leibniz, *New Essays on Human Understanding*, ed. Peter Remnant and Jonathan Bennett (Cambridge: Cambridge University Press, 1996), 55.

32. Baumgarten, *Metaphysica*, § 518: "Status animae, in quo perceptiones dominantes obscurae sunt, est regnum tenebrarum, in quo clarae regnant, regnum lucis."

33. Johannes Tauler, *Die Predigten Taulers*, ed. Ferdinand Vetter (Berlin: Weidmann, 1910; repr.: Frankfurt: Minerva, 1968), 367 (my trans.).

34. Tauler, *Predigten*, 176; trans. in McGinn, *The Harvest of Mysticism*, 263.

35. Tauler, *Predigten*, 350 (my trans.).

36. Hendrik Herp, *Directorium aureum contemplativorum. Directorio de contemplativos*, ed. Juan Martin Kelly (Madrid: Fundacion Universitaria Española, 1974), 647–649; Hendrik Herp, *Theologia mystica cum speculativa* (Cologne: Ex officina Melchioris Nouesiani, 1538; repr.: Farnborough, UK: Gregg, 1966), 169F.

37. In addition to Herp, see Rudolf of Biberach, *De septem itineribus aeternitatis*. Compare Largier, "Tactus."

38. For a discussion of the significance of touch in the eighteenth century, compare Inka Mülder-Bach, *Im Zeichen Pygmalions: Das Modell der Statue und die Entdeckung der "Darstellung" im 18. Jahrhundert* (Munich: Fink, 1998); Ulrike Zeuch, *Umkehr der Sinneshierarchie: Herder und die Aufwertung des Tastsinns seit der frühen Neuzeit* (Tübingen: Niemeyer, 2000); Georg Braungart, *Leibhafter Sinn: Der andere Diskurs der Moderne* (Tübingen: Niemeyer, 1995); Natalie Binczek, *Kontakt: Der Tastsinn in Texten der Aufklärung* (Tübingen: Niemeyer, 2007).

39. See Nuzzo, "Kant and Herder," 594.

40. Herder, *Werke,* 8:363.

41. Herder, *Werke,* 8:363.

42. Quoted in Mülder-Bach, *Im Zeichen Pygmalions,* 71 (my trans.).

43. Mülder-Bach, *Im Zeichen Pygmalions,* 74.

44. Mülder-Bach, *Im Zeichen Pygmalions,* 74 (my trans.).

45. Johann Gottfried Herder, *Sämtliche Werke,* ed. Bernhard Suphan (Berlin: Weidmann, 1877–1913; repr.: Hildesheim: Olms, 1967–1968), 4:52.

46. Johann Gottfried Herder, "<Entwurf (1769)> Von der Bildhauerkunst fürs Gefühl," in *Bibliothek der Kunstliteratur. Vol. 3: Klassik und Klassizismus,* ed. Helmut Pfotenhauer and Peter Sprengel (Frankfurt: Deutscher Klassiker Verlag, 1995), 101 (my trans.).

47. Jacob Grimm and Wilhelm Grimm, *Deutsches Wörterbuch* (Leipzig: S. Hirzel, 1854–1961), 8:1002–1003.

48. Herder, "<Entwurf (1769)>," 95 (my trans.).

49. Herder, *Werke,* 2:517.

50. Cage, *Silence,* 35.

51. Cage, *Silence,* 39.

52. Cage, *Silence,* 39.

53. Cage, *Silence,* 92.

CHAPTER 7

1. Huysmans, *Against Nature,* 1.

2. Huysmans quotes from the French translation in Ernest Hello, *Rusbroek l'admirable* (Paris: Poussielgue frères, 1869).

3. Huysmans, *Against Nature,* 117.

4. Huysmans, *Against Nature,* 129.

5. Huysmans, *Against Nature,* 128.

6. Huysmans, *Against Nature,* 117.

7. Huysmans, *Against Nature,* 117.

8. Georges Bataille, *Inner Experience,* trans. Leslie Anne Boldt (Albany: State University of New York Press, 1988), 8. Compare Carter, "Black Malpractice," 70–74.

9. See Huysmans, *À rebours,* 101, 394.

10. Bataille, *Inner Experience,* 8–9.

11. Bataille, *Inner Experience,* 8.

12. See Hollywood, *Sensible Ecstasy,* 68–75.

13. Compare Bruce Holsinger, *The Premodern Condition: Medievalism and the Making of Theory* (Chicago: University of Chicago Press, 2005), 33–34. For a short characterization of Angela's works, compare Bernard McGinn, *The Flowering of Mysticism,* 143–151.

14. Bataille, *Inner Experience*, 7.

15. Carl Girgensohn, *Der seelische Aufbau des religiösen Erlebens. Eine religionspsychologische Untersuchung auf experimenteller Grundlage* (Leipzig: Hirzel, 1921). Compare Susanne Reichlin and Robert Leucht, "'Ein Gleichgewicht ohne festen Widerhalt, für das wir noch keine rechte Beschreibung gefunden haben.' Robert Musils 'anderer Zustand' als Ort der Wissensübertragung," in *Medien, Technik, Wissenschaft. Wissensübertragung bei Robert Musil und in seiner Zeit*, ed. Ulrich J. Beil, Michael Gamper, and Karl Wagner (Zürich: Chronos, 2011), 289–322.

16. Musil, *The Man without Qualities*, 1:10–11.

17. Musil, *The Man without Qualities*, 1:265–266.

18. For a critical review, see Robert Sharf, "The Rhetoric of Experience and the Study of Religion," *Journal of Consciousness Studies* 7 (2000): 267–287.

19. Musil, *The Man without Qualities*, 1:266.

20. Musil, *The Man without Qualities*, 1:266.

21. Musil, *The Man without Qualities*, 1:265. Compare 2:828–831.

22. I am translating these sentences from the early twentieth-century modern German adaptation by Herman Büttner in Meister Eckhart, *Schriften und Predigten* (Jena: Diederichs, 1919), 1:206.

23. Robert Musil, "Ansätze zu neuer Ästhetik. Bemerkungen über eine Dramaturgie des Films," in Béla Balázs, *Der sichtbare Mensch, oder die Kultur des Films* (Frankfurt: Suhrkamp, 2001), 161 (my trans.). English translation: "Toward a New Aesthetic: Observations on a Dramaturgy of Film," in *Precision and Soul: Essays and Addresses*, ed. and trans. Burton Pike and David S. Luft (Chicago: University of Chicago Press, 1990), 203.

24. Musil, *The Man without Qualities*, 2:826.

25. Musil, *The Man without Qualities*, 2:827.

26. Musil, *The Man without Qualities*, 2:827.

27. Musil, *The Man without Qualities*, 2:828.

28. Musil, *The Man without Qualities*, 2:828–829.

29. Quoted in Helmut H. Diederich's afterword to Balázs, *Der sichtbare Mensch*, 129 (my trans.).

30. Balázs, *Der sichtbare Mensch*, 31 (my trans.).

31. Balázs, *Der sichtbare Mensch*, 44–45 (my trans.).

32. Musil, "Toward a New Aesthetic," 198-199.

33. Musil, "Toward a New Aesthetic," 194.

34. Musil, "Toward a New Aesthetic," 196.

35. Musil, "Toward a New Aesthetic," 204.

36. Kracauer, "Bücher vom Film," in Balázs, *Der sichtbare Mensch*, 172 (my trans.).

CHAPTER 8

1. See Derek Krueger, *Symeon the Holy Fool: Leontius's Life and the Late Antique City* (Berkeley: University of California Press, 1996).

2. Rosalind B. Brooke, ed., *Scripta Leonis, Rufini et Angeli sociorum S. Francisci* (Oxford: Clarendon Press, 1970), 288.

3. Butler, "What Is Critique?," 224.

4. Foucault, "What Is Critique?," 73–74.

5. Butler, "What Is Critique?," 224.

6. Foucault, "What Is Enlightenment?," 117.

7. Foucault, "What Is Enlightenment?," 117, quoting from Charles Baudelaire, *The Painter of Modern Life, and Other Essays*, ed. and trans. Jonathan Mayne (New York: Phaidon, 1964).

8. Alexander Weheliye, *Habeas Viscus: Racializing Assemblages, Biopolitics, and Black Feminist Theories of the Human* (Durham, NC: Duke University Press, 2014), 130, referring to Giorgio Agamben, *Potentialities: Collected Essays in Philosophy*, ed. Daniel Heller-Roazen (Stanford, CA: Stanford University Press, 1999), 182–183.

9. Weheliye, *Habeas Viscus*, 130–131.

10. Foucault, "What Is Enlightenment?," 124.

11. Leontios of Neapolis, "The Life of Symeon the Fool," in Krueger, *Symeon the Holy Fool*, 148.

12. Krueger, *Symeon the Holy Fool*, 126.

13. Krueger, *Symeon the Holy Fool*, 127.

14. Leontius of Neapolis, "The Life of Symeon the Fool," 150–154.

15. Walter Benjamin, "The Paris of the Second Empire in Baudelaire," in *Selected Writings*, 4:25.

Bibliography

Adam of Dryburgh. "Liber de quadripertito exercitio cellae." In *Patrologia Latina*, edited by Jean-Paul Migne, 153:787–884. Paris: Migne, 1880.

Agamben, Giorgio. *Potentialities: Collected Essays in Philosophy*. Edited, translated, and with an introduction by Daniel Heller-Roazen. Stanford, CA: Stanford University Press, 1999.

Agamben, Giorgio. *The Signature of All Things: On Method*. Translated by Luca D'Isanto with Kevin Attell. New York: Zone Books, 2009.

Albert the Great. *Commentarii in tertium librum sententiarum*. Edited by Stephanus Borgnet. Opera Omnia, vol. 28. Paris: Vivès, 1894.

Albert the Great. *De caelestis hierarchia*. Edited by Stephanus Borgnet. Opera Omnia, vol 14. Paris: Vivès, 1892.

Angela of Foligno. *Complete Works*. Translated and with an introduction by Paul Lachance. Preface by Romana Guarnieri. New York: Paulist Press, 1993.

Angelus Silesius. *Der Cherubinische Wandersmann*. Edited by Louise Gnädinger. Stuttgart: Reclam, 1984.

Angenendt, Arnold, Thomas Braucks, Rolf Busch, Thomas Lentes, and Hubertus Lutterbach. "Gezählte Frömmigkeit." *Frühmittelalterliche Studien* 29 (1995): 1–71.

Auerbach, Erich. *Dante als Dichter der irdischen Welt*. Edited by Kurt Flasch. Berlin: De Gruyter, 2001.

Auerbach, Erich. *Dante: Poet of the Secular World*. Translated by Ralph Manheim. Chicago: University of Chicago Press, 1961.

Auerbach, Erich, "*Figura*." In *Gesammelte Aufsätze zur Romanischen Philologie*, 55–92.

Auerbach, Erich. "*Figura*." In *Time, History, and Literature*, 65–113.

Auerbach, Erich. *Gesammelte Aufsätze zur Romanischen Philologie*. Bern: Francke, 1967.

Auerbach, Erich. "Giambattista Vico und die Idee der Philologie." In *Gesammelte Aufsätze zur Romanischen Philologie*, 233–241.

Auerbach, Erich. *Literary Language and Its Public in Late Latin Antiquity and in the Middle Ages.* Translated by Ralph Mannheim. Princeton, NJ: Princeton University Press, 1993.

Auerbach, Erich. *Literatursprache und Publikum in der lateinischen Spätantike und im Mittelalter.* Bern: Francke, 1958.

Auerbach, Erich. *Mimesis: Dargestellte Wirklichkeit in der abendländischen Literatur.* Bern: Francke, 1988.

Auerbach, Erich. *Mimesis: The Representation of Reality in Western Literature.* Translated by Willard R. Trask. Introduction by Edward W. Said. Princeton, NJ: Princeton University Press, 2003.

Auerbach, Erich. *Time, History, and Literature: Selected Essays of Erich Auerbach.* Edited and with an introduction by James I. Porter. Translated by Jane Newman. Princeton, NJ: Princeton University Press, 2014.

Auerbach, Erich. "Vico and Aesthetic Historism." In *Time, History, and Literature,* 36–45.

Auerbach, Erich. "Vico and Herder." In *Time, History, and Literature,* 11–23.

Auerbach, Erich. "Vico and the Idea of Philology." In *Time, History, and Literature,* 24–35.

Auerbach, Erich. "Vico's Contribution to Literary Criticism." In *Time, History, and Literature,* 3–10.

Auerbach, Erich. *Vier Untersuchungen zur Geschichte der französischen Bildung.* Bern: Francke, 1951.

Auerbach, Erich, Martin Elsky, Martin Vialon, and Robert Stein. "Scholarship in Times of Extremes: Letters of Erich Auerbach (1933–46), on the Fiftieth Anniversary of His Death." *PMLA* 122 (2007): 742–762.

Augustine of Hippo. *Confessions.* With an English translation by William Watts. 2 vols. Cambridge, MA: Harvard University Press, 1988.

Bachmann, Ingeborg. "The Thirtieth Year." In *The Thirtieth Year: Stories by Ingeborg Bachmann,* translated by Michael Bullock, 18–55. New York: Knopf, 1987.

Bahr, Hermann. *Studien zur Kritik der Moderne.* Frankfurt: Rütten and Loening, 1894.

Bahti, Timothy. "Auerbach's *Mimesis.*" In *Allegories of History: Literary Historiography after Hegel,* 154–155. Baltimore: Johns Hopkins University Press, 1992.

Bailey, Michael D., and Sean L. Field, eds. *Late Medieval Heresy: New Perspectives. Studies in Honor of Robert E. Lerner.* York, UK: York Medieval Press, 2018.

Balázs, Béla. *Der Geist des Films.* Frankfurt: Suhrkamp, 2001.

Balázs, Béla. *Der sichtbare Mensch, oder die Kultur des Films.* Frankfurt: Suhrkamp, 2001.

Baldwin of Canterbury. "Tractatus de Duplici Resurrectione." In *Patrologia Latina,* edited by Jean-Paul Migne, 204:429–442. Paris: Migne, 1855.

Balthasar, Hans Urs von. *Herrlichkeit. Eine theologische Ästhetik.* 3 vols. Einsiedeln, Switzerland: Johannes, 1961–1969.

Barad, Karen. "Transmaterialities: Trans*/Matter/Realities and Queer Political Imaginings." *GLQ: A Journal of Lesbian and Gay Studies* 21 (2015): 387–422.

Barrès, Maurice. *Un homme libre.* Edited by Ida-Marie Frandon. Paris: Imprimerie Nationale, 1988.

Bataille, Georges. *Inner Experience.* Translated by Leslie Anne Boldt. Albany: State University of New York Press, 1988.

Baudelaire, Charles. *The Painter of Modern Life, and Other Essays.* Edited and translated by Jonathan Mayne. New York: Phaidon, 1964.

Baumgarten, Alexander Gottlieb. *Aesthetica.* Edited and translated by Dagmar Mirbach. Hamburg: Meiner, 2007.

Baumgarten, Alexander Gottlieb. *Metaphysica.* Halle: Hemmerde, 1779. Reprint: Hildesheim: Olms, 1982.

Beckman, Frida, and Charlie Blake. "Shadows of Cruelty: Sadism, Masochism, and the Philosophical Muse. Part One." *Angelaki* 14, no. 3 (2009): 1–9.

Beckman, Frida, and Charlie Blake. "Shadows of Cruelty: Sadism, Masochism, and the Philosophical Muse. Part Two." *Angelaki* 15, no. 1 (2010): 1–12.

Belting, Hans. *Bild und Kult: Eine Geschichte des Bildes vor dem Zeitalter der Kunst.* Munich: Beck, 1990.

Benjamin, Walter. "Doctrine of the Similar." In *Selected Writings,* edited by Michael W. Jennings, Howard Eiland, and Gary Smith, vol. 2, part 2, 694–698. Cambridge, MA: Harvard University Press, 2005.

Benjamin, Walter. "On the Image of Proust." In *Selected Writings,* edited by Michael W. Jennings, Howard Eiland, and Gary Smith, vol. 2, part 1, 237–247. Cambridge, MA: Harvard University Press, 2005.

Benjamin, Walter. *Origin of the German Trauerspiel.* Translated by Howard Eiland. Cambridge, MA: Harvard University Press, 2019.

Benjamin, Walter. "The Paris of the Second Empire in Baudelaire." In *Selected Writings,* edited by Michael W. Jennings, Howard Eiland, and Gary Smith, 4:3–92. Cambridge, MA: Harvard University Press, 2005.

Binczek, Natalie. *Kontakt. Der Tastsinn in Texten der Aufklärung.* Tübingen: Niemeyer, 2007.

Blumenberg, Hans. *Theorie der Unbegrifflichkeit.* Edited by Anselm Haverkamp. Frankfurt: Suhrkamp, 2007.

Bodmer, Johann Jakob, and Johann Jakob Breitinger. *Schriften zur Literatur.* Edited by Volker Meid. Stuttgart: Reclam, 2014.

Boersma, Hans. *Nouvelle Théologie and Sacramental Ontology: A Return to Mystery.* Oxford: Oxford University Press, 2009.

Böhme, Jacob. *De signatura rerum.* In *Werke,* edited by Ferdinand van Ingen, 509–791. Frankfurt: Deutscher Klassiker Verlag, 1997.

Böhme, Jacob. *The Signature of All Things, and Other Writings*. Translated by Clifford Bax. London: Clarke, 1969.

Bonaventure. "Itinerarium mentis in deum." In *Opera Theologica Selecta*, edited by Augustinus Sépinski, 5:179–214. Florence: Collegium s. Bonaventurae, 1964.

Bonaventure. "The Soul's Journey into God." In *The Soul's Journey into God; The Tree of Life; The Life of Saint Francis*, translated and introduced by Ewert Cousins, preface by Ignatius Brady, O.F.M., 51–116. Mahwah, NJ: Paulist Press, 1978.

Braungart, Georg. *Leibhafter Sinn: Der andere Diskurs der Moderne*. Tübingen: Niemeyer, 1995.

Brooke, Rosalind B., ed. *Scripta Leonis, Rufini et Angeli Sociorum S. Francisci*. Oxford: Clarendon Press, 1970.

Bruno, Giordano. *Cause, Principle, and Unity, and Essays on Magic*. Edited by Richard J. Blackwell and Robert de Lucca. Introduction by Alfonso Ingegno. Cambridge: Cambridge University Press, 2004.

Bruno, Giordano. *De la cause, du principe et de l'un*. Edited by Giovanni Aquilecchia. Translated by Luc Hersant. Introduction by Michele Ciliberto. In *Oeuvres complètes*, vol. 3. Paris: Les Belles Lettres, 1997.

Bruno, Giordano. *Le souper des cendres*. Edited by Giovanni Aquilecchia. Translated by Yves Hersant. Introduction by Adi Ophir. In *Oeuvres complètes*, vol. 2. Paris: Les Belles Lettres, 1994.

Buñuel, Luis. *Là-bas: Guión cinematográfico de Luis Buñuel y J.-C. Carrière, basado en la novela homónima de J.-K. Huysmans*. Teruel, Spain: Instituto de Estudios Turolenses, 1990.

Buñuel, Luis. *My Last Sigh*. Translated by Abigail Israel. Minneapolis: University of Minnesota Press, 2003.

Butler, Judith. *The Psychic Life of Power: Theories in Subjection*. Stanford, CA: Stanford University Press, 1997.

Butler, Judith. "What Is Critique? An Essay on Foucault's Virtue." In *The Political*, edited by David Ingram, 212–226. Malden, MA: Blackwell, 2002.

Bychkov, Victor V. "The Symbolology of Dionysius the Areopagite." *Russian Studies in Philosophy* 51 (2012): 28–63.

Bynum, Caroline. *Christian Materiality: An Essay on Religion in Late Medieval Europe*. New York: Zone Books, 2011.

Caciola, Nancy. *Discerning Spirits: Divine and Demonic Possession in the Middle Ages*. Ithaca, NY: Cornell University Press, 2003.

Cage, John. *Silence: Lectures and Writings*. Hanover, NH: Wesleyan University Press, 1961.

Canévet, Mariette. "Sens spirituels." In *Dictionnaire de spiritualité ascétique et mystique*, edited by Marcel Viller, Ferdinand Cavallera, and Joseph de Guibert, 13:598–617. Paris: Cerf, 1989.

Carruthers, Mary. *The Book of Memory: A Study of Memory in Medieval Culture.* Cambridge: Cambridge University Press, 2008.

Carruthers, Mary. "The Concept of 'Ductus'; or, Journeying through a Work of Art." In *Rhetoric beyond Words: Delight and Persuasion in the Arts of the Middle Ages*, 190–213. Cambridge: Cambridge University Press, 2010.

Carruthers, Mary. *The Craft of Thought: Meditation, Rhetoric, and the Making of Images, 400–1200.* Cambridge: Cambridge University Press, 2000.

Carter, J. Kameron. "Black Malpractice (a Poetics of the Sacred)." *Social Text* 37, no. 2 (2019): 67–107.

Cassirer, Ernst. "The Concept of Symbolic Form in the Construction of the Human Sciences." In *The Warburg Years: Essays on Language, Art, Myth, and Technology*, translated and with an introduction by S. G. Lofts with A. Calgagno, 72–100. New Haven, CT: Yale University Press, 2013.

Celan, Paul. *Gesammelte Werke.* Edited by Stefan Reichert and Beda Allemann. 2 vols. Frankfurt: Suhrkamp, 1986.

Certeau, Michel de. *La fable mystique, XVIe–XVIIe siècle.* 2 vols. Paris: Gallimard, 1982, 2013.

Certeau, Michel de. *The Mystic Fable.* Translated by Michael B. Smith. 2 vols. Chicago: University of Chicago Press, 1992, 2015.

Châtillon, Jean. "Nudum Christum Nudus Sequere." In *S. Bonaventura 1274–1974*, 4:719–772. Grottaferrata (Rome): Collegio S. Bonaventura, 1974.

Coolman, Boyd Taylor. *Knowing God by Experience: The Spiritual Senses in the Theology of William of Auxerre.* Washington, DC: Catholic University of America Press, 2016.

Coolman, Boyd Taylor. *Knowledge, Love, and Ecstasy in the Theology of Thomas Gallus.* Oxford: Oxford University Press, 2017.

Corbin, Henry. *Alone with the Alone: Creative Imagination in the Sufism of Ibn 'Arabi.* With a new preface by Harold Bloom. Princeton, NJ: Princeton University Press, 1997.

Coulter, Dale M. "Contemplation as 'Speculation.'" In *From Knowledge to Beatitude: St. Victor, Twelfth-Century Scholars, and Beyond*, edited by E. Ann Matter and Lesley Smith, 204–228. Notre Dame, IN: Notre Dame University Press, 2013.

Daniélou, Jean. *Les origines du Christianisme Latin.* Paris: Cerf, 1978.

David of Augsburg. *Die sieben Staffeln des Gebets.* Edited by Kurt Ruh. Munich: Fink, 1965.

David of Augsburg. "Septem gradus orationis." Edited by Jacques Heerinckx. *Revue d'ascétique et de mystique* 14 (1933): 146–170.

Debaise, Didier. *Speculative Empiricism: Revisiting Whitehead.* Translated by Tomas Weber. Edinburgh: Edinburgh University Press, 2017.

Deleuze, Gilles. "Coldness and Cruelty." In *Masochism*, translated by Jean McNeil, 7–138. New York: Zone Books, 1989.

Deleuze, Gilles. *The Fold: Leibniz and the Baroque.* Foreword and translation by Tom Conley. Minneapolis: University of Minnesota Press, 1992.

Deleuze, Gilles. "Mysticism and Masochism." In *Desert Islands and Other Texts, 1953–1974*, translated by Mark Taormina, 131–136. New York: Semiotext(e), 2004.

Deleuze, Gilles, and Félix Guattari. *A Thousand Plateaus.* Minneapolis: University of Minnesota Press, 1987.

Deleuze, Gilles, and Félix Guattari. *What Is Philosophy?* New York: Columbia University Press, 1994.

Derrida, Jacques. "How to Avoid Speaking: Denials." Translated by Ken Frieden. In *Languages of the Unsayable: The Play of Negativity in Literature and Literary Theory*, edited by Sanford Budick and Wolfgang Iser, 3–70. New York: Columbia University Press, 1989.

Derrida, Jacques. *On the Name.* Edited by Thomas Dutoit. Translated by David Wood, John P. Leavey, and Ian McLeod. Stanford, CA: Stanford University Press, 1995.

Descola, Philippe. "Presence, Attachment, Origin: Ontologies of 'Incarnates.'" In *A Companion to the Anthropology of Religion*, edited by Janice Boddy and Michael Lambek, 35–49. Oxford: Wiley Blackwell, 2013.

Dionysius the Areopagite. *The Complete Works.* Translated by Colm Luibheid. Notes by Paul Rorem. Preface by René Roques. Introduction by Jaroslav Pelikan, Jean Leclercq, and Karlfried Froehlich. New York: Paulist Press, 1987.

Dionysius the Areopagite. *De ecclesiastica hierarchia.* In *Patrologia Graeca*, edited by Jean-Paul Migne, 3:369–584. Paris: Migne, 1857.

Dionysius the Areopagite. *La hiérarchie céleste.* Edited by Maurice de Gandillac, René Roques, and Günter Heil. Paris: Cerf, 1958.

Dionysius the Areopagite. *Les noms divins. La théologie mystique* (*De divinis nominibus. De mystica theologia*). Edited by Isabel de Andia. 2 vols. Paris: Cerf, 2016.

Dohm, Burkhard. "Radikalpietistin und 'schöne Seele': Susanna Katharina von Klettenberg." In *Goethe und der Pietismus*, edited by Hans-Georg Kemper and Hans Schneider, 111–133. Tübingen: Niemeyer, 2001.

Dubilet, Alex. *The Self-Emptying Subject: Kenosis and Immanence, Medieval to Modern.* New York: Fordham University Press, 2018.

Fast, Heinold. *Der linke Flügel der Reformation: Glaubenszeugnisse der Täufer, Spiritualisten, Schwärmer und Antitrinitarier.* Bremen: C. Schünemann, 1962.

Fetzer, Karl A. *Der Flagellantismus und die Jesuitenbeichte: Historisch-psychologische*

Geschichte der Geisselungsinstitute, Klosterzüchtigungen und Beichtstuhlverirrungen aller Zeiten. Leipzig: J. Scheible, 1834.

Finch, Jeffrey D. "Neo-Palamism, Divinizing Grace, and the Breach between East and West." In *Partakers of Divine Nature: The History and Development of Deification in the Christian Traditions*, edited by Michael J. Christensen and Jeffery A. Wittung, 233–249. Madison, WI: Fairleigh Dickinson University Press, 2007.

Flasch, Kurt. "Procedere ut imago. Das Hervorgehen des Intellekts aus seinem göttlichen Grund bei Meister Dietrich, Meister Eckhart und Berthold von Moosburg." In *Abendländische Mystik im Mittelalter*, edited by Kurt Ruh, 125–134. Stuttgart: Metzler, 1986.

Flaubert, Gustave. *La tentation de saint Antoine.* Edited by Jacques Suffel. Paris: Flammarion, 1967.

Foucault, Michel. *Dits et écrits.* 4 vols. Paris: Gallimard, 1994.

Foucault, Michel. *The Order of Things.* New York: Vintage Books, 1966.

Foucault, Michel. "What Is Critique?" In *The Politics of Truth*, edited by Sylvère Lotringer and Lysa Hochroth, 23–82. New York: Semiotext(e), 1997.

Foucault, Michel. "What Is Enlightenment?" In *The Politics of Truth*, edited by Sylvère Lotringer and Lysa Hochroth, 101–134. New York: Semiotext(e), 1997.

Fraigneau-Julien, Bernard. *Les sens spirituels et la vision de dieu selon Syméon le Nouveau Théologien.* Paris: Flammarion, 1985.

Frostin, Per. *Luther's Two Kingdoms Doctrine.* Lund: Lund University Press, 1994.

Frugoni, Chiara. *Francesco e l'invenzione delle stimmate. Una storia per parole e immagini fino a Bonaventura e Giotto.* Turin: Einaudi, 1993.

Fumaroli, Marc. *L'école du silence: Le sentiment des images au XVIIe siècle.* Paris: Flammarion, 1994.

Garb, Jonathan. *Shamanic Trance in Modern Kabbalah.* Chicago: University of Chicago Press, 2011.

Gavrilyuk, Paul L., and Sarah Coakley, eds. *The Spiritual Senses: Perceiving God in Western Christianity.* Cambridge: Cambridge University Press, 2012.

Gerson, Jean. "De distinctione verarum revelationum a falsis." In *Oeuvres complètes*, edited by Palémon Glorieux, 3:36–56. Paris: Desclée, 1962.

Gerson, Jean. "De probatione spirituum." In *Oeuvres complètes*, edited by Palémon Glorieux, 9:177–185. Paris: Desclée, 1973.

Giesecke, Michael. *Der Buchdruck in der frühen Neuzeit: Eine historische Fallstudie über die Durchsetzung neuer Informations- und Kommunikationstechnologien.* Frankfurt: Suhrkamp, 1991.

Girgensohn, Carl. *Der seelische Aufbau des religiösen Erlebens. Eine religionspsychologische Untersuchung auf experimenteller Grundlage.* Leipzig: Hirzel, 1921.

Glissant, Édouard. *Poetics of Relation.* Translated by Betsy Wing. Ann Arbor: University of Michigan Press, 1997.

Grégoire, Réginald. "L'adage ascétique 'Nudus nudum Christum sequi.'" In *Studi storici in onore di Ottorino Bertolini*, 1:395–409. Pisa: Pacini, 1972.

Gregory of Nyssa. *Commentary on the Song of Songs.* Translated by Casimir McCambley. Brookline, MA: Hellenic College Press, 1987.

Gregory of Nyssa. *In Canticum Canticorum.* Edited by Hermann Langerbeck. In *Gregorii Nysseni Opera*, vol. 6. Leiden: Brill, 1960.

Gregory of Nyssa. *La vie de Moïse.* Edited by Jean Daniélou. Paris: Cerf, 1987.

Gregory of Nyssa. *The Life of Moses.* Translated, with an introduction and notes by Abraham J. Malherbe and Everett Ferguson. New York: Paulist Press, 1978.

Gregory the Great. *Gregory the Great on the Song of Songs.* Translation and introduction by Mark DelCogliano. Collegeville, MN: Liturgical Press, 2012.

Gregory the Great. *XL Homiliarum in Evangelia libri duo.* In *Patrologia Latina*, edited by Jean-Paul Migne, vol. 76. Paris: Migne, 1849.

Grimm, Jacob, and Wilhelm Grimm. *Deutsches Wörterbuch.* Leipzig: S. Hirzel, 1854–1961.

Guarnieri, Romana. "Il movimento del Libero spirito dalle origini al secolo XVI." *Archivio italiano per la storia della pietà* 4 (1965): 353–499.

Guigo II the Carthusian. *The Ladder of Monks and Twelve Meditations: A Letter on the Contemplative Life.* Translated, with an introduction by Edmund Colledge and James Walsh. Garden City, NY: Doubleday, 1978.

Guigo II the Carthusian. *Lettre sur la vie contemplative (L'échelle des moines). Douze méditations.* Introduction and critical text by Edmund Colledge and James Walsh. Paris: Cerf, 2001.

Guigo II the Carthusian. "Scala claustralium, sive tractatus de modo orandi." In *Patrologia Latina*, edited by Jean-Paul Migne, 184:475–484. Paris: Migne, 1862.

Haas, Alois. *Der Kampf um den Heiligen Geist: Luther und die Schwärmer.* Freiburg: Universitätsverlag, 1997.

Haas, Alois. *Gottleiden—Gottlieben: Zur volkssprachlichen Mystik im Mittelalter.* Frankfurt: Insel, 1989.

Haas, Alois. *Kunst rechter Gelassenheit. Themen und Schwerpunkte von Heinrich Seuses Mystik.* Bern: Lang, 1995.

Haas, Alois. *Offene Horizonte: Gott, Engel, Mensch.* Einsiedeln, Switzerland: Johannes, 2020.

Haas, Alois. *Sermo mysticus.* Freiburg: Universitätsverlag, 1979.

Hadewijch. *The Complete Works.* Translation and introduction by Columba Hart. New York: Paulist Press, 1980.

Hadot, Pierre. *Philosophy as a Way of Life: Spiritual Exercises from Socrates to Foucault.* Translated by Michael Chase, edited and with an introduction by Arnold I. Davidson. Oxford: Blackwell, 1995.

Hamburger, Jeffrey. "Speculations on Speculation: Vision and Perception in the

Theory and Practice of Mystical Devotion." In *Deutsche Mystik im abendländischen Zusammenhang. Neu erschlossene Texte, neue methodische Ansätze, neue theoretische Konzepte. Kolloquium Kloster Fischingen, 1998*, edited by Walter Haug and Wolfram Schneider-Lastin, 535–408. Tübingen: Niemeyer, 2000.

Harman, Graham, and Manuel Delanda. *The Rise of Realism*. Cambridge: Polity, 2017.

Heidegger, Martin. *Discourse on Thinking: A Translation of Gelassenheit*. Translated by John M. Anderson and E. Hans Freund. Introduction by John M. Anderson. New York: Harper and Row, 1966.

Heidegger, Martin. *The Principle of Reason*. Translated by Reginald Lilly. Bloomington: Indiana University Press, 1991.

Hello, Ernest. *Rusbroek l'Admirable*. Paris: Poussielgue frères, 1869.

Herder, Johann Gottfried. "<Entwurf (1769)> Von der Bildhauerkunst fürs Gefühl." In *Bibliothek der Kunstliteratur. Vol. 3: Klassik und Klassizismus*, edited by Helmut Pfotenhauer and Peter Sprengel, 95–107. Frankfurt: Deutscher Klassiker Verlag, 1995.

Herder, Johann Gottfried. *Sämtliche Werke*. Edited by Bernhard Suphan. Berlin: Weidmann, 1877–1913. Reprint: Hildesheim: Olms, 1967–1968.

Herder, Johann Gottfried. *Werke*. Edited by Wolfgang Pross. Munich: Hanser, 1984.

Herder, Johann Gottfried. *Werke in zehn Bänden*. Edited by Hans Dietrich Irmscher. Frankfurt: Deutscher Klassiker Verlag, 1991.

Herp, Hendrik. *Directorium aureum contemplativorum. Directorio de contemplativos*. Edited and with an introduction by Juan Martin Kelly. Madrid: Fundacion Universitaria Española, 1974.

Herp, Hendrik. *Theologia mystica cum speculativa*. Cologne: Ex officina Melchioris Nouesiani, 1538. Reprint: Farnborough, UK: Gregg, 1966.

Hinten, Wolfgang von, ed. *Der Franckforter (Theologia Deutsch): Kritische Textausgabe*. Munich: Artemis, 1982.

Hoff, Johannes. *The Analogical Turn: Rethinking Modernity with Nicholas of Cusa*. Grand Rapids, MI: B. Eerdmans, 2013.

Hollywood, Amy. *Sensible Ecstasy: Mysticism, Sexual Difference, and the Demands of History*. Chicago: University of Chicago Press, 2002.

Holsinger, Bruce. *The Premodern Condition: Medievalism and the Making of Theory*. Chicago: University of Chicago Press, 2005.

Hugh of Saint Victor. "De modo dicendi et meditandi." In *Patrologia Latina*, edited by Jean-Paul Migne, 176:875–880. Paris: Migne, 1854.

Hugh of Saint Victor. "De sacramentis." In *Patrologia Latina*, edited by Jean-Paul Migne, 176:173–617. Paris: Migne, 1854.

Hugh of Saint Victor. "De virtute orandi." In *L'œuvre de Hugues de Saint-Victor*, edited and translated by P. Sicard, H. B. Feiss, D. Poirel, and H. Rochais, 1:117–173. Turnhout, Belgium: Brepols, 1997.

Hugh of Saint Victor. "On the Power of Prayer." In *Writings on the Spiritual Life: A Selection of Works of Hugh, Adam, Achard, Richard, Walter, and Godfrey of St Victor*, edited by Christopher P. Evans, 315–348. Hyde Park, NY: New City Press, 2014.

Hugh of Saint Victor (Pseudo-?). "*Miscellanea.*" In *Patrologia Latina*, edited by Jean-Paul Migne, 177:469–897. Paris: Migne, 1854.

Huysmans, Joris-Karl. *À rebours.* Edited by Marc Fumaroli. Paris: Gallimard, 1977.

Huysmans, Joris-Karl. *Against Nature.* Translated by Margaret Mauldon. Oxford: Oxford University Press, 1998.

Ignatius of Loyola. *Spiritual Exercises and Selected Works.* Edited by Parmananda Divarkar and Edward J. Malatesta. New York: Paulist Press, 1991.

Jauss, Hans Robert. "Über religiöse und ästhetische Erfahrung. Zur Debatte um Hans Beltings 'Bild und Kult' und George Steiners 'Von realer Gegenwart.'" *Merkur* 45 (1991): 934–946.

Javelet, Robert. *Image et ressemblance au XIIe siècle. De saint Anselme à Alain de Lille.* Paris: Letouzey et Ané, 1967.

Kant, Immanuel. "An Answer to the Question: What Is Enlightenment?" In *Perpetual Peace and Other Essays*, translated and with an introduction by Ted Humphrey, 41–48. Indianapolis: Hackett, 1983.

Kant, Immanuel. "Beantwortung der Frage: Was ist Aufklärung?" In *Werke*, edited by Wilhelm Weischedel, 6:51–61. Frankfurt: Insel, 1964.

Kant, Immanuel. *Critique of Judgment.* Translated by Werner S. Pluhar. Indianapolis: Hackett, 1987.

Kant, Immanuel. "On a Newly Arisen Superior Tone in Philosophy." In *Raising the Tone of Philosophy: Late Essays by Immanuel Kant, Transformative Critique by Jacques Derrida*, edited by Peter Fenves, 51–81. Baltimore: Johns Hopkins University Press, 1993.

Kant, Immanuel. "Von einem neuerdings erhobenen vornehmen Ton in der Philosophie." In *Werke*, edited by Wilhelm Weischedel, 3:375–397. Frankfurt: Insel, 1964.

Karnes, Michelle. *Imagination, Meditation, and Cognition in the Middle Ages.* Chicago: University of Chicago Press, 2011.

Kemper, Hans-Georg. *Deutsche Lyrik der frühen Neuzeit.* 6 vols. Tübingen: Niemeyer, 1987–1991.

Kierkegaard, Søren. *The Lily of the Field and the Bird of the Air: Three Godly Discourses.* Translated and with an introduction by Bruce H. Kirmmse. Princeton, NJ: Princeton University Press, 2016.

Klossowski, Pierre. *Roberte ce Soir; and, The Revocation of the Edict of Nantes.* Translated by Austryn Wainhouse. Chicago: Dalkey Archive Press, 2002.

Kracauer, Siegfried. "Bücher vom Film." In *Der sichtbare Mensch, oder die Kultur des Films*, by Béla Balázs, 170–174. Frankfurt: Suhrkamp, 2001.

Krueger, Derek. *Symeon the Holy Fool: Leontius's Life and the Late Antique City.* Berkeley: University of California Press, 1996.

Largier, Niklaus. "Allegorie und Figur. Figuraler Realismus bei Heinrich Seuse und Erich Auerbach." *Paragrana* 21 (2012): 36–46.

Largier, Niklaus. "Die Applikation der Sinne: Mittelalterliche Ästhetik als Phänomenologie rhetorischer Effekte." In *Das fremde Schöne: Dimensionen des Ästhetischen in der Literatur des Mittelalters*, edited by Manuel Braun and Christopher Young, 43–60. Berlin: De Gruyter, 2007.

Largier, Niklaus. *Die Kunst des Begehrens: Dekadenz, Sinnlichkeit und Askese.* Munich: C. H. Beck, 2007.

Largier, Niklaus. "Die Kunst des Weinens und die Kontrolle der Imagination." *Querelles. Jahrbuch für Frauenforschung* 7 (2002): 171–186.

Largier, Niklaus. "Die Phänomenologie rhetorischer Effekte und die Kontrolle religiöser Kommunikation." In *Literarische und religiöse Kommunikation in Mittelalter und Früher Neuzeit. DFG-Symposion 2006*, edited by Peter Strohschneider, 953–968. Stuttgart: Metzler, 2009.

Largier, Niklaus. *In Praise of the Whip: A Cultural History of Arousal.* New York: Zone Books, 2007.

Largier, Niklaus. "Inner Senses—Outer Senses: The Practice of Emotions in Medieval Mysticism." In *Codierung von Emotionen im Mittelalter / Emotions and Sensibilities in the Middle Ages*, edited by Stephen Jaeger and Ingrid Kasten, 3–15. Berlin: De Gruyter, 2003.

Largier, Niklaus. "Intellekttheorie, Hermeneutik und Allegorie bei Meister Eckhart." In *Geschichte und Vorgeschichte der Subjektivität*, edited by Roland Hagenbüchle, Reto L. Fetz, and Peter Schulz, 1:460–486. Berlin: De Gruyter, 1998.

Largier, Niklaus. "Kontextualisierung als Interpretation. Gottesgeburt und *speculatio* im *Paradisus anime intelligentis.*" In *Meister Eckhart in Erfurt*, edited by Andreas Speer and Lydia Wegener, 298–313. Berlin: De Gruyter, 2005.

Largier, Niklaus. "The Media of Sensation." In *The Anthropology of Catholicism: A Companion Reader*, edited by Valentina Napolitano, Maya Mayblin, and Kristin Norget, 316–325. Berkeley: University of California Press, 2017.

Largier, Niklaus. "Medieval Mysticism." In *The Oxford Handbook of Religion and Emotion*, edited by John Corrigan, 364–379. Oxford: Oxford University Press, 2008.

Largier, Niklaus. "Mysticism, Modernity, and the Invention of Aesthetic Experience." *Representations* 105 (2009): 37–60.

Largier, Niklaus. "Negativität, Möglichkeit, Freiheit: Zur Differenz zwischen der Philosophie Dietrichs von Freiberg und Meister Eckharts." In *Dietrich von Freiberg: Neue Perspektiven seiner Philosophie, Theologie und Naturwissenschaft*, edited by Karl-Heinz Kandler and Burkhard Mojsisch, 149–168. Amsterdam: B. R. Grüner, 1999.

Largier, Niklaus. "The Plasticity of the Soul: Mystical Darkness, Touch, and Aesthetic Experience." *Modern Language Notes* 125 (2010): 536–551.

Largier, Niklaus. "Praying by Numbers: An Essay on Medieval Aesthetics," *Representations* 104 (2008): 73–92.

Largier, Niklaus. "Rhetorik des Begehrens: Die 'Unterscheidung der Geister' als Paradigma mittelalterlicher Subjektivität." In *Inszenierungen von Subjektivität in der Literatur des Mittelalters*, edited by Martin Baisch, 249–270. Königstein, Germany: Helmer, 2005.

Largier, Niklaus. *Spekulative Sinnlichkeit. Kontemplation und Spekulation im Mittelalter.* Zürich: Chronos, 2018.

Largier, Niklaus. "Spiegelungen: Fragmente einer Geschichte der Spekulation." *Zeitschrift für Germanistik*, n.s., 3 (1999): 616–636.

Largier, Niklaus. "Tactus. Le sens du toucher et la volupté au Moyen Age." *Micrologus* 13 (2004): 233–249.

Latour, Bruno, *Facing Gaia: Eight Lectures on the New Climate Regime.* Translated by Cathy Porter. London: Polity, 2017.

Leibniz, Gottfried Wilhelm. *New Essays on Human Understanding.* Edited by Peter Remnant and Jonathan Bennett. Cambridge: Cambridge University Press, 1996.

Lenk, Werner, ed. *Dokumente aus dem deutschen Bauernkrieg.* Röderberg, Germany: Aufbau, 1980.

Leontios of Neapolis. "The Life of Symeon the Fool." In *Symeon the Holy Fool: Leontius's Life and the Late Antique City*, by Derek Krueger, 131–171. Berkeley: University of California Press, 1996.

Lerner, Robert. *The Heresy of the Free Spirit in the Later Middle Ages.* Berkeley: University of California Press, 1972.

Lispector, Clarice. *The Passion according to G. H.* Translated, with a note, by Idra Novey. New York: New Directions, 2012.

Lohenstein, Daniel Casper von. *Sophonisbe.* Edited by Rolf Tarot. Stuttgart: Reclam, 1985.

Lorde, Audre. "Poetry Is Not a Luxury." In *Sister Outsider: Essays and Speeches*, 71–77. Berkeley: Crossing Press, 2007. [eBook]

Lorde, Audre. "Uses of the Erotic: The Erotic as Power." In *Sister Outsider: Essays and Speeches*, 103–114. Berkeley: Crossing Press, 2007. [eBook]

Lukács, Georg. *Heidelberger Notizen (1910–1913). Eine Textauswahl.* Edited by Béla Bacsó. Budapest: Akadémiai Kiadó, 1997.

Lukács, Georg. *Soul and Form*. Edited by John T. Sanders and Katie Terezakis. Translated by Anna Bostock. Introduction by Judith Butler. New York: Columbia University Press, 2010.

Lukács, Georg. "Von der Armut am Geiste. Ein Gespräch und ein Brief." *Neue Blätter* 1 (1912): 67–92.

Luther, Martin. *D. Martin Luthers Werke: Kritische Gesamtausgabe*. Weimar: Hermann Böhlau, 1883–2009.

Luther, Martin. "The Freedom of a Christian." In *Martin Luther's Basic Theological Writings*, edited by Timothy F. Lull and William R. Russell, 403–427. Minneapolis, MN: Augsburg Fortress Publishers, 1989.

Luther, Martin. "Temporal Authority: To What Extent It Should Be Obeyed." In Lull and Russell, *Martin Luther's Basic Theological Writings*, 428–455.

Mangin, Eric. "La lettre du 13 août 1317 écrite par l'évêque de Strasbourg." *Revue des Sciences Religieuses* 75 (2001): 522–538.

Mansfield, Nick. *Masochism: The Art of Power*. Westport, CT: Praeger, 1997.

Mantey, Volker. *Zwei Schwerter—Zwei Reiche: Martin Luthers Zwei-Reiche-Lehre vor ihrem spätmittelalterlichen Hintergrund*. Tübingen: Mohr Siebeck, 2005.

McGinn, Bernard. *The Flowering of Mysticism*. New York: Herder, 1998.

McGinn, Bernard. "The Four Female Evangelists of the Thirteenth Century: The Invention of Authority." In *Deutsche Mystik im abendländischen Zusammenhang. Neu erschlossene Texte, neue methodische Ansätze, neue theoretische Konzepte. Kolloquium Kloster Fischingen, 1998*, edited by Walter Haug and Wolfram Schneider-Lastin, 175–194. Tübingen: Niemeyer, 2000.

McGinn, Bernard. *The Harvest of Mysticism in Medieval Germany*. New York: Herder, 2005.

McGinn, Bernard. "Love, Knowledge, and Mystical Union: Twelfth to Sixteenth Centuries." *Church History* 56 (1987): 7–24.

McGinn, Bernard, ed. *Meister Eckhart and the Beguine Mystics: Hadewijch of Brabant, Mechthild of Magdeburg, and Marguerite Porete*. New York: Continuum, 1997.

McGinn, Bernard. *The Varieties of Vernacular Mysticism, 1350–1550*. New York: Herder, 2012.

McGuckin, J. A. "The Strategic Adaptation of Deification." In *Partakers of Divine Nature: The History and Development of Deification in the Christian Traditions*, edited by Michael J. Christensen and Jeffery A. Wittung, 95–114. Madison, WI: Fairleigh Dickinson University Press, 2007.

McInroy, Mark J. "Karl Rahner and Hans Urs von Balthasar." In *The Spiritual Senses: Perceiving God in Western Christianity*, edited by Paul L. Gavrilyuk and Sarah Coakley, 257–274. Cambridge: Cambridge University Press, 2012.

Mechthild von Magdeburg. *Das fliessende Licht der Gottheit*. Edited by Gisela Vollmann-Profe. Frankfurt: Deutscher Klassiker Verlag, 2003.

Mechthild of Magdeburg. *The Flowing Light of the Godhead.* Translated by Frank Tobin. New York: Paulist Press, 1998.

Meillassoux, Quentin. *Après la finitude. Essai sur la nécessité de la contingence.* Paris: Seuil, 2006.

Meister Eckhart. *The Essential Sermons, Commentaries, Treatises, and Defense.* Translation and introduction by Edmund Colledge and Bernard McGinn. Preface by Huston Smith. New York: Paulist Press, 1986.

Meister Eckhart. *German Sermons and Treatises.* Translated and with an introduction by Maurice O'C. Walshe. 3 vols. London: Watkins, 1979–1985.

Meister Eckhart. *Meister Eckhart: Teacher and Preacher.* Edited and translated by Bernard McGinn, with the collaboration of Frank Tobin and Elvira Borgstädt. Preface by Kenneth Northcott. New York: Paulist Press, 1981.

Meister Eckhart. *Schriften und Predigten.* Edited by Herman Büttner. 2 vols. Jena: Diederichs, 1919.

Meister Eckhart. *Selected Writings.* Selected and translated by Oliver Davies. London: Penguin Books, 1994.

Meister Eckhart. *Werke.* Edited by Niklaus Largier. 2 vols. Frankfurt: Deutscher Klassiker Verlag, 1993.

Merleau-Ponty, Maurice. *Phenomenology of Perception.* Translated by Donald A. Landes. New York: Routledge, 2012.

Meur, Diane. "Auerbach and Vico. Die unausgesprochene Auseinandersetzung." In *Erich Auerbach. Geschichte und Aktualität eines europäischen Philologen*, edited by Karlheinz Barck and Martin Treml, 57–70. Berlin: Akademie, 2007.

Meyer, Birgit. "Mediation and Immediacy: Sensational Forms, Semiotic Ideologies and the Question of the Medium." In *A Companion to the Anthropology of Religion*, edited by Janice Boddy and Michael Lambek, 309–326. Oxford: Wiley-Blackwell, 2015.

Meyer, Birgit. *Mediation and the Genesis of Presence: Towards a Material Approach to Religion.* Utrecht: Universiteit Utrecht, 2012.

Meyer, Birgit, and Mattijs van de Port, eds. *Sense and Essence: Heritage and Cultural Construction of the Real.* Oxford: Berghahn, 2018.

Miquel, Pierre. *Le vocabulaire de l'expérience spirituelle dans la tradition patristique grecque du IVe au XIVe siècle.* Paris: Beauchesne, 1989.

Mormando, Franco. "'Nudus nudum Christum sequi': The Fransciscans and Differing Interpretations of Male Nakedness in Fifteenth Century Italy." *Fifteenth-Century Studies* 33 (2008): 171–197.

Moten, Fred. "Blackness and Nothingness (Mysticism in the Flesh)." *South Atlantic Quarterly* 112 (2013): 737–780.

Mülder-Bach, Inka. *Im Zeichen Pygmalions: Das Modell der Statue und die Entdeckung der "Darstellung" im 18. Jahrhundert.* Munich: Fink, 1998.

Mülder-Bach, Inka. *Robert Musil. Der Mann ohne Eigenschaften: Ein Versuch über den Roman.* Munich: Hanser, 2013.

Müller, Gerhard. *Die Mystik oder das Wort? Zur Geschichte eines Spannungsverhältnisses.* Stuttgart: Akademie der Wissenschaften und der Literatur, 1999.

Müntzer, Thomas. "Auslegung des anderen Unterschieds Danielis." In *Schriften und Briefe: Kritische Gesamtausgabe,* edited by Günther Franz, 241–263. Gütersloh, Germany: Gütersloher Verlagshaus Gerd Mohn, 1968.

Musil, Robert. "Ansätze zu neuer Ästhetik. Bemerkungen über eine Dramaturgie des Films." In *Der sichtbare Mensch, oder die Kultur des Films,* by Béla Balázs, 148–167. Frankfurt: Suhrkamp, 2001.

Musil, Robert. "Der deutsche Mensch als Symptom." In *Gesammelte Werke,* 8:1353–1400.

Musil, Robert. *Der Mann ohne Eigenschaften.* Edited by Adolf Frisé. 2 vols. Reinbek: Rowohlt, 1978.

Musil, Robert. "The German as Symptom." In Pike and Luft, *Precision and Soul,* 150–192.

Musil, Robert. *Gesammelte Werke in neun Bänden.* Edited by Adolf Frisé. 9 vols. Reinbek: Rowohlt, 1978.

Musil, Robert. *The Man without Qualities.* Translated by Sophie Wilkins. 2 vols. New York: Knopf, 1995.

Musil, Robert. *Precision and Soul: Essays and Addresses.* Edited and translated by Burton Pike and David S. Luft. Chicago: University of Chicago Press, 1990.

Musil, Robert. "Toward a New Aesthetic: Observations on a Dramaturgy of Film." In Pike and Luft, *Precision and Soul,* 193–208.

Nancy, Jean Luc. "The Sublime Offering." In *Of the Sublime: Presence in Question. Essays by Jean-Francois Courtine, Michel Deguy, Eliane Escoubas, Philippe Lacoue-Labarthe, Jean-Francois Lyotard, Louis Marin, Jean-Luc Nancy, and Jacob Rogozinski,* translated and with an afterword by Jeffrey S. Librett, 25–53. Albany: State University of New York Press, 1993.

Newman, Barbara. *From Virile Woman to WomanChrist: Studies in Medieval Religion and Literature.* Philadelphia: University of Pennsylvania Press, 1995.

Nicolaus Cusanus. *De apice theoriae. Die höchste Stufe der Betrachtung.* Edited and translated by Hans Gerhard Senger. Hamburg: Meiner, 1986.

Nicolaus Cusanus. "De filiatione dei." In *Opuscula,* edited by Paul Wilpert. Hamburg: Meiner, 1959.

Nicolaus Cusanus. *De visione dei.* Edited by Adelaida D. Riemann. Opera Omnia, vol. 6. Hamburg: Meiner, 2000.

Nicolaus Cusanus. *Directio speculantis seu de non aliud.* Edited by Ludovicus Baur and Paulus Wilpert. Opera Omnia, vol. 13. Leipzig: Meiner, 1944.

Nicolaus Cusanus. *Trialogus de possest. Dreiergespräch über das Können-Ist.* Edited by Renate Steiger. Hamburg: Meiner, 1991.

Nicolin, Günther, ed. *Hegel in Berichten seiner Zeitgenossen.* Hamburg: Meiner, 1970.

Nietzsche, Friedrich. *The Birth of Tragedy and Other Writings.* Edited by Raymond Geuss and Ronald Speirs. Translated by Ronald Speirs. New York: Cambridge University Press, 1999.

Novalis. *Philosophical Writings.* Edited by Margaret M. Stoljar. Albany: State University of New York Press, 1997.

Noyes, John. *The Mastery of Submission: Inventions of Masochism.* Ithaca, NY: Cornell University Press, 1997.

Nuzzo, Angelica. "Kant and Herder on Baumgarten's *Aesthetica.*" *Journal of the History of Philosophy* 44 (2006): 577–597.

Origen. *Commentaire sur le Cantique des Cantiques.* Edited by Luc Brésard, Henri Crouzel, and Marcel Borret. Paris: Cerf, 1991.

O'Sullivan, Robin Anne. "The School of Love: Marguerite Porete's *The Mirror of Simple Souls.*" *Journal of Medieval History* 32 (2006): 143–162.

Otten, Willemien. *Thinking Nature and the Nature of Thinking: From Eriugena to Emerson.* Stanford, CA: Stanford University Press, 2020.

Pandolfo, Stefania. *Knot of the Soul: Madness, Psychoanalysis, Islam.* Chicago: University of Chicago Press, 2018.

Paracelsus. *Essential Theoretical Writings.* Edited, translated, and with an introduction and commentary by Andrew Weeks. Leiden: Brill, 2008.

Peter of Ailly. *Compendium contemplationis.* In *Opuscula Spiritualia.* Douai, France: apud Viduam Marci Wyon, 1634.

Porete, Marguerite. *The Mirror of Simple Souls.* Translated by Ellen Babinsky. New York: Paulist Press, 1993.

Porter, James. "Disfigurations: Erich Auerbach's Theory of Figura." *Critical Inquiry* 44 (2017): 80–113.

Proust, Marcel. *In Search of Lost Time.* Vol. 2: *Within a Budding Grove.* Translated by C. K. Scott Moncrieff and Terence Kilmartin. Revised by D. J. Enright. New York: Modern Library, 1992.

Rabbow, Paul. *Seelenführung: Methodik der Exerzitien in der Antike.* Munich: Kösel, 1954.

Rahner, Karl. "La doctrine des 'sens spirituels' au Moyen-Age, en particulier chez Bonaventure." *Revue d'ascétique et de mystique* 14 (1933): 263–299.

Rahner, Karl. "Le début d'une doctrine des cinq sens spirituels chez Origène." *Revue d'ascétique et de mystique* 13 (1932): 113–145.

Reichlin, Susanne, and Robert Leucht. "'Ein Gleichgewicht ohne festen Widerhalt, für das wir noch keine rechte Beschreibung gefunden haben.' Robert Musils 'anderer Zustand' als Ort der Wissensübertragung." In *Medien, Technik, Wissenschaft. Wissensübertragung bei Robert Musil und in seiner Zeit,* edited by Ulrich J. Beil, Michael Gamper, and Karl Wagner, 289–322. Zürich: Chronos, 2011.

Retucci, Fiorella. "On a Dangerous Trail: Henry Suso and the Condemnations of Meister Eckhart." In *A Companion to Meister Eckhart*, edited by Jeremiah Hackett, 587–606. Leiden: Brill, 2012.

Roth, Cornelius. *Discretio spirituum. Kriterien geistlicher Unterscheidung bei Johannes Gerson.* Würzburg: Echter, 2001.

Rudolf of Biberach. *De septem itineribus aeternitatis. Nachdruck der Ausgabe von Peltier 1866 mit einer Einleitung in die lateinische Überlieferung und Corrigenda zum Text.* Edited by Margot Schmidt. Stuttgart-Bad Cannstatt: Frommann-Holzboog, 1985.

Rudy, Gordon. *The Mystical Language of Sensation in the Later Middle Ages.* London: Routledge, 2002.

Schoeller, Donata. *Gottesgeburt und Selbstbewusstsein: Denken der Einheit bei Meister Eckhart und G. W. F. Hegel.* Hildesheim: Morus, 1992.

Schweitzer, Franz-Josef. *Der Freiheitsbegriff der deutschen Mystik: Seine Beziehung zur Ketzerei der "Brüder und Schwestern vom Freien Geist," mit besonderer Rücksicht auf den pseudoeckhartischen Traktat "Schwester Katrei."* Frankfurt: Lang, 1981.

Senner, Walter. "Meister Eckhart's Life, Training, Career, and Trial." In *A Companion to Meister Eckhart*, edited by Jermiah Hackett, 7–83. Leiden: Brill, 2012.

Seznec, Jean. *Nouvelles études sur "La tentation de saint Antoine."* London: Warburg Institute, 1949.

Sharf, Robert H. "The Rhetoric of Experience and the Study of Religion." *Journal of Consciousness Studies* 7 (2000): 267–287.

Silverman, Kaja. *Male Subjectivity at the Margins.* New York: Routledge, 1992.

Simon, Karl, ed. *Deutsche Flugschriften zur Reformation (1520–1525).* Stuttgart: Reclam 1980.

Sithole, Tendayi. *The Black Register.* New York: Polity, 2020.

Skafish, Peter. "The Descola Variations: The Ontological Geography of *Beyond Nature and Culture*." *Qui Parle* 25 (2016): 65–93.

Smith, Chris L. "Text and Deployment of the Masochist." *Angelaki* 14, no. 3 (2009): 45–57.

Snyder, James. *Hieronymus Bosch.* New York: Excalibur Books, 1977.

Spreitzer, Brigitte. "Meister Musil: Eckharts deutsche Predigten als zentrale Quelle des Romans 'Der Mann ohne Eigenschaften.'" *Zeitschrift für deutsche Philologie* 119 (2000): 564–588.

Stépanoff, Charles. *Voyager dans l'invisible: Techniques chamaniques de l'imagination.* Paris: La Découverte, 2019.

Stevens, Wallace. *Collected Poetry and Prose*. Edited by Frank Kermode and Joan Richardson. New York: Library of America, 1997.

Suso, Henry. *Das Buch der Wahrheit*. Edited by Loris Sturlese and Rüdiger Blumrich. Hamburg: Meiner, 1993.

Suso, Henry. *Deutsche Schriften*. Edited by Karl Bihlmeyer. Stuttgart: Kohlhammer, 1907. Reprint: Frankfurt: Minerva, 1961.

Suso, Henry. *The Exemplar, with Two German Sermons*. Edited and translated by Frank Tobin. Preface by Bernard McGinn. New York: Paulist Press, 1989.

Suso, Henry. *The Little Book of Truth*. In Suso, *The Exemplar*, 305–331.

Tauler, Johannes. *Die Predigten Taulers*. Edited by Ferdinand Vetter. Berlin: Weidmann, 1910. Reprint: Frankfurt: Minerva, 1968.

Teresa of Ávila. *The Life of Saint Teresa of Ávila by Herself*. London: Penguin, 1957.

Thomas of Celano. *Vita prima S. Francisci Assisiensis*. Edited by PP Collegii S. Bonaventurae. Florence: Collegium S. Bonaventurae, 1926.

Thysell, Carol. *The Pleasure of Discernment: Marguerite de Navarre as Theologian*. Oxford: Oxford University Press, 2000.

Valéry, Paul. "La tentation de (saint) Flaubert." In *Variété V*, 197–207. Paris: Gallimard, 1982.

Vaneigem, Raoul. *The Movement of the Free Spirit: General Considerations and Firsthand Testimony concerning Some Brief Flowerings of Life in the Middle Ages, the Renaissance and, Incidentally, Our Own Time*. New York: Zone Books, 1994.

Vico, Giambattista. *The New Science*. Translated and edited by Jason Taylor and Robert Miner. With an introduction by Giuseppe Mazzotta. New Haven, CT: Yale University Press, 2020.

Voaden, Rosalynn. *God's Words, Women's Voices: The Discernment of Spirits in the Writing of Late-Medieval Women Visionaries*. Woodbridge, Suffolk, UK: Boydell and Brewer, 1999.

Vries, Hent de. *Miracles et métaphysique*. Paris: Puf, 2019.

Vries, Hent de. *Philosophy and the Turn to Religion*. Baltimore: Johns Hopkins University Press, 2019.

Warburg, Aby. *Werke*. Edited by Martin Treml, Sigrid Weigel, and Perdita Ladwig. Frankfurt: Suhrkamp, 2018.

Warnock, Robert G. "'Von den vier Einsprüchen'—Die volkssprachliche Überlieferung." In *Der Traktat Heinrichs von Friemar über die Unterscheidung der Geister. Lateinisch-mittelhochdeutsche Textausgabe mit Untersuchungen*, edited by Robert G. Warnock and Adolar Zumkeller, 39–145. Würzburg: Augustinus, 1977.

Weheliye, Alexander. "After Man." *American Literary History* 20 (2008): 321–336.

Weheliye, Alexander. *Habeas Viscus: Racializing Assemblages, Biopolitics, and*

Black Feminist Theories of the Human. Durham, NC: Duke University Press, 2014.

Weil, Simone. *Waiting for God.* Translated by Emma Craufurd. New York: HarperCollins, 1951.

White, Hayden. "Auerbach's Literary History: Figural Causation and Modernist Historicism." In *Figural Realism: Studies in the Mimesis Effect,* 92–97. Baltimore: Johns Hopkins University Press, 1999.

White, Hayden. "Figural Realism in Witness Literature." *Parallax* 10 (2004): 113–124.

Whitehead, Alfred North. *Science and the Modern World.* New York: Free Press, 1967.

William of Saint Thierry. *Epistola ad fratres de Monte Dei.* Edited by Jean Déchanet. Paris: Cerf, 2004.

William of St. Thierry. *Meditativae orationes.* Edited by Jacques Hourlier. Paris: Cerf, 1985.

Williams, G. H. *Spiritual and Anabaptist Writers: Documents Illustrative of the Radical Reformation.* London: Westminster John Knox Press, 1957.

Wynter, Sylvia. "Beyond the World of Man: Glissant and the New Discourse of the Antilles." *World Literature Today* 63 (1989): 637–658.

Wynter, Sylvia, with Greg Thomas. "PROUD FLESH Inter/Views: Sylvia Wynter." *ProudFlesh: New Afrikan Journal of Culture, Politics and Consciousness* 4 (2006). https://www.africaknowledgeproject.org/index.php/proudflesh/article/view/202.

Zeuch, Ulrike. *Umkehr der Sinneshierarchie: Herder und die Aufwertung des Tastsinns seit der frühen Neuzeit.* Tübingen: Niemeyer, 2000.

Zum Brunn, Émilie, ed. *Voici Maître Eckhart.* Grenoble: Jérôme Millon, 1998.

Index

Adam of Dryburgh (Adam Scotus), 82, 83
Adorno, Theodor, 44
Aesthetica (Baumgarten), 201, 202–3, 204
Aesthetic experience (*aisthesis*), 2, 12, 18, 19, 34, 68, 71, 73, 81, 112, 137, 204–6, 207; dance as, 214–17; ground of the soul, 188, 189, 201–2; of liturgy, 69–70; soul and, 203, 213
Against the Grain; Against Nature (Huysmans), 97–98, 218, 220
Agamben, Giorgio, 198–99
Albert the Great, 78, 258n21
Alcher of Clairvaux, 79
Allegory, allegoresis, 2, 52, 60, 62, 86, 126, 133, 156, 185–86, 216; Suso on, 130–31
Anabaptists, 165, 167
Andrei Rublev (Tarkovsky), 246–47
Angela of Foligno, 110, 159, 219, 220, 221
Angelus Silesius, Johannes, 48, 159–60, 174, 175, 177, 179
Angels: as tropes, 24–25
"An Answer to the Question: What Is Enlightenment?" (Kant), 180–81
Anthony, Saint, 105, 107, 110, 111; hagiography of, 102–3; temptation of, 76, 82, 95–96, 101–2, 103–4
Apokatatastasis, 26, 71, 80
Apophatic moment, 155; Suso on, 123–24
Aristotle, 40, 54
Arousal: prayer and, 75–76
"On the art of sculpture in view of feeling" (Herder), 214
Asceticism; ascetic practices, 39, 94, 97, 174–75; prayer and, 102, 109–10
Assimilation, 15, 19, 24, 34, 68, 77, 92, 94, 96, 126, 142, 156, 164, 191; mimetic, 6, 66–67; mirroring and, 189–90; practices of, 18, 123
Asymmetry, 9, 10, 18, 34, 40, 41, 44–45, 49, 57; affective and sensual, 76–77; figural, 12–13, 17
Auerbach, Erich, 10, 12, 34, 50, 57, 105, 133, 224, 256n11; on concrete, 62–63; on Dante, 51, 52–53; energetic realism, 73, 90, 137; "*Figura*," 9, 16, 53–56; on genealogy, 59–60; on Vico, 58–59, 60–61
"Von dem auffrurischen geyst" (Luther), 166–67
Augustine, Saint, 30, 240

Baader, Franz von, 159
Bachmann, Ingeborg, 159
Bahr, Hermann, 97, 99, 259n6
Balázs, Béla, 18, 19–20, 39, 227, 229; on film, 225–26, 235–36; *Visible Man*, 232–34
Baldwin of Canterbury, 82–83
Barad, Karen, 186–87, 188, 197
Baroque period, 186; drama, 191, 192; mysticism, 173, 190, 191
Barrès, Maurice, 99, 260n9
Barthes, Roland, 26
Bataille, Georges, 1, 19, 20, 49, 143, 159,

219, 237, 238; *Inner Experience*, 66, 220, 221
Baudelaire, Charles, 51, 54, 56, 58, 176, 218, 219, 241, 242
Baumgarten, Alexander Gottlieb: on aesthetic experience, 18, 19, 201–2, 213; on ground of the soul, 187–88, 202–3, 204–6
Benjamin, Walter, 24, 28, 44, 56, 58, 192, 199; on allegory, 185–86; monadology and, 190–91; on written word, 50–51
Bernhard of Clairvaux, 79
Bernini, Gian Lorenzo, 115
Bible, 56, 76; vernacular, 166, 171, 172
Birth: God and, 120–21, 122, 123
Blumenberg, Hans, 161
Böhme, Jacob, 2, 3, 32, 35, 175, 179, 186, 187, 238; cosmopoetics, 18, 19, 200; on mysticism, 191–92; on signature, 193–94, 197–99; on transcription in, 196–97; on will, 194–95
Bonaventure, 78, 93, 124
The Book of the True Believers' Experience (Angela of Foligno), 221
Bosch, Hieronymus, 95, 143
Breviloquium (Bonaventure), 78
Brueghel, Pieter, 103; *Hunters in the Snow*, 27–28, 29–30
Bruno, Giordano, 39; *Concerning the Cause, Principle, and One*, 41–43
Büchlein der Ewigen Weisheit (Suso), 128–29
Buñuel, Luis, 109; on prayer, 99, 107; *Simon of the Desert*, 94–97
Butler, Judith, 20, 240
Büttner, Herman, 225, 228

Cage, John, 1, 39, 40, 159, 216–17
Cassirer, Ernst, 62
Celan, Paul, 159
Cézanne, Paul, 39
The Cherubic Wanderer: Sensual Description of the Four Final Things (Angelus Silesius), 160
Chora (Majce and Man), 23–24
Christ, 76, 96, 127, 131, 135, 243; imitation of, 103–4, 105; Saint Francis and, 92–93
Christianity, 9, 13, 15; *figura* in, 53–56; mystical tradition, 2, 63–64
"Composition as Process" (Cage), 216–17
Conceptualization, 7, 8, 15, 111, 189
Concerning the Cause, Principle, and One (Bruno), 41–43
Concrete, concreteness, 2-3, 8-9, 52, 55, 56, 62–63, 137
Condillac, Abbé de, 209–10
Confessions (Saint Augustine), 30
Contemplation, 17, 63, 72, 83, 127, 133; figures in, 65–66; Medieval, 11, 74–81; Scriptures and, 70–71
Contributions to a Critique of Modernity (Bahr), 97, 259n6
Corbin, Henry, 24
Corinthians, first letter to, 27
"Correspondences" (Baudelaire), 176
Cosmopoetics, 2, 18, 19, 200
Coulter, Dale M., on speculation, 137–38
Council of Constance, 171
Creation, 130, 131, 195; of man and world, 121–22
Creativity, divine, 68, 120-23, 131, 227
Cusanus, Nicolaus, 47, 49, 124

Dance, as aesthetic experience, 23-24, 214–17
Dante: Poet of the Secular World (Auerbach), 51, 52–53
Dante Alighieri, 9, 51; poetic style, 52–53
Darkness/nothingness, 36, 83–84, 213, 220; and ground of the soul, 205–6, 217
d'Aurevilly, Barbey, 101
David of Augsburg, 74, 78; on knocking, 106, 107, 109
de Certeau, Michel, 173

Defamiliarization, 64–65, 156
Deification, 13, 37, 67
Delacroix, Eugène, 242
Delay, and desire, 110–11
Deleuze, Gilles, 1, 2, 111, 112, 118; folding, 195–96
Denys the Carthusian, 157, 164
Derrida, Jacques, 48, 159
Desert, 47, 97; Saint Anthony in, 95–96
des Esseintes, Jean, 97, 98–99, 109, 218, 219
Desire, 47–48, 66, 69, 89, 112, 115, 194; and delay, 110–11
Detachment, 38, 41, 124, 135, 141, 147, 157, 158–59, 229
Dialogue, 150–51
Diogenes the Cynic, 39, 41, 242, 243
Dionysius the Areopagite, 46, 47, 77, 78, 83, 146, 205, 221; negative theology of, 121, 165
Discernment of spirits, 157–58, 163–64, 168–69, 170
Disfiguration, 24, 70, 105–6, 128, 132; reshaping perception, 100–101; temptation of St. Anthony and, 101–104
Dis-imagination, 121, 122, 124, 125, 131, 132
Dispossession, 10, 20
Divine, 1, 12, 13, 18, 71, 74, 83, 89, 130, 147, 149–50, 208; creativity of, 120, 121, 122; engagement with, 66–68; experiential knowledge of, 63–64, 78–79; love of, 117–18
Divine Names, On the (Dionysius the Areopagite), 46, 221
Drama, Baroque, 190–91, 192
Dramatization, drama, 204; musical imagery and, 82–83; *Song of Songs* as, 81–82
Du Bois, W.E. B. 13
Duchamp, Marcel, 159
De duplici resurrectione (Baldwin of Canterbury), 82–83

Eastern Orthodoxy, 37, 47, 239
Ecce homo, 120, 124
Eckhart von Hochheim, 4, 13, 41, 48, 127, 132, 143, 159, 163, 195, 203, 225, 226, 235; Cage on, 216–17; censorship of, 144, 149; detachment and dis-imagination, 124, 157; ground of the soul, 204–5; on incarnation, 120–23, 125; Musil on, 227–28, 229–30; on nothingness, 83–84; on reason, 37–38; on soul, 188, 205; Suso on, 141–42; thought and reason, 228–29
Ekphrastic production, 84, 126
Emblems, emblematic tension 184-86, 191, 221
Emergence, 32, 191
Energeia, 55, 56, 61
Engagement, 18, 52, 124, 163, 229
Enlightenment, 180, 186, 240
Enumeration, 33, 76, 77, 106; as ascetic exercise, 109–10; Mechthild on, 107–8; metonymical structure of, 108–9
Eroticism, 36, 155, 211, 221
Essayism, 222; utopias of, 223–25, 228, 229–30
Excitatio: prayer and, 75–76
Exegetic practice: of Origen of Alexandria, 71–72, 73–74
Experience, 15, 71, 84, 153, 159; divine and, 78–79; mystical, 163–64; and prayer, 79–80; sensations and, 73–74
Experimentation, 2; generative, 153–54

Ficino, Marsilio, 35
"*Figura*" (Auerbach), 9, 16; on Christian use of, 53–56
Figural play, 32, 35–36
Figuration: perception and, 4-10, 52-56; possibility and, 4-7, 10, 18, 188-89, 202-05, 220, 222-30, 242
Film, 234; Balázs's theory of, 235–36; visibility of, 39, 233
Flaubert, Gustave, 107, 109, 260n15; *The Temptation of Saint Anthony*, 101–2, 103

The Flowing Light of the Godhead (*Das fliessende Licht der Gottheit*) (Mechthild of Magdeburg), 81–82, 149, 164; enumeration in, 107–8; experimental writing in, 150–51; metonymical structure in, 108–9
Flugschriften, 165, 167
Folding, 195–96
Foolishness, 241, 242
Fools: gestures of, 242–43; holy, 239–40
Foucault, Michel, 20, 41, 44, 48, 102, 261n16; on freedom, 240–41; *The Order of Things,* 186, 198
On the Fourfold Exercise of the Cell (Adam of Dryburgh), 82
Franciscan tradition, 79, 133
Francis of Assisi, 39, 105, 117, 241, 242; as holy fool, 239, 240; visionary experience of, 91–93
Freedom, 29, 141, 157, 172, 180, 242; moral norms and, 143–44; visual poetics of, 132–33
The Freedom of a Christian (Luther), 165, 168
A Free Man (Barrès), 99, 260n9
Free spirit(s), 143, 154, 157, 161; hermeneutics of, 146–47; identification of, 148–49; Porete on, 145–46; Suso on, 141–42, 144–45
To the Friend Who Did Not Save My Life (Guibert), 243
Frugoni, Chiara, 91

Garden of Earthly Delights, The (Bosch), 143
Genealogy, 58, 59–60
Gerson, Jean, 157, 164, 170, 171
Giles of Assisi, 104, 105
Giotto di Bondone, 133
Glissant, Edouard, 27
Gnosis, 34, 36, 67-68, 73, 191
God, 46, 129, 135; creation and, 121–22; incarnation and, 120–21
Gothic: dance and, 214–15, 216
Grace, 13, 35, 40, 107, 136
Gregory of Nyssa, 73, 80; *Life of Moses,* 66, 67; material mimesis, 67, 68, 69
Gregory the Great, 84, 85, 86
Greiffenberg, Katharina Regina von, 174, 175, 177
Ground of the soul, 187–89, 208, 209, 211, 212, 213; as aesthetic experience, 201–2; Baumgarten on, 202–3, 204; Cage and, 216–17; darkness and, 205–6
Guattari, Félix, 111
Guigo II the Carthusian, 74–75

Hadewijch of Antwerp, 110, 163, 164; visionary experience of, 86–88, 89, 90
Hagiography: of Saint Anthony, 102–3
The Hammer of Witches (Kramer), 169
Harnack, Adolf von, 55
Hegel, Georg Wilhelm Friedrich, 43, 60, 159, 161, 162, 185, 194
Heidegger, Martin, 48, 159–60, 161, 162, 173–74
Heidelberger Notizen (Lukács), 226
Hello, Ernest, 218–19
Hellweg, Martin, 50
Henry of Friemar, 157, 164
Henry of Langenstein, 157, 164
Herder, Johann Gottfried, 48, 216; aesthetic experience, 18, 19, 201, 202, 214, 215; on ground of the soul, 187–88, 211, 213, 217; on sensation, 210–11, 212; on soul, 208–9
Heresy, heresiology, 143–44, 147–48, 158; "free spirits," 141–42, 157; Porete's, 145–46
Herp, Hendrik, 74, 131, 140, 208; on senses, 206–7
Hexameron, 82
History: Auerbach on, 60–61; materialist view, 28–29
Un homme libre (Barrès), 99, 260n9
Horologium sapientiae (Suso), 128
Hugh of Saint Victor, 79, 163; on prayer and meditation, 75–78, 82, 118

Hume, David, 24
Hunters in the Snow (Brueghel), as film trope, 27–28, 29–30
Huysmans, Joris-Karl, 1, 18, 19, 20, 71, 99, 100, 101, 109, 219, 237, 238; *Against Nature*, 97–98, 218, 220

Iconoclasm, 10, 121, 124, 159; Suso on, 125–26, 132, 133, 147
Ignatius of Loyola, 86, 124; *Spiritual Exercises*, 70, 99–100, 104
Image(s), 26–27, 35, 47, 121, 124, 128, 130; and imagination, 126–27; as representation, 131–32; text and, 184–85
Imagination, 3, 24, 31, 32, 52, 58, 121, 175–77, 188, 200, 261n16; use of, 126–27; visual, 116–17
Imitatio Christi (Thomas a Kempis), 78
Imitation, 50-51, 55, 91, 93, 105
Immanence, 11-12, 36, 45, 51, 79-80, 93, 122, 125, 129, 133, 174, 178, 204, 238
Immersion, 27–28, 29
Incarnation, 131; Eckhart on, 120–23; Suso on, 125, 129
Inner Experience (Bataille), 66, 220, 221
Inner man, 177, 180–81
Intellect: freedom of, 122–23
Inversion, 43–44
Itinerarium mentis in deum (Bonaventure), 78, 93

Javelet, Robert, 137, 264n78
La Jetée (Marker), 39
John of Damascus, 74
Jubilus, 137, 138, 139

Kant, Immanuel, 19, 43, 161, 162, 170, 183, 185, 201; on mystical tropes, 179–82
Khlebnikov, Velimir: on language, 38–39
Kierkegaard, Søren, 38
Klettenberg, Susanna Katharina von, 179; on imagination, 176–77
Klossowski, Pierre, 159
Knocking, 106–7, 109
Knowledge, 14, 19, 36, 41, 43, 135, 142, 148, 178, 201; body of, 220–21; experiential, 63, 64, 71, 84; signature and, 197–98
Kracauer, Siegfried, 236
Kramer, Heinrich, 169

The Ladder of Monks (Guigo II), 74–75
Landscapes: of soul and flesh, 30
Language, 44, 47, 155, 176; in experimental writing, 157, 158; German, 195, 199; revolution of, 38–39
Lectures on Aesthetics (Hegel), 161
Leibniz, Gottfried Wilhelm, 160, 161, 162, 196, 204, 205
Leontius of Neopolis: on Simeon the Holy Fool, 243–46
Liber de vere fidelium experientia (Angela of Foligno), 221
Liberty, 146, 148, 193
El libro de la vida (*The Life Written by Herself*) (Teresa of Ávila), 114, 115, 117; ascetic suffering, 118–19; rapture in, 119–20
Life of Moses (Gregory of Nyssa), 66, 67
Lispector, Clarice, 2
Literary Language and Its Public in Late Latin Antiquity and in the Middle Ages (Auerbach), 57
The Little Book of Eternal Wisdom (Suso), 126–27, 128–29; on praise, 134–35
The Little Book of Truth (Suso), 141, 144, 146–47, 154
Liturgy: aesthetic experience of, 68, 69–70; visual experience and, 86–88, 89
Lives of Saints, 76
Lohenstein, Daniel Casper von: *Sophonisbe*, 190–91
Lorde, Audre, 33; "Poetry Is Not a Luxury," 25–26
Love, 40, 41, 75, 115; asymmetry of, 117–18

Lucretius, 35, 39, 41
Lukács, Georg, 1, 18, 19, 20, 42, 44, 226, 227
Luther, Martin, 18, 161, 171, 174, 267n36; on discernment of spirits, 168–69; on mysticism, 162, 164–65; on inner and outer man, 177, 180–81; on radical reform, 167–68; on secular vs. spiritual, 170, 179, 182–83; *Theologia Germanica*, 172–73; "On the revolutionary spirit," 166–67
Lutheranism, 172; orthodoxy, 176–77

Majce, Moritz: *Chora*, 23–24
Malleus Maleficarum (Kramer), 169
Man, Sandra: *Chora*, 23–24
The Man without Qualities (Musil), 4–5, 7, 225, 232; encounters in, 8–9; figuration in, 12–13; negative theology in, 230–31; themes in, 222–23; utopianism in, 223–24, 227–28, 229–30
Marcion of Sinope, 55
Marker, Chris, 40
Martyrdom, martyrs, 104, 111, 118; of Teresa of Ávila, 114–17, 119
Marx, Karl: on inversion, 43–44
Mary, 128; incarnation, 121, 122
Masochism, 110, 111; figuration of, 112–13
Materialism, 11, 46; history in, 28–29
McLuhan, Marshall, 48
Mechthild of Magdeburg, 110, 111, 158, 163; enumeration in, 107–8; experimental writing of, 151–52, 153–57; *The Flowing Light of the Godhead*, 81–82, 149–51, 164; metonymics of, 108–9
Meditation, 127, 129, 139, 151; as practice, 135, 138; and prayer, 74, 75–76, 237, 238; as rhetorical practice, 76–77; writing as, 154–55
Melancholia (von Trier), 29–30, 247
Melancholy: Baroque, 51
Memory: house of, 27
Metakritik der sogenannten Transzendental-Ästhetik (Metacritique of the so-called transcendental aesthetics) (Herder), 208–9
Metaphors: metonymical structure of, 108–9
Metaphysica (Baumgarten), 201, 202, 204
Metaphysics, 4, 34
Methexis, 23
Metonymical structures, 108–9
Mies van der Rohe, Ludwig, 39
Mimesis, 23, 50, 105; material, 67–69, 83
Mimesis (Auerbach), 60
Mimetic practice, 69; assimilation and, 66–67; material, 67–68
Mirroring, 27, 67, 70, 135, 189–90, 203, 208
Mirror of Simple Souls (Porete), 145–46, 149, 157, 164
Modernity, 182–83, 212, 225, 241
Modernism, 62-63, 98, 102, 218
Monadology, 19, 189, 190–91, 208
Monastic tradition, 104; sensual experiences in, 72–73
Montagne Sainte Victoire (Cézanne), 39
Moral norms: freedom from, 13, 143–44
Moses, 66, 67, 68–69
Movement of the Free Spirit (Vaneigem), 144
Mülder-Bach, Inka, 211
Müntzer, Thomas, 167, 172, 175
Music: imagery of, 82–83, 215
Musil, Robert, 1, 10, 14, 16, 18, 19, 20, 42, 48, 159, 226, 235; figuration in, 12–13; *The Man without Qualities*, 4–5, 6, 7–9, 222, 231–32; on utopianism, 223–25, 227–28, 229–30
On Mystical Theology (Dionysius the Areopagite), 46, 221
Mysticism, 1, 10, 12, 13, 14, 17, 124, 141, 163, 178, 179, 187, 219, 228, 237; Baroque, 173, 190, 191; Böhme on, 191–92; Kant on, 179–82;

languages of, 161–62; Luther on, 164–65; medieval, 63–64, 141, 174; Scriptures, 88–89
Mystics, 36, 37, 74, 110, 159

Name, On the (Derrida), 159
Narrative, narration, 45, 76, 77; Mechthild's, 151–52
Nature, 12-13, 134, 135, 175, 218
New Testament, 55, 56
Nielsen, Asta, 233
Nietzsche, Friedrich, 54, 58, 62, 73, 143, 221
Nominalism: Medieval, 162–63
Nothingness/darkness, 83–84, 208–9
Nouvelle théologie, 53
Novalis, 178–79

Old Testament, 56, 146, 256n11
The Order of Things (Foucault), 186, 198
Origen of Alexandria, 81, 93, 109, 207; on aesthetic experience, 68–69; exegetic practice of, 71–72, 73–74
The Origin of the German Trauerspiel (Benjamin), 190
Outer man, 177, 180–81

The Painter of Modern Life (Baudelaire), 241
Painting(s), 25, 39, 126; Brueghel's, 27–28, 29–30, 103
Pamphlets, 165; production of, 171–72
Paracelsus, 175, 199
Paradisus anime intelligentis (Paradise of the intelligent soul), 123
Participation, partaking in the divine, 2-3, 7-8, 13, 25, 28, 35-37, 40, 47-48, 50, 55-56, 63, 66-72, 77, 83-84, 89, 93, 99, 105, 109, 115, 210, 234
Passion(s), 103, 104, 106, 139
Passion according to G. H. (Lispector), 2
Paul, apostle, 1, 27, 93, 135, 144; Damascus vision, 83–84; letter to the Romans, 169, 172
Pedagogy: spiritual, 126–27
Pentecost, 88, 89
Perception, 1, 3, 30, 62, 161, 177, 178, 179, 189
Peter of Ailly, 78, 79, 157, 164
Phenomenology, 50, 52, 84, 102–3, 220, 238
Philosophy, 31, 179, 182
Plastic effect, 30, 48
Plato: allegory of the cave, 41
Poems in Stanzas (Hadewijch), 164
Poetics, 34, 151, 161, 221; Dante's, 52–53; visual, 124, 125, 126, 131–33, 137
Poetry, 25–26, 33, 79, 174, 175, 176
"Poetry Is Not a Luxury" (Lorde), 25–26
Porete, Marguerite, 143, 147, 158; *Mirror of Simple Souls,* 145–46, 149, 157, 164
Pornographic novels, 105
Porter, James, 60, 256n11
Possibility. *See* Figuration
"On Poverty in Spirit" (Lukàcs), 225
On the Power of Prayer (Hugh of Saint Victor), 75–76
Praise: Suso on, 134–35
Prayer, 63, 72, 81, 82, 99, 104, 118; amplification techniques in, 77–78; ascetic practice of, 102, 109–10; enumeration in, 76, 109–10; meditative, 237, 238; metonymics of, 108–9; practice of, 74–75, 79–80; repetition in, 106–8; sensation and, 207–8
The Principle of Reason (Heidegger), 159–60
Printing press, 165, 171–72
De probatione spirituum (Gerson), 157
Prophecy: false, 146
The Protestant Ethic and the "Spirit" of Capitalism (Weber), 165
Proust, Marcel, 6
Psalms: singing of, 76, 151

Rapture: Teresa of Ávila on, 119–20
Reading, 74, 90, 139, 151, 157, 164; Luther on, 166–67; as surrender, 113–14

Real, 31, 34, 44
Realism, 46; agential, 186–87; energetic, 9, 54–55, 73, 90, 137, 139; figural, 57, 238; texts and, 51–52
Reason, 37, 141, 229; Eckhart on, 37–38
À rebours (Huysmans), 97–98, 218, 220
Reformation, 170, 171–72
Reform movement: Luther on, 166–68
Repetition, 107–10
De rerum natura (Lucretius), 35
"On the revolutionary spirit" (Luther), 166–67
Rhetoric (Aristotle), 54
Rhetorical practices, 1, 54, 174–75; in prayer, 77–78, 107–8
Rilke, Rainer Maria, 25
Roberte ce soir (Klossowski), 159
Romanticism, 11, 178, 185–86
Rothko, Mark, 39
Rudolf of Biberach, 74, 78, 79, 139–40
Ruusbroec, Jan, 109, 218, 219

From Sacher-Masoch to Masochism (Deleuze), 118
Salon de 1859 (Baudelaire), 242
Salvation, 107, 112
Sans Soleil (Marker), 40
Der Satz vom Grund (Heidegger), 159–60
Scala claustralium (Guigo II), 74–75
Scheffler, Johann. *See* Angelus Silesius, Johannes
Schelling, Friedrich, 35, 194
Science, 34, 79, 176
Scriptures, 2, 11, 16, 55, 56, 76, 77, 86, 93, 141, 153, 158, 169, 172, 185; contemplative reading of, 70–71; enactment of, 175–76; figural reading of, 90, 103; hermeneutical frame of, 177–78; Mechthild's use of, 154, 156, 157; meditation and, 151, 155; mimesis, 67–68; mystical tropes in, 88–89, 182–83; prayer and, 79–80, 104; reading of, 166–67, 173; sensual experiences of, 72–73
Sculptural figures: dance and, 214–15
Secular, 172; Luther on, 168, 169, 170, 179, 180, 182
Secular order, 165–66
Self, 128, 175; formation of, 155–56
Senses, sensation, 7, 14, 18, 70, 78, 79, 80, 97, 102, 161, 202, 212, 213; dramatic production of, 81–83; five spiritual, 71–72; Herder on, 210–11; mystical/spiritual, 88–89; and prayer, 207–8; refiguration of, 105–6, 118–19; role of, 206–7; technological production of, 98–99
Sensuality, 72–73, 103, 104, 105, 204, 208–9
Sensus mysticus, 88–89, 90
Septem gradus orationis (*Seven Degrees of Prayer*) (David of Augsburg), 78
De septem itineribus aeternitatis (*Seven Paths of Eternity*) (Rudolf of Biberach), 78, 79
Sexuality, 110, 112
Der sichtbare Mensch, oder die Kultur des Films (Balàzs), 225–26, 232–34
Siglo de Oro, 74
Signatura rerum, 198, 199, 200–201
Signatures, 199–200; and knowledge, 197–98
The Signature of Things (Böhme), 193–94
Silence (Cage), 39
Simeon Stylites, Saint, 94, 95
Simeon the Holy Fool, 243–46
Simón del desierto (*Simon of the Desert*) (Buñuel), 94–97, 107, 109, 111
Smith, Chris L., 112
Solaris (Tarkovsky), 26; immersion theme in, 27–28, 29
Song of Songs, 76, 88, 174, 207; dramatization of, 81–82; visualization in, 84, 85–86, 90
Sophonisbe (von Lohenstein), 190–91
Soul, 30, 35, 70, 74, 120; arousal of, 211–12, 215; ground of the, 187–89, 203, 204–6, 216–17; Herder on, 208–9;

life of, 78, 82–83, 85; plasticity of, 202, 213
On the Soul (Aristotle), 40
The Soul's Journey into God (Bonaventure), 93
The Souls of Black Folk (Du Bois), 13
Speculation, 34, 52, 135–36, 137–38
Speech, 126, 152; mystical, 181–82
Spirit(s), 32, 215; discernment of, 157–58, 163–64, 168–69, 170
Spiritual: vs. secular, 170, 182
The Spiritual Espousals (Ruusbroec), 218
Spiritual exercises, 16, 70, 86, 99–100, 185
Spiritual Exercises (Ignatius), 70, 99–100, 104
Spirituality, spiritualism, 51, 52, 55, 56, 57, 60, 72, 205; senses and, 88–89
Stagel, Elsbeth, 125, 135
Stevens, Wallace, 25
Stigmata, stigmatization: of Saint Francis, 91–93
Studien zur Kritik der Moderne (Bahr), 97, 259n6
Styles of encounter, 5–6
Subjugations, 25–26, 29, 31, 127–28
Suffering, 118–19, 135
Summa Atheologica (Bataille), 159
Summa theologiae (Thomas Aquinas), 220–21
Supernatural state/word, 138–39, 241
Surrender, 119, 128; acts of, 113–14, 116
Suso, Henry, 74, 110, 120, 166; on allegory, 130–31; apophatic moment, 123–24; on free spirits, 141–42, 144–45, 148, 154, 157; on iconoclasm, 125–26; *Little Book of Eternal Wisdom,* 126–27, 128–29, 134–37; *Little Book of Truth,* 146–47; on supernatural state, 138–39; visual poetics, 131–33

Tarkovsky, Andrei, 30; *Andrei Rublev,* 246–47; *Solaris,* 26–28, 29
Tauler, Johannes, 120, 206, 209
Technology: in production of sensation, 98–99
"Temporal Authority: To What Extent It Should Be Obeyed" (Luther), 167
Temptation of Saint Anthony, The (Bosch), 95
Temptation: of Saint Anthony, 76, 82, 95–96, 101–2, 103
La tentation de saint Antoine (*The Temptation of Saint Anthony*) (Flaubert), 101–2, 103
Teresa of Ávila, 110: ascetic suffering, 118–19; asymmetry of love, 117–18; martyrdom of, 114–17; on rapture, 119–20; on reading, 113–14
Tertullian, 9, 56, 256n11; on figural typology, 53, 54–55
On the Testing of the Spirits (Gerson), 157
Texts: and image, 184–85; Mechthild's, 149–50; mystical, 158–59, 169–70; and realism, 51–52; vernacular, 144, 155–56, 171
Theologia Germanica (*Theologia Deutsch*) (Luther), 172–73
Theological teachings: threats to, 144, 149–50
Theology, 2, 9, 13, 31, 37, 56, 63, 147, 171; negative, 10, 17, 36, 121, 146, 159, 165, 185, 205, 230–31
"The Theorem of Human Formlessness" (Musil), 224
Things, 34, 36, 37, 39; effects produced by, 32–33
Thomas a Kempis, 78
Thomas Aquinas: *Summa theologiae,* 220–21
Thomas of Celano, 91, 92, 93
Tolokonnikova, Nadezhda, 239, 243
Touch, 202, 206, 207, 208, 209, 210, 211, 212, 213, 215
Transcendence, 11-12, 35-36, 52, 62, 65, 80
Transcription, 196–97
Transfiguration, 70, 105, 130, 241; practices of, 18, 214–15

Transformation, 72, 139, 191
Treatise of Sister Katrei, 144
Trier, Lars von, 30–31; *Melancholia,* 29–30, 247
On the Twofold Resurrection (Baldwin of Canterbury), 82–83

Utopianism, 5; Musil on, 223–24, 227–28, 229–30

Valèry, Paul, 101, 102, 260n15
Vaneigem, Raoul, 144
Vico, Giambattista, 16, 43, 57; Auerbach on, 60–61; figuration, 58, 59
"Vico's Contribution to Literary Criticism" (Auerbach), 58
Violence, 24, 46, 117; of martyrdom, 115, 116
De virtute orandi (Hugh of Saint Victor), 75–76
Visible Man, or the Culture of Film (Balázs), 225–26, 232–34
Visibility, 39, 232–33
Visionary experiences, 90; Francis of Assisi on, 91–93; Hadewijch of Antwerp on, 86–88, 89
Visuality, visualization, 87–90, 210, 233; in *Song of Songs,* 84, 85–86
Vita (Suso), 125, 135, 138
Voice, 4, 40; in Mechthild's writings, 152, 155
"Von der Bildhauerkunst fürs Gefühl" (Herder), 214

Warburg, Aby, 48, 62
Weber, Max, 165
Weheliye, Alexander, 29, 242
Weil, Simone, 38
"What Is Enlightenment?" (Kant), 180–81
William of Saint Thierry, 163, 261n17
Wolff, Christian, 204
Writing, 116; Benjamin on 50–51; decadent, 96–97; experimental, 150–54, 156–57; meditative, 154–55
Wynter, Sylvia, 29

Cultural Memory in the Present

Mihaela Mihai, *Political Memory and the Aesthetics of Care: The Art of Complicity and Resistance*
Ethan Kleinberg, *Emmanuel Levinas's Talmudic Turn: Philosophy and Jewish Thought*
Willemien Otten, *Thinking Nature and the Nature of Thinking: From Eriugena to Emerson*
Michael Rothberg, *The Implicated Subject: Beyond Victims and Perpetrators*
Hans Ruin, *Being with the Dead: Burial, Ancestral Politics, and the Roots of Historical Consciousness*
Eric Oberle, *Theodor Adorno and the Century of Negative Identity*
David Marriott, *Whither Fanon? Studies in the Blackness of Being*
Reinhart Koselleck, *Sediments of Time: On Possible Histories*, translated and edited by Sean Franzel and Stefan-Ludwig Hoffmann
Devin Singh, *Divine Currency: The Theological Power of Money in the West*
Stefanos Geroulanos, *Transparency in Postwar France: A Critical History of the Present*
Sari Nusseibeh, *The Story of Reason in Islam*
Olivia C. Harrison, *Transcolonial Maghreb: Imagining Palestine in the Era of Decolonialization*
Barbara Vinken, *Flaubert Postsecular: Modernity Crossed Out*
Aishwary Kumar, *Radical Equality: Ambedkar, Gandhi, and the Problem of Democracy*
Simona Forti, *New Demons: Rethinking Power and Evil Today*
Joseph Vogl, *The Specter of Capital*
Hans Joas, *Faith as an Option*
Michael Gubser, *The Far Reaches: Ethics, Phenomenology, and the Call for Social Renewal in Twentieth-Century Central Europe*
Françoise Davoine, *Mother Folly: A Tale*
Knox Peden, *Spinoza Contra Phenomenology: French Rationalism from Cavaillès to Deleuze*
Elizabeth A. Pritchard, *Locke's Political Theology: Public Religion and Sacred Rights*
Ankhi Mukherjee, *What Is a Classic? Postcolonial Rewriting and Invention of the Canon*

Jean-Pierre Dupuy, *The Mark of the Sacred*
Henri Atlan, *Fraud: The World of* Ona'ah
Niklas Luhmann, *Theory of Society, Volume 2*
Ilit Ferber, *Philosophy and Melancholy: Benjamin's Early Reflections on Theater and Language*
Alexandre Lefebvre, *Human Rights as a Way of Life: On Bergson's Political Philosophy*
Theodore W. Jennings, Jr., *Outlaw Justice: The Messianic Politics of Paul*
Alexander Etkind, *Warped Mourning: Stories of the Undead in the Land of the Unburied*
Denis Guénoun, *About Europe: Philosophical Hypotheses*
Maria Boletsi, *Barbarism and Its Discontents*
Sigrid Weigel, *Walter Benjamin: Images, the Creaturely, and the Holy*
Roberto Esposito, *Living Thought: The Origins and Actuality of Italian Philosophy*
Henri Atlan, *The Sparks of Randomness, Volume 2: The Atheism of Scripture*
Rüdiger Campe, *The Game of Probability: Literature and Calculation from Pascal to Kleist*
Niklas Luhmann, *A Systems Theory of Religion*
Jean-Luc Marion, *In the Self's Place: The Approach of Saint Augustine*
Rodolphe Gasché, *Georges Bataille: Phenomenology and Phantasmatology*
Niklas Luhmann, *Theory of Society, Volume 1*
Alessia Ricciardi, *After* La Dolce Vita*: A Cultural Prehistory of Berlusconi's Italy*
Daniel Innerarity, *The Future and Its Enemies: In Defense of Political Hope*
Patricia Pisters, *The Neuro-Image: A Deleuzian Film-Philosophy of Digital Screen Culture*
François-David Sebbah, *Testing the Limit: Derrida, Henry, Levinas, and the Phenomenological Tradition*
Erik Peterson, *Theological Tractates*, edited by Michael J. Hollerich
Feisal G. Mohamed, *Milton and the Post-Secular Present: Ethics, Politics, Terrorism*
Pierre Hadot, *The Present Alone Is Our Happiness, Second Edition: Conversations with Jeannie Carlier and Arnold I. Davidson*
Yasco Horsman, *Theaters of Justice: Judging, Staging, and Working Through in Arendt, Brecht, and Delbo*
Jacques Derrida, *Parages*, edited by John P. Leavey
Henri Atlan, *The Sparks of Randomness, Volume 1: Spermatic Knowledge*
Rebecca Comay, *Mourning Sickness: Hegel and the French Revolution*
Djelal Kadir, *Memos from the Besieged City: Lifelines for Cultural Sustainability*
Stanley Cavell, *Little Did I Know: Excerpts from Memory*
Jeffrey Mehlman, *Adventures in the French Trade: Fragments Toward a Life*
Jacob Rogozinski, *The Ego and the Flesh: An Introduction to Egoanalysis*
Marcel Hénaff, *The Price of Truth: Gift, Money, and Philosophy*
Paul Patton, *Deleuzian Concepts: Philosophy, Colonialization, Politics*
Michael Fagenblat, *A Covenant of Creatures: Levinas's Philosophy of Judaism*

Stefanos Geroulanos, *An Atheism That Is Not Humanist Emerges in French Thought*
Andrew Herscher, *Violence Taking Place: The Architecture of the Kosovo Conflict*
Hans-Jörg Rheinberger, *On Historicizing Epistemology: An Essay*
Jacob Taubes, *From Cult to Culture*, edited by Charlotte Fonrobert and Amir Engel
Peter Hitchcock, *The Long Space: Transnationalism and Postcolonial Form*
Lambert Wiesing, *Artificial Presence: Philosophical Studies in Image Theory*
Jacob Taubes, *Occidental Eschatology*
Freddie Rokem, *Philosophers and Thespians: Thinking Performance*
Roberto Esposito, *Communitas: The Origin and Destiny of Community*
Vilashini Cooppan, *Worlds Within: National Narratives and Global Connections in Postcolonial Writing*
Josef Früchtl, *The Impertinent Self: A Heroic History of Modernity*
Frank Ankersmit, Ewa Domanska, and Hans Kellner, eds., *Re-Figuring Hayden White*
Michael Rothberg, *Multidirectional Memory: Remembering the Holocaust in the Age of Decolonization*
Jean-François Lyotard, *Enthusiasm: The Kantian Critique of History*
Ernst van Alphen, Mieke Bal, and Carel Smith, eds., *The Rhetoric of Sincerity*
Stéphane Mosès, *The Angel of History: Rosenzweig, Benjamin, Scholem*
Pierre Hadot, *The Present Alone Is Our Happiness: Conversations with Jeannie Carlier and Arnold I. Davidson*
Alexandre Lefebvre, *The Image of the Law: Deleuze, Bergson, Spinoza*
Samira Haj, *Reconfiguring Islamic Tradition: Reform, Rationality, and Modernity*
Diane Perpich, *The Ethics of Emmanuel Levinas*
Marcel Detienne, *Comparing the Incomparable*
François Delaporte, *Anatomy of the Passions*
René Girard, *Mimesis and Theory: Essays on Literature and Criticism, 1959–2005*
Richard Baxstrom, *Houses in Motion: The Experience of Place and the Problem of Belief in Urban Malaysia*
Jennifer L. Culbert, *Dead Certainty: The Death Penalty and the Problem of Judgment*
Samantha Frost, *Lessons from a Materialist Thinker: Hobbesian Reflections on Ethics and Politics*
Regina Mara Schwartz, *Sacramental Poetics at the Dawn of Secularism: When God Left the World*
Gil Anidjar, *Semites: Race, Religion, Literature*
Ranjana Khanna, *Algeria Cuts: Women and Representation, 1830 to the Present*
Esther Peeren, *Intersubjectivities and Popular Culture: Bakhtin and Beyond*
Eyal Peretz, *Becoming Visionary: Brian De Palma's Cinematic Education of the Senses*
Diana Sorensen, *A Turbulent Decade Remembered: Scenes from the Latin American Sixties*

Hubert Damisch, *A Childhood Memory by Piero della Francesca*
José van Dijck, *Mediated Memories in the Digital Age*
Dana Hollander, *Exemplarity and Chosenness: Rosenzweig and Derrida on the Nation of Philosophy*
Asja Szafraniec, *Beckett, Derrida, and the Event of Literature*
Sara Guyer, *Romanticism After Auschwitz*
Alison Ross, *The Aesthetic Paths of Philosophy: Presentation in Kant, Heidegger, Lacoue-Labarthe, and Nancy*
Gerhard Richter, *Thought-Images: Frankfurt School Writers' Reflections from Damaged Life*
Bella Brodzki, *Can These Bones Live? Translation, Survival, and Cultural Memory*
Rodolphe Gasché, *The Honor of Thinking: Critique, Theory, Philosophy*
Brigitte Peucker, *The Material Image: Art and the Real in Film*
Natalie Melas, *All the Difference in the World: Postcoloniality and the Ends of Comparison*
Jonathan Culler, *The Literary in Theory*
Michael G. Levine, *The Belated Witness: Literature, Testimony, and the Question of Holocaust Survival*
Jennifer A. Jordan, *Structures of Memory: Understanding German Change in Berlin and Beyond*
Christoph Menke, *Reflections of Equality*
Marlène Zarader, *The Unthought Debt: Heidegger and the Hebraic Heritage*
Jan Assmann, *Religion and Cultural Memory: Ten Studies*
David Scott and Charles Hirschkind, *Powers of the Secular Modern: Talal Asad and His Interlocutors*
Gyanendra Pandey, *Routine Violence: Nations, Fragments, Histories*
James Siegel, *Naming the Witch*
J. M. Bernstein, *Against Voluptuous Bodies: Late Modernism and the Meaning of Painting*
Theodore W. Jennings, Jr., *Reading Derrida / Thinking Paul: On Justice*
Richard Rorty and Eduardo Mendieta, *Take Care of Freedom and Truth Will Take Care of Itself: Interviews with Richard Rorty*
Jacques Derrida, *Paper Machine*
Renaud Barbaras, *Desire and Distance: Introduction to a Phenomenology of Perception*
Jill Bennett, *Empathic Vision: Affect, Trauma, and Contemporary Art*
Ban Wang, *Illuminations from the Past: Trauma, Memory, and History in Modern China*
James Phillips, *Heidegger's* Volk*: Between National Socialism and Poetry*
Frank Ankersmit, *Sublime Historical Experience*
István Rév, *Retroactive Justice: Prehistory of Post-Communism*
Paola Marrati, *Genesis and Trace: Derrida Reading Husserl and Heidegger*
Krzysztof Ziarek, *The Force of Art*

Marie-José Mondzain, *Image, Icon, Economy: The Byzantine Origins of the Contemporary Imaginary*
Cecilia Sjöholm, *The Antigone Complex: Ethics and the Invention of Feminine Desire*
Jacques Derrida and Elisabeth Roudinesco, *For What Tomorrow . . . : A Dialogue*
Elisabeth Weber, *Questioning Judaism: Interviews by Elisabeth Weber*
Jacques Derrida and Catherine Malabou, *Counterpath: Traveling with Jacques Derrida*
Martin Seel, *Aesthetics of Appearing*
Nanette Salomon, *Shifting Priorities: Gender and Genre in Seventeenth-Century Dutch Painting*
Jacob Taubes, *The Political Theology of Paul*
Jean-Luc Marion, *The Crossing of the Visible*
Eric Michaud, *The Cult of Art in Nazi Germany*
Anne Freadman, *The Machinery of Talk: Charles Peirce and the Sign Hypothesis*
Stanley Cavell, *Emerson's Transcendental Etudes*
Stuart McLean, *The Event and Its Terrors: Ireland, Famine, Modernity*
Beate Rössler, ed., *Privacies: Philosophical Evaluations*
Bernard Faure, *Double Exposure: Cutting Across Buddhist and Western Discourses*
Alessia Ricciardi, *The Ends of Mourning: Psychoanalysis, Literature, Film*
Alain Badiou, *Saint Paul: The Foundation of Universalism*
Gil Anidjar, *The Jew, the Arab: A History of the Enemy*
Jonathan Culler and Kevin Lamb, eds., *Just Being Difficult? Academic Writing in the Public Arena*
Jean-Luc Nancy, *A Finite Thinking*, edited by Simon Sparks
Theodor W. Adorno, *Can One Live after Auschwitz? A Philosophical Reader*, edited by Rolf Tiedemann
Patricia Pisters, *The Matrix of Visual Culture: Working with Deleuze in Film Theory*
Andreas Huyssen, *Present Pasts: Urban Palimpsests and the Politics of Memory*
Talal Asad, *Formations of the Secular: Christianity, Islam, Modernity*
Dorothea von Mücke, *The Rise of the Fantastic Tale*
Marc Redfield, *The Politics of Aesthetics: Nationalism, Gender, Romanticism*
Emmanuel Levinas, *On Escape*
Dan Zahavi, *Husserl's Phenomenology*
Rodolphe Gasché, *The Idea of Form: Rethinking Kant's Aesthetics*
Michael Naas, *Taking on the Tradition: Jacques Derrida and the Legacies of Deconstruction*
Herlinde Pauer-Studer, ed., *Constructions of Practical Reason: Interviews on Moral and Political Philosophy*
Jean-Luc Marion, *Being Given That: Toward a Phenomenology of Givenness*
Theodor W. Adorno and Max Horkheimer, *Dialectic of Enlightenment*
Ian Balfour, *The Rhetoric of Romantic Prophecy*

Martin Stokhof, *World and Life as One: Ethics and Ontology in Wittgenstein's Early Thought*

Gianni Vattimo, *Nietzsche: An Introduction*

Jacques Derrida, *Negotiations: Interventions and Interviews, 1971–1998*, ed. Elizabeth Rottenberg

Brett Levinson, *The Ends of Literature: The Latin American "Boom" in the Neoliberal Marketplace*

Timothy J. Reiss, *Against Autonomy: Cultural Instruments, Mutualities, and the Fictive Imagination*

Hent de Vries and Samuel Weber, eds., *Religion and Media*

Niklas Luhmann, *Theories of Distinction: Redescribing the Descriptions of Modernity*, ed. and introd. William Rasch

Johannes Fabian, *Anthropology with an Attitude: Critical Essays*

Michel Henry, *I Am the Truth: Toward a Philosophy of Christianity*

Gil Anidjar, *"Our Place in Al-Andalus": Kabbalah, Philosophy, Literature in Arab-Jewish Letters*

Hélène Cixous and Jacques Derrida, *Veils*

F. R. Ankersmit, *Historical Representation*

F. R. Ankersmit, *Political Representation*

Elissa Marder, *Dead Time: Temporal Disorders in the Wake of Modernity (Baudelaire and Flaubert)*

Reinhart Koselleck, *The Practice of Conceptual History: Timing History, Spacing Concepts*

Niklas Luhmann, *The Reality of the Mass Media*

Hubert Damisch, *A Theory of /Cloud/: Toward a History of Painting*

Jean-Luc Nancy, *The Speculative Remark: (One of Hegel's bon mots)*

Jean-François Lyotard, *Soundproof Room: Malraux's Anti-Aesthetics*

Jan Patočka, *Plato and Europe*

Hubert Damisch, *Skyline: The Narcissistic City*

Isabel Hoving, *In Praise of New Travelers: Reading Caribbean Migrant Women Writers*

Richard Rand, ed., *Futures: Of Jacques Derrida*

William Rasch, *Niklas Luhmann's Modernity: The Paradoxes of Differentiation*

Jacques Derrida and Anne Dufourmantelle, *Of Hospitality*

Jean-François Lyotard, *The Confession of Augustine*

Kaja Silverman, *World Spectators*

Samuel Weber, *Institution and Interpretation: Expanded Edition*

Jeffrey S. Librett, *The Rhetoric of Cultural Dialogue: Jews and Germans in the Epoch of Emancipation*

Ulrich Baer, *Remnants of Song: Trauma and the Experience of Modernity in Charles Baudelaire and Paul Celan*

Samuel C. Wheeler III, *Deconstruction as Analytic Philosophy*

David S. Ferris, *Silent Urns: Romanticism, Hellenism, Modernity*

Rodolphe Gasché, *Of Minimal Things: Studies on the Notion of Relation*
Sarah Winter, *Freud and the Institution of Psychoanalytic Knowledge*
Samuel Weber, *The Legend of Freud: Expanded Edition*
Aris Fioretos, ed., *The Solid Letter: Readings of Friedrich Hölderlin*
J. Hillis Miller / Manuel Asensi, *Black Holes / J. Hillis Miller; or, Boustrophedonic Reading*
Miryam Sas, *Fault Lines: Cultural Memory and Japanese Surrealism*
Peter Schwenger, *Fantasm and Fiction: On Textual Envisioning*
Didier Maleuvre, *Museum Memories: History, Technology, Art*
Jacques Derrida, *Monolingualism of the Other; or, The Prosthesis of Origin*
Andrew Baruch Wachtel, *Making a Nation, Breaking a Nation: Literature and Cultural Politics in Yugoslavia*
Niklas Luhmann, *Love as Passion: The Codification of Intimacy*
Mieke Bal, ed., *The Practice of Cultural Analysis: Exposing Interdisciplinary Interpretation*
Jacques Derrida and Gianni Vattimo, eds., *Religion*

Lightning Source UK Ltd.
Milton Keynes UK
UKHW030642100222
398444UK00003B/157